Y0-EBM-686

MINORITIES AND THE CANADIAN STATE

MINORITIES AND THE CANADIAN STATE

Edited by
Neil Nevitte
and
Allan Kornberg

MOSAIC PRESS
OAKVILLE NEW YORK LONDON

Canadian Cataloguing in Publication Data

Main entry under title:
Minorities & the Canadian state

Bibliography: p.
Includes index.
ISBN 0-88962-278-7 (bound). - ISBN 0-88962-277-9 (pbk.)

1. Minorities - Canada - Addresses, essays, lectures.
2. Civil rights - Canada - Addresses, essays, lectures. I. Nevitte, Neil. II. Kornberg, Allan, 1931-

JC599.C3M56 1985   323.1'71   C85-098772-5

No part of this book may be reproduced or transmitted in any form, by any means, electronic or mechanical, including photocopying and recording, information storage and retrieval systems, without permission in writing from the publisher, except by a reviewer who may quote brief passages in a review.

Published by Mosaic Press, P.O. Box 1032, Oakville, Ontario, L6J 5E9, Canada. Offices and warehouse at 1252 Speers Road, Unit 10, Oakville, Ontario, L6L 5N9, Canada.

Published with the assistance of the Canada Council and the Ontario Arts Council.

Copyright © Neil Nevitte and Allan Kornberg, 1985
Printed and bound in Canada.

ISBN 0-88962-278-7 cloth
ISBN 0-88962-277-9 paper
MOSAIC PRESS:
In the United States:
Flatiron Book Distributors, 1170 Broadway, Suite 807, New York, N.Y. 10001, U.S.A.
In the U.K.:
John Calder (Publishers) Ltd., 18 Brewer Street, London, W1R 4AS, England.
In New Zealand:
Pilgrims South Press, P.O. Box 5101, Dunedin, New Zealand.
In Australia:
Bookwise International, 1 Jeanes Street, Beverley, 5009, South Australia, Australia

CONTENTS

1. Introduction: Minorities in Canada: An Overview — 11

PART I: Minority Rights, Human Rights and the Charter

2. DALE GIBSON — 31
   Protection of Minority Rights Under the Canadian Charter of Rights and Freedoms: Can Politicians and Judges Sing Harmony?

3. MARY EBERTS — 53
   The Use of Litigation Under the Canadian Charter of Rights and Freedoms as a Strategy for Achieving Change

4. F.L. MORTON — 71
   Group Rights Versus Individual Rights in the Charter: The Special Cases of Natives and Quebecois

5. RAINER KNOPFF — 87
   The Statistical Protection of Minorities: Affirmative Action Policy in Canada

6. THOMAS FLANAGAN — 107
   The Manufacture of Minorities

7. DALE GIBSON — 125
   Stereotypes, Statistics and Slippery Slopes: A Reply to Professors Flanagan & Knopff and Other Critics of Human Rights Legislation

8. WILLIAM REEVES, J.S. FRIDERES — 139
   The Resolution of Complaints Based on Race and Origin: The Canadian Human Rights Commissions

PART II: Minorities in Canadian Society: Problems, Prospects, Perspectives

9. LEO DRIEDGER — 155
   Conformity Vs. Pluralism: Minority Identities and Inequalities

10. RONALD S. DICK — 157
    Minorities and the Canadian Visual Media

11. FRANK MacKINNON — 193
    When "Rights" Are Wrong: With Examples from Atlantic Canada

12. BARRY COOPER — 203
    The West: A Political Minority

13. JOEL SMITH, ALLAN KORNBERG, BETH RUSHING — 221
    The Changing Political Situation of Women in Canada

14. FRANCES ABELE — 239
    Dene-Government Relations: The Development of a New Political Minority

15. NEIL NEVITTE, ROGER GIBBINS 257
   Minorities as an Attitudinal Phenomenon: A Comparative Analysis of Youth Elites

16. HAROLD D. CLARKE, ALLAN KORNBERG, MARIANNE C. STEWART 275
   Politically Active Minorities: Political Participation in Canadian Democracy

Notes on Contributors

INDEX: Persons

INDEX: Subjects

LIST OF TABLES

6.1	Prohibited Grounds of Discrimination in Canada	110
8.1	Enquiries by regions and selected subjects for 1983 (percentage)	142
8.2	Complaints accepted by regions by grounds, 1983 (percentage)	143
8.3	Results of cases submitted for decision by year (including percentage of total)	145
8.4	Results of cases submitted for decision in 1983 (percentages)	146
13.1	Distribution of Gender, Age and Marital Status of Respondents in Trois Rivières, Peterborough, and Lethbridge	233
13.2	Number of Items for which Response Patterns Indicate Age-Related Changes in Gender Differences	235
15.1	Comparative Orientations to Visible Minorities	261
15.2	Item Inter-Correlation for Questions on Blacks/Racial Minorities	262
15.3	Attitudinal Linkage Between Minority Relations and Gender Issues	264
15.4	Mean Correlation Between Minority Relations and Gender Issues: Controlled for Gender of Respondent	266
15.5	Ideological Linkages with Minority Relations	268
15.6	Canadian Issue Linkages to Minority Relations	270
16.1	Frequency of Participation in Conventional Political Activities	280
16.2	Unconventional Political Activities — Approval, Effectiveness, Participation	280
16.3	Factor Analysis of Conventional Political Activities	281
16.4	Factor Analyses of Approval, Perceived Effectiveness and Participation in Unconventional Political Activities	282
16.5	Multiple Regression Analyses of Conventional Political Activities	285
16.6	Multiple Regression Analyses of Unconventional Political Activities: Petitions, Boycotts, Rallies	286
16.7	Multiple Regression Analyses of Unconventional Political Activities: Demonstrations, Strikes	287
16.8	Joint Distributions of Unconventional and Conventional Political Activities	289
16.9	Summary of Logit Analyses of Selected Contrasts of Conventional Activities v. Petitions, Boycotts and Rallies	291
16.10	Summary of Logit Analyses of Selected Contrasts of Conventional Activities v. Demonstrations, Strikes	292

LIST OF FIGURES

8.1	Organization Chart of Federal Human Rights Commission	140
9.1	The Assimilationist-Pluralist Continuum	165
9.2	A Conformity-Pluralist Conceptual Model	170
16.1a	Extent of Participation in Demonstrations and Wildcat Strikes	283
16.1b	Extent of Participation in Petitions, Boycotts, and Rallies	283

ACKNOWLEDGEMENTS

Organizing conferences and editing conference papers are often tedious tasks; in this case they were not. In large part this was due to the cooperation and support of several organizations and individuals. We would like to acknowledge those involved; they all contributed generously and graciously.

The Conference on Minorities in Canada held in Banff, Alberta, in May 1984, brought together people from across Canada and the United States. The Conference would not have been possible without the financial support which came from several sources: the Government of Canada, Secretary of State, Multiculturalism; the Government of Alberta, Ministry of Advanced Education, and the Alberta Cultural Heritage Foundation; the University of Calgary: Conference Grant, Special Projects Fund, Faculty of Social Sciences and Department of Political Science; and Duke University's Canadian Studies Center, Center for International Studies and Department of Political Science.

Successful conferences also require the complementary efforts of a large number of individuals. At the University of Calgary, Norman Wagner, President of the University, Don Seastone, Dean of the Faculty of Social Sciences, and Tom Flanagan, Head of the Department of Political Science were an active and continual source of encouragement. At Duke University, Richard Leach, Chairman of the Center for Canadian Studies, provided support and assistance that were instrumental in bringing this project to a successful conclusion.

We would be remiss if we did not acknowledge the valuable but sometimes invisible logistical assistance provided by Miriam Carey, Marc Arnal, Herman Van Reekum and Collette Arnal.

Much of the Conference's organizational load, as is probably typical, fell on the shoulders of the secretarial staff. We wish to express our appreciation to Dot Weathers, who coordinated Conference-related matters at Duke. The secretarial staff of the Department of Political Science at the University of Calgary had the pleasure of being at the hosting end of the Conference. We would like to extend a special thank you to Cecile Calverley, whose organizational skill, eye for detail, patience and good humour were instrumental to the whole enterprise.

Finally, we wish to thank the conferees who brought their experience and intellectual insight to the Conference table in a spirit of goodwill and in so doing contributed to an enormously educational experience. These thanks extend to the Honourable David Collenette, Secretary of State, Multiculturalism; the Honourable Bob Daudlin, Chairman of the Special Committee on Participation of Visible Minorities in Canadian Society, House of Commons; Gary Caldwell, Institut Québécoise de Recherche sur la Culture, Montréal; and Howard Palmer, Department of History, the University of Calgary. Their contributions, while not represented in this volume, were nonetheless valuable. Those conferees whose papers do appear in this volume responded courteously, patiently and promptly to editorial questions and suggestions. We appreciate their efforts greatly.

INTRODUCTION

MINORITIES IN CANADA:
AN OVERVIEW

The essays in this book are concerned with various aspects of the status and condition of minorities in Canada. This focus immediately raises the question of "what is a minority?" Does the concept hinge on the proportion in a population which a group constitutes relative to other groups, or does it instead hinge on substantial inequality with a respect to valued social positions and resources? A definition which emphasizes proportionality runs afoul of the fact that groups which can be considered are arbitrarily defined. Usually some frame of reference relevant only to a particular problem of interest defines group categories. Thus, for example, one can move from Christian-Nonchristian to Protestant-Catholic-Jewish-Muslim-Other, to even more refined religious group categories. All may be relevant from one perspective or other. However, the more extensive the system of categories, the smaller a minority each group becomes and the greater the likelihood that every group eventually will be a "minority," in the sense of comprising less than half the population. For this reason, groups which apparently are in a disadvantaged position in terms of an established distribution of socially valued resources, or which believe they are in such a position, also have been considered minorities. This perspective, however, has foundered on the grounds that virtually every group at one time or another either has been seriously disadvantaged, or believes it has been disadvantaged.

Given these definitional problems, in a preliminary communication to the group of scholars who were invited to prepare conference papers on topics pertinent to minorities and the Canadian state, the editors of this book suggested that they conceive of minorities as groups which generally have been distinguished by at least two of the following attributes:

1. Other than women, minorities constitute statistically small proportions of the Canadian population;
2. Irrespective of whether they reside in cohesive communities or are geographically dispersed, and whether they are or are not distinguished by distinctive physical characteristics, they have identified themselves and been identified by others as minorities.
3. They generally believe themselves to have been the objects of *prolonged* discrimination which — although varying in its intensity — has prevented their equitable and effective participation in one or more of the political, legal, economic and educational systems of the Canadian state.

The papers we were calling for would be subjected to critical analysis at a conference to be held in May 1984 at Banff, Alberta. A perusal of several of the papers in this volume (all of which were presented at the conference) will reveal that several invitees did not accept our characterization of a minority group. Their disagreement notwithstanding, they experienced little difficulty in selecting and developing topics for papers. This is because the problems generated by the relationships between minorities (however defined) and the Canadian state are hardly novel. Indeed, it is no great exaggeration to assert that they have had a significant influence on politics and governance since well before Confederation.

A number of explanations have been offered to account for this condition. The two most general are structured in terms of conquest and immigration. The first contends that one of the two Charter groups, the conquering English, was able to relegate the other, the vanquished French, to a position of social and economic inferiority from which it only now is beginning to emerge. Somewhat differently, the second explanation argues that political elites representing *both* Charter groups were able to determine which other groups would follow them, as well as the conditions of their entry. Inevitably, invidious comparisons were made about the qualities and aptitudes of new arrivals. Over time, these evaluations led to social, economic, and even legal-political differentiations which encumbered certain groups with the attributes associated with minority status.

A third (and related) explanation is that certain groups — either because of their distinct physical characteristics (e.g., native peoples and orientals) or their religious practices and cultural norms (e.g., Mennonites and Doukhobors) were never really accorded full membership in the Canadian political community. Consequently, they have suffered different but persistent forms of discrimination. Still another "social-structural" explanation contends that Canadian political authorities, like those of other democracies characterized by substantial degrees of social and political pluralism, long have tolerated the existence of organized groups. Indeed, it usually is argued that they actually encourage them as part of the "normal political process" to press their self-interested claims upon government and upon other groups in society. It follows that certain groups become and remain minorities because they lack the sheer numbers, social and political cohesion, material resources, political acumen, and skilled and resourceful leadership which would enable them effectively to press their claims on government and the public.

A more sinister variation of this particular explanation is that the fault lies not with these groups but with the Canadian public and its political leaders. Although it is acknowledged that some groups (e.g., Hutterites) may not have wanted to participate in the societal mainstream, in fact most have. The difficulty is that local majorities have employed different social and economic pressures, and political authorities have employed a variety of social controls — including the discrediting or co-opting of group leaders and the threatened or actual application of force — to prevent certain of them from organizing and articulating their interests.

Although scholars may differ in their explanations of the conditions under which certain groups become and remain minorities, most would agree that the status of minorities, as we have characterized them, improved markedly during the period 1950-74 largely because sustained economic growth and the expansion of the repertoire of acceptable political actions combined to enhance the democratic and participatory character of Canadian society. This improvement notwithstanding, they might also agree that the dynamic of minority-state relations may change markedly in the relatively near future because of two events that have occurred during the past decade. The first is the decade-long economic recession that in part is a consequence of the enormous increase in energy costs. Prolonged periods of stagflation and continuing record budget deficits may

INTRODUCTION

sharply constrain the ability of even the best intentioned government to respond to public needs and demands. The second and more recent event is the ratification of the Constitution with its Charter of Rights and Freedoms. The April 1985 implementation of the Charter not only may significantly expand the array of minority rights that will receive constitutional protection, it also may expand the role of the courts in this process and in the political process more generally. Given these possibilities, we asked the conferees to consider the directions any changes might take and what their implications might be for the status of minorities in Canadian society. Their papers are organized into two sections in this book. The papers in section one focus on the state's role in protecting minority rights and the manner in which this role may change after the implementation of the Charter of Rights and Freedoms. The second section papers are concerned with variations in the status and activities of particular minority groups.

In the first essay of section one, "Protection of Minority Rights under the Canadian Charter of Rights and Freedoms," Dale Gibson delineates the manner in which the Charter has expanded the range of constitutionally entrenched minority rights. It is difficult to assess the eventual impact of the Charter on minority rights, however, because it stands against the backdrop of the courts' passive tradition of self-restraint. Historically, the courts in Canada have deferred to democratically elected representatives and restricted government's legal accountability to matters of procedural form rather than substance. By way of illustration, the courts did not actively exploit the potential of legislation such as the Canadian Bill of Rights. Unlike the Bill of Rights though, the Charter is a constitutional instrument capable of placing significant constraints on legislatures and governments. How the courts will react to this new opportunity to advance minority rights, in Gibson's judgement, "depends on the extent to which judges are prepared to second-guess politicians."

The fundamental dilemma is clear: in a democratic system such as our own, politicians are likely to respond to the wishes of the majority. Minorities, therefore, must look to the courts for protection. Gibson does not argue that the courts should supplant elected decision makers. He suggests, instead, that "a balance is needed: judges should generally respect the decisions of those with the democratic mandate; but they must be willing to intervene, even on matters of substance, where the deep rooted values enshrined in the Charter — including respect for minority rights are imperilled by government action."

Gibson's paper analyses and evaluates the proper domains of legislative and judicial decison makers with respect to general rights and freedoms and particular minority rights. He notes, for example, that the Reasonable Limits clause of the Charter (Section 1) may have the salutary effect of encouraging lawmakers to think more carefully about the purpose and impact of laws. Section 33, however, which allows Parliament to opt out of some key Charter rights, may have deleterious consequences for minorities, exposing them to the political will of an unsympathetic majority.

Although key sections of the Charter (e.g., the general equality clause, Section 15, clause 24 which gives the courts generous remedial powers, and clauses which affect language groups, women and so on) may be regarded as important expansions of minority rights and an invitation to judges to change course, it is unclear whether the courts will accept the invitation. In Gibson's view "the major obstacle to obtaining effective positive remedies from the courts is rooted in judicial inclinations rather than in the law." Gibson does not call for unbridled activism on the part of courts since such a course ultimately could produce a backlash limiting their effectiveness. But, he observes, this does not mean the judiciary must be passive. After all, the courts are uniquely placed to protect minorities in majoritarian regimes. The answer lies in a "creative balance" where the courts collaborate in harmonious duets with politicians.

Mary Eberts' paper, "The Use of Litigation under the Canadian Charter of Rights and Freedoms as a Strategy for Achieving Change," develops one of the central themes introduced by Gibson, namely, the relationship between law and politics, or, more specifically, between legislation and litigation. Eberts expects that the extensive provisions and reach of the Charter hold out considerable promise and encouragement to minority groups in two respects. First, minorities will invoke Charter provisions in order to shape legislation. Second, minorities now will have clear recourse to the courts to measure existing legislation against a constitutional standard.

The fact that there is no obvious overarching definition of "minority" informing the Charter is potentially problematic because it raises the possibility that some minorities, such as language groups, whose rights are specifically enumerated, may enjoy greater protection than groups whose characteristics are not enumerated. Nonetheless, Eberts is optimistic, given the internal structure of the Charter, that minorities will have in it an important new lever for redressing grievances and achieving change.

Eberts calls for the development of coherent, focused litigation *strategies*. Strategic approaches mobilize resources more effectively by spreading the costs of long proceedings — costs which tend to hamper individuals more than governments. Sophisticated strategic approaches also involve the careful selection of cases that meet two criteria: they are winnable on the facts and they provide sound building blocks for the development of the law.

As do other constitutional experts, Eberts anticipates that there will be difficulties in interpreting the Charter. Since the Courts have not developed a sophisticated theoretical apparatus for dealing with egalitarian concepts, they may be expected to play a limited role in resolving conflicts involving egalitarian principles. The Charter, in her view, does not confront indirect inequalities. That is, it does not deal with the actual differential impacts which are at the root of social and economic inequalities. It is unclear, too, how the courts will resolve the question of individual vs. group rights. Notwithstanding these problems, Eberts makes a compelling case that intelligently employed litigation strategies provide a realistic springboard for lobbying and remedial legislation.

Historically, governments in Canada have taken the following policy orientations toward minorities: non-discrimination policies; special treatment policies based on a group's unique legal status; and group self-government policies. F.L. "Ted" Morton's paper, "Group Rights Versus Individual Rights in the Charter," suggests that Section 15 of the Charter reinforces, but significantly complicates, policies affecting minorities. In the past, in the absence of a constitutionally entrenched rights clause such as Section 15 of the Charter, federal and provincial legislatures were responsible for resolving competing demands. Under Section 15 of the Charter, however, minority group members are in a position to challenge these policies as violations of one or more of the several equality rights. They will be encouraged to do so because all government policies concerning minorities potentially are subject to judicial review.

Morton argues that the aforementioned complication results from the compression by the framers of the Charter of two contrary principles. One principle draws on the group rights tradition, a tradition that entails the use of status classifications. The other principle prohibits such classifications. His paper explores the legal and political implications of these conflicting notions of rights by examining the cases of two minority groups — natives and French Canadians. Unlike minorities which strive for assimilation into the social and economic mainstream of Canadian life, the traditional goals of both native and French Canadian minorities have been oriented toward maintaining group identity and maximizing autonomy. Morton suggests that the pursuit of these goals through the courts inevitably will precipitate a confrontation between individual and group rights, forcing judges to choose between the competing notions of minority rights built into Section 15 of the Charter.

The implications of "judicializing" issues of fundamental political disagreement, Morton argues, are rather disturbing. On the one hand, the courts, unlike other political institutions, are not suited to facilitate political accommodation. On the other, the courts are being asked to solve problems that other institutions have been unable to solve successfully. What, for example, will happen if the courts are forced to choose between individual and group rights, or between competing group rights, in which parties are not willing to accept adverse decisions? Will Canadians support federal enforcement of Supreme Court decisions? What will be the costs of such federal enforcement?

Rainer Knopff's paper, "Statistical Protection of Minorities: Affirmative Action Policy in Canada," starts with the assertion that the age of affirmative action is upon us. The paper analyses the major components of the new affirmative action programs and the reasons by which they are justified — particularly the claim that affirmative action is a necessary remedy for discrimination. The author argues that these reasons amount to tendentious rhetoric — that they cannot really justify what has come to be a central component in virtually all affirmative action programs: the emphasis on the setting and achievement of numerical "goals" or "targets."

This statistical orientation, he suggests, is rhetorically (and hence politically) difficult to justify because it suggests that proportional representation of groups is the norm and that any deviations from proportionality are due to discrimination. However, common sense indicates that discrimination, as it is commonly understood, does not account for all statistical imbalance. Further, the setting of numerical targets by reference to a standard of statistical balance appears to run afoul of the publicly supported merit principle.

Proponents of affirmative action have an answer to both of these objections. In order to make discrimination account for more of the observable statistical imbalance, they expand the definition of the term, adding what is called "systemic discrimination." But even systemic discrimination cannot account for all of the remaining imbalance and so the affirmative action rhetoric makes its peace with common sense, the author argues, by disclaiming any belief in the norm of proportionality. Indeed, affirmative action programs go to great lengths to develop an elaborate methodology to control for that degree of imbalance that is *not* due to discrimination. This, it is argued, allows the setting of realistic "goals," lower and more flexible than the "quotas" that would be required to produce complete demographic proportionality. Unlike quotas, moreover, such moderate goals are alleged not to violate the merit principle.

In fact, Knopff asserts, this "methodology of moderation" is nothing more than pseudo-scientific mystification. It is part of "the underhandedness of affirmative action." The premise on which it is based — that not all imbalance is caused by discrimination — undermines the case not only for quotas, but for any numerical emphasis. The only truly compelling case for the prevailing statistical mania is faith in the norm of proportionality, and ultimately the rhetoricians of affirmative action admit as much. The paper argues that if this is true, then one can continue to attribute statistical imbalance to discrimination only by expanding the definition of the term to such an extent that it loses all meaning. It thus becomes apparent that the utility of the term for affirmative action programs is primarily rhetorical, a utility it derives from its unexpanded, common sense meaning.

Thomas Flanagan's paper "The Manufacture of Minorities" examines the relationship between what the author terms "the legal manufacture of minorities" and the activities of the eleven Human Rights Commissions in Canada. Flanagan begins by arguing that the meaning of the word "minority" has been broadened by social scientists so that currently a generally accepted definition is that it is a group characterized by identifiability, differential power, pejorative treatment, and group awareness. Consequently, mere statistical minorities, for example, left-handed people, can become genuine minority groups "if they become aware of their powerlessness and mistreatment at the hands of a statistical majority and if they can gain a degree of public recognition of their group trait."

Ontario created the first Human Rights Commission in 1962 and all other provinces as well as the federal government had created similar commissions by 1977. Despite variations in detail among individual commissions, Flanagan contends that one may speak of a distinctly Canadian approach to protecting minorities against discrimination. The main features of the approach are: (1) enactment of a comprehensive code rather than passage of several anti-discrimination statutes; (2) entrusting all enforcement within a jurisdiction to a single body rather than dividing it among several agencies; (3) mandating a conciliation stage before adversary proceedings begin in a dispute; (4) except in Québec, creating quasi-judicial tribunals to settle disputes, with ultimate appeal to the courts; and (5) delegating public education to the same commission that oversees enforcement.

Although the Canadian approach has many advantages, it also has led to a marked tendency on the part of commissions to expand their jurisdiction. Although no single commission lists all of them, there currently are thirty prohibited grounds of discrimination, which Flanagan classifies as "stigmata," "life cycle" and "life style." Stigmata are group characteristics that are regularly passed from one generation to the next through genetic inheritance. Life cycle criteria are biologically based but are not transmitted in the same way as stigmata (e.g., women bear both male and female children). Life style criteria are the result of personal choice.

INTRODUCTION

There is a clear pattern, the author argues, in the way in which these thirty criteria have entered into legislation. The stigmata came first, being largely adopted in the 1960s. The life cycle criteria were largely accepted in the 1970s and early 1980s and — although no single life style criterion has yet succeeded in gaining acceptance by a majority of commissions — Flanagan predicts that they will dominate the human rights agenda in the 1980s.

Flanagan offers several explanations for the expansion of the jurisdiction of Human Rights Commissions. Among these are that the staffs of Human Rights Commissions have a vested interest in expansion. Another contributing factor is that the several commissions keep in touch with one another and an amendment in one jurisdiction is likely to be imitated elsewhere. The existence of commissions also provides a lobbying target for organized pressure groups who seek to advance their cause by getting it accepted as a human rights issue. Finally, many groups seek a "risk free" society and look to the state to provide it. The provision of insurance against even everyday risks, the author suggests, is not "manna from heaven." Rather, it involves considerable costs which are not less real or substantial because they are known primarily through abstract reasoning.

In a paper, "Stereotypes, Statistics and Slippery Slopes," in which he responds to Flanagan and Knopff, Dale Gibson identifies three main methods used by governments to redress the unequal opportunities facing minorities: prohibition of discrimination based on group stereotypes, affirmative action, and education programs. All three, he suggests, are under siege and in the paper he confronts both Flanagan's critique of the prohibitionary approach and Knopff's reservations about affirmative action.

Gibson questions Flanagan's assertion that it is dangerous to extend human rights legislation to encompass broader categories of minorities. He feels the use of statistics and stereotypes is risky. Stereotypes may be convenient, he says, but "against the convenience of basing business decisions on statistically supportable stereotypes must be weighed the fact that some applicants will have been deprived of an equal opportunity to compete for the job or benefit on their own individual merits."

Gibson also rejects the usefulness of Flanagan's typology which classifies minorities according to stigmatic, life cycle and life style criteria and challenges the practical validity of the voluntaristic and non-voluntaristic distinction that underpins minority group membership. He argues that Flanagan "fails to explain satisfactorily why the prohibition of discrimination is justified in one category but not in others." In the final analysis, he contends, Flanagan "fails to demonstrate any real difference in cost, or indeed any other convincing distinction sufficient to justify prohibiting discrimination by race, religion, nationality or ethnicity, but permitting other forms."

Gibson defends affirmative action, the second arrow in the government's equal opportunity quiver, from Knopff's criticism by arguing that affirmative action is a "no fault" catch-up approach to remedy inequality. He points out that unlike anti-discrimination laws "affirmative action employs the very statistical methods that anti-discrimination laws condemn." If affirmative action programs were driven by a statistical engine they would be unfair because individual differences would not be taken into account. Fortunately, Gibson claims, "few affirmative action plans are absolute"; most take into account individual factors while giving special consideration to members of minority target groups.

Although affirmative action necessarily involves a measure of favouritism based on group affiliation, he argues that much of the kind of criticism Knopff makes — which focuses on the apparent inconsistency between collective and individual treatment — is not merited. Since "inequality results from the societal tendency to treat minorities collectively, collective measures are needed to address that inequality."

In Gibson's view, the kind of analysis offered by Flanagan and Knopff is informed by concerns, widely held, that further government intrusion into the private sphere is unwarranted and that Human Rights Commissions are an advance down the slippery slope to a "totalitarian abyss." He counters that many human rights initiatives are, in fact, voluntary and that public sector activities in general are justifiable if they promote important social goals. Finally, Gibson argues that those who attack Human Rights Commissions for being intrusive arms of government miss two points. First, the commissions serve, in part, to control government excesses. Second, notwithstanding some glaring exceptions, most commissions are sufficiently independent of governments, in practice, to do so effectively. Indeed, far from representing a threatening form of government intervention, Human Rights Commissions can be regarded as deterrents to such intrusion.

In their paper, "The Resolution of Complaints Based on Race and Origin: The Canadian Human Rights Commission," William Reeves and James S. Frideres focus on the activities of one such commission. More specifically, they examine the disposition of the files of 49 cases of complaints of discrimination investigated by the Canadian Human Rights Commission during the period 1979-1983. The commission was established by an act of Parliament in 1977 and although a number of changes were made in the original act in 1983, its basic structure remains unchanged. The commission deals with complaints falling into one or more proscribed grounds: race, colour, national or ethnic origins, religion, age, sex, marital status, family status, disability, and conviction for which a pardon has been granted. Its jurisdiction extends to federal bodies such as government departments and to private sector areas subject to federal regulation such as chartered banks. In addition, organizations doing business with the federal government must meet federal standards of anti-discrimination. The Complaints and Compliance Branch deals with all formal complaints lodged with the commission.

The pursuit of formal complaints usually begins in one of the commission's regional offices. A determination is first made as to whether the complaint falls within federal jurisdiction and involves discrimination as defined in the act. If these two conditions are met, an investigator collects data from the complainant and the respondent and may augment these with information from other witnesses and sources. The investigator's report and recommendations are presented to the commission for a final decision. The commission decides whether the complaint is substantiated, whether a settlement will be proposed, and, if so, what it will be.

Reeves and Frideres' analysis of the case files indicated that cases involving race/colour and national/ethnic origins were dismissed substantially more frequently than were complaints based on other grounds. For all types of cases, documentation had an important bearing on their resolution. Generally, documents were used by investigators to substantiate the claims of the

INTRODUCTION

complainants. The exceptions to this general practice were complaints alleging discrimination on the bases of national/ethnic origins. In the latter cases, documentation tended to be used by investigators to establish the reasonableness of the actions of respondents. As a consequence documentation for complaints based on national/ethnic origins tended to be associated more often with dismissals.

Both race/colour and national/ethnic origins complaints tended to be resolved in a rather ad hoc fashion. Conclusions as to whether discrimination had occurred were avoided and dismissals of complaints usually were justified by references to the particulars of interpersonal relationships between the complainants and respondents.

The authors offer several reasons why complaints based on national/ethnic or race/colour discrimination tended to be disposed of in a different fashion from complaints based on other grounds. They make clear that there is no evidence that differences in the disposition of cases were the product of some conscious plan or the objective of the commission. Indeed, it was the commission itself which initially drew the attention of others to the possibility of a differential disposition of cases. Notwithstanding this fact, Reeves and Frideres argue that the differences in disposition noted are a matter of serious concern meriting continued monitoring and, if necessary, additional, more intensive investigation.

Leo Driedger's paper, "Conformity vs. Pluralism: Minority Identities and Inequalities," the first in the second section of this book, contends that although two models, which he terms "assimilationist" and "pluralist," have been developed to describe relationships between the Anglo-Celtic majority and minority groups in Canada, in fact there are numerous variants of these pure types and different groups can be located in positions between the polar models. The author focuses on several such, which he terms Franco-conformity, amalgamation, modified assimilation, conflict, modified pluralism and segregated enclavic identity. He goes on to discuss the conditions required to maintain the identity of a minority group such as a segregated territory, separate ethnic institutions, charismatic leadership and a religious or political ideology. He notes, however, that a majority often forces a separate existence upon certain minorities by creating majority-minority social distance through devices such as stereotyping, prejudice and discrimination. As a consequence, a voluntary-involuntary as well as an assimilationist-pluralist continuum can be utilized to generate a five-cell conformity-pluralist conceptual model of majority-minority relations. He concludes by discussing the three directions — assimilation, amalgamation, and pluralism — these relations may take in Canada and suggests that the new Charter of Rights and Freedoms may facilitate the maintenance of the latter relationship.

In "Minorities and the Canadian Visual Media" Ronald Dick focuses on interactions between the visual media and minorities in Canada. More specifically, he is concerned with addressing three questions: (1) how have ethnic and visible minorities been portrayed over time by the visual media? (2) how have the visual media responded to minority complaints regarding their (minority) representation? and, (3) how have minorities evaluated changes in media representations of, and policies toward, them?

Regarding the visual media's treatment of minorities, a review of fifty years of American films indicates that ethnic and visible minorities long were subjected to negative stereotyping. Since the Canadian film market until very recently was entirely an extension of the American, Canadian audiences were equally exposed to these depictions. By way of illustration, French Canadians, Métis, and Indians invariably were represented as irresponsible, unreliable, lazy, childish, gullible, and amoral, with a marked tendency to violent and uncontrollable fits of passion. Asiatics, in an endless stream of films, were depicted as sinister, cunning, devious, cowardly, sexually immoral, ruthless, and possessed of a natural gift for complicated crime. Other minorities were also subjected to negative stereotyping, ranging from the malevolently racist to the offensively paternalistic.

Because of consistent complaints by minority leaders regarding their depiction in films and television, overt expressions of racism largely have ended and there has been a steady reduction in the production of the most blatant types of misrepresentation. Notwithstanding these changes, representatives of visible and ethnic minorities have continued to complain about the existence of negative stereotypes, residual racism, ignorance, invisibility, and the misuse or nonuse of minorities in advertising. Especially irritating to minorities — as overt expressions of prejudice toward them have diminished — have been the latter two conditions. Regarding their relative invisibility, minorities complain that they are being hurt by not being represented among decision makers in public and private media organizations and among the "gatekeepers" in the production, news-gathering, and writing staffs who control what goes on and what does not. With respect to advertising, their complaint has been that they are "left out" as actors and consumers alike. Moreover, when they do appear in advertisements, they continue to be stereotyped (e.g., Chinese sell tea and blacks sell basketballs).

According to Dick, the liberal attitudes which nourished the ethnic revival of the 1970s and the sensitivity to criticism of media officials who regard themselves as "progressive" helped insure that most minority complaints would be found valid. The response of the media was a virtual torrent of materials on the minority experience in Canada. Although those efforts have drawn only mixed reviews from minority spokesmen and more dispassionate academic observers, the author argues (any shortcomings notwithstanding) that the materials have had a significant and positive impact on public attitudes toward visible and ethnic minorities. "I believe that the 'people with the funny names' and the 'odd looks' will be less ill at ease, perhaps no more so than the McTavishes and the Poiriers. As a result we will all have come at least to like, understand, and even enjoy one another a bit more. If so, that will be a gain indeed."

Frank MacKinnon's paper, "When 'Rights' are Wrong: With Examples from Atlantic Canada," concerns the enthusiastic and emotional atmosphere that surrounds fashionable causes such as minority rights. The minority game is easy to play. People are easily moved to support petitions without comprehending the subjects or understanding the motives behind them. Their sympathies may be inspired by genuine compassion but they can become political capital for those wishing to exploit them. MacKinnon argues that the strong temptation to take the moral high road on minority issues should be resisted. There are inherent dangers in being swept along by the increasing tendency "to enhance groups by calling them minorities and conjuring up privileges disguised as rights." Certainly, MacKinnon argues, "we should respect thinking minorities and

INTRODUCTION

promote deserved rights." However, the examination of high sounding abstract ideas such as "rights" and "minorities" should be conducted in a balanced way, with an eye to flexibility and by engaging in dialogue.

It is easy to advocate the benefits of extending rights to minorities but a genuine dialogue serving both minorities and the Canadian community can take place only if the costs of extending minority rights are given serious and open consideration. We pay lip service to the axiom that Canada will thrive on unity and find strength in diversity but, the author suggests, "unity must be developed, not forced, and diversity respected, not exaggerated." The author argues that the public needs protection against unscrupulous minorities — "against groups that must promote organized loyalty as a psychological crutch to keep and control their membership; against ideological and dogmatic gurus who train members to admit no mistakes and compromise no 'principles'; and against the fact that promoting minorities and rights always involves hunting for villains, and going too far makes villains of everyone."

MacKinnon contends that the Atlantic region illustrates the problems of politicized status minorities found elsewhere in Canada. In the east, he points out, pump priming is a popular phrase, but priming is useless unless it is followed by vigorous pumping. The efforts of status seekers and privilege gatherers, however, are devoted to priming and the dangers and costs of this misguided preoccupation are legion. People, he suggests, become accustomed to being sustained rather than being creative, the emphasis is on getting over doing, politicization over productivity and membership over citizenship. Initiative is suffocated and obstructed, small matters become inflated; it is a case of macro politics for micro events. These preoccupations amount to a massive handicap for more productive, efficient cooperative enterprises which, in the long run, benefit everyone. The tragedy, MacKinnon suggests, is that by world standards we have little to complain about, yet we must find villains among ourselves.

In contrast to most discussions of minorities which deal with social realities, Barry Cooper's paper, "The West: A Political Minority," deals with the West as a political minority within the Canadian federation. The author notes that a federal regime attempts to reconcile representation of territorially based interests with interests that arise from sheer numbers of citizens. From the beginning of its association with Canada, the West has encountered considerable difficulty in defending its interests when they have conflicted with the numerically larger East. But conflicting interests are the substance of politics, just as conciliation of them is its highest purpose.

Politics is not only the activity of conciliating interests; it is also controversy — words, speeches, discourses. Conflicts are considered meaningful, and those meanings are expressed in accounts, stories, and myths. Taken as an ensemble, stories, including the stories of persistent conflicts over public policy, constitute, in Northrop Frye's words, a sense of identity, an expression of how a territory becomes a home, a familiar place, a "here." A sense of identity is common to all regions of Canada, but it is not a common identity precisely because it is local. The sense of identity is nourished and conditioned by the environment, but mostly it is sustained by stories that give meaning to historical experience. Cooper argues that on the basis of literary evidence — of stories, symbols, and myths that express local experiences of place — it seems clear that no common story unites East and West. This enormously complicates the question of Canadian federalism because expectations and assumptions alter the emotional meaning of common words: the CPR does not, to a Saskatchewan wheat farmer, evoke a national dream.

According to Cooper, a final factor that alters the sense of an already complex understanding of how the imaginative reality of the West exists as a political minority within the federation is given by technology. Technology tends to erode all sense of identity by eclipsing the importance of particular locale in favour of a universal and homogeneous milieu. That is, it alters the meaning of East-West conflict by depriving both terms of their former sense, which was one of opposition, of particularity and heterogeneity. The same process, moreover, is altering the sense of the federation by turning political conflicts — the conflicts of high ambition and public interests — into disputes of administrative jurisdiction and the management of social policies, including the manufacture of social minorities. The author predicts that if Western regionalism continues to exist under such circumstances, it will be in an altered political form.

In their paper, "The Changing Political Situation of Women in Canada," Joel Smith, Allan Kornberg, and Beth Rushing focus on women and their participation in the political process. They examine the situation of women because women, despite their numerical majority, have been identified as a social group that suffers from a wide range of social, economic and political disadvantages. Their analysis deals with behavioural and attitudinal involvement in politics because politics is the socially approved means for accomplishing changes in ascribed status in democratic polities. It is complicated by the fact that some generally accepted beliefs about women, namely that women are more conservative than men, that they participate in politics less than do men, and that when they do participate their beliefs and actions primarily reflect the influence of men on them, are based on research that may be flawed by a fundamental male bias in its topical orientations. Further, much of the research that supports these generalizations is quite old and the burgeoning feminist movement may have changed things even if the characterization of women's political involvement once was correct.

To explore these possibilities, information concerning the political opinions and behaviour of men and women in Trois Rivières, Peterborough and Lethbridge at the time of the Quebec referendum on sovereignty association were examined for evidence of spuriousness and change. Despite difficulties in measurement, Smith, Kornberg, and Rushing judge that the weight of evidence suggests that gross indications of greater male interest and activity are spurious products of differences in the age structure and marital statuses of the two gender groups. Using age as a proxy for change since earlier studies were done, they also find indications of the disappearance of any gender differences that might have existed some years ago. Given the experience of their analysis, they assert that it is clear that if women are less involved and more disadvantaged politically, it is not because of any unalterable biological differences or unchangeable social norms or structural arrangements that are gender-based. In addition, they suggest that changes in women's political involvement and participation attributable to pressures for such change may have been accomplished not only through legal means and publicity, but as a consequence of the role of women's groups in refocusing the agenda of concerns that are at the centre of political attention.

INTRODUCTION

Frances Abele's paper, "Dene-Government Relations: The Development of a New Political Minority," explores the process by which the Dene aboriginal peoples of the Northwest Territories became a politicized minority and how that politicization transformed the relationship between the Dene and the state. Historically, southern Canada's interest in the North has been a function of the changing geopolitical and economic significance of the region. By the mid-twentieth century the region had experienced extensive contacts with southern culture and the contacts had had debilitating effects on northern aboriginal life styles. However, those contacts largely were episodic and had not generated highly organized, coherent collective responses from native peoples. It was the proposed construction of the Mackenzie Valley Pipeline through the Dene's traditional lands which focused and mobilized the political energy of the Dene. Abele explains that it was in the face of the Pipeline crisis that the Dene were able to overcome cultural differences which had traditionally divided them, to emphasize their similarities, and to develop a common public interpretation of their collective history. The paper argues that the Dene's ability to forge a common interpretation provided an essential basis for a strategy which called for a common defense of their collective interests, interests which revolved around the preservation of aspects of their traditional culture.

Using evidence presented before the Berger Inquiry, Abele illustrates that while there were important generational differences within the Dene community, and differences in political perspectives towards representatives of the Canadian South, the common ground of opposition to the project was effectively communicated. The effectiveness of that communication and the success the Dene achieved in the courts represented successful adaptive responses to the hitherto unfamiliar hierarchical institutional structures of the Canadian state. But the very use of those institutional structures at least implicitly suggests acceptance of the legitimacy of the state apparatus. However, this was achieved without forfeiting traditional claims and traditional cultural values. Abele is confident that "the institutional arrangements now in place guarantee that the passage of the Dene from a position of silence and virtual powerlessness to one which their influence over at least regional affairs is assured will not be reversed."

Government efforts in North America to advance the causes and protect the rights of minorities were facilitated by landmark judicial decisions made in response to the political activism of the American civil rights movement. The Canadian government, like its United States counterpart, has adopted a broad range of policies intended to assist groups such as racial minorities, women and the handicapped. In their paper, "Minorities as an Attitudinal Phenomenon: A Comparative Analysis of Youth Elites," Neil Nevitte and Roger Gibbins argue that it would be a mistake for Canadian governments to follow the American approach because there is no Canadian equivalent to the civil rights experience which informed American policy making. They suggest that in the absence of an equivalent history, Canadian orientations towards minorities will be fundamentally different from American orientations. The paper explores this contention using survey data on the attitudes of two matched samples of senior college undergraduates in the United States and Canada.

Analysis of the data indicates a number of significant differences between Canadian and American respondents. Canadians are less likely to identify achieving equality for black/racial minorities as an important social priority and are less likely to support the use of quotas as a tool for giving minorities access to education or the job market. And, although American respondents show a generalized support for a host of minority related issues, Canadians do not. Moreover, among Canadians, support for one minority group is not a good predictor of support for others. Canadians are also significantly less likely to see any connection between support for minority causes and other fundamental social and political issues such as the use of government intervention to redistribute income. It is noteworthy, too, that neither Anglophone nor Francophone respondents see the French-English language division as a minority concern.

The authors conclude that Canadian students do not offer generalized support for minority causes. They make sharp distinctions between minority groups and the term "minority" is not a powerful organizer of Canadian opinion. This finding alone raises questions about the political utility of the label. The authors suggest that their findings "challenge the assumption that minority legislation in Canada will be able to draw from the same kind of political support that is clearly in place in the United States." The implication is that in Canada there may be less potential for political coalitions across minority groups and that there may be little advantage to groups in representing themselves as "minorities." By the same token, because there is less linkage between minority and other issues, governments in Canada may have the freedom to take on minority issues without encountering the kind of broader ideological resistance that their American counterparts have confronted.

As noted above, in Canada (and in other advanced industrial societies with democratic political systems) the repertoire of political action has expanded during the past twenty years to encompass activities such as protest marches, sit-ins, and so forth. Because it has, and because the minority of people who have engaged in such actions periodically have been able to effect significant changes in public policy, Harold Clarke, Allan Kornberg and Marianne Stewart focus on both the extent and correlates of unconventional political activity in Canada in their paper, "Politically Active Minorities: Participation in Canadian Democracy." They feel Canada is a particularly appropriate site for this type of investigation because "almost nothing is known about the 'whos' and 'whys' of unconventional or protest political activities and their relationship to more conventional kinds of political action." They attempt to illuminate these matters by employing data drawn from a 1983 national study in which respondents were asked whether they approved of and had participated in six unconventional activities ranging from signing a petition to taking part in a protest or demonstration that could have turned violent. Members of the public also were asked whether they felt such activities were effective.

As is the case with conventional participation, the level of the public's involvement in protest activities varied widely. People were more likely to approve than disapprove, and to find effective rather than ineffective, relatively "safe" activities such as signing a petition or joining a boycott. In contrast, they were less likely to approve of and regard as effective more extreme acts such as participating in a wildcat strike or sitting in a public or private building. Although a total of only 15 percent of the respondents stated they had participated in more extreme forms of protest behaviour, those who had tended

INTRODUCTION

to be disproportionately young, well educated, interested in politics, residents of Québec, less willing to comply with the decisions of government, and less supportive of the national political community.

With regard to the patterns of political activities, combining patterns of conventional and unconventional actions indicated that the traditional dichotomy counterposing a large majority of political "spectators" to a relative handful of inveterate political activists is inadequate. A more accurate characterization is one that juxtaposes *several* active minorities against a small group of inactives and a modal category of minimal participants. Significantly, however, the latter group is itself a minority.

The authors speculate that one reason protest activities such as the ones on which they focus have achieved varying degrees of social acceptance is the extensive coverage they have received in the media, especially television. Notwithstanding their varying degree of acceptance, protest actions of the extreme variety still carry with them a degree of risk to which most people are unwilling to expose themselves. More important, most Canadians understand that protest activities resulting in serious or frequent disruptions of public order eventually threaten a democratic political order. Consequently, they voluntarily refrain from engaging in actions that eventually might require even the most permissive public officials to employ coercive countermeasures. This mind of self-denying behaviour has enabled a democratic political order to be maintained in Canada, even as the delicate balance continues to shift between political stability and governmental effectiveness on the one hand, and enhanced democratization and citizen participation on the other.

We noted above that relations between minority groups and the state may well be approaching a significant juncture. Canadians currently live in an economic environment in which the national debt is large, unemployment is high, and the economic pie is shrinking. On the one hand these conditions may constrain the efforts of government at all levels to respond to public needs and demands, including those of minority groups. On the other hand, the Charter of Rights and Freedoms that will be implemented shortly may increase — perhaps dramatically — both the number of group demands and the role of the courts in addressing them. Some of the papers in this volume have attempted to analyse events that may ensue from the concatenation of these conditions. Others have been concerned with the status of minority groups more generally. None offers definitive answers, but together they may have shed light on some of the problems pertinent to minority-state relations, the complexities of which will continue to offer strong intellectual and emotional challenges to all Canadians of good will.

Neil Nevitte
Calgary, Alberta
Allan Kornberg
Durham, North Carolina
December 1984

MINORITY RIGHTS, HUMAN RIGHTS AND THE CHARTER

2

PROTECTION OF MINORITY RIGHTS UNDER THE CANADIAN CHARTER OF RIGHTS AND FREEDOMS: CAN POLITICIANS AND JUDGES SING HARMONY?

DALE GIBSON

INTRODUCTION

The Canadian Charter of Rights and Freedoms, enacted in 1982, offers new constitutional protections for minority rights. Constitutional guarantees for minority rights are not a complete novelty for Canada; sections 93 and 133 of the Constitution Act, 1867, established important protections for both Roman Catholic and Protestant minority schools (Schmeiser 1964:125), and the right to use the English and French languages in certain limited situations (Sheppard 1971; *A.-G. Quebec v. Blaikie* 1981). The new Charter has greatly expanded the range of constitutionally entrenched minority rights, however.

It would be unwise to place too much importance on these new constitutional provisions yet. The disillusionment caused by the courts' failure to exploit the full potential of the Canadian Bill of Rights is still too fresh to expect high hopes from libertarians (Tarnopolsky 1975). On the other hand, the Charter is, unlike the Bill, a constitutional instrument, capable of placing significant constraints on the actions of both Parliament and the provincial legislatures, as well as of their respective governments. It would be an even greater error, at this early stage, to assume that the Charter has added little to the fundamental rights of Canadians.

It all depends on the extent to which judges are prepared to second-guess politicians. Canadian courts have a tradition of deference to the decisions of democratically elected representatives; they have generally refused to interfere with political decisions unless they exceed by a very wide margin what most Canadians would regard as permissible bounds. They have tended to restrict governments' legal accountability to matters of form, rather than of substance; if proper procedures have been followed, substantive unfairness has not usually concerned the courts. For Canadian judges the medium has indeed been the message.

Where minority rights are concerned, the danger of placing too much faith in the democratic process is obvious. Politicians understandably respond to what they perceive as the wishes of the majority. It is to the courts that minorities must generally look for protection of their constitutional rights. New Charter protections of minority rights will be of little real value if the courts persist in their tendency to defer unduly to political judgements.

This is not to suggest that courts should supplant the elected decision makers. That would negate the democratic nature of the Canadian Constitution. A balance is needed: judges should generally respect the decisions of those with the democratic mandate; but they must be willing to intervene, even on matters of substance, where the deep-rooted values enshrined in the Charter — including respect for minority rights — are imperilled by governmental actions.

The Charter has created numerous new opportunities for judicial scrutiny of governmental conduct. This paper will examine the major opportunities affecting minority rights. It will deal first with a number of general questions, applicable to all guaranteed rights and freedoms, and will then turn to a consideration of specific minority rights. In both sections the focus will be on the proper ambits of political and judicial decision making, in a democratic nation concerned about the rights of its minorities.

SOME GENERAL ISSUES

REASONABLE LIMITS

No right is absolute. In part, this is so because most rights, if fully exercised, would conflict with other equally important rights. My right to freedom of expression is subject, for example, to your right to be protected from defamation. Your freedom of assembly is subject to my liberty to pass freely through public streets. Moreover, the protection and convenience of the community often require restrictions on individual rights and freedoms. Rights and freedoms guaranteed by every constitution of the world are limited by these facts of life. In many cases the limitations are not explicitly articulated in the constitutional documents, but they are nevertheless recognized by the courts that interpret them. Under the Canadian Charter of Rights and Freedoms, the recognition of these limitations is explicit (Conklin 1982; Christian 1982; Morel 1983; Marx 1982).

Section 1 reads as follows:

> The Canadian Charter of Rights and Freedoms guarantees the rights and freedoms set out in it subject only to such reasonable limits prescribed by law as can be demonstrably justified in a free and democratic society.

This section makes manifest the relationship between lawmakers and judges that was contemplated by the drafters of the Charter: the legislators may place restrictions on Charter rights, so long as the courts agree that the restrictions are "reasonable limits." Whenever a court is called upon to decide whether the Charter has been violated by some legal ordinance, it must make a determination about whether that ordinance constitutes a "reasonable limit ... in a free and democratic society." While it would be possible for the courts to abdicate their supervisory role by holding that any restriction enacted by a democratically elected legislature is, ipso facto, a reasonable limit ... the early decisions show no inclination to do so. They indicate a willingness to examine the reasonableness of each restriction on a case-by-case basis.

To a greater extent than ever before, therefore, Canadian courts must now consider the consonance of the laws they administer with fundamental values of Canadian society. I believe this will require them to be more open than they have in the past to "social testimony": evidence about the purpose intended to be served by particular legal restrictions, and about the impact those restrictions have or are likely to have on Canadian society. That exercise is likely to have at least two beneficial side effects: the need to articulate goals and impacts when judicially challenged should cause governmental policy makers to think more deeply about proposed new laws before putting them into effect; and exposure of the courts to evidence about the likely societal impact of their decisions should

PROTECTION OF MINORITY RIGHTS

lead to more realistic and humane judicial decision making.

An important characteristic of section 1 that is sometimes overlooked is that it applies only to such limits as are "prescribed by law." This means that a practice or procedure adopted by a governmental organization would not be protected by section 1 from a Charter attack, no matter how reasonable the practice or procedure might be, unless it were embodied in a "law" of some kind. While an authoritative definition of "law" for this purpose has not yet been provided by the courts, it seems likely that it includes a wide range of legal ordinances: statutes, regulations, by-laws, orders-in-council, as well as the common law and other judge-made law.

"Prescribed" means "written in advance," and the reason for requiring Charter limitations to be prescribed must be to ensure that they are capable of being known, accepted and complied with by the community. Some courts have held that section 1 does not justify laws which bestow general undefined discretionary powers on public authorities, because limitations on rights and freedoms that result from discretionary powers are not written in advance, and are therefore not "prescribed" (*Ontario Film & Video Appreciation Society and Ontario Board of Censors* 1983). This approach, if upheld by the Supreme Court of Canada, would impose a constitutional requirement of certainty on Canadian laws which restrict Charter rights.

While section 1 would not, strictly speaking, apply to a governmental practice or procedure that was not embedded in law, it is possible that such a practice or procedure, if reasonable, would nevertheless survive a Charter attack on the ground that, even apart from section 1, Charter rights are qualified rights. Suppose, as a matter of practice, rather than of law, prison authorities refused to employ guards of the opposite sex for duties which would bring them into intimate contact with the prisoners. Section 15 of the Charter prohibits "discrimination" based on sex, among other factors. The likelihood is great, I believe, that a court would nevertheless uphold the practice, if it found it to be reasonable, on the ground that it would not involve "discrimination" in the pejorative sense intended by section 15.

It will be noted that section 1 uses the term "limits" to describe the permitted restriction of Charter rights. The view has been expressed by some, including a prominent Quebec judge in an important early Charter decision, that the term "limits" does not include a total *denial* of a right or freedom. In the case in question, a law of the province of Quebec completely denied to certain Anglophone parents the right to English language education for their children in accordance with section 23 of the Charter. Lawyers for the province argued that this was a "reasonable limit" imposed in the interests of preserving the French language in Quebec. Among other reasons advanced for rejecting that argument, Chief Justice Deschênes expressed the view that no law which completely denies a right can qualify as a "limit" under section 1 of the Charter (*Quebec Association of Protestant School Boards v. A.-G. Quebec* 1984). If this point of view should be upheld by the Supreme Court of Canada, it would place an important restriction on section 1.

LEGISLATIVE OPT-OUT

Section 33 of the Charter permits either the Parliament of Canada or a provincial legislature to remove from the scope of most Charter protections any legislative provision which they choose to declare operative notwithstanding the Charter (Marx 1982:70; Scott 1982; Slattery 1983). This opt-out procedure does not apply to all Charter rights; it does not apply, for example, to minority language provisions or to aboriginal and treaty right provisions. It does, however, operate with respect to the all-important general equality right contained in section 15. While each opt-out has a maximum duration of five years, it may be renewed every five years for an indefinite period.

This controversial section was one of the prices of agreement to the 1982 constitutional amendments extracted during negotiations by provinces that were opposed to or suspicious about the constitutional entrenchment of fundamental rights and freedoms (Sheppard & Valpy 1982). It was eventually accepted by those who supported the entrenchment of rights, on the theory that governments would rarely be willing to face the intense public criticism likely to be provoked by a deliberate setting aside of Charter rights. The difficulty with this theory is that the democratic pressures upon which it depends reflect the views of the majority, while it is usually minority rights with which the Charter is concerned. As Canada's shameful treatment of its Japanese Canadian population during World War II demonstrates, the majority becomes quite insensitive to minority interests during times of perceived threats to the nation or to the community. At such times, governments are readier than normal to sacrifice minority rights, and most citizens are reluctant to criticize such "emergency measures."

Although no other government has yet seen fit to employ the opt-out mechanism, the Legislature of Quebec has already opted-out of the Charter on a wholesale basis, by a single legislative provision to the effect that *all* Quebec statutes operate notwithstanding the provisions of the Charter with respect to which it is possible to opt-out (An Act Respecting the Constitution Act 1982). It would be hard to imagine a more dramatic illustration of the fact that the opt-out mechanism can be easily employed by a government which enjoys the support of its constituency on that issue.

It is possible that Quebec's omnibus opt-out, and other unreasonable attempts to avoid the operation of the Charter, could be ruled unconstitutional. There are some who believe, for example, that section 33 contemplates an individualized opting-out process, whereby each separate statutory provision and relevant Charter right is listed. Another approach would be to treat section 33 as being subject to section 1, which would mean that courts have the power to determine whether statutes opting-out of the Charter are "reasonable limits" in a "free and democratic society." Both approaches were rejected by Chief Justice Deschênes in the first challenge of Quebec's opt-out (*Alliance des Professeurs de Montréal v. A.-G. Quebec* 1984). That decision was based on the view that section 33 was intended to give legislators the power, so long as they observe the prescribed form, to escape judicial scrutiny altogether.

Even if that view ultimately prevails, it strengthens the case of searching judicial scrutiny of restrictive laws enacted without the support of an opt-out clause. If the elected lawmakers wish to avoid Charter scrutiny they may employ section 33. If they choose not to do so the courts cannot be accused of intruding into the democratic process by examining the substantive reasonableness of legislation; the legislators have implicitly agreed to it.

APPLICATION OF CHARTER TO PRIVATE SECTOR
Threats to minority rights come from both governmental and non-governmental sources. The orthodox view of the Canadian Charter of Rights and Freedoms appears to be that it applies only to the former, and that those who seek protection from rights violations by the private sector must be content with private law and the human rights legislation of the jurisdiction in question (Tarnopolsky 1982:423; Swinton 1982:44; Hogg 1982/1:75). I have argued elsewhere that it is both desirable and legally possible to extend the scope of the Charter to private as well as public activities (Gibson 1982/1). The question awaits judicial determination.

Even if the Charter were not held to be directly applicable to the activities of the private sector, there would undoubtedly be a massive indirect impact on those activities. All laws are clearly subject to the Charter, and governmental regulation of or cooperation with private sector activities is so extensive that Charter considerations are likely to effect a sweeping array of "private" transactions (Gibson 1983).

APPLICATION OF CHARTER TO PUBLIC SECTOR
Whatever may be the case for the private sector, it is beyond doubt that the Charter protects individuals' rights with respect to governmental activities. Section 32(1) reads as follows:

> This Charter applies
> (a) to the Parliament and government of Canada in respect of all matters within the authority of Parliament including all matters relating to the Yukon Territory and Northwest Territories; and
> (b) to the legislature and government of each province in respect of all matters within the authority of the legislature of each province.

It will be noted that there is no explicit reference to the municipal level of government. Most observers are confident that the Charter will be interpreted to apply to local governments, however — probably by placing a generous construction on the words "government of each province."

It is unlikely that every governmental decision will be found to be subject to Charter scrutiny. Mention has already been made of the fact that in the past, respect for the democratic tradition has caused Canadian judges to exercise great (some would say undue) self-restraint when reviewing decisions made by elected governmental authorities. While the Charter now calls upon Canadian judges to play a more active role when scrutinizing governmental actions, it is likely that they will continue to exhibit considerable deference to political judgement. One way of doing this would be to permit the politicians a wide margin of error when determining whether a given law is a "reasonable limit" within the meaning of section 1.

Another possible, and more radical, technique of judicial self-restraint would be to hold that certain kinds of governmental decisions are completely beyond the reach of judicial review. The Supreme Court of the United States has occasionally adopted such an approach with respect to what it has labelled "political questions": matters more appropriate to determination by political processes than by adjudication (Tribe 1978:71; Sawer 1963; Strayer 1983: 195).

While that principle is sometimes said to derive from the peculiarly American constitutional concept of "separation of powers," and has never been forthrightly adopted by Canadian courts, there is Canadian precedent for both judicial deference to political judgement in certain types of politically sensitive legal disputes (*Temple v. Bulmer* 1943) and refusal by the courts to deal with issues not regarded as "judiciable" (*A.-G. Nova Scotia v. Bedford Service Commission* 1977).

The issue arose in one of the first politically controversial Charter cases to face the courts: *Operation Dismantle Inc., et al v. The Queen et al* (1984). It concerned the alleged constitutional invalidity of a decision by the government of Canada to participate in the testing of United States cruise missiles in Canadian airspace. The plaintiffs contended that the decision jeopardized their "liberty" and "security of the person," contrary to section 7 of the Charter. The Federal Court of Appeal rejected this claim. While this decision was based on several alternate grounds, a major reason advanced by three judges of the Federal Court was that the issue is "non-judiciable." Mr. Justice Ryan put it this way:

> The problem is whether this question is susceptible of proof one way or another in a judicial proceeding.... The accuracy of the government's estimate of what national security and national defence require is, of course, open to debate in our society, and the government is responsible for their decision under the principle of responsible government. But can the rightness or wrongness of their decision to permit testing be proved in a court case? The decision would obviously be based essentially on policy considerations, including questions of strategy. Whether the testing of the Cruise Missile should or should not be permitted, and more particularly, whether the Canadian government should authorize its testing in Canada, would depend upon the evaluation of a vast range of factors and on a delicate balancing of interests.... For these reasons, I conclude that the Statement of Claim does not raise a triable issue and should, therefore, be struck.

Mr. Justice LeDain expressed similar sentiments:

> Despite the enlarged scope of judicial review which the Charter imposes it cannot ... have the effect of requiring the courts to determine issues which are inherently non-judiciable because they are not capable of adjudication by a court of law. The central issue raised by ... the Respondents' Statement of Claim is the effect of the proposed testing and availability of the Cruise Missile on the risk of nuclear conflict. That is manifestly not a question which is judiciable. It is not susceptible of adjudication by a court. It involves factors, considerations and imponderables, many of which are inaccessible to a court or of a nature which a court is incapable of evaluating or weighing.

Although these judges took pains to deny that they were invoking the American "political questions" doctrine, there can be little doubt that the principles are essentially identical.

The mere fact that a Charter dispute has a major political aspect is not what is relevant here. The American use of the term "political questions" to describe the principle is somewhat deceptive, since American courts have undertaken to deal with many cases having intensely political overtones. As Mr. Justice Brennan said in a leading American decision: "The doctrine of which we treat is one of 'political questions,' not one of 'political cases.'" (*Baker v. Carr* 1962). The essential factor is not whether the matter is a political "hot potato," but whether it is suitable for judicial determination.

Judiciability appears to involve two principal factors: (a) the existence of a body of consistent guidelines or norms in accordance with which individual disputes may be determined, and (b) appropriateness of judicial procedures and remedies to the determination of particular disputes. The absence of the first factor caused the Appeal Division of the Nova Scotia Supreme Court, in *A.-G. Nova Scotia v. Bedford Service Commission* (1977) to reject a claim that a regional planning authority had chosen an improper site for landfill purposes. The Court pointed out that since the principles which the plaintiff sought to have the Court apply were those of fairness rather than of law, the matter was not judiciable. This aspect of judiciability is not likely to create a problem in Charter cases, since the Charter itself lays down a body of universal norms, appropriate for interpretation and application by the judiciary.

It is the other aspect of judiciability — the appropriateness of judicial procedures and remedies — that could present obstacles to judicial Charter scrutiny of some governmental decisions. This is what seemed to concern the judges of the Federal Court of Appeal in the *Operation Dismantle* case. Where governmental decisions involve state secrets or the need to act rapidly in the interest of national security, particularly when the questions at issue are very complex, courts are understandably reluctant to interfere unduly in governmental decision making. It is submitted, however, that situations in which the need for such judicial deference arises should be very rare.

Where a court decides that a particular Charter issue is non-judiciable, that decision need not apply for all time. Many of the procedural-remedial reasons for non-judiciability will dissipate with the passage of time. This would not be so in a case like the cruise missile situation, where injunctive relief is being sought, but it would be true of a situation like the World War II displacement of Japanese Canadians, where considerations of state security would diminish as time went by. In such circumstances, it might be appropriate for a court, rather than dismissing the non-judiciable claim outright, merely tostpone the hearing until a time when it could be dealt with effectively.

It may also be possible in some non-judiciable situations for courts to provide at least partial relief to victims of the action in question on a "no-fault" basis, without having to examine the justification for the action. Suppose a recurrence of circumstances like those that led to Quebec's "October Crisis" in 1970. Federal and provincial governments have reason to believe that a scheme is afoot to overthrow democratic government in a certain province. The War Measures Act is invoked overnight, and hundreds of people are rounded up and detained for several days. Charges are eventually laid against a handful of the detainees, but most are released without charge. The propriety of the action is a matter of vigorous controversy, and the government claims that it cannot provide a full public explanation without compromising national security. If legal proceedings were launched against the government by one or more of the detainees, the likelihood is high that the courts would refuse to consider whether the detentions were justified in general. That would be a non-judiciable question, for the time being at least. But it would be necessary to deal with that general question in order to provide relief to individuals detained — perhaps because their unorthodox political associations placed them under temporary suspicion — and then set free without being charged. In such cases the known facts would speak for themselves: the plaintiffs' release would have demonstrated that they had been arbitrarily detained without justification, and that they had therefore been deprived of a freedom guaranteed by the Charter. Compensation could be awarded to such individuals without even considering the non-judiciable question of whether the government was generally justified in acting as it did.

REMEDIES

As the last two paragraphs indicate, the impact of the Charter cannot be realistically discussed without considering remedial questions — the types of relief the courts are able and willing to award to those whose Charter rights have been violated.

Unlike equivalent constitutional guarantees in many other countries, the Canadian Charter is explicit and generous in the remedial powers it bestows on the courts. Section 24 states:

> (1) Anyone whose rights or freedoms, as guaranteed by this Charter, have been infringed or denied may apply to a court of competent jurisdiction to obtain such remedy as the court considers appropriate and just in the circumstances.

> (2) Where, in proceedings under subsection (1), a court concludes that evidence was obtained in a manner that infringed or denied any rights or freedoms guaranteed by this Charter, the evidence shall be excluded if it is established that, having regard to all the circumstances, the admission of it in the proceedings would bring the administration of justice into disrepute.

The full meaning of these involves a number of difficult legal questions that will require considerable litigation to resolve (Gibson 1982/2). Even greater uncertainty resides in the breadth of the discretionary power given to judges. Will they choose to exercise the power widely? Let us consider, by way of example, the extent to which they may and should be willing to order positive conduct.

Courts are much more familiar with "shalt nots" than with "shalts." Although the Charter is expressed in terms of positive rights and freedoms rather than of duties and responsibilities, the remedies sought by persons alleging violation of their Charter rights are most often of a negative type: striking down a law or governmental action that offends the Charter, rejecting evidence obtained in violation of the Charter, acquitting an accused who was denied his or her Charter rights.

In some circumstances, however, especially where minority rights are involved, the most appropriate remedy may involve positive action by the defendant to restore the plaintiff's Charter rights, or to compensate for their deprivation. Several of the Charter's substantive rights would mean little if the courts were unable or unwilling to enforce them by positive remedies. These include the right to vote (section 3), the right to an interpreter in court (section 14), the right to certain public services in either French or English (section 20), and the right to minority language instruction and educational facilities (section 23).

The simplest positive remedy is the payment of monetary damages: to make up for income lost due to a discriminatory refusal to employ someone, for example, or to compensate for the cost of a private school resorted to when minority language instruction was improperly refused in the public school system. More elaborate forms of positive relief might sometimes be suitable also: an order to provide employment or a denied service to a victim of discrimination, or to provide educational or governmental services to members of a minority language community, or perhaps to carry out an affirmative action program for the benefit of historically disadvantaged groups.

In my view, the courts have the power under the Charter to award such positive forms of relief where appropriate. The award of compensatory damages is one of the most common civil remedies available in the courts. The judicial arsenal also includes such positive measures as mandatory injunctions and writs of mandamus. Section 24 of the Charter seems clearly to contemplate the courts' use of every remedy within their normal powers.

The major obstacle to obtaining effective positive remedies from the courts is rooted in judicial inclinations rather than in law. The traditional deference of judges toward the elected arm of government looms large here. Courts regard it as less intrusive to tell the government that it may not pass a particular law or pursue a specific line of action than to tell it what law should be enacted or what line of action should be taken. Another reason for judicial reticence is a long-standing reluctance to order conduct which would require detailed or long-lasting judicial supervision. Although the Canadian and Commonwealth courts have shown increasing willingness to design and supervise complex mandatory orders, they have not yet gone as far as their American counterparts in this regard (Gibson 1982/2: 505).

This does not mean that positive orders are likely to be denied in all Charter actions, however. Damage awards have already been made in a number of cases. Even where mandatory injunctions are involved there is reason to believe that they will be employed, though no doubt sparingly, in situations where they would be relatively straightforward and easy to enforce (e.g., "Provide a bilingual receptionist at the office of the Canadian Human Rights Commission in Winnipeg"). Where a matter is more complex, and a court is reluctant to select among several possible ways of providing a positive remedy, it doesn't have to opt-out entirely; it could simply make an order stipulating the *result* to be achieved, and leave to the defendant the manner in which it should be carried out (e.g., "Put into effect in Winnipeg School Division No. 1 a French language instruction program capable of providing the children of Winnipeg Francophones instruction in the French language equal in quality to instruction available in the English language to the children of Winnipeg Anglophones").

There are, in other words, ways in which courts can employ a wide range of remedies — including mandatory orders — in Charter cases without getting themselves unduly embroiled in administrative details.

MINORITY RIGHTS

EQUALITY RIGHTS
The most significant minority rights bestowed by the Canadian Charter of Rights and Freedoms are likely to be those contained in section-15 (Tarnopolsky 1982; Gold 1982; Vickers 1983; Polyviou 1980). This provision which comes into force in April 1985 reads as follows:

> (1) Every individual is equal before and under the law and has the right to the equal protection and equal benefit of the law without discrimination and, in particular, without discrimination based on race, national or ethnic origin, colour, religion, sex, age or mental or physical disability.

> (2) Subsection (1) does not preclude any law, program or activity that has as its object the amelioration of conditions of disadvantaged individuals or groups including those that are disadvantaged because of race, national or ethnic origin, colour, religion, sex, age or mental or physical disability.

The roots of this provision lie in the egalitarian writings of John Locke and Jean Jacques Rousseau, and their predecessors. Those same roots have produced very different constitutional flora in the United Kingdom and the United States. Dr. Jill Vickers has reduced the welter of equality ideas to two basic prototype approaches: (a) the "equality of *rights*" approach, which stresses *fair play*, and is primarily concerned that procedural rules apply equally to everyone; and (b) the "equality of *condition*" approach, which seeks fair *shares*, and attempts to ensure equal distribution to everyone of the substantive benefits of life (Vickers 1983). These are caricatures, of course; Dr. Vickers acknowledges that the positions of most individuals and organizations are somewhere between the extremes. It would not be unfair, however, while acknowledging the exaggeration involved, to identify the traditional British approach to legal equality with Model (a), and the American approach with Model (b) (Tarnopolsky 1982:399). As is too often the case with Canadian constitutional law, it is not yet possible to be sure whether the British or American approach will ultimately be adopted by Canadian courts.

The Canadian Charter of Rights and Freedoms is not the only legally enforceable libertarian Charter in operation in Canada. Several provinces have their own Bills or Charters of Rights, and, for the federal order of government, the Canadian Bill of Rights has been in effect since 1960 (Tarnopolsky 1975; Hogg 1982/2). Section 1(b) of the Canadian Bill of Rights guarantees, as against the federal order of government, "the right of the individual to equality before the law and the protection of the law." Judicial interpretation of this provision by the Supreme Court of Canada has been very restrictive, and so inconsistent as to defy rational explanation. While the section was used on one occasion to strike down a section of the federal Indian Act which discriminated against native persons with respect to certain drinking offences (*R. v. Drybones* 1970), the Supreme Court soon appeared to repent that decision and found no occasion thereafter to invalidate laws alleged to be unequal in their impact. At times, the majority of the Court appeared to adopt an extreme version of Dr. Vickers' Model (a) (*A.-G. Canada v. Lavell* 1973). More recently, the Court invented, out of whole cloth, the principle that a law would not be regarded as unequal if it were designed "to achieve a valid federal objective" (Tarnopolsky, 1982/1:415). A variation of that test was suggested by Mr. Justice McIntyre (with whom Dickson J. agreed) in his concurring reasons for judgement in *McKay v. R.* (1981):

> I would be of the opinion ... that as a minimum it would be necessary to inquire whether any inequality ... has been created rationally in the sense that it is not arbitrary or capricious and not based on any ulterior motive or motives offensive to the provisions of the Canadian Bill of Rights, and whether it is a necessary departure from the general principle of universal application of the law for the attainment of some necessary and desirable social objective. Inequalities created for such purposes may well be acceptable under the Canadian Bill of Rights.

While the McIntyre gloss on the "valid federal objective" test has been hailed by some as a significant liberalization (Tarnopolsky 1982/1:418), both formulae appear to indicate that the individual's right of equality may be overridden by Parliament whenever it can put forward a plausible reason for doing so. It was with an apparent intention to escape from this narrow approach to the interpretation of equality rights that the Charter of Rights adopted a much fuller formulation of the right, requiring equality "before *and under* the law and ... *equal* protection and *equal benefit* of the law...." Whether the judges will act upon this invitation to change direction is impossible to tell at this point.

The remainder of this section will be devoted to discussion of a few problems with which the courts will have to struggle before an authoritative interpretation of section 15 emerges.

LEVELS OF SCRUTINY

Judicial interpretation of the American "equal protection of the laws" constitutional protection over the past quarter century has developed a variable approach, keyed to the perceived importance of the particular equality right in question (Tarnopolsky 1982/1:403). Three levels of judicial "scrutiny" have developed: strict, intermediate, and minimal. Where discrimination based on race, religion or nationality is involved, the courts have exercised "strict scrutiny," and have treated the discriminatory provisions as being "inherently suspect," and liable to being struck down unless the government can prove "an overriding state interest," that requires discrimination. Where discrimination is based on gender or age, there has been a tendency to be more tolerant, retaining the onus on those who seek to uphold the law, but requiring only proof that the discrimination serves "important governmental objectives." This is the so-called "intermediate scrutiny" category. The third group, embracing alleged inequality in situations not covered by the other two categories, is marked by "minimal" judicial scrutiny. The burden of persuasion in that category is on the person who alleges constitutional inequality, and the burden can only be met by establishing that there are no facts that "reasonably may be conceived to justify" the discrimination.

It has been pointed out that the "valid federal objective" test developed by the Supreme Court of Canada with respect to the equality rights provision of the Canadian Bill of Rights is very close to the approach taken by the American courts in the "minimal scrutiny" category (Tarnopolsky 1982/1:421). Some

Canadian writers have suggested that the Supreme Court will, or should, adopt the American stratified approach even more fully when interpreting section 15 of the Canadian Charter of Rights and Freedoms (Tarnopolsky 1982/1:422; Gold 1982:148). At least, they contend, two levels of scrutiny may be appropriate for Canada: strict scrutiny for those forms of discrimination which are referred to explicitly in section 15; and minimal scrutiny for other forms of inequality, covered by the more general opening words of section 15(1).

I submit that this would be a mistake. There is no room for differing levels of entrenchment under the Canadian Charter, at least not with respect to the burden of persuasion. Section 1 disposes of any need for either a "valid federal objective" concept or gradations of judicial surveillance. It sets a single test for "limits" on all constitutional rights: "such reasonable limits prescribed by law as can be demonstrably justified in a free and democratic society." The onus is *always* on those who uphold the law to establish that a limit is "reasonable," regardless of the constitutional right affected. While the courts might well be more willing to treat certain kinds of *limits* as reasonable than others, it seems to me dangerous to invite them to treat certain of the entrenched *rights* as being more important than others. To treat the specified forms of discrimination under section 15 as more important than the general right of equality not only lacks any grammatical or logical justification, but also runs the risk of locking constitutional interpretation into a mold determined by current social patterns, which would be unlikely to serve well in the unforeseeable future.

EQUAL BENEFIT OF LAW

There are many who hope that the "equal benefit" clause of section 15, which is entirely new to Canada, will result in greater opportunity for members of all minorities to benefit from governmental programs. I hope they will not be disappointed.

The initial interpretative difficulty to be overcome is that section 15 speaks of "equal benefit of the *law*," not "equal benefit of government *programs*." If the term "the law" were construed to refer only to legal processes, and not to governmental activities in general, the significance of the protection would be markedly diminished. A broader interpretation is also possible, however. Since most governmental programs are authorized by a law of some kind, whether it be a statute, a regulation, a by-law, or an order-in-council, it would not be unreasonable to hold that unequal application of the program for which the law provides constitutes denial of "equal benefit of the law." This could mean, for example, that a local school board, carrying out its responsibility under provincial educational legislation to provide educational facilities for the district, would be in violation of the Charter if it did not provide deaf children within the district education facilities as satisfactory as those provided for other children.

This raises the question of whether the Charter obligation of equality can be met by measures that are "different but equal." Could a school board that did not feel justified in incurring the expense of educational facilities for deaf children satisfy the Charter by making arrangements to bus deaf children from its area to suitable facilities in another district? The courts would probably answer that question in the affirmative if the alternative facilities were satisfactory, and if there were good reason for not duplicating them within the district. The notion of "reasonable accommodation," developed under Human Rights legislation, recognizes that alternate facilities for those with special needs cannot be regarded as discriminatory if they are reasonable in the circumstances (*Canadian Odeon Theatres v. Saskatchewan Human Rights Commission* 1982). It is probable that the notion of "reasonable accommodation" will be put to use, where appropriate, in determining whether a law that calls for differential treatment of a minority is a "reasonable limit" under section 1 of the Charter.

Related to the last question is the problem of whether differences of approach to the needs of minorities from one area (province or school division) to another will be tolerated. The probable answer is that they will, so long as the arrangements, though different, are reasonably satisfactory. It is a characteristic of the "free and democratic society" that prevails in Canada that many social programs are the responsibility of provincially or locally elected representatives. This form of decentralization is an important part of our constitutional structure; it cannot be ignored when deciding whether a particular law is or is not "reasonable" under section 1 of the Charter. The fact that school district A provides local facilities for deaf pupils but school district B buses its deaf children to another district is not likely to be treated as unreasonable inequality unless there is a marked disparity in the quality of the programs.

LANGUAGE RIGHTS

Concern for the linguistic rights of English and French speaking minorities was evident even in Canada's original constitution. The Constitution Act, 1867, guaranteed, in section 133, the right to use either language in the Parliament of Canada, the Legislature of Quebec, their respective records and journals, the courts of Canada and Quebec, and their respective pleadings and processes — as well as the right to have the laws of both those jurisdictions expressed in both languages. When Manitoba became a province in 1870, linguistic protections similar to those applicable to Quebec were extended to it (Manitoba Act 1870: s. 23). The Charter confirms those minimal initial protections, and expands them in several respects. At the federal level, it adds a provision that "English and French are the official languages of Canada and have equality of status and equal rights and privileges as to their use in all institutions of the Parliament and government of Canada" (section 16), as well as a right of members of the public to communicate in French or English with any head or central office of a federal government institution if there is a "significant demand," or if it is otherwise "reasonable" that services be provided in both languages by that office (section 20). For the province of New Brunswick, the Charter makes applicable all the language guarantees available in Quebec and Manitoba, plus all rights applicable to federal governmental institutions. In fact, the constitutionally entrenched language rights of New Brunswick citizens are more sweeping than those of all other Canadians, in that they include the right to communicate with *every* office of a New Brunswick governmental institution (sections 16[2], 17[2], 18[2], 19[2] and 20[2]).

Additional provisions permit the Parliament of Canada or provincial legislatures to add legislatively to these bilingual rights (section 16[3]), confirm existing constitutional bilingual rights (section 21), and provide that nothing in the above protections "abrogates or derogates from any legal or customary right or privilege acquired or enjoyed ... with respect to any language that is not English or French" (section 22).

The most interesting of the linguistic rights created by the Charter are those that related to minority language education. Section 23 of the Charter gives to members of the Anglophone or Francophone linguistic minorities in any province or territory the right to have their children educated, at both primary and secondary school levels, in that minority language, provided that the number of children of persons having that right in the particular province or territory is "sufficient to warrant the provision to them out of public funds of minority language instruction." While this provision will require considerable judicial interpretation before its significance is fully understood, some things are evident immediately. The right applies only to "citizens of Canada." This means that landed immigrants in Canada do not have access to these rights for their children, even if they are permanently resident members of the English or French linguistic minority in a particular province or territory. Another indisputable and important feature of section 23 is that it includes the right to both "instruction" and appropriate "educational facilities," both of which are to be "provided out of public funds." The "public funds" provision is particularly important, since it will prevent the courts doing what they did with respect to the guarantee of religious schooling under section 93: interpreting it so as merely to permit privately funded schools (*City of Winnipeg v. Barrett* 1892).

The greatest uncertainty surrounding section 23 involves the meaning of the words "wherever in the province the number of children of citizens who have such a right is sufficient to warrant" minority language instruction and educational facilities. The first question is whether the decision is to be made by politicians or by judges. Those who ascribe minimal legal significance to the Charter suggest that section 23 is too vague to be enforced judicially, and is intended, instead, as a mere exhortation to the elected representatives responsible for education (a provincial matter in Canada) to do the best they can with respect to minority language education. That view is unlikely to prevail. It will be recalled that section 24(1) of the Charter gives every "Court of competent jurisdiction" the power to award those whose Charter rights are infringed "such remedy as the court considers appropriate and just in the circumstances." There being no relevant exceptions to that provision, it seems clear that section 23 is judicially enforceable (*Quebec Association of Protestant School Boards v. A.-G. Quebec* 1984).

What is less clear is the extent to which the courts will, in practice, defer to the judgement of politicians when deciding whether "numbers warrant." There is a risk that when asked to enforce this important but vaguely worded new minority right judges will fall back on their traditional disinclination to second-guess politicians, and simply rubber-stamp the conclusions of the elected representatives. This would be regrettable. Section 23 would be of little real significance if the courts, which have been authorized to supervise its practical application, merely delegated the task to those they are supposed to supervise.

The process must begin with the politicians, of course. It is for the elected representatives to design the detailed arrangements for minority language education, and for the courts merely to determine, after the event, whether those arrangements satisfy the requirements of section 23. This raises another difficult question: which politicians are responsible? Constitutionally speaking, education is a responsibility of the provincial legislatures. In practice, however, most educational facilities are designed, administered, and to a large extent paid for at the local level by locally elected school boards. Does section 23, by calling for minority language education "wherever in the province the number of children ... is sufficient to warrant" such education, refer to a province-wide test, or to one which is applicable to a particular school district or region of the province? It would appear that the test is intended to be applied locally. Although the English text of section 23 is grammatically capable of either interpretation, the French text seems clearly to indicate a localized approach ("... partout dans la province où le nombre ... est significant..."). This would seem to indicate that the initial responsibility for carrying out section 23 lies with local school boards, and that it imposes an obligation only on those boards whose districts include fairly high concentrations of minority language residents.

If that were the *sole* political responsibility under section 23, it would be unfortunate for the minority language residents of areas where there are very few who speak that language. It is, I think, possible to interpret section 23 as imposing a *second level* of political responsibility — on the government of the province involved — to deal with such situations. Whereas the numbers of minority language users within any given school district might be insufficient to warrant minority language educational facilities at the local level, the numbers resident in several contiguous school districts might well be sufficient to warrant the provision by the province of facilities to which children from those several districts could be transported. If section 23 is to accomplish linguistic preservation as effectively as intended, it will be necessary for the courts to recognize that it imposes a responsibility on both local and provincial politicians.

ABORIGINAL AND TREATY RIGHTS

The constitutional position of Canada's native population has never been entirely clear (Lysyk 1967). Constitutional jurisdiction to make laws concerning "Indians, and lands reserved for the Indians" was given to the Parliament of Canada by section 91(24) of the Constitution Act, 1867. Although the term "Indians" in that section has been interpreted to include the Inuit (*In Re Indians* 1939), it is still not certain whether it also covers laws concerning the mixed-blood Métis population. While many aboriginal tribes entered into treaties with representatives of the Crown in which they surrendered claims to suzerainty over the areas they inhabited in return for reservations and other treaty rights, the very existence and legal significance of the aboriginal title they claimed has never been conclusively established by the courts (*Calder v. A.-G. British Columbia* 1973). Although certain native hunting rights appeared to be protected, either constitutionally or legislatively, from encroachment by provincial laws, nothing in the Constitution prior to 1982 prevented the restriction or denial of those or other aboriginal rights by the Parliament of Canada (*R. v. George* 1966). Before enactment of the Charter there was not even any unequivocal constitutional protection for native persons against discrimination based on their ancestry; indeed, some argued that the existence of section 91(24) in the Constitution Act provided constitutional authority to discriminate (*A.-G. Canada v. Lavell* 1973:489, per Ritchie J.)

The Charter, as well as other provisions of the Constitution Act, 1982, introduced what appear to be major changes to this situation, but the generality and incompleteness of the language employed make it impossible to assess confidently the impact of those changes (Sanders 1983/1; McNeil 1982; Slattery

1983; Green 1983).

At one point in the complex negotiations leading to the enactment of the Constitution Act, 1982, it was proposed to include only the protection now provided by section 25:

> The guarantee in this Charter of certain rights and freedoms shall not be construed so as to abrogate or derogate from any aboriginal, treaty or other rights or freedoms that pertain to the aboriginal peoples of Canada including
> (a) any rights or freedoms that have been recognized by the Royal Proclamation of October 7, 1763; and
> (b) any rights or freedoms that may be acquired by the aboriginal peoples of Canada by way of land claims settlement."

This is not an insignificant section, since it ensures that the "equality rights" section of the Charter, section 15, will not be used to strike down any of the traditionally recognized rights of native people on the ground that they discriminate against non-natives. It does nothing, however, to advance the position of native persons. Representatives of Canadian native organizations accordingly mounted a massive and ultimately successful campaign to obtain more from the Charter than mere preservation of the status quo (Sanders 1983/2).

Their most important victory was the inclusion in the Constitution Act, 1982, of section 35:

> (1) The existing aboriginal and treaty rights of the aboriginal peoples of Canada are hereby recognized and affirmed.
>
> (2) In this Act, "aboriginal peoples of Canada" includes the Indian, Inuit and Metis peoples of Canada.
>
> (3) For greater certainty, in subsection (1) "treaty rights" includes rights that now exist by way of land claims agreements or may be so acquired.
>
> (4) Notwithstanding any other provisions of this Act, the aboriginal and treaty rights referred to in subsection (1) are guaranteed equally to male and female persons.

It should be noted that this section is not a part of the Canadian Charter of Rights and Freedoms; the Charter ends with section 34. Those who were negotiating on behalf of native persons were fearful that the hectic federal/provincial bargaining about the contents of the constitutional amendment might result in a last-minute abandonment of the Charter proposal; so in order to ensure that aboriginal and treaty rights would not be jettisoned along with the Charter, they managed to secure an independent position for them in the Constitution Act, 1982. This means that these rights have a slightly different constitutional status than the Charter rights: they are merely "recognized and affirmed," rather than "guaranteed," and they are beyond the reach of the Charter's remedial provisions in section 24. They are, nevertheless, constitutionally entrenched, and probably as effectively enforceable by the courts as Charter rights (Gibson 1982/2).

The word "existing," by which the section 35 rights are modified, has been a source of considerable controversy and confusion. It was inserted, at the insistence of some provincial governments, shortly before the constitutional amendment was agreed upon. Some observers saw the addition of the word as meaningless, arguing that the section would have been interpreted to apply to existing rights only, even if the word had not been used explicitly. Others, more skeptical, contended that the intention was to gut the guarantee altogether. As usual, the truth probably lies somewhere between these extremes, but exactly where is not easy to say. The key question seems to be whether "existing" rights can include rights which have been legislatively restricted, or even abolished, without extinguishment by treaty. Most observers agree that rights which have been extinguished by treaty cannot be resurrected under section 35. But what about rights, such as the right to hunt for migratory birds out of season, which have been restricted by federal legislation? If the legislation were repealed, the aboriginal right would presumably revive. Some writers have argued, therefore, that such rights continue to exist, even though they have been temporarily suspended by legislation, and that the suspending legislation is therefore open to a constitutional attack on the basis of section 35 (McNeil 1982:257).

Section 35 involves a number of difficult definitional problems as well. As mentioned earlier, there has never been legal agreement about the content of "aboriginal rights." Section 35 confirms the existence of these rights, without defining their content. This leaves the courts with an extremely difficult future task. Similarly, although the term "aboriginal peoples" has been defined (and has broken new ground by including the Métis) the courts are left to their own resources (in the absence of clarification by future amendments) to determine the criteria for qualifying as an Indian, an Inuit, or a Métis.

The other major constitutional concession wrested from the politicians by the negotiators for native organization, was the inclusion in section 37 — which called for a future constitutional conference — of a requirement that native representatives be involved, and that the agenda include discussion of native constitutional rights. That conference was held in March 1983. Although the most serious problems of interpretation remained unresolved when the conference ended, some progress was made. Agreement was reached to clarify both sections 25 and 35 in some minor respects, and to provide for two more similar conferences, before the third and fifth anniversaries of the Charter. A proclamation amending the Constitution in those respects was issued in June 1984.

MULTICULTURAL RIGHTS
Canada's cultural quilt is made up of much more than Anglophone, Francophone, and native patches. The distinctiveness of Canadian society results from the presence of many cultures. There has been a growing awareness on the part of Canadian politicians of the value of encouraging Canadians to preserve, propagate, and celebrate their individual cultural heritages. One product of that new awareness is section 27 of the Charter:

> This Charter shall be interpreted in a manner consistent with the preservation and enhancement of the multicultural heritage of Canadians.

As a statement of political and social purpose, section 27 is undoubtedly significant. As a tool to be used in the legal protection of the constitutional rights of Canadians, its importance is much less obvious. Its language is too general to support a legally enforceable obligation to provide specific multicultural programs. (Tarnopolsky 1982/1:437)

This is not to say that section 27 is legally meaningless. It embodies a principle of interpretation which could possibly assist courts to resolve uncertainties in the application of some Charter provisions. Suppose, for example, that a provincial legislature decided to advance multiculturalism by requiring school authorities to hire teachers, from among those who satisfy the minimum vocational qualifications, on the basis not of individual merit, but of ensuring that every school has teachers representing a broad range of ethnic backgrounds. A law of that kind would offend the equal rights provision in section 15 of the Charter unless it could be said, under section 1, to be a "reasonable limit in a free and democratic society." In deciding whether the law in question were a reasonable limit, the court would be required by section 27 to take account of the fact that the preservation of our multicultural heritage is one of Canada's constitutionally enshrined national goals.

SEXUAL EQUALITY

Prior to the enactment of the Charter, representatives of women's organizations lobbied intensely for the inclusion of protection against sexual discrimination more effective than the general right to equality covered by section 15. The result was section 28:

> Notwithstanding anything in this Charter, the rights and freedoms referred in it are guaranteed equally to male and female persons.

The apparent intention of this provision was to protect the right of sexual equality from the limitations to which other Charter rights are subject by virtue of section 1 and section 33 (Tarnopolsky 1982/1:436; Gold 1982:151; Hosek 1983). It is not at all certain, however, that the section will be found to have that effect.

Suppose a province were to pass a statute requiring that adult females keep their bosoms covered at bathing beaches or other public places, or that pregnant women not be employed in work involving possible radiation hazards to fetuses. Would the courts strike these laws down without even considering whether they constitute "reasonable limits" under section 1? Would a legislature be judicially denied the power to exempt those laws from the ambit of the Charter? It would depend upon whether the court interpreted the words "rights and freedoms" in section 28 as referring to *absolute* rights, or rather, as indicating rights and freedoms *qualified* by sections 1 and 33. I suspect that the courts would adopt the latter interpretation, and that section 28 will, accordingly, not serve its apparent intended purpose.

Of even greater concern is the possibility that section 28 will be interpreted in a manner that would significantly undermine the interests of the very groups that secured its enactment. Section 15, which prohibits discrimination on the basis of sex and other group factors, contains, in subsection 2, an assurance that this prohibition does not preclude affirmative action programs designed to ameliorate the conditions of persons or groups who are disadvantaged because of sex or other factors. It could be argued that an affirmative action program in favour of women, though permitted by section 15(2), is prohibited by section 28, since it would involve preferential treatment of one sex.

One constitutionalist has argued persuasively against that interpretation, by asserting that section 15(2) does not create a right to affirmative action, but merely explains or qualifies the substantive right of equality set out in section 15(1) (Tarnopolsky 1982/1:436). Again, it comes down to the definition of "rights and freedoms." It is certainly possible to treat section 15(2) as bestowing the right to have the benefit of affirmative action without contravening section 15(1). If so, section 28 would appear to raise a significant obstacle to affirmative action in favour of women. On the other hand, if section 28 were given that meaning it would appear to make nonsense of the explicit authorization of sex-based affirmative action in section 15(2). Rather than interpret the inclusion of "sex" in section 15(2) as meaningless, it seems likely to me that the courts would adopt the argument outlined above for excluding section 15(2) from the impact of section 28. Another way of arriving at the same result would be to decide that affirmative action does not involve discrimination in the first place, but is merely a method of attempting to overcome the effects of past discrimination. That approach involves a very complex historical, philosophical, and definitional debate, however.

Section 28 may turn out to have created more difficulties than it resolved.

CONCLUSION

In a democracy, representatives of the majority are, in good times, generally tolerant of minority interests. On ceremonial occasions they sometimes even salute them. But when the exercise of minority rights would be perceived as conflicting in any significant way with majority interests, minorities cannot expect support from the tribunes. In such circumstances enforcement of minority rights can come from only two sources: self-help and judicial review. Since most effective self-help requires either economic power or a willingness to act illegally, its usefulness is limited. That leaves only the courts.

The protection that courts can provide for minority rights under the authority of the Canadian Charter of Rights and Freedoms, if they choose to do so, is real, but restricted. If they attempt to encroach excessively upon the domain of the politicians, they are apt to find themselves stripped of their powers, as President Roosevelt made the judges of the United States Supreme Court in 1937. Yet if they allow the fear of political backlash to deter them entirely from challenging the political will when Charter rights are seriously affected, they will have to bear the responsibility for aborting minority legal rights and eviscerating the Charter generally.

Both extremes are avoidable. A creative balance can often be achieved between contrasting modes. George Burns and Gracie Allen proved it. So did the person who discovered that gin and vermouth in the right combination produces a distinct and distinguished beverage; and, of course, the one who first teamed four contrasting voices in a barbershop quartet.

If the Canadian judiciary can be persuaded that the role assigned to it under the Charter of Rights and Freedoms is neither that of spectator nor of soloist, but of collaborator in harmonious duets with the politicians, there will be reason for optimism about the legal status of minority rights in Canada.

REFERENCES

Alliance des Professeurs de Montréal v. Attorney-General of Québec 5 D.L.R. (4th) 157 (Q.S.C.) (1984).
Attorney-General of Canada v. Lavell. 38 D.L.R. (3d) 481 (S.C.C.) (1973).
Attorney-General of Nova Scotia v. Bedford Service Commission. 72 D.L.R. (3d) 639 (N.S.S.C.-App.) (1977).
Attorney-General of Quebec v. Blaikie et al. 123 D.L.R. (3d) 14 (S.C.C.) (1981).
Baker v. Carr. 369 U.S. 186 (U.S.S.C) (1962).
Calder v. Attorney-General of British Columbia. 34 D.L.R. (3d) 145 (S.C.C.) (1973).
Canadian Odeon Theatres v. Saskatchewan Human Rights Commission. 137 D.L.R. (3d) 759 (Sask. Q.B.) (1982).
Christian, T. "The Limitation of Liberty: A Consideration of Section 1 of the Charter of Rights and Freedoms," U.B.C.L.R. (1982) 105.
City of Winnipeg v. Barrett. A.C. 445 (P.C.) (1892).
Conklin, W.E. "Interpreting and Applying the Limitations Clause: An Analysis of Section 1." In Belobaba and Gertner (eds.), *The New Constitution and the Charter of Rights*, (1982).
Drybones, R. v. 9 D.L.R. (3d) 473 (S.C.C.) (1970).
George, R. v. 55 D.L.R. (2d) 386 (S.C.C.) (1966).
Gibson, Dale: (1) "The Charter of Rights and the Private Sector." Man. L.J. 12 (1982): 213; (2) "Enforcement of the Canadian Charter of Rights and Freedoms." In Tarnopolsky and Beaudoin (eds.) *The Canadian Charter of Rights and Freedoms: Commentary*, 1982; (3) "Distinguishing the Governors from the Governed: The Meaning of 'Government' Under Section 32(1) of the Charter." Man. L.J. 13 (1983): 505.
Gold, M. "A Principled Approach to Equality Rights: A Preliminary Inquiry." In Belobaba and Gertner, *op. cit.*
Green, L.C. "Aboriginal Peoples, International Law and the Canadian Charter of Right and Freedoms." Can. Bar Rev. 61 (1983): 339.
Hogg, P.W. (1) *Canada Act Annotated*, 1982; (2) "A Comparison of the Canadian Charter of Rights and Freedoms With the Canadian Bill of Rights." In Tarnopolsky and Beaudoin, *op cit.*
Hosek, C. "Women and the Constitutional Process." In Banting and Simeon, *And No One Cheered*, 1983.
Indians, In Re. S.C.R. 104 (S.C.C.) (1939).
Lysyk, K. "The Unique Constitutional Position of the Canadian Indian." Can. Bar Rev. 45 (1967): 513.
Marx, H. "Entrenchment, Limitations and Non-Obstante." In Tarnopolsky and Beaudoin, *op. cit.*
McKay v. R. 114 D.L.R. (3d) 393 (S.C.C.) (1981).
McNeil, K. "The Constitutional Rights of the Aboriginal Peoples of Canada." In Belobaba and Gertner, *op. cit.*

Morel, A. "La Clause Limitative de l'Article 1 de la Charte Canadienne des Droits et Libertés: Une Assurance Contre le Gouvernement des Juges." Can. Bar Rev. 61 (1983): 81.

Ontario Film and Video Appreciation Society and Ontario Board of Censors, Re. 147 D.L.R. (3d) 58 (Ont. Div. Ct.) (1983).

Operation Dismantle Inc. v. The Queen et al. 3 D.L.R. (4th) 193 (F.C.A.) (1984).

Polyviou, P.G. *The Equal Protection of Laws*, 1980.

Québec Association of Protestant School Boards v. Attorney-General of Québec 1 D.L.R. (4th) 573 (Que. C.A.) (1984).

Sanders, D. (1) "The Rights of the Aboriginal Peoples of Canada." 61 Can. Bar. Rev. (1983): 314; (2) "The Indian Lobby." In Banting and Simeon, *op. cit.*

Sawer. G. "Political Questions." U.T.L.J. 15 (1963): 49.

Schmeiser, P.A. *Civil Liberties in Canada*, 1964.

Scott, S.A. "Entrenchment by Executive Action: A Partial Solution to 'Legislative Override.'" In Belobaba and Gertner, *op. cit.*

Sheppard, C.-A. *The Law of Languages in Canada*, 1971.

Sheppard, R., and Valpy, M. *The National Deal: The Fight For a Canadian Constitution*, 1982.

Slattery, B. "Canadian Charter of Rights and Freedoms — Override Clauses Under Section 33." 61 Can. Bar Rev. (1983): 391.

Strayer. B.C. *The Canadian Constitution and the Courts.* 2d ed. 1983.

Swinton, K. "Application of the Canadian Charter of Rights and Freedoms." In Tarnopolsky and Beaudoin, *op. cit.*

Tarnopolsky, W.S. (1) *Canadian Bill of Rights*, 1975; (2) "The Equality of Rights," in Tarnopolsky and Beaudoin, *op cit.*

Temple v. Bulmer. 3 D.L.R. 649 (S.C.C.) (1943).

Tribe, L.H. *American Constitutional Law*, 1978.

Vickers, J.M. "Major Equality Issues of the Eighties." Can. Human Rights Yearbook (1983) 47.

3
THE USE OF LITIGATION UNDER THE CANADIAN CHARTER OF RIGHTS AND FREEDOMS AS A STRATEGY FOR ACHIEVING CHANGE

MARY EBERTS

INTRODUCTION

The Canadian Charter of Rights and Freedoms has attracted the interest of members of minority groups wanting change in their legal or socio-economic status. In particular, section 15 of the Charter dealing with "Egalitarian Rights" is the focus of much hopeful expectation. Section 15, which will come into force on April 17, 1985, provides that:

> (1) Every individual is equal before and under the law and has the right to the equal protection and equal benefit of the law without discrimination and, in particular, without discrimination based on race, national or ethnic origin, colour, religion, sex, age or mental or physical disability.

> (2) Subsection (1) does not preclude any law, program or activity that has as its object the amelioration of conditions of disadvantaged individuals or groups including those that are disadvantaged because of race, national or ethnic origin, colour, religion, sex, age or mental or physical disability.

There are, of course, other provisions of the Charter which have a bearing on what might, generally speaking, be called "minority" rights; these are canvassed briefly below, and in more detail in Professor Gibson's paper. These constitutional rights fundamentally affect both the legislative and the judicial process. Because the rights are entrenched, they set standards for government action, and the courts have been made the arbiters of whether legislation, the other governmental action, accords with the commands of the Charter.

The reach of the Charter thus gives minority groups two major ways of influencing government behaviour. During the legislative process itself, advocates of a particular minority interest will invoke the provisions of the Charter in an effort to shape the content of legislation. With regard to legislation already in place, advocates now have a clear recourse to the courts to seek measurement of a legislative provision against the constitutional standard. Canada's history is rich in both these types of pressure group activity: neither political lobbying nor interest-group litigation is an entirely new creature, spawned by the Charter of Rights. One can expect, however, that the provisions of the Charter will add new energy and forcefulness to efforts already underway, and inspire new directions or new activity.

Considered in this paper are some of the promises and pitfalls of litigation as a way of using the Charter to seek change. In spite of some real shortcomings as a strategy, litigation will surely be resorted to, particularly once section 15 comes into force. This paper suggests that the most effective use of the provisions of the Charter will come through the development of some coherent litigation strategy, focussing on development over time of a line of cases aiming at the achievement of particular goals. This planned approach differs from the fairly reactive and random approach which has characterized "equality" litigation up to this point.[1]

WHOSE RIGHTS: MINORITY RIGHTS IN THE CHARTER OF RIGHTS

The term "minority" is not used in a general sense in the Charter of Rights; it is used, specifically with reference to the linguistic minority, in the context of the educational guarantees in section 23:

(1) Citizens of Canada
(a) whose first language is that of the English or French linguistic minority population of the province in which they reside, or

(b) who have received their primary school instruction in Canada in English or French and reside in a province where the language in which they received that instruction is the language of the English or French linguistic majority population of the province,

have the right to have their children receive primary and secondary school instruction in that language in that province.

(2) Citizens of Canada of whom any child has received or is receiving primary or secondary school instruction in English or French in Canada have the right to have all their children receive primary and secondary school instruction in the same language.

(3) The right of citizens of Canada under subsections (1) and (2) to have their children receive primary and secondary school instruction in the language of the English or French linguistic minority population of a province

(a) applies wherever in the province the number of citizens who have such a right is sufficient to warrant the provision to them out of public funds of minority language instruction; and

(b) includes, where the number of those children so warrants, the right to have them receive that instruction in minority language educational facilities provided out of public funds.

There is, however, no overarching definition of the term "minority" included in the Charter, from which one might derive an idea of what, if any, theory of minority rights motivated the framers of the document. An overview of the provisions of the Charter shows that the constitutional guarantees touch all three of the types of minority described by Professor Flanagan: stigmata-based, life cycle, and life style.[2]

USE OF LITIGATION

Section 28 of the Charter provides that

Notwithstanding anything in this Charter, the rights and freedoms referred to in it are guaranteed equally to male and female persons.

Section 27 requires that the Charter "shall be interpreted in a manner consistent with the preservation and enhancement of the multicultural heritage of Canadians."

Sections 16 to 22, inclusive, provide certain guarantees with respect to official languages. They provide:

Official Languages of Canada

16. (1) English and French are the official languages of Canada and have equality of status and equal rights and privileges as to their use in all institutions of the Parliament and government of Canada.

(2) English and French are the official languages of New Brunswick and have equality of status and equal rights and privileges as to their use in all institutions of the legislature and government of New Brunswick.

(3) Nothing in this Charter limits the authority of Parliament or a legislature to advance the equality of status or use of English and French.

17. (1) Everyone has the right to use English or French in any debates and other proceedings of Parliament.

(2) Everyone has the right to use English and French in any debates and other proceedings of the legislature of New Brunswick.

18. (1) The statutes, records and journals of Parliament shall be printed and published in English and French and both language versions are equally authoritative.

(2) The statutes, records and journals of the legislature of New Brunswick shall be printed and published in English and French and both language versions are equally authoritative.

19. (1) Either English or French may be used by any person in, or in any pleading in or process from, any court established by Parliament.

(2) Either English or French may be used by any person in, or in any pleading in or process issuing from, any court of New Brunswick.

20. (1) Any member of the public in Canada has the right to communicate with, and to receive available services from, any head or central office of an institution of the Parliament or government of Canada in English or French, and has the same right with respect to any other office of any such institution where

55

(a) there is a significant demand for communications with and services from that office in such language; or

(b) due to the nature of the office, it is reasonable that communications with and services from that office be available in both English and French.

(2) Any member of the public in New Brunswick has the right to communicate with, and to receive available services from, any office of an institution of the legislature or government of New Brunswick in English or French.

21. Nothing in sections 16 to 20 abrogates or derogates from any right, privilege or obligation with respect to the English and French languages, or either of them, that exists or is continued by virtue of any other provision of the Constitution of Canada.

22. Nothing in sections 16 to 20 abrogates or derogates from any legal or customary right or privilege acquired or enjoyed either before or after the coming into force of this Charter with respect to any language that is not English or French.

Section 29 of the Charter provides that

Nothing in this Charter abrogates or derogates from any rights or privileges guaranteed by or under the Constitution of Canada in respect of denominational, separate, or dissentient schools.

The reference in this context is to section 93 of the Constitution Act, 1867:

Education

93. In and for each Province the Legislature may exclusively make Laws in relation to Education, subject and according to the following Provisions:—

(1) Nothing in any such Law shall prejudically affect any Right or Privilege with respect to Denominational Schools which any Class of Persons have by Law in the Province at the Union:

(2) All the Powers, Privileges, and Duties at the Union by Law conferred and imposed in Upper Canada on the Separate Schools and School Trustees of the Queen's Roman Catholic Subjects shall be and the same are hereby extended to the Dissentient Schools of the Queen's Protestant and Roman Catholic Subjects in Quebec:

(3) Where in any Province a System of Separate or Dissentient Schools exists by Law in the Union or is thereafter established by the Legislature of the Province, an Appeal should lie to the Governor General in Council from any Act or Decision of any Provincial Authority affecting any Right

or Privilege of the Protestant or Roman Catholic Minority of the Queen's Subjects in relation to Education:

(4) In case any such Provincial Law as from Time to Time seems to the Governor General in Council requisite for the due Execution of the Provisions of this Section is not made, or in case any Decision of the Governor General in Council on any Appeal under this Section is not duly executed by the proper Provincial Authority in that Behalf, then and in every such Case, and as far only as the Circumstances of each Case require, the Parliament of Canada may make remedial Laws for the due Execution of the Provisions of this Section and of any Decisions of the Governor General in Council under this Section.

There are, moreover, certain provisions in the "fundamental freedoms" and "democratic rights" parts of the Charter which should be noted.

Section 2(a) of the Charter provides that everyone has the fundamental freedom of "freedom of conscience and religion." Section 3 provides that

Every citizen of Canada has the right to vote in an election of members of the House of Commons or of a legislative assembly and to be qualified for membership herein.

In the legal rights section of the Charter is the proviso that

14. A party or witness to any proceedings who does not understand or speak the language in which the proceedings are conducted or who is deaf has the right to the assistance of an interpreter.

All of the guarantees of the Charter are subject to the provision in section 1 that:

The *Canadian Charter of Rights and Freedoms* guarantees the rights and freedoms set out in its subject only to such reasonable limits prescribed by law as can be demonstrably justified in a free and democratic society.

My comments here will focus on section 15 although, as I shall outline, section 15 will be read in light of other guarantees described above. The guarantees of equality in subsection 15(1) are general ones, although the language of the subsection also refers to certain specific characteristics. Can it be predicted that the courts will afford more protection against legislative distinctions drawn on the basis of one of the enumerated grounds than on the basis of a non-enumerated ground? Should the courts treat the enumerated grounds differently? Indeed, is it possible that there will emerge a sort of "caste system" even among the enumerated grounds themselves, as was feared by some when the grounds of "age" and "mental and physical handicap" — thought by some to be reasonable grounds for drawing numerous kinds of legislative distinctions — were added to the section?[23]

The first of these questions surfaced in jurisprudence dealing with subsection 1(b) of the Canadian Bill of Rights, which provides:

1. It is hereby recognised and declared that in Canada there have existed and shall continue to exist without discrimination by reason of race, national origin, colour, religion or sex, the following human rights and fundamental freedoms, namely,

    (b) the right of the individual to equality before the law and the protection of the law;...

In *Curr v. The Queen*, S.C.R. 889 (1972), Mr. Justice Laskin held at p. 896 that the enumerated ground was "an additional lever" to which the Court should respond; it was clear that a case would not be rejected merely because the basis upon which the legislature made the distinction complained of was not enumerated in the Bill of Rights. Indeed, many of the cases dealing with equality rights which reached the Supreme Court of Canada were ones which did not involve denial of equality on a ground specifically mentioned in the Bill.[4] Unfortunately, the Supreme Court gave both enumerated and non-enumerated grounds very cautious treatment, ruling in favour of an argument based on section 1(b) only once in the twenty-four-year history of the Bill of Rights.[5] Accordingly, it is impossible to say what, if any, theoretical or practical difference there was between an enumerated and a non-enumerated ground under the Canadian Bill of Rights jurisprudence.

I differ from Professor Gibson on the issue of whether the courts should make a distinction between enumerated and non-enumerated grounds in determining the validity of a legislative limit on section 15 rights. As outlined below, my preferred approach to analysing sections 15 and 1 **is first to determine** whether there is a distinction which *prima facie* seems to have the result of denying a section 15 right, and then to determine whether that limit on the right is a "reasonable limit imposed by law and demonstrably justifiable in a free and democratic society." It seems reasonable to accord considerable weight to the fact that a characteristic has been specifically protected in the constitution, when analysing whether an infringement on the rights of those sharing that characteristic might be "demonstrably justifiable." On the other hand, however, the fact that a particular ground is not enumerated in section 15 should not always relieve the government from having to show under section 1 why a limitation based on that ground is demonstrably justifiable. Thus, while non-enumeration should not have a major role in determining, under section 15, whether there is a distinction that *prima facie* denies a section 15 right, yet it should have significance in determining whether a limit is demonstrably justifiable.

In that context, what might one say about the proper test to be applied in assessing whether a limit on equality fashioned around a non-enumerated ground is demonstrably justifiable? Surely not all non-enumerated grounds are alike. Some, like sexual preference, geographical location or marital status, are what Professor Flanagan would call "life style"; some, like pregnancy, are arguably "life cycle" characteristics; and others, like eye colour, are stigmata. Still others, like height, may be difficult to categorize, for height may be at least partially affected by different factors: e.g., race, sex, or age. What these examples do show is that sometimes non-enumerated grounds are stand-ins for enumerated ones: distinctions on the basis of pregnancy may be seen as distinctions on the basis of sex, because only women get pregnant; distinctions on the basis of height may in a particular case be taken to be racially-based distinctions, because a statistical link can be shown between the characteristic and a racial group. In those kinds of situations, the case may be dealt with as an example of "indirect" discrimination on an enumerated ground, and the analytical problem is of a different sort. Where no such substitutional relationship can be discerned, however, the question remains whether one should accord to non-enumerated grounds greater or lesser weight depending, for example, on whether they are stigmata-based, life cycle, or life style.

In my view, it would be unduly restrictive to evaluate a case only on the basis of the weight or protection to be accorded to the characteristic itself. The relationship between the characteristic and the purpose of the legislation is surely relevant. Indeed, one of the main differences between the enumerated grounds in section 15 and the non-enumerated is that the framers of the Charter have, in effect, said that very few kinds of legislative objects are going to justify a curb on equality based on an enumerated ground, whereas, in the case of a non-enumerated ground, there is much greater scope for the legitimizing influence of the legislative purpose. It may be that, over time, there will emerge from the case law certain non-enumerated grounds which are invariably given strong protection against curtailment, so that they become in effect "suspect classifications" like race and alienage in U.S. constitutional law; but that development should properly proceed incrementally.

Throughout the foregoing discussion, I have proceeded on the basis that all the enumerated categories in section 15 would receive the same treatment. As mentioned above, some feared that the addition of "age" and "mental and physical disability" would dilute the protection offered by section 15. Their reasoning was that there are so many more reasonable reasons for distinguishing on the basis of age and disability than there are for distinguishing on the basis of any other of the grounds in section 15 that any jurisprudential doctrine developed to accommodate those many legitimate exceptions would allow incursions into the other areas as well. In particular, there was concern that doctrine might emerge which justified distinctions on the basis that the law or program is for the *benefit* of the young, or old, or disabled person; the vestiges of paternalism in the treatment of Indians, other racial minorities, and women might thereby be given a constitutional foothold.

That this danger exists is not to be denied. However, it may be even worse to invite the courts to start ranking the grounds contained in section 15. Individual theories of the importance of certain values might take over in an area where the constitutional command, on the plain face of the document, seems clear. If a "justification" for certain distinctions must be found, let it be found according to the standard in section 1 of the Charter, and not in rearranging or weighting the list of grounds in section 15.

The approach I have outlined above is, if you will, very much a non-theoretical one, which stays very close to the legislation, to such materials as the Court may want to consider regarding the legislative purpose, and to the constitution itself. Should one embrace a more activist stance, arguing that the Court should indeed rank the characteristics set out in section 15 by some criteria other than the internal ones of the constitution, or should rank the non-enumerated grounds according to criteria outside the constitution, then one meets the interesting fact that most of the theoretical work in this area is done by political scientists and sociologists, not jurists. Nor are political scientists and sociologists *ad idem* on how to define minorities, or which minority characteristics should attract state protection. To what extent will, or should, a court become involved in the theoretical differences of other disciplines? Here is one interesting instance of the blurring of the line between political science and the practice of law which is affected by an entrenched constitution.

THE ADVANTAGES OF CHARTER LITIGATION

In the short term, it can probably be safely assumed that whatever the theoretical underpinnings of the concept of 'minority,' persons who see themselves as somehow disadvantaged by a particular provision, and also see themselves as possessing one or more of the characteristics protected in the Charter, will seriously consider litigation as a means of vindicating their rights.

Let us consider the advantages of Charter litigation, first of all by looking at certain features of the Charter and the Constitution Act, 1982.

The supremacy clause in subsection 52(1) of the Constitution Act, 1982, provides that

> The Constitution of Canada is the supreme law of Canada and any law that is inconsistent with the provisions of the Constitution is, to the extent of the inconsistency, of no force or effect.

By reason of subsection 52(3), amendments to the constitution of Canada shall be made only in accordance with the authority contained in the constitution of Canada.

Section 33 of the Charter provides, in subsection (1), that

> Parliament or the legislature of a province may expressly declare an Act of Parliament or the legislature, as the case may be, that the Act or a provision thereof shall operate notwithstanding a provision included in section 2 or sections 7 to 15 of the Charter.

There is, in subsection 33(3), a five-year limitation on any such override enacted pursuant to subsection 33(1), but the override may be re-enacted for successive five-year terms.

Section 24 of the Charter provides one means for enforcement of its guarantees:

> 24(1) Anyone whose rights or freedoms, as guaranteed by this Charter, have been infringed or denied may apply to a court of competent jurisdiction to obtain such remedy as the court considers appropriate and just in the circumstances.

This is not the only means of seeking redress for a Charter violation, of course. The validity of a law or regulation may be challenged directly in a number of proceedings which have traditionally been available to challenge the legitimacy of government action (proceedings to obtain a declaration, mandamus, prohibition, certiorari, habeas corpus) and may also be raised as a collateral issue in other proceedings (e.g., as a defence in a criminal prosecution, or in a proceeding by the state to collect taxes owing). Section 24 adds to this array of procedural devices; it does not replace them.

Let us consider how these, and the other provisions mentioned above, enhance the appeal of resorting to litigation under the Charter. My comments here focus mainly on section 15 of the Charter.

Section 15 and the other sections apply by reason of subsection 32(1) of the Charter to the Parliament and government of Canada, and the legislature and government of each province, and the territories. The reach of the Charter to the provinces is an improvement over the scope of the Canadian Bills of Rights, which dealt only with the federal government and the territories.

The entrenchment and supremacy provisions of section 52 also represent a strengthening of the Bill of Rights approach. Section 52 requires that provisions inconsistent with the Charter be considered inoperative, a result which was not achieved by the Supreme Court of Canada under the Bill of Rights in any case but the exceptional *R. v. Drybones*.

One must also consider as a positive feature of section 15 that a number of the problems with the "equality before the law" guarantees of subsection 1(b) of the Canadian Bill of Rights, which emerged from the case law, were addressed during the process of drafting and redrafting section 15, and seem to have been eliminated. For example, subsection 15(1) guarantees equality before *and under* the law, a term that has its genesis in adverse reaction to the holding by the Supreme Court in *Attorney-General of Canada v. Lavell; Isaac et al. v. Bedard*, S.C.R. 1349 (1974), at p. 1373, that equality before the law means only equality in the enforcement and application of the law and does not reach the substance of legislation. Similarly, the decision in *Bliss v. Attorney General of Canada*, S.C.R. 183 (1979), that the provisions of subsection 1(b) do not prevent unequal bestowing of a benefit, caused there to be inserted into subsection 15(1) a guarantee of a right to the equal benefit of the law. The attractiveness of the jurisprudence under the equal protection provisions of the U.S. Bill of Rights resulted in the incorporation into subsection 15(1) of the right to the equal protection of the law.

One cannot leave any survey of the positive aspects of litigation under section 15 without mentioning that there appear in it a number of prohibited grounds of drawing legislative distinctions, which did not appear in subsection 1(b) of the Bill of Rights: age, mental disability, and physical disabilty.

It is well recognized that there must be some distinctions drawn in law; otherwise all legislation would have to apply to all people, regardless of their situation. It is also recognized that courts will themselves decide whether the basis for a particular distinction is, to use a neutral word, "acceptable." American jurisprudence under the Fourteenth Amendment, with its strict scrutiny, intermediate scrutiny, and reasonable basis tests, has functioned on that assumption; so, too, has case law developed under the equality before the law guarantees of the Canadian Bill of Rights.

In Canada, the exercise of judicial discretion about whether a limit is acceptable has been structured by section 1 of the Charter. That section requires that limits on Charter rights be "reasonable" and be "imposed by law." Further, they must be "demonstrably justifiable in a free and democratic society." Jurisprudence under the Charter to date has established that this last requirement places the burden of proof on the party seeking to uphold the limitation: in most cases, this will be the government or at least an emanation of it, like a regulatory tribunal.[6] The channeling of judicial discretion achieved by section 1 is, in many respects, an improvement over both the American and the Canadian Bill of Rights jurisprudence.

Some of the other provisions of the Charter "double-track" the protections offered in section 15: for example, section 28 (sex equality), sections 2 and 29 (religion), sections 27, and 16 to 23 (race, ethnic origin). It is not entirely clear that these additional sections will always, or necessarily, strengthen the protection available through section 15, but often they may. Clearly, they must be taken into account in attempting to develop a comprehensive and principled approach to the application of section 1 to section 15.

So far, these comments upon the positive aspects of litigation under the Charter with respect to minority rights have focussed on the Charter itself. There are, moreover, positive attributes of litigation as a means of approach generally. One of the main ones is that litigation can be an effective *minority* strategy. Achieving results in litigation does not depend on having a consensus of public opinion in favour of the argument put forward. Judges do not ask, at least not explicitly, how many of their constituents will favour this approach. One person or group, even with limited popular support, can prevail in a court with the "right" argument. This freedom from the majority will is an important characteristic of the judicial process.

One must acknowledge, however, that the discretion to consider what is demonstrably justifiable in a free and democratic society does invite judicial consideration of the public temper, even if such consideration is not likely to be either as dispositive or as extensive as that in the minds of elected politicians. In one way, however, the majority will could have a significant impact on judges in Charter cases. Section 33 does allow the legislature to cancel out a judicial decision by declaring that a particular piece of legislation operates notwithstanding the Charter. There may be pressure on the legislature to use the override if a judicial interpretation is unpopular. Thus, it is possible that courts may feel constrained to be cautious in their approach to equality arguments if they feel that their decisions in favour of equality would attract use of the override. Such caution might operate not only in a particular case, but also, across the board, if courts expect frequent legislative resort to the override provision. Accordingly, while a litigant need not demonstrate political support to win a case, he or she might lose a case because of supposed "political" opposition to the point being put forward, or to the type of case generally. One hopes, of course, that this type of anticipatory caution will not figure largely in judicial deliberations; the experience of a judge, who is required to be apolitical, arguably does not equip him or her to become involved in second-guessing the legislature in this fashion.

A second desirable feature of litigation is that it can be, and often is, a principled debate. The appeals of counsel are not solely to emotion; logic and precedent play a significant role in the proceedings. Coupled with the fact that courts are public, this principled debate in judicial proceedings can perform a useful function of public education. A recent example of such a function is the test case concerning the validity under section 7 of the Charter of cruise missile testing in Canada.[7]

The experience of the Canadian women's movement following the decisions of the Supreme Court in *Murdoch v. Murdoch*,[8] *Bedard and Lavell*, and

Bliss, has shown that the ability to focus and generate publicity around a major court case can make litigation a useful element in an overall strategy for change. All three of these cases actually produced negative decisions for the individuals involved, yet making manifest the injustice and illogic of the "successful" position provided useful impetus for lobbying efforts. These efforts have produced legislative changes in the case of pregnancy leave[9] (*Bliss*), and have furthered the cause of changes to the Indian Act[10] (*Bedard and Lavell*), as well as producing the language of section 15 referred to above. The *Murdoch* decision touched off a series of family property law reform statutes: in many cases, the subject had been under review by the provincial law reform commission for many years before citizens' groups' representations caused provincial legislatures to re-order their priorities and bring the studies forward to action.[11]

Because of the "public forum" aspect of the court, litigation as a strategy differs from proceedings before Human Rights Commissions. If a complaint is made to a Commission, that body has a statutory obligation to try to settle, or conciliate, the complaint. It is only if the complain cannot be settled, and the Human Rights Commission is of the view that the case merits the appointment of a Board of Inquiry, that there will be a public airing of the issues at the heart of the complaint. There are no such barriers to public awareness at the outset of a court proceeding; except in very rare instances, no one must obtain consent of a government official to begin a court case.[12] The parties to a court proceeding also have more control over the action than does the complainant in a human rights proceeding. The complainant in a human rights proceeding may retain a lawyer, but neither the complainant nor the lawyer has significant impact on whether a Board of Inquiry will be appointed: the Commission and its officers have the major voice in that decision. Similarly, the Commission decides who will sit as the Board of Inquiry and who will represent it (and the complainant if the complainant does not have resources to retain counsel) before the Board of Inquiry, and it is the Commission which decides about the strategy of conducting the case.

To summarize the advantages of Charter litigation outlined above, there are substantive protections that have been broadened, the Court has power to render legislation inoperative or, possibly, fashion creative remedies under section 24, and standards to guide judicial discretion in determining the appropriateness of a restriction on Charter rights have been placed in the Charter itself. The litigation process itself offers the opportunity for principled public debate, with a comparatively high degree of control over the process vested in the parties.

What, then are the significant drawbacks to Charter litigation?

DRAWBACKS TO CHARTER LITIGATION
First of all, let us consider some of the shortcomings of the litigation approach itself (wherever it is carried on) and the potential for these shortcomings occurring in the Charter context.

Court proceedings are, inevitably, long and costly. In most Charter cases, the entity seeking to uphold a limitation on minority rights will be the government itself. In such a situation, the private individual is more likely than the government to be hampered by cost considerations. In many kinds of litigation under the Charter, it is possible that gathering evidence (statistics about the impact of a law, for example) either to present a case or to challenge the government's case for justifiability will involve large expenses.

Under section 24 of the Charter, it seems to be the "individual affected" who must bring the challenge in court. The plaintiff must be "anyone whose rights or freedoms, as guaranteed by this Charter, have been infringed or denied." A public interest group, or an unaffected individual, would not have the "standing" under that section to challenge legislation.

Section 24 provides only one of the methods for raising the issue of the validity of legislation. It may well be that courts dealing with the other methods described above, or some of them, will not require a violation of the plaintiff's or applicant's own Charter rights as a basis for standing. The decision of the Supreme Court of Canada in *Borowski* sets the standing requirements in certain kinds of constitutional cases at a low level: Joseph Borowski, a former cabinet minister in the provincial government, was given standing to challenge section 250 of the Criminal Code providing for therapeutic abortions although he was neither the father nor grandfather of the foetus *in utero* threatened by a planned abortion.[13]

The potential pitfall is, however, that a group or individual seeking to raise the issue of the validity of a law by which it is not affected could spend its limited resources fighting the standing issue before it ever reaches the merits of its challenge.

One of the limitations of most litigation is that it relates only to a particular case; ordinarily, a court will abstain from making sweeping policy statements. While the decision in a particular case could conceivably have wide ramifications, it is unlikely that one could regard that case as the total answer to the difficulties posed by an area of law. The development of legal doctrine through case law is an incremental process.

In Charter litigation, this difficulty of the scope of the decision is compounded. The Court may invalidate a particular legislative provision, to the extent that it is inconsistent with the Charter. It may, pursuant to a generous interpretation of its mandate under section 24, give creative remedies in the individual case. Yet it cannot redraft the legislation to fill the lacuna caused by the declaration of invalidity. A range of questions will be raised any time a legislative provision is declared inoperative pursuant to the Charter, and these must be dealt with by the legislature. Consider the case of paragraph 12(1)(b) of the Indian Act, which takes Indian status from Indian women who marry non-Indians. Suppose it were declared inoperative by a court. The legislature would still have to consider whether to remedy the inequality by depriving Indian men of their status when they marry non-Indians, or by refusing so to deprive Indian women. The legislature must also contend with the question of reinstatement of women who have hitherto been deprived of their status, and the effect any reinstatement is to have on Indian bands, and on the women's children.[14]

Thus, except in certain quite pointed cases, a litigation result is merely the beginning of another process. Success in establishing that a piece of litigation violates the Charter simply opens up the legislative agenda, so that changes to the legislation may be debated. However, these changes will not always necessarily consolidate the victory achieved in the court case. If a legislature decides that making the changes consequent on a court case is too difficult, or politically unpalatable, it can avail itself of the option of using the override bestowed by section 33 of the Charter in order to declare that the provision just declared void by the Court will operate notwithstanding the Charter.

The incremental nature of developing law by the case method raises yet another potential drawback to relying on the Charter as a strategy for achieving change. The Charter guarantees mentioned above might be invoked by litigants in a number of inappropriate contexts; these inappropriate arguments could produce adverse rulings on the merits or the nature of the guarantee, which would inhibit resort to it for quite some time. Moreover, the Charter argument need not be inappropriate in order to have this result: a quite appropriate argument could be rejected by the judge of the first instance, and if the party does not have the funds to bring an appeal, that case would stand as an authoritative interpretation of the provision until another case comes forward on the same point, or a similar one, and the parties have the resources to pursue avenues of appeal.

It is because of these drawbacks in particular that I suggest that minority groups should seek to employ a strategic approach to litigation, that would bring forward at first cases which are not only "winnable" on their facts and on the law, but also good building blocks for future development of the law. Group action, by way of such a strategy, could thus to some extent contain the possibly adverse effects of advancing the 'wrong' case first. It can, by mobilizing funds, alleviate the difficulties of cost involved in litigating against the government. Without such a strategy, there is some risk that the first few years of section 15 might witness only the hardening of precedent against full exploitation or implementation of the Charter guarantees.

SUBSTANTIVE DIFFICULTIES IN CHARTER INTERPRETATION

Experience with judicial interpretation of section 1(b) of the Canadian Bill of Rights does not give rise to much optimism that Canadian courts will take a vigorous approach to the elaboration of rights under section 15 of the Charter. Under the Canadian Bill of Rights, the courts were manifestly uneasy at the idea that egalitarian goals could or should be furthered in judicial interpretation. Some of the conservatism can be attributed to the unclear mandate bestowed on the courts by the Bill of Rights. The sway of the doctrine of parliamentary supremacy was not reduced by any command in the Bill, as it is by section 52 of the Charter.

Be that as it may, however, the legacy of the Bill of Rights is a judiciary that is not schooled in handling egalitarian, and a jurisprudence that is lacking any sophisticated theories of equality rights in the Canadian context.

It has almost been assumed automatically that jurisprudence under section 15 will develop along one of two lines. Professor Marc Gold sees, and advocates, a limited role for the courts, and envisions a regime much like the "reasonable basis" analysis which was a feature of the last few years of the Canadian Bill of Rights.[15] Upholding limitations on equality where there is a reasonable basis for them means a judiciary which continues to be very deferential to the role of Parliament. Mr. Justice Walter Tarnopolsky is one commentator who sees, by contrast, a likelihood that Canadian courts will use the "three-tier" analysis devised by American courts working with the Fourteenth Amendment.[16] Distinctions based on race or sex would, according to his theory, require strict scrutiny; they would in almost no circumstances be justifiable. Distinctions based on, for example, age or mental or physical handicap would call for a lesser degree of scrutiny.

It seems to me that neither of these theories pays sufficient attention to the internal lines of the Charter itself. Section 1 of the Charter is the principle formula for determining justifiability; taken on its face, it does not appear to mandate a three-level analysis like that of the American jurisprudence. It does, however, clearly require more than the sort of "reasonable basis" analysis developed under the Bill of Rights, for section 1 requires that the "reasonable limit" be one that is "demonstrably justifiable." Moreover, under the old "reasonable basis" analysis of the Canadian Bill of Rights jurisprudence, the person challenging the law was obliged to prove that it served no valid federal object, or had no reasonable basis. Under the Charter the ultimate onus is on the party seeking to rely on the law to justify its limitations.

To locate the authority for a U.S. type three-tier analysis in section 15 itself seems to focus over much on the guarantee of "equal protection" in that section. The equal protection guarantee is only one out of four apparently equally weighted guarantees. There is nothing in the Charter itself to suggest that a three-tier analysis like that used in American equal protection jurisprudence is necessary to determine the legitimacy of limits challenged under section 15 when the challenge is based on, say, denial of equal benefit of the law. Moreover, it is difficult to see how one could first require a plaintiff under section 15 to establish a *prima facie* case that there is no reasonable basis for a limit on equality and then, call on the government to show that the limit is demonstrably justifiable. The first process seems to pre-empt the second. Such a pre-emption is certainly contrary to the tendency in the cases to require the Crown to establish that the limit is demonstrably justifiable.

It is my hope that a common sense reading of section 15 will prevail. That is, a person relying on section 15 would have to establish certain elements as part of his/her *prima facie* case. These might include showing that one's group is either specifically enumerated under section 15 or under the wide "non-enumerated ground" rubric. One could show that there is a differential in treatment between the applicant's group and another (the "discrimination" in its simple meaning of "distinction"). One might then also be required to show that the distinction has the effect of denying, say, the "protection" or "benefit" afforded to the other group or that there is a lack of sameness (equality) between what is afforded to the applicant and the other. This part of the analysis, focussing on the four kinds of equality, is similar in some respect to what some commentators are doing when they seek the "adverse impact" of the differentiation being complained of. This analysis, within the embrasure of section 15, does not contain any element of justification analysis. That is left to section 1.

Within the context of section 1, one would inquire whether the limit on equality identified under section 15 is reasonable, given not only the purpose of the legislation, but also the level of constitutional protection given to the group characteristic forming the basis of the distinction (i.e., is the characteristic specifically identified in section 15, specifically mentioned in any other section of the Charter, and so on). By this analysis, age or physical or mental disability would at least *prima facie* be entitled to the same degree of protection as, for example, ethnic origin (on the assumption that section 27 does not add appreciably to the protection afforded that latter ground). The real test would then be whether the Crown can demonstrably justify the departure from the norm.

It is not suggested that handling even that sort of simple analysis would be free of difficulty. Even as sophisticated a commentator as Justice Tarnopolsky assumes that there will be *more* justifiable distinctions on the basis of age and disability than on the other grounds;[17] as judges' assumptions are a powerful, and difficult to predict, factor in any analysis of rights under the Charter, one cannot feel easy about the task facing minority groups' advocates.

Moreover, it may be some time before the courts are prepared to accept some lines of argument. One such instance has already been described: the problem of indirect inequality, where a law is apparently neutral on its face but has a different impact on some minority groups than on those in the mainstream. There is also the question of whether the Charter imposes an obligation not just to redress imbalances (lack of sameness) in legislative provisions, but also to legislate in a positive way. For example, women may successfully argue that the explicit differentials in some statutory pension legislation will fall before the command of equality in the Charter. However, consider that elderly women are, in fact, economically unequal to men because of their years in unpaid work as housewives, their low wages in the work force, and the failure of some pension plans to ensure adequate survivor benefits. Can a challenge under the Charter result in a finding that the government must pass legislation to redress these imbalances in fact?

Third are situations where there is a conflict between group and individual rights, both within a "minority group" context. The present Charter is, for example, as ill suited as the Canadian Bill of Rights to deal with the position of Indian women, when one considers the conflict between sections 15 and 28 on the one hand, and section 25 of the Charter and section 35 of the Constitution Act on the other hand. Sections 25 and 35 provide as follows:

> 25. The guarantee in this Charter of certain rights and freedoms shall not be construed so as to abrogate or derogate from any aboriginal, treaty or other rights or freedoms that pertain to the aboriginal peoples of Canada including
>
> > (a) any rights or freedoms that have been recognized by the Royal Proclamation of October 7, 1763; and
> > (b) any rights or freedoms that now exist by way of land claims settlement or may be so acquired.
>
> 35. (1) The existing aboriginal and treaty rights of the aboriginal peoples of Canada are hereby recognized and affirmed.
> (2) In this Act, "aboriginal peoples of Canada" includes the Indian, Inuit and Métis peoples of Canada.
> (3) For greater certainty, in subsection (1) "treaty rights" includes rights that now exist by way of land claims agreements or may be so acquired.
> (4) Notwithstanding any other provision of this Act, the aboriginal and treaty rights referred to in subsection (1) are guaranteed equally to male and female persons.

The federal government has taken the position that section 15 will prevail to ensure that section 12(1)(b) should be ruled inoperative, yet at least one well-respected scholar takes a diametrically opposed view.[18]

The long-term solution to these difficulties may be in the legislative will. The three-year moratorium on implementation of section 15 was said to be to allow governments a chance to review legislation for compliance with the Charter. It was, perhaps, expected that amending legislation could be prepared which would deal comprehensively with the various interests to be balanced. In drafting such legislation, one would expect that governments convinced of the need to redress imbalances in fact need not be deterred by the possible absence from the Charter of a clear command to redress them.

Unfortunately, these "statute audits," as some call them, have not progressed as quickly or on as comprehensive a basis as one would wish, although the results of some of them are beginning to be known.[19] Often, it seems, the responsibility for identifying compliance problems in existing legislation has been given to the government departments charged with its administration: the very government departments who would be instructing Crown lawyers in the defence of challenges to the legislation under the Charter.

CONCLUSION

In my view, it is essential that organized minority communities become involved in the scrutiny of legislation for compliance with the Charter. Such work would form the basis not only for lobbying efforts to secure passage or remedial legislation, but also of litigation programs. Given the shortcomings of litigation as a strategy, intelligent use of the method is indicated if its advantages are to be seized and the costs of doing so are to be minimized.

FOOTNOTES

[1] A survey of litigation in the past fifty years relating to women's rights in Canadian public law is included in M.E. Atcheson et al. *Women and Legal Action*, Ottawa: Canadian Advisory Council on the Status of Women, 1984.

[2] (The reference is to Tom Flanagan's paper in this volume.)

[3] One early expression of this concern is in the "Summary of Those Resolutions Passed at The Ad Hoc Conference on Women and The Constitution which deal with Required Amendments to the Proposed Charter of Rights and Freedoms, together with commentary on the significance of the amendments for Women and the proposed wording of the Charter as amended, prepared pursuant to the Ad Hoc Conference on Canadian Women and the Constitution held on February 14th and 15th, 1981."

[4] Consider, for example, *Morgentaler v. The Queen* (1975), 20 C.C.C. (2d) 499 (geographical location); *R.v. Burnshine*, (1975) 1 S.C.R. 693 (age and geographical location); *Prata v. Minister of Manpower and Immigration*, (1976) 1 S.C.R. 376 (citizenship and domicile); *MacKay v. The Queen* (1980), 114 D.L.R. (3d) 393 (military).

[5] In *R.v. Drybones*, (1970) S.C.R. 282.

[6] *Re Federal Republic of Germany and Rauca* (1983), 41 O.R. (2d) 225 and *Re Southam and The Queen* (No. 1) (1983), 3 C.C.C. (3d) 515 (Ontario Court of Appeal).

[7] *Operation Dismantle Inc. et al v. Government of Canada et al.* (1983), 49 N.R. 363 (Fed. C.A.).
[8] *Murdoch v. Murdoch*, (1975) 1 S.C.R. 423.
[9] Changes in pregnancy leave were introduced by: *An Act to Amend the Unemployment Insurance Act, 1971*, S.C. 1980-81-82-83, c. 150.
[10] A bill formulating changes to the Indian Act failed to pass the Senate early in 1984: *An Act to Amend the Indian Act*, Bill C-47, Second Session, Thirty-second Parliament, First reading in the Commons June 18, 1984.
[11] See M.E. Atcheson et al. *op. cit.*, note 1, at pp. 27-28.
[12] Some statutes require that consent of the Minister or Attorney-General is necessary before a prosecution for an offence under the Act can be brought, but no consent is required to bring an ordinary civil action.
[13] *Borowski v. Minister of Justice for Canada*, (1982) 1 W.W.R. 97 (S.C.C.).
[14] See the discussion in *The Elimination of Sex Discrimination from the Indian Act* (Ottawa: Indian Affairs and Northern Development, 1982).
[15] Marc Gold, "A Principled Approach to Equality Rights: A Preliminary Inquiry," (1982) 4 *Supreme Court L.R.* 132.
[16] W.S. Tarnopolsky, "The Equality Rights," in W.S. Tarnopolsky and G.A. Beaudoin, eds., *The Canadian Charter of Rights and Freedoms: Commentary* (Toronto: The Carswell Company Limited, 1982), at pp. 421-422.
[17] *Op. cit., supra*, note 16, p. 422.
[18] Douglas Sanders, in an essay to be published in Bayefsky and Eberts, eds., *Equality Rights and the Canadian Charter of Rights and Freedoms*, (Toronto: The Carswell Company, forthcoming).
[19] See, Dale Gibson, *Impact of Canadian Charter of Rights and Freedoms on Manitoba Statutes*, Legal Research Institute of the University of Manitoba, 1982; Mary Eberts, *Preliminary Study: Equality Rights under the Canadian Charter of Rights and Freedoms and the Statutes of Canada* (Ottawa, March 1983); *An Act respecting Compliance of Acts of the Legislature with the Canadian Charter of Rights and Freedoms*, S.N.B. 1984, c.4 (effective date of s. 16 is April 1, 1984; effective date of the balance is June 30, 1983).

4
GROUP RIGHTS VERSUS INDIVIDUAL RIGHTS IN THE CHARTER: THE SPECIAL CASES OF NATIVES AND THE QUEBECOIS

F.L. MORTON

INTRODUCTION

With the adoption of the Charter of Rights in 1982, the political issues raised by government policies toward minorities in Canada became inextricably linked with the constitutional issues raised by the equality rights provisions of section 15. What were once essentially policy issues to be resolved through the political accommodation of the parliamentary process have taken on a new constitutional dimension and are now subject to judicial resolution. The mandates of section 15 reinforce but also complicate Canadian public policies toward minority groups. This paper identifies and analyzes the political and legal problems raised by section 15 for government policy toward two specific minority groups — natives and the Québecois.

Historically, Canadian public policies toward minorities can be roughly placed into three distinct categories: non-discrimination, special treatment based on a group's unique legal status, and group self-government. The notion of minority group rights as the right against discrimination is the oldest and most fundamental, and is shared by all other liberal democracies. Despite the rubric of "group right," its focus is essentially individualistic. It attempts to assure that individuals are not arbitrarily discriminated against by the government because of their membership in a racial, ethnic, or religious minority group. This policy has always been an integral part of "the rule of law" in Canada's unwritten constitution. (Dawson 1969:77,78) It was given explicit statutory force in the 1960 Bill of Rights, and has been made part of Canada's written constitution by the "equality before the law" clause of section 15.

A new and much broader scope was added to the meaning of non-discrimination and legal equality by section 15. Additional language was used to extend its original meaning of non-discrimination in the "application and administration of the law" to a substantive meaning of non-discriminatory laws. The additional rights to equality "under the law" and "equal protection of the law" were added to proscribe the use of certain designated minority group characteristics as legislative classifications, or at least to place a heavy burden of proof on the government to justify the use of such classifications before the courts. The additional equality right to the "equal benefit of the law" was intended to prohibit laws or policies that have a discriminatory or unequal impact upon minority groups. (Hogg 1982:51)

The notion of minority group rights as a group's possession of a special legal status is also well-entrenched in Canadian law and politics. Unlike the non-discrimination right, which essentially is the claim of an individual to be treated the *same* as everyone else *regardless* of minority group membership, special legal status amounts to the claim of an individual to be treated *differently* than everyone else *because* of minority group membership. The British North America Act proclaimed special denominational rights with respect to religious education (s. 93) and language rights (s. 130). These were reaffirmed and, in the case of language rights, extended by sections 16-23 and section 29, respectively, of the Charter. Section 91(24) of the B.N.A. Act clearly authorized Parliament to create a special legal status for Indians and the governance of affairs on Indian reserves, which Parliament has done in the form of the Indian Act. Section 25 of the Charter reaffirms the validity of a special legal status for Indians, and, together with section 35, goes on to recognize and protect "existing aboriginal and treaty rights." A novel form of special legal status — known as "affirmative action" — is given constitutional legitimacy by the second part of section 15. Section 15(2) authorizes the government to designate certain groups as "disadvantaged," and to enact laws, programs, and activities designed to better the condition of such groups. Its recognized purpose is to create a category of exceptions to the non-discrimination principle of section 15(1).

The third and final notion of minority group rights is the right of a group to be self-governing. While not explicitly recognized in the B.N.A. Act, the form of federalism was clearly adopted to accommodate regional demands for a degree of self-government. In the case of Quebec, the concept of provincial rights has always had added significance because of the ethnic, linguistic, and religious homogeneity of that province's Francophone majority. With varying degrees of intensity, Quebec governments have always maintained that the protection of Quebec's provincial rights is equivalent to the protection of the French minority's rights within Canada. (See section 4, below.) Native groups have long claimed a similar right to self-government, and now argue that this right is recognized in the declaration of "aboriginal rights" in sections 25 and 35 of the Charter. (See section 3, below.)

There are strong tensions and sometimes outright conflicts between these three different kinds of minority group policies. To grant special education status to Catholics and Protestants is to deny "equal" treatment to other religious groups. Does a law that treats individuals differently because of their race or sex constitute an undesirable form of invidious discrimination or a desirable form of special treatment justified by special needs? Does the right to group self-government allow groups to enact discriminatory policies within their jurisdiction?

In the past, in the absence of a constitutionally entrenched equality rights clause, responsibility for reconciling these competing demands and values rested with the federal and provincial legislatures. A government was able to pursue a pragmatic mixture of these different kinds of policies. It need not have worried about such tensions and conflicts, other than the political unpopularity that they might incur. The Charter changes this. Under section 15, a minority group member, representing either himself or his group, may challenge a government policy, or absence of policy, as violating one of the various equality rights mandated by section 15. In deciding these cases, judges will be forced to choose between the competing notions of minority rights. After April 17, 1985, the date that section 15 takes effect, all government policies respecting minority groups will potentially be subject to judicial review and possible reversal by the courts.

The equality rights section of the Charter raises a number of potential problems for government policies toward minorities. This paper addresses only one: the tension between group rights and individual rights as it affects public policy toward natives and French Canadians in Quebec. Both of these groups share the conception of *their* group rights as a form of the right to self-government and self-determination. Unlike a group such as women, whose putative goal is economic and social assimilation into the Canadian mainstream, Natives and French Canadians (or at least their leaders) define their goals as avoiding such assimilation and maintaining their group identity through the process of self-government. In both instances this leads to conflicts with the competing conception of non-discrimination as the basic principle of group equality.

Through an analysis of these two groups, this paper argues that the courts have been given a nearly impossible task in reconciling the group rights and individual rights requirements of Canada's amended constitution. Legally, it is suggested that the courts will be unable to devise a "principled" approach to interpreting the section 15 equality rights clause of the Charter. Judges will be forced to make so many exceptions to the non-discrimination principle of the section 15 equality clause that the exceptions will destroy the rule. Without the support of principle, judicial interpretation will degenerate into an *ad hoc* style of judicial decision making, a practice likely to erode the courts' authority. Politically, it is suggested that the Charter places the courts in an equally difficult position, by creating inevitable conflicts between group rights and individual rights, in which competing parties are not willing to accept an adverse decision.

NATIVE RIGHTS: SELF-GOVERNMENT AND CULTURAL AUTONOMY VERSUS INDIVIDUAL FREEDOM

> The social situations in *Brown v. Board of Education* and the instant cases are, of course, very different, but the basic philosophic concept is the same. The Canadian Bill of Rights is not fulfilled if it merely equates Indians with Indians in terms of equality before the law, but can have validity and meaning only when ... it is seen to repudiate discrimination in every law of Canada by reasons of race, national origin, colour, religion or sex....[1]

These were the words of Justice Emmett Hall in the 1969 *Drybones* case, a case which voided a conviction under section 94(b) of the Indian Act as a violation of the 1960 Bill of Rights guarantee to "equality before the law." They were broad indeed, and, together with the opinions of five other judges, they were hailed as ushering in a "brave new world" of Canadian jurisprudence. Parliamentary supremacy was to be replaced, or at least modified, by the new primacy of the 1960 Bill of Rights, interpreted and enforced by a vigilant Supreme Court. Discrimination in government policy on any of the prohibited grounds could now be successfully attacked through the courts.

These hopes and expectations were shortlived. They were dashed by a series of subsequent Supreme Court decisions that revived and reinstated Dicey's interpretation of "equality before the law" as a procedural not a substantive requirement — as equality in the application and administration of laws, not equal laws. In a 1975 case that effectively completed the destruction of the *Drybones* legacy, Justice Beetz attempted to explain the source of the Court's difficulties with the equality clause:

> The principle of equality before the law is generally hostile to the very nature of status and it is no easy task to reconcile the two in Canada when the one is enshrined in a quasi-constitutional statute and the other forms part of the fundamental law of the land. This the courts have attempted to do in *Drybones* and *Lavell*.[2]

The experience under the 1960 Bill of Rights demonstrated a basic incompatibility between the tradition of "group rights" in Canadian political experience and an American-style equality clause. The tradition of group rights entails the use of status classifications, while a non-Diceyean equality principle prohibits such classifications. The unhappy experience of the Bill of Rights notwithstanding, the framers of the new Charter of Rights and Freedoms have now compressed these two contrary principles into Canada's written constitution.

No area of law caused more problems for judicial interpretation of the 1960 Bill of Rights than the Indian Act. Three of the five major equality decisions of the Supreme Court dealt with provisions or effects of the Indian Act: *Drybones, Lavell,* and *Canard*.[3] The Court's inability to reconcile the special status conferred through the Indian Act and authorized by the B.N.A. Act with a substantive definition of "equality before the law" effectively undermined the potential for any American-style, *Brown v. Board* equality jurisprudence under the 1960 Bill of Rights. Unwilling to adopt a definition of "equality before the law" that would deny the validity of the Indian Act, the Court quickly abandoned the broad, substantive notion of "equality before the law" articulated in *Drybones*, and returned to the procedural definition of Dicey.

The drafters of the equality clause of the Charter went to great lengths to avoid a repeat of this experience. In addition to the traditional right to "equality before the law," section 15 goes on to proclaim rights to equality "under the law ... equal protection (of the law) and equal benefit of the law." This "new improved," four-tier equality clause was designed to make it clear to even the most traditional of judges that the Charter requires much more than the Bill of Rights precedents provide. It is intended, in short, to resurrect Justice Hall's brave new vision articulated in *Drybones*: "to repudiate discrimination in every law of Canada by reason of race, national origin, colour, religion or sex."

Since the Indian Act is clearly a law that discriminates "by reason of race," does this mean that it is now (or will be in 1985, when section 15 takes effect) unconstitutional? The answer, one hopes, is certainly not. There are insuperable legal and political obstacles to such an interpretation. Legally, the use of Indian status is certainly authorized by the terms of section 91(24) of the B.N.A. Act, "to make laws for ... Indians, and Lands reserved for Indians." In addition, sections 25 and 35 of the Constitution Act, 1981, proclaim the continued validity of any and all aboriginal and treaty rights of native peoples. This constitutional sanction for the continued use of race as a legislative classification, combined with the "reasonable limitations" clause of section 1 of the Charter, would seem to provide more than enough legal support for the continued validity of the Indian Act.

The political obstacle is even more obvious. Neither the federal government, nor native groups themselves, would allow the Indian Act to be unilaterally cast out by a group of judges claiming to enforce the equality provisions of the Charter of Rights. While neither party may be content with the status quo under the Indian Act, each has a vested interest in participating directly in any process that changes the status quo.

Does the Charter thus solve the problem that so perplexed the judges under the Bill of Rights? Is Justice Beetz's lament in *Canard* no longer applicable? Civil libertarian enthusiasts certainly think so. For the reasons reviewed above, the Indian Act can be treated as *sui generis*, "a special and limited exception" to the non-discrimination command of section 15. This answer can be provisionally accepted, but it raises in turn a second question. How many exceptions can a constitutional principle have before it ceases to be a principle? Constitutional principles, after all, are supposed to lay down the basic ground rules for the conduct of government. At what point do the exceptions swallow the rule? We will return to this problem at the end of the paper.

The guarantees of existing aboriginal and treaty rights in sections 25 and 35 of the Constitution Act, 1982, may resolve the problem of reconciling the Indian Act with the non-discrimination principle of section 15. But they raise even more serious problems. Just what these "aboriginal rights" mean in practice is notoriously ambiguous. At a minimum they include only the existing rights and privileges bestowed by positive law and treaties. At a maximum, many native leaders claim that "aboriginal rights" include the right to complete self-government and political autonomy, on large tracts of land presently under the control of non-Indians, and all this on the basis of natural or "higher" law. (Flanagan 1984; and Sanders 1983:225)

The native claims to self-government and political autonomy pose critical problems for the application of the Charter of Rights, and especially the equality clause, to the "internal" policy affairs of Indian bands. This "right to self-government" essentially means the right of native groups to conduct all the internal affairs of the band free from "outside" interference, including judicial interference. This is a problem, because inevitably some of these internal practices and policies will conflict with the provisions of the Charter.

The fundamental freedoms (s. 1) and equality sections of the Charter are designed for a "liberal" society, a society that accepts the "natural equality" of all members, and a corresponding right to participate equally in the process of government. A liberal society relegates religion to a secondary or "private" matter, and prohibits any direct government support of religion or punishment of "nonbelievers." It places a premium on the rights of the individual and not the group. Individual liberty, including the use of private property, cannot be restricted legitimately, unless it can be shown that they directly harm some other individual. Suffice it to say that most of these concepts are absent from, if not in direct conflict with, the traditions and values of native societies. These non-European, and thus non-liberal, traditions and values would inevitably, and in some cases purposely, be included in the internal policies of self-governing Indian bands. Indeed, a central purpose of the native claim to self-government, free from "outside" interference, is precisely to protect and to promote aspects of traditional native culture that are perceived to be threatened by the norms and practices of Canadian society.

The conflict between native rights as the right to greater self-government and the Charter is not merely hypothetical. The *Lavell* and *Bedard* cases, and the ensuing controversy, are a good example of this problem. Lavell and Bedard were both Indian women who married non-Indians and, pursuant to s. 12(1)(b) of the Indian Act, lost their Indian status. There is no similar loss of status for Indian men who marry non-Indians. Lavell and Bedard argued that s. 12(1)(b) discriminated against them on the basis of sex, and thus violated the "equality before the law" provision of the 1960 Bill of Rights. The Supreme Court rejected this argument by interpreting the Bill of Rights as requiring only equality in "the application and administration of the law." Since Lavell and Bedard were treated the same as all other Indian women, there was no proscribed inequality of treatment.

Referred to as the "*Plessy v. Ferguson* of Canadian civil liberties," this case has become something of a "cause célèbre" amongst civil libertarians and feminist groups. The *Lavell* decision marked the beginning of the end of the broad, non-discrimination principle announced in *Drybones*, and is, along with the *Bliss* case, the direct cause of the four-tier wording of the "new improved" equality clause in section 15 of the Charter. Feminists and civil libertarians were determined to guarantee that when the next *Lavell* or *Bliss* cases arrived at the Supreme Court, they would be decided very differently.

That day may not be far off. In the 10 years since the *Lavell* decision, there has been no legislative resolution of the controversy. Despite many promises (and eventually threats) by the federal government to amend the Indian Act, s. 12(1)(b) remains intact. The reason is intense opposition by native leaders to any changes to s. 12(1)(b) without accompanying financial assistance and additional land to accommodate the potential influx of an estimated 15,000 Indian women and 57,000 Indian children. While the federal government has indicated a willingness to pick up the financial costs associated with such a policy change — costs estimated at $35 million for the first year and amounting to $312.1 million by year 40 of the program — provincial governments have been unwilling to cede disputed land claims that make up the second half of the package.[4] Without both, Indian leaders refuse to cut a deal. The result has been an absolute stalemate, as witnessed by the failure of the second Constitutional Conference on Aboriginal Rights in March, 1984.

While native leaders have tirelessly denounced both the federal and provincial governments for creating and prolonging this admittedly discriminatory practice, they have been equally adamant about not allowing the issue to be resolved by the courts. Eleven of the twelve Indian associations that intervened in the original *Lavell* case supported the legal validity of s. 12(1)(b). Native leaders have repeatedly rejected the idea that it is simply an issue of "individual rights." (Cardinal 1977:109-112) George Manuel, president of the National Indian Brotherhood, pointedly identified the native's fear of any judicial involvement in this issue: "... we cannot accept a position where the only safeguards we have can be struck down by a court that has no authority to put something better in its place." (Manuel and Posluns 1974:241) In the wake of the bitterly unsuccessful March, 1984 Constitutional Conference, the Assembly of First Nations ran half-page advertisements in major Canadian newspapers declaring:

> Although the problem has been described as discrimination against women, sexual equality is not the issue.... The proposed change to

eliminate discrimination would create more problems than it solves, as it only addresses one of the many and varied problems confronting First Nations. This is a complex matter involving real issues such as the right of individual First Nations to determine their own citizenship, the preservation of their cultural identities and the right to exercise self-government.[5]

While the same advertisement went on to claim that, "We have always believed in and praticed sexual equality," and blame the federal government for creating the problem, the fact remains that Indian leaders prefer the status quo to any court-ordered solution. Unilateral control of band membership is an essential element of the collective right to self-government embraced by the native conception of "aboriginal rights." While they may be willing to bargain with the federal government for changes in band membership in exchange for financial and land claims compensation, they are vehemently opposed to any unilateral "judicial law reform" under section 15 of the Charter.

As a result, s. 12(1)(b) is a Charter case just waiting to happen, and there is no doubt that it will. There are disenfranchised Indian women such as Mary Two-Axe Early, formerly from the Mohawk Caughnawaga reserve, who have actively campaigned for abolition of s. 12(1)(b), with or without the consent of native leaders. According to Two-Axe, native leaders have too many other priorities. "They are worried about land claims. How many years will it take them to worry about us?"[6] Feminist groups strongly support this position, and are willing and able to organize and pay for the required lawsuits.

How, it must be asked, are Canadian judges supposed to decide this case? Legally, both sides can point to explicit Charter language supporting their case: Indian leaders to the guarantee of "aboriginal rights" in sections 25 and 35; disenfranchised Indian women and feminist groups to the non-discrimination principle in section 15. Politically, neither side is willing to accept an adverse decision. A decision either way will be bitterly condemned by the losing side, and possibly not complied with by native leaders.

GROUP RIGHTS AS PROVINCIAL RIGHTS: THE CASE OF THE QUEBECOIS

The concept of group rights is hardly new in Canadian law and politics. It can be traced back to the terms under which Canada's two founding nations, the English and the French, agreed to union, or rather, confederation. The British North America Act provided three different constitutional protections for collective or minority rights. The section 93 denominational school provisions were intended to protect the Protestant minority in Quebec and the Catholic minority in the other provinces. Similarly, section 133 provided protection for the English-speaking minority within Quebec and the French-speaking minority within Canada in the conduct of the affairs of the new national government. Finally, and perhaps most importantly, section 92 as a whole, and especially subsection 13, provided for the protection of the French minority in Canada as a whole, by providing a significant degree of political autonomy for Quebec, the home of over 85 percent of all French-speaking Canadians.

The political history of Canada since 1867 might well be summarized as the struggle between which of these two ways of protecting and expressing the

"French fact" in Canada should prevail. From Laurier's refusal to intervene in the Manitoba school crisis in the 1890s to Trudeau's confrontation with Levesque in the 1980 Quebec Referendum, the alternatives of an essentially provincial presence versus a national presence have competed with one another for dominance, especially among French Canadian leaders.

The Charter of Rights now overlays a constitutional principle of non-discrimination on this 100-year tradition of collective rights for French and English, Catholic and Protestant minorities. It thus raises in a new form the dilemma complained of by Justice Beetz in *Canard*: how to reconcile the constitutional prohibition of legal status — assigning different rights to individuals based upon their ethnic background or religious affiliation — with other clauses of the constitution that explicitly provide for such treatment.

In the context of this well-established tradition of collective or group rights, the Charter raises two very distinct kinds of problems. The first is the more obvious but less serious problem of how to deal with the claims of ethnic or religious groups that do not, or choose not to, fit into either the English Protestant or French Catholic legal categories. If Catholics have a right to direct their property taxes to Catholic schools, should not Jews or Fundamentalist Christians enjoy "equal right"? When an ethnic group comes to dominate a certain neighbourhood or community, should they not have an "equal right" to educate their children in their mother tongue? These claims are certainly given added plausibility by section 27 of the Charter, which declares that the Charter "shall be interpreted in a manner consistent with the preservation and enhancement of the multicultural heritage of Canadians."

Under the traditional Diceyean interpretation of "equality before the law," these claims could be dispensed with easily. But as we have already seen, the "new improved" equality clause of the Charter is purposely stacked with language to discourage a merely procedural interpretation. Individuals are guaranteed the additional rights of "equal protection and equal benefit of the law." And there is little question that a provincial education act that allocates property taxes to the Catholic schools but no other denomination hardly provides the "equal benefit of the law." Once again, Canadian judges are confronted with a dilemma.

There are basically three possible solutions to this problem. The first would be to abolish, by judicial fiat, any and all preferential treatment of linguistic or religious minorities. This would be the most consistent and thus the most "judicial" application of the non-discrimination principle of section 15, and is essentially the constitutional practice in the United States.[7] Of course, this approach is neither legally nor politically feasible in present-day Canada. Legally, section 93 of the B.N.A. Act is still the law of the land. Moreover, it is reinforced by section 29 of the Charter, which affirms all traditional "rights or privileges guaranteed by or under the Constitution of Canada in respect of denominational, separate or dissentient schools." The political furor created by such a decision need not be elaborated.

A second option would be for the courts to embark on a broad course of judicial policy making, ordering provinces and school districts to accommodate the demands of linguistic and religious minorities on an "equal" footing with English Protestant and French Catholic minorities. While this may well be unavoidable in cases raising section 23 claims to English or French language educational facilities, the judges would be well advised to steer clear of setting innovative education policies for other minorities under section 15 of the Charter. While principle would again be served by this approach, it raises a host of practical difficulties. In addition to the obvious problem of judicial control of the public purse, the American school desegregation experience strongly suggests that when judges take over the administration of school systems, neither the judges nor the schools prosper. (Glazer 1974) Finally, given the proven cautiousness of the Canadian judiciary in civil liberties cases, it is highly improbable that this approach would be adopted in the foreseeable future.

The third option, and the one most likely to be adopted, is simply to maintain the status quo. This is not only the path of least resistance politically, but it can be defended on the basis of tradition, combined with the "reasonable limits" clause of section 1.[8] This course of action does not preclude a province or a school board from voluntarily expanding its school policies to accommodate other ethnic or religious minorities in Canadian society. It simply states that there are no "rights" in these matters, but only questions of policy, properly determined by local political accommodation.

The drawback to this approach is that it is yet another exception to the non-discrimination "principle" of section 15. In effect, this approach says to other ethnic or religious minorities, "Sorry, you came too late. Only French and English, Catholics and Protestants, enjoy any special educational rights in this country." While this solution is defensible on policy grounds and a prudent course of action for the judges, it further erodes the claim that section 15 establishes a *judicially enforceable* non-discrimination policy. How many exceptions can a principle have before it ceases to be a principle?

The second problem is the accurate perception of the Charter as a direct challenge to the claim of Quebec to be the true or best representative of French interests in Canadian politics and society. This is a more serious problem than the first, because it drags the courts into an area where the political battle lines are old and well established, and places the courts squarely on the side of the federal government. Once again the Charter places the courts, especially the Supreme Court, in an exceedingly difficult position. The Charter explicitly authorizes the courts to enforce the enumerated rights against any offending provincial legislation. Yet any attempts to do so against Quebec legislation will be widely regarded within the province as further attacks on and erosion of the collective rights of French Canadians. The perception of the Supreme Court as impartial and politically neutral will be damaged, and thus its authority within Quebec further diminished.

Quebec's misgivings about the Charter have been eloquently summarized by Gordon Robertson:

> As far as the point about collective rights is concerned, it seems to me that it would be a mistake to assess the protection of collective rights only in terms of clauses like section 92(13) or section 93 or section 133 of the BNA Act, that formally and directly protect specific rights. The powers of the government of Quebec are seen in Quebec as being in themselves important protections of the collective rights of the French-speaking people of the province. Those people in Quebec constitute eighty-five percent of the French-speaking people of Canada. Their continuity as a vibrant, healthy, French-speaking society is seen as a *sine qua non* for the

survival of French-speaking communities in the rest of Canada. In short, the rights and powers of the government of Quebec become a very important instrument of protection for the entire French-speaking minority in Canada. (McKercher 1983:149)

The Charter, he concludes, actually "diminishes the powers of the Assemblé Nationale de Québec."

This is essentially the view of Premier Levesque and his Parti Québecois, who have treated the Charter with open contempt. Because they did not consent to the constitutional amendments of which the Charter was one part, they regard the entire Constitution Act, 1982, as itself "unconstitutional" and illegitimate. Their contempt for the Charter was manifested in Bill 62, enacted in June, 1982, immediately after the Charter took effect. Taking avantage of the section 33 legislative override clause in an unanticipated and extreme form, Bill 62 purports to exempt retroactively and in a blanket-fashion all existing Quebec statutes from sections 2 and 7 to 15 of the Charter.[9]

This view of the meaning and desirability of collective rights as provincial rights in Canadian politics is certainly not unanimous. As M. James Penton has effectively argued, "from an historical standpoint collective rights have often become collective wrongs for those groups not in the mainstream of Canadian politics." (McKercher 1983:174) Penton documents this claim through such examples as Quebec's persecution of the Jehovah's Witnesses during the forties; the prairie provinces' mistreatment of Catholics and Francophones and, more recently, discriminatory legislation directed at Hutterites, Mennonites, and Doukhobors; and anti-Chinese legislation at various times in British Columbia. From Penton's perspective, there is an irreconcilable tension between individual rights and group rights, and he is generally critical of the Charter's various concessions to the latter, especially the section 33 legislative override. On balance, however, he sees the various protections of individual rights as "a major buttress in defense of civil liberties in Canada," and hails the Charter's "enactment and entrenchment as a positive step in the history of our nation." (McKercher 1983:183)

The judges are left with the task of trying to reconcile these two very different views on the relative meaning and desirability of collective rights and individual rights in the Canadian polity. This will be no easy task, for underlying these opposing judgements are two very different understandings of the very meaning and purpose of politics. Penton's views, which are basically those of all civil libertarians, are based on a very individualistic view of society and a radical narrowing of the purpose of government. Individual liberty is the primary political fact, and government's main purpose is to protect its exercise from infringement by other individuals or the government itself. There are no collective or group rights, other than the collective right of the entire society to be governed by their consent, because there are no collective goods, other than the sum of all disparate individual goods. Each individual defines for himself the meaning of "the good life," or happiness. What in pre-liberal thought was called the "health of the soul" is banished from the public agenda and made a purely private affair. The function of the state is reduced to providing security — collective security from hostile foreign nations, and domestic security for the "life, liberty, and property" of each individual citizen.

Such is the political theory implicit in those sections of the Charter championed by its civil libertarian supporters, and it is a very liberal, and a very American, view of political life. Needless to say, it does not fit comfortably with the Canadian political experience. As Hartz, Horowitz, Grant and others have all said in different ways, Canada has retained a sense of collective good, a "tory touch," a sense that the political whole is more than the sum of its parts. This is especially true of Quebec nationalism, and a central purpose of the federal form of government has been to give scope and life to the different regions' sense of collective identity and purpose.

It is in the context of this dimension of Canadian political experience that the protests of the Quebec nationalists find their source and moral force. For them, group rights do not mean the right of an individual not to be discriminated against because of his race or religion. Rather, in the words of André Tremblay,

> To my mind, collective rights mean justice for minorities who want to survive, who want to develop. I am not against the protection of individual rights, but Quebec's legitimate demands for collective rights have yet to be met.... What worries me is that this constitution is the product of confrontation and means few collective rights, less justice for minorities, and more bitterness for Quebec. (McKercher 1983:142)

Tremblay's remarks make arguably clear that the Quebec nationalist understanding of the purpose of politics is not limited to a narrow Lockean liberalism of the protection of individual liberty. It includes facilitating the "survival" and "development" of a collective way of life, a shared language and a shared culture. This "politics of culture" is a modern version of the old "regime politics" rejected and eventually overthrown by modern political liberalism. And as the founders of modern liberalism well understood, when a government undertakes actively to promote through law and public policies a distinctive "way of life," it inevitably impinges on the sense of equal treatment and equal participation of those minorities who are not part of the community and who do not share in their sense of collective good. The "politics of culture" presupposes a homogeneous community, while the Charter is designed to protect the equal treatment of individuals in a heterogeneous society.[10]

Predictably, the conflict between the political liberalism of the Charter and the "regime politics" of the Levesque nationalists has already come to a head in a Charter of Rights case. The Quebec Association of Protestant School Boards has challenged the constitutional validity of the French language education sections of Bill 101, the centrepiece of the Levesque government's language and culture program.[11] Since the section 23 education language rights provisions are not subject to any provincial override, the Levesque government has been forced to fight this issue in the courts. It lost at trial and again on appeal in the Quebec courts, and the case is now pending decision by the Supreme Court of Canada.

Unlike other institutions of government decision making, the Supreme Court must provide an answer to this dispute. It cannot call for a Royal Commission to study the matter, or call a first ministers conference to negotiate a compromise settlement. It must make a ruling and make it now. Since the language of relevant Charter sections is relatively clear on this issue, the Court will almost certainly rule against the challenged education provisions of Bill 101, and thus the heart of the Parti Quebecois agenda.

While the Supreme Court's decision is quite predictable in this case, the response of the Quebec government is not. Will Levesque comply with such a decision? Andre Tremblay has pointedly stated the Parti Québécois perspective: "The question is, to what extent is the minority bound to respect a decision which will remove its collective rights?" (McKercher 1983:142) If compliance is not forthcoming, would the federal government "force" compliance? More interesting still, could the federal government force Quebec to obey?[12]

It is these latter questions — and their disturbing implications — that point to the risks involved in "constitutionalizing," or, what is the same thing, "judicializing" issues of fundamental political disagreement. Do collective rights mean "justice for minorities who want to survive, who want to develop"? Or are collective rights a code word for discrimination against minorities? If Canadian society cannot answer this question, it is very doubtful that the Supreme Court can.

American experience sheds some light on the problems involved in "constitutionalizing" issues of fundamental political disagreement. In the 1857 *Dred Scott* case, the American Supreme Court tried to resolve once and for all the slavery issue that had divided the new American nation since its founding. The result was the formation of the Republican Party, a wholly regional party, the election of a Republican — that is, a regional — president three years later, and the beginning of a civil war. Almost one hundred years later, in the *Brown v. Board of Education* case, the American Supreme Court once again attempted to impose a solution to the legacy of slavery — the legal system of racial desegregation in the South. Despite strong "states' rights" protests, this Supreme Court decision was obeyed, but only after President Eisenhower called in the National Guard to force the integration of Central High School in Little Rock, Arkansas. If Quebec refuses to comply with the Supreme Court's decision in the Bill 101 case, would Canadians support a similar form of federal enforcement?

The point is not that the U.S. Court's decision in *Brown v. Board* was a mistake. Obviously it was a most necessary decision. Try to imagine contemporary American society without it. The point is that the decision had a high cost — the destruction of the remaining constitutional supports of states' rights and federalism. "States' rights" was the consitutional vehicle for segregation. "States' rights" was the constitutional vehicle for segregation, and it had to be destroyed if "equal protection of the laws" was to be enforced. Americans (the majority of whom lived outside the South) were willing to pay this price. Would a majority of Canadians be willing to pay a similar price to enforce bilingual education in Quebec?

A still more relevant political precedent can be drawn from Canadian political history. Historian Kenneth McNaught, in describing Sir Wilfred Laurier's decision not to use the federal government's power to legislate a settlement to the Manitoba School Crisis in the 1890s, writes:

> Knowing that the principal shoal to avoid was a permanent division on racial lines, he saw also that "rights" depended more upon mutual accommodation than upon law. (McNaught 1960:187)

Historically, the federal structure of Canada's political system has served arguably well to facilitate such political accommodations. Unfortunately, judicial interpretation of "entrenched rights" is a uniquely ill-suited process for this purpose.

CONCLUSION

The courts have been given a near impossible task in reconciling the group rights and individual rights provisions of the Charter. The language of section 15, combined with the other guarantees of group rights, new and old, simply point in different directions. There is no single "principle of equality" that the judges can appeal to as a ground for their decisions. Recommendations for tests of "judicial balancing of competing values" just obfuscate this problem, and come from civil liberties enthusiasts whose "result oriented" jurisprudence permits them to ignore this problem.

The logical problems of interpreting section 15 are further compounded by political problems. If the judges simply ignore the four-tier wording of the equality clause and persist in a Diceyean interpretation of equality as equality in the application and administration of the laws (which at least has the merit of permitting on principle "affirmative action" policies), they will be excoriated by civil libertarian interest groups, feminists, academic legal commentators, and the press. If, on the other hand, the courts strike out with "bold" and "creative" substantive interpretations of the equality guarantees, sweeping aside "archaic" and "overbroad" legislative classifications, they will shortly butt up against the cold reality of the section 33 legislative override power. Provincial political leaders are not likely to be reluctant to use their section 33 override powers to disobey "legally" court decisions that are generally perceived as contrary to common sense, sound policy, or both.

The courts are thus in a very difficult situation. No matter what they do with section 15, they will be roundly condemned by one faction or another. This unenviable predicament provokes the obvious question of why — or how — did this ever happen in the first place? The answer seems to be in the political wheeling and dealing by the Trudeau government during the constitution-making process of 1980 to 1982. Their protestations of innocence notwithstanding, the federal negotiators not only traded "fish for rights," but they also traded "rights" for timely political support against the "Gang of Eight." The original wording of section 15 and some of the legal rights sections were significantly broadened in the direction advocated by feminist and civil liberties groups. In the end, the Charter had something for everyone — a politician's dream come true, but a judicial nightmare.

Before contemptuously dismissing Trudeau for creating such a legal and political morass, it must be asked whether there might not be some method in his madness. For whatever his vices might be, no one has ever accused the Prime Minister of being stupid. Upon closer analysis, there are really two different categories of "group rights" in the Charter: the section 15 equality rights and the sections 16-23 minority language and education rights. The principal difference is that the former are all subject to the section 33 legislative override, while the latter are not. This reinforces the view that Trudeau's "concessions" to feminists and other civil libertarian groups on the wording of section 15 and certain of the legal rights sections were tactical maneuvers designed to gain wider political support for the overall constitutional package. It also suggests that perhaps from Trudeau's perspective, they were not very significant concessions.

From this perspective, the fundamental or preferred freedoms of the Charter are not the universal rights and freedoms associated with the practice of liberal democracy everywhere, but rather those rights and freedoms that are unique to Canadian experience. Rather than "cluttering up" the Charter as some commentators have critically remarked, these uniquely Canadian elements may be its heart and soul. Nor, perhaps, is it coincidence that they correspond closely to, and indeed promote, Trudeau's vision of a more unified Canada based on a national policy of bilingualism.

FOOTNOTES

[1] *The Queen v. Drybones* S.C.R. 282 (1970).
[2] *Attorney-General of Canada v. Canard*, 52 D.L.R. (3d) 548 (1975).
[3] The other two cases are *Regina v. Burnshine*, 44 D.L.R. (3d) 584 (1974), and *Bliss v. Attorney-General of Canada*, 92 D.L.R. (3d) 417 (1979).
[4] These figures are from Minister for Indian Affairs, Hohn Munro's "secret report" of September, 1983, "Amendments to Remove the Discriminatory Sections of the Indian Act." The unwillingness of provincial leaders to cede disputed land claims was predicted in this report, and demonstrated at the Constitutional Conference of March, 1984. See *Calgary Herald*, March 10, 1984, "Ministers' Meet Collapses."
[5] See *Calgary Herald*, April, 1984.
[6] *Calgary Herald*, March 10, 1984.
[7] This is certainly true as far as religious sects are conerned. Historically it has been true of race as well, until the beginning of "affirmative action" policies in the late sixties. Much of the opposition to "affirmative action" comes from old-style American liberals (now known as "neo-conservatives") who see it as a dangerous deviation from the "colour-blind" constitutional policy announced in *Brown v. Board of Education* in 1954.
[8] The section 23 educational language rights are quite explicit, and cannot be avoided by the courts.
[9] It was originally speculated that Bill 62 was itself unconstitutional, but it recently withstood a legal challenge. See *Re: Alliance des Professeurs de Montréal et al. v. A.-G. Québec*, Superior Court of Québec, unreported.
[10] For an insightful elaboration of the "non-liberal" character of the Parti Quebecois' culture policies, see Rainer Knopff's two articles: "Language and Culture in the Canadian Debate: The Battle of the White Papers," *Canadian Review of Studies in Nationalism* (Spring, 1979): 66-82; and "Liberal Democracy and the Challenge of Nationalism in Canadian Politics," *Canadian Review of Studies in Nationalism* (Spring, 1982): 23-42.
[11] *Québec Association of Protestant School Boards et al. v. A.-G. Quebec* 140 D.L.R. (3d) (1982), 23-42.
[12] These questions are all raised but of course not answered in the "roundtable" section of McKercher, (1983): 139-150.

REFERENCES

Cardinal, Harold. *The Rebirth of Canada's Indians*. Edmonton: Hurtig Publishers, 1977

Dawson, R. MacGregor. *The Government of Canada*. Revised by Norman Ward, 4th edition. Toronto: University of Toronto Press, 1963.

Flanagan, Thomas. "What are Aboriginal Rights, and Do They Exist?" Paper presented at the Western Canadian Legal History Conference, University of Calgary. April 25-27, 1984.

Glazer, Nathan. *Affirmative Discrimination*. New York: Basic Books, 1974.

Hogg, Peter. *Canada Act 1982 Annotated*. Toronto: Carswell, 1982.

Manuel, George and Michael Posluns. *The Fourth World — An Indian Reality*. Toronto: Collier-Macmillan Canada, 1974.

McKercher, William R., ed. *The U.S. Bill of Rights and the Canadian Charter of Rights and Freedoms*. Toronto: Ontario Economic Council, 1983.

McNaught, Kenneth. *The Pelican History of Canada*. London: Penguin Books, 1960.

Sanders, Douglas. "Prior Claims: An Aboriginal People in the Constitution of Canada." In Stanley M. Beck and Ivan Bernier, *Canada and the New Constitutiton: The Unfinished Agenda*. Vol. 1, Montreal. The Institute for Research on Public Policy, 1983.

5
THE STATISTICAL PROTECTION OF MINORITIES: AFFIRMATIVE ACTION POLICY IN CANADA

RAINER KNOPFF

INTRODUCTION

The age of affirmative action in Canada is upon us. It is fast becoming one of the leading policy responses to the political claims of Canadian women and minorities. In June of 1983 Treasury Board President Herb Gray "announced that an affirmative action program, under the direction of the Treasury Board, is being implemented across the Public Service of Canada."[1] Many provincial governments have similar programs, as do a number of municipalities. While these public sector programs are mandatory, affirmative action in the private sector remains largely voluntary.[2] Governments are actively promoting private sector affirmative action, however. In 1979 the Affirmative Action Directorate of the Canada Employment and Immigration Commission (CEIC) was established to act as a consultant to private industry in the creation and implementation of affirmative programs; it does this for businesses under both federal and provincial jurisdiction. Some of the provincial human rights commissions have been doing the same thing. The response to these initiatives has not been overwhelming: from 1979 to 1983 only 49 of the 1130 firms approached by CEIC entered into agreements to establish affirmative action programs, a fact that led the Special House of Commons Committee on Visible Minorities to recommend the imposition of mandatory affirmative action in five years "if insufficient progress is detected under voluntary programs." (Daudlin, 1984:35)

The first affirmative action program in Canada, although it was not then known by that name, was the federal government's effort, beginning in the late 1960s, to increase the proportion of Francophones in the public service. The "target groups" benefitting from the most recent wave of affirmative action are women, indigenous people, the handicapped and blacks (in Nova Scotia). In March of 1984 the Commons Committee on Visible Minorities recommended extension of the policy to racial minorities in general.

In light of these developments, affirmative action becomes an important subject for a volume on minorities in Canada. Since the policy, in most of its current applications, has been borrowed somewhat uncritically from the United States, it is especially important for Canadians to assess its theoretical and practical validity. As a contribution to this task, this paper analyses the major components of the new affirmative action programs and the reasons by which they are justified — particularly the claim that affirmative action is a necessary remedy for discrimination. I argue that these reasons amount to tendentious rhetoric, and that they cannot really justify what has come to be a central component in virtually all affirmative action programs — the emphasis on the setting and achievement of numerical "goals" or "targets."

This statistical orientation is rhetorically (and hence politically) difficult to justify to the extent that it suggests that proportional representation of groups is the norm and that any deviations from proportionality are due to discrimination. This is so for two reasons. First, common sense indicates that discrimination, as it is commonly understood, does not account for all statistical imbalance. Second, the setting of numerical targets by reference to a standard of statistical imbalance appears to run afoul of the publicly supported merit principle. Proponents of affirmative action have an answer to both of these objections. In order to make discrimination account for more of the observable statistical imbalance, they expand the definition of the term, adding what is called "systemic discrimination." Not even systemic discrimination can account for all of the remaining imbalance, however, and so the affirmative action rhetoric apparently makes its peace with common sense by disclaiming any belief in the norm of proportionality. Indeed, affirmative action programs go to great lengths to develop an elaborate methodology to control for that degree of imbalance that is *not* due to discrimination. This, it is argued, allows the setting of realistic "goals," lower and more flexible than the "quotas" that would be required to produce complete demographic proportionality. Unlike quotas, moreover, such moderate goals are alleged not to violate the merit principle.

In fact, this "methodology of moderation," as one might call it, is nothing more than pseudo-scientific mystification; it is part of what Harvey Mansfield, Jr. calls "the underhandedness of affirmative action." (Mansfield, 1984) The premise on which it is based — that not all imbalance is caused by discrimination — undermines the case not only for quotas, but for any numerical emphasis. The only truly compelling case for the prevailing statistical mania is faith in the norm of proportionality, and ultimately the rhetoricians of affirmative action admit as much. But if this is true, then one can continue to attribute statistical imbalance to discrimination only by expanding the definition of the term to such an extent that it loses all meaning and hence its utility as an explanatory concept. It thus becomes apparent that the utility of the term for affirmative action programs is primarily rhetorical — a utility it derives from its unexpanded, common sense meaning.

AFFIRMATIVE ACTION & SYSTEMIC DISCRIMINATION

Advocates of affirmative action typically describe its purpose as the achievement of a more proportional representation of groups than currently exists. According to one formulation,

> Affirmative Action is a comprehensive planning process designed to ensure not only an equality of opportunity but also an equality of results. Its primary objective is to ensure the Canadian workforce is an accurate reflection of the composition of the Canadian population given the availability of required skills. (Phillips, 1981:2)

Depending on how one defines discrimination, this policy can be understood either as a remedial response to discrimination or as something separate from and additional to an anti-discrimination policy. In the early days of anti-discrimination legislation, when it was generally thought that the legal prohibition extended only to direct and intentional discrimination "because of"[3] an individual's group affiliation, affirmative action was understood in the latter sense. Since not all group underrepresentation could be attributed to direct discrimination, the prohibition of such discrimination could be expected to have a less than adequate impact on the problem of disproportionality. A policy designed to bring about proportional representation had therefore to be understood as overcoming factors other than legally prohibited discrimination, not as a remedy to such discrimination. It followed that the enforcers of anti-discrimination legislation had no authority to compel affirmative action; at best, they could recommend voluntary implementation. Peter Robertson, now a consultant to CEIC, recalls that this was the understanding with which he began his career in the enforcement of anti-discrimination legislation. Upon his appointment as Executive Director of the Missouri Human Rights Commission, he was briefed by a group of experts, one of whom told him, "If *all* you do is remedy discrimination, you will fail. The wave of the future is *affirmative action.*" Says Robertson,

> Thus, I started out in this field with the idea that affirmative action was entirely different from remedying discrimination and that it was really a sort of quasi-charitable activity which I would ask employers to engage in — out of the kindness of their hearts; but which I could not insist that they implement to comply with the law. (Robertson, 1980:4)

The second way of understanding affirmative action — as a remedy for discrimination — requires an expanded definition of discrimination. One must include in the concept those factors other than direct intentional discrimination that contribute to the underrepresentation affirmative action is designed to overcome. Proponents of affirmative action argue that such a transformation of the definition is logically required by the purpose to which anti-discrimination policy is directed. In this view, the legislation was enacted precisely to bring about greater proportionality, and the discrimination it prohibits must therefore be defined in a manner adequate to this end. Again, Peter Robertson summarizes this thinking:

> ... when we in the U.S. initially confronted the different unemployment rates, occupational distribution, and disparate income levels of minorities and women we attempted to change the situation by making it illegal to discriminate. When we discovered that eliminating discrimination (as it was then defined) was having no impact on the problem we began to talk about affirmative action and to perceive that action as something above and beyond eliminating discrimination. [However] that failure to change the underlying facts which had confronted Congress was not a failure of the anti-discrimination legislation but was, instead, a failure to understand the real nature of discrimination. It was only when we began to perceive discrimination in a totally different fashion that we began to have a real impact on the problem ... on the facts. (Robertson, 1980:4-5)

The main way in which the concept of discrimination was expanded was by including in it neutral rules, procedures or requirements that are not implemented in order to exclude members of a group — and thus escape a prohibition of direct, intentional discrimination — but that have an "adverse impact" on the group nevertheless. A common example is a height and weight requirement for police work, which, while neutral on its face, excludes many more women than men, thereby contributing to the underrepresentation of women in the police force. In Canada such barriers have come to be known as "systemic discrimination." Other, less common labels include "adverse effect discrimination," "indirect discrimination," and "constructive discrimination." Affirmative action, understood as a policy of increasing the proportional representation of groups, is generally described as a response to this kind of discrimination. One CEIC report, for example, defines affirmative action as "a comprehensive result-oriented plan adopted by an employer as a remedy for employment discrimination with special emphasis on systemic discrimination." (CEIC, 1979:1) Another states that

> The affirmative action approach to the problem of inequity and inefficient utilization of target group workers is based on the concept of systemic discrimination. That is, this approach identifies discrimination in the workplace in terms of the impact of employment practices on the employment of target group members. (CEIC, 1982:41)

The prohibition of systemic discrimination is said to make it possible to conceive of affirmative action not only as a policy response to underrepresentation, but also, in appropriate circumstances, as a legal, and hence obligatory, remedy. We shall have to consider whether this conclusion is justified.

FROM EQUAL OPPORTUNITY TO NUMERICAL TARGETS
According to CEIC, an affirmative action program cannot achieve its goal of proportionality unless it is composed of both an "equal opportunity response" and "special measures." By an "equal opportunity response" CEIC means the cessation of direct discrimination and the dismantling of systemic barriers in favour of practices that do not have a disparate impact on target groups. Special measures are of two types: remedial and support. "A remedial measure is any action designed to redress past discrimination by providing a preferential benefit to a designated group." Examples of such measures include the preferential hiring of women from a pool of otherwise equally qualified applicants, and special training programs for natives in order to help them qualify for certain jobs. A support measure is designed to alleviate "an employment problem specifically affecting a particular group" but is not preferential because members of non-target groups can avail themselves of the benefit. An alcoholic counselling program, for example, may have been designed with the problem of a particular minority in mind, but would be available to any alcoholic, whatever his group affiliation. (CEIC, 1982:41) Whereas equal opportunity responses, and some support measures, constitute permanent changes in employment practices, remedial measures are usually conceived of as being temporary.

The reason affirmative action must include both "equal opportunity" and "remedial" measures is that it "has as its primary objective a change in the existing employment distribution. Equality of results is of paramount concern," (CEIC, 1979:1) and such "results" cannot be achieved by an equal opportunity response alone. Equality of opportunity gives free rein to actual inequalities and leads inevitably to inequality of result. To the extent that actual inequalities are not natural, but the consequence of past discrimination, equality of opportunity perpetuates the effects of past injustice. The mere cessation of discrimination is therefore not enough. As one commentator observes, "The federal Public Service Commission, after four years of implementing an equal opportunity program, reported little improvement in women's status, and an actual decrease in some occupational areas." (Bruce, 1983:2)

If an equal opportunity response is not sufficient for the achievement of affirmative action's goals, it is nevertheless necessary. A remedial program designed to upgrade the qualifications of a particular group will not achieve the desired result if the employer continues to base hiring decisions on prejudiced stereotypes or if systemic barriers, such as seniority systems, prevent the promotion of the program's beneficiaries.

In addition to an equal opportunity response and special measures, most of the literature stresses that a properly constructed affirmative action program must set numerical goals or targets and establish timetables for achieving them. The Commons Committee on Visible Minorities distinguished between voluntary and mandatory affirmative programs partly in terms of the emphasis placed on achieving these goals. "While it is not obligatory (in a voluntary program) to meet the goals, good faith efforts to hire minorities must be demonstrated." In a mandatory program, on the other hand, "An employer is obligated to employ a fixed number or percentage of visible minority workers." (Daudlin, 1984:33). Although such goals are to be flexible even in mandatory programs, the success of a program is measured in terms of achieving them, and program managers are evaluated in terms of this measure of success — if they don't get results, they must expect to be penalized. Thus one of the criteria for evaluating the Treasury Board's affirmative action programs is "the level of attainment of the quantitative goals set by departments and agencies..."; success "will be considered a priority item in evaluating the performance of deputy heads."[4] For CEIC, such "accountability" is important **even in voluntary** private sector programs. (CEIC, 1982:54)

Many proponents of affirmative action are at great pains to distinguish "goals" from "quotas," which are considered an evil to be avoided for reasons set out by the Ontario Human Rights Commission:

> Some jurisdictions, particularly in the United States, have attempted to remedy long-established patterns of discrimination against various groups by requiring employers to hire quotas of people belonging to those groups. The Commission believes that this is a crude and simplistic approach to a complex problem. Such an approach casts doubt on the legitimacy of minority group achievements. Moreover, it betrays the basic principle of equality of opportunity if people are given jobs or promoted not because they are competent, but because they belong to a minority group. Such reverse discrimination, though well-intentioned, is discrimination none the less. It still spells condescension and, in the long run, it may do far more harm than good. At bottom, it is the antithesis of human rights legislation. (OHRC, 1977:35)

Goals allegedly escape this criticism because, unlike quotas, they do not constitute "an absolute preference based on [group affiliation] without regard to qualifications." They are flexible, temporary, reasonable, and "they never require hiring the *unqualified*" (emphasis in the original). Instead of absolutely requiring the selection of definite numbers of target group members — a policy that could lead to the hiring of unqualified candidates — "they require a ratio from among qualified or qualifiable individuals." (Robertson, 1980:21-22)

Critics of affirmative action tend to reject this reasoning. Writing in *Saturday Night*, David Frum contends that the distinction founders on the rock of self-interest — in this case the self-interest of those who are responsible for the success of affirmative action programs.

> The distinction between quotas and goals turns out to be meaningless mostly because ... success in hiring women, natives, and handicapped in [the civil service] will be a "priority item in evaluating the performance of deputy heads [of departments]." (Frum, 1984:11)

The American writer Paul Seabury is more acerbic, expressing his contempt for the distinction by coining the new labels "quoals" and "gotas," the former being "a slow-moving quota-goal" and the latter, "a supple, fast-moving quota-goal." (Reported in Roche, 1976:148) Even friends of affirmative action sometimes question the distinction. For example, Russell Juriansz, legal counsel for the Canadian Human Rights Commission, has written that "It is difficult to make sense of a statement such as 'We are not imposing quotas, we are adopting goals and timetables." (Juriansz, 1983:1) Elaborating orally, he insisted that the distinction was "mumbo jumbo; you're either playing the numbers game or you're not."[5] The question of who is right in this debate about goals and quotas turns on assessment of the validity of the methods by which proponents of the distinction propose to ensure that "goals" will never undermine the merit principle — what I have called the "methodology of moderation."

THE METHODOLOGY OF MODERATION

Although affirmative action is intended to increase the proportional representation of groups, the standard of proportionality is not usually the demographic composition of the population as a whole. Recall that the "primary objective" of affirmative action "is to ensure the Canadian workforce is an accurate reflection of the composition of the Canadian population *given the availability of required skills*" (emphasis added). Thus, in order to determine whether an affirmative action program is warranted, and to set the numerical targets at which the program aims, the representation of a group in the workforce is compared not to its presence in the population as a whole but to a figure generated by what is called "availability analysis." (CEIC, 1982: 60-63)

Availability analysis attempts to control for non-discriminatory causes of underrepresentation in order to ascertain the degree of proportionality, short of complete demographic balance, to be aimed at as a remedy for discrimination. It is based on the assumption that discrimination is only one of several causes of demographic statistical imbalance, which is not, therefore, conclusive proof of discrimination. As Thomas Sowell points out, "Even a disease that is fatal 100 percent of the time provides no automatic explanation of death if there are many other fatal diseases, along with accidents, murder, and suicide.... Even if A is known to cause Z, we still cannot infer A whenever we find Z, if B, C, D, etc. also cause Z." (Sowell, 1984:17) Availability analysis seeks to ascertain the degree of Z that is caused by A, by separating out the amount caused by B, C, D, etc. As Sowell remarks elsewhere, "If discrimination is to mean unequal treatment of equal individuals, then comparisons must be made between individuals who are similar with respect to the variables which generally determine employment, pay, and promotion. Only insofar as we succeed in specifying all these variables can we confidently refer to the remaining economic differences as 'discrimination'." (Sowell, 1975:13)

CEIC identifies three such non-discriminatory variables. The first is geography, which is important because groups tend not to be evenly distributed across the country. Thus an employer who draws his workforce from a region in which the target group's representation is significantly less than its national average cannot be accused of discriminatory underutilization if the workforce representation of the group falls short of demographic proportionality. By the same token, an employer who draws from an area in which the target group is concentrated may be guilty of underutilization even if demographic balance is approximated in his workforce. Utilization must be measured by reference to target group representation in the employer's recruitment area, not in the population as a whole. On the other hand, an unnecessarily small recruitment area may be open to challenge as systemic, or even intentional, discrimination if it avoids areas in which target groups predominate. "Comparison of local and wider population patterns may reveal that by widening its recruitment area somewhat, the company could reach a greater proportion of target group members." (CEIC, 1982:62)

The second factor considered in availability analysis is skill or qualifications. If the proportion of qualified target group members in the relevant recruitment area is less than the group's total representation in that area, underutilization based on the latter figure could be remedied only at the cost of subverting the merit principle. Again, however, a requirement of unnecessarily high qualifications is open to the charge of systemic discrimination.

The third major component of availability analysis is the institutional source of candidates. Candidates for any position can be recruited either internally, from "the pool of people next in line in the organizational hierarchy," or externally, from qualified non-employees. Both factors must be included in an assessment of availability. To consider only the proportion of qualified target group members in the geographically relevant area would be to discount experience within the organization; yet internal experience is clearly a relevant and non-discriminatory consideration in making many employment decisions. On the other hand, to limit one's search to internal sources will do nothing to overcome the statistical effects of past discrimination in the organization as a whole. (CEIC, 1982:62,69)

Although it is not mentioned in CEIC's *Affirmative Action Technical Training Manual*, another element in some availability analyses is what might be called the "time-lag" factor. This factor attempts to give weight to target group availability at the time that most of the present employees were hired. Consider, for example, a government department whose employees are only 20 percent female while women constitute 40 percent of the qualified geographical labour pool. It would hardly be fair to describe this "underutilization" as the result of departmental discrimination, systemic or otherwise, if most of the present employees were hired 20 years ago, and if women then comprised only 20 percent of the qualified labour pool.[6]

The result of this attempt to control for non-discriminatory causes of underrepresentation is a measure of the degree of representation one would expect in the absence of past or present discrimination. This measure, which is called the "utilization standard," is then increased on the basis of a "pull factor" to produce an "augmented utilization standard." "The pull factor is a means of compensating for disproportionately low participation rates of target groups stemming from the effects of past discrimination; and of giving recognition to the unused and under-utilized skills possessed by target group members." (CEIC, 1982:64) For CEIC, the pull factor is 10 percent of the ratio of working-age target group members to the total working-age population in the relevant recruitment area. "For example, if the Native population of the island of Newfoundland is close to zero, the pull factor will be zero. On the other hand, if the Native population of northern Manitoba is 23 percent, the pull factor will be 10 percent of 23, or 2.3 percent." (CEIC, 1982:65)

The comparison of workforce representation with "availability" (which I will hereafter use as a convenient synonym for the "augmented utilization standard") results in a measure of the "utilization" of a group. "Underutilization," or "adverse impact," occurs when workforce representation is lower than availability. Obviously, the latter figure will generally be lower than one based on a comparison of workforce representation with overall population statistics. It is reduced even further by the fact that underutilization is not generally defined as *any* workforce representation falling short of availability, but as representation that is less than some specified proportion of availability. For CEIC, the cutoff figure is 80 percent of availability. (CEIC, 1982:58) The measure of underutilization arrived at in this way also constitutes the basis of the targets to be aimed at. The numerical goal of an affirmative action program, in other words, is 80 percent of availability, which is in turn less than simple demographic representation.

It is the moderation of the goals thus generated that forms part of the distinction between goals and quotas. We have seen that goals, unlike quotas, are understood as not abandoning the merit principle. This is so because "availability analysis" ensures that only the qualified are included in the population upon which goal-setting calculations are based. Goals, therefore, require the preferential treatment of target group members only within a pool of otherwise equally qualified candidates. In short, one of the differences between goals and quotas is that the latter are too high to accommodate the merit principle, and they are too high because they are derived not from "availability" but from total population statistics. Thus, the Treasury Board's new affirmative action program, while clearly requiring the use of numerical targets, does not "countenance any infringement upon the merit principle or the imposition of quotas of targets based simply on demographics."[7]

THE IMMODERATE SUBSTRATUM
The moderation apparent on the surface of the affirmative action rhetoric is belied by its deeper and truer inclinations. This is brought to light by certain

contradictions within the "methodology of moderation" itself. In CEIC's *Training Manual* one's suspicions are first aroused by the declaration that a finding of underutilization does not by itself prove the existence of discrimination, that it is merely an indicator alerting one to the possibility of discrimination, and that further investigation (called "employment systems analysis") is necessary to uncover the systemic barriers to which one can reasonably attribute the underutilization. (CEIC, 1982:58) Since underutilization does not prove discrimination, one must assume that the employment systems analysis will not always find discrimination, or that not all underutilization is caused by discrimination. At first glance, this seems to be a praiseworthy extension of the methodology of moderation, but upon reflection one realizes that it is moderation overreaching itself. If underutilization does not prove the existence of discrimination, the distinction between goals and quotas is undermined; it either collapses, or can be saved only at the cost of calling the necessity of goals into question. In CEIC's case, the problem is solved by surreptitiously abandoning the distinction and by more explicitly abandoning the premise upon which it is based — that not all imbalance is caused by discrimination.

It would certainly make sense to say that underutilization does not prove the existence of discrimination if one were basing the measure of underutilization on total population statistics, but it becomes problematic in light of the painstaking availability analysis that is undertaken, and from which underutilization is derived. After all, availability analysis is a way of controlling for the non-discriminatory causes of underrepresentation in order to isolate the degree of disproportionality attributable to discrimination. If this analysis were truly comprehensive, the measure of underutilization based on it *would* be sufficient proof of discrimination, and employment systems analysis would be necessary not to provide a missing proof, but only to identify the foci of an "equal opportunity response." Moreover, the 20 percent discount can be seen as an attempt to accommodate unanticipated non-discriminatory causes, or those that are methodologically difficult to assess. The statement that underutilization is an insufficient proof of discrimination thus amounts to an admission that non-discriminatory causes of underrepresentation sufficiently important to outweigh the 20 percent discount may be left out of the availability analysis.

One such non-discriminatory cause of underrepresentation can conveniently be labelled the "interest factor." Ronald Manzer points out that, "As with class groups, the existence of distinctive occupational patterns for ethnic groups does not necessarily signify unequal access to occupations, since differences in the distribution of members of each ethnic group might simply reflect the preferences and cultural characteristics of people in each ethnic group." (Manzer, 1974:212) In fact, the affinity of ethnic groups for different occupations is well known. Nor is it easy to describe this phenomenon as the result only of discrimination, at least of direct or systemic discrimination as we have defined them, because many of these affinities persist across time and political boundaries, often manifesting themselves not only where the group is a minority, but also in the country of origin. (Sowell, 1984:26-29)

The press release announcing the Treasury Board's new affirmative action programs in the federal public service asserted that the objective of affirmative action was "to ensure that target groups participate and are represented equitably in the Public Service, based on their representation within the available, qualified and *interested* workforce."[8] There is no mention of interest in the CEIC *Training Manual*'s discussion of availability analysis, yet it would certainly affect one's assessment of the degree of underrepresentation due to discrimination. If interest among qualified members of a target group was less than among qualified members of the majority, even after equal opportunity and special measures were implemented, then not all of the underutilization could be attributed to discrimination. The reverse is also true: just as lack of interest can account for underrepresentation even in the absence of discrimination, so proportional representation may occur despite the presence of systemic barriers. For example, a minority may be disproportionately burdened by a job qualification but its qualified members may apply in disproportionately large numbers.[9] In short, a measure of proportionality or disproportionality tells one little about the presence or absence of discrimination unless one knows something about the effect of the "interest factor."

Differences in the average age of groups can also account for underrepresentation. A group whose members are disproportionately young will inevitably be underrepresented in the workforce in general and in higher level occupations in particular. This is another dimension of availability that is left out of CEIC's availability analysis.

Even if one assumes complete equality among groups in terms of acquired skills, interests, age, etc., the phenomenon of statistical variance, which certainly cannot be attributed to discrimination, leads one to expect statistical imbalances in any particular firm or industry. If one flips a balanced coin an infinite number of times, for example, it will come up heads or tails about half the time. On any particular sequence of 10 tosses, however, every conceivable combination of heads and tails is possible, and combinations other than 5 and 5 are highly probable. Similarly, even if one expects the random distribution of groups within the national workforce as a whole, it is an unwarranted leap of logic to contend that, absent discrimination, it should also occur in the smaller scale workforce of individual employers. Simple statistical variance ensures that it will not. (Sowell, 1984:53-56)

There are undoubtedly many other non-discriminatory causes of statistical underrepresentation that are left out of the typical availability analysis. Indeed, it is probably impossible to include or even to predict every relevant non-discriminatory cause, and some, such as the interest factor, would be methodologically difficult to handle. In any case, CEIC's statement that underutilization does not prove discrimination is coherent only if one assumes that significant dimensions of "availability" have been left out of the availability analysis.

This poses a critical problem. The numerical goals of affirmative action programs are based on a measure of underutilization, which is in turn dependent on a measure of availability. To the extent that dimensions of availability sufficient to outweigh the 20 percent discount are excluded from the latter figure, the goals will be set too high. At this point we should remind ourselves that one of the central distinctions between goals and quotas is that the latter are too high.

The most obvious solution to this problem lies in the vaunted flexibility of goals, which would appear to allow downward adjustment of those goals that can be achieved only by transforming them into quotas. Upon reflection, however, this solution is not without difficulty. If the employment systems analysis is well done and the affirmative action program is otherwise well-constructed, any failure to meet goals must be due to some non-discriminatory factor that was left out of the availability analysis. To the extent that this is so, a goal would always have to be lowered to fit reality, in which case one wonders why numerical goals are necessary at all.

The same difficulty is inherent in another of the common ways in which goals are distinguished from quotas. As Herb Gray said, in introducing the Treasury Board's programs, "The numerical goals which we will be introducing as part of affirmative action are not quotas. They are rather an estimate of what can be achieved when systemic barriers are eliminated and some special measures are put in place...."[10] But why should one settle for a mere estimate when one can and will have the real thing? All one needs to do in order to know precisely what can be achieved by an affirmative action program is to put it in place and see what happens. The prior estimate of what will happen would seem to be superfluous. Stated differently, an estimate is logically inferior to the reality it projects and must be replaced by the latter.

One could defend goals against this charge of redundancy by arguing that they are necessary to indicate whether the employment systems analysis was completely and thoroughly done. This defence downplays the possibility that the failure to reach goals is due to non-discriminatory elements left out of the availability analysis in favour of a more energetic second (or third or fourth) look for discriminatory causes. The assumption on which this defence is built — that failure to achieve goals is most likely to flow from undiscovered or unremedied discriminatory causes — is required to justify the emphasis on the "accountability" of those responsible for the achievement of goals. If lack of achievement were generally an indication of unanticipated non-discriminatory causes, such accountability would be unnecessary; it only makes sense as an incentive for the affirmative action manager to work harder to discover additional discriminatory causes and to develop additional affirmative responses.

One way of supporting the assumption that failure to achieve goals is seldom due to unanticipated non-discriminatory causes is by reference to the widespread suspicion of affirmative action. In this hostile climate, it might be argued, one cannot assume that the job of employment systems analysis will be well done or that affirmative responses will be enthusiastically implemented, and one must attribute most of the underachievement to this half-heartedness. From this perspective, goals are hardly redundant; affirmative action managers need an incentive to do more than pay lip-service to the principles of their programs, and numerical goals, for the achievement of which they are held accountable, are the best way of providing this incentive. As the affirmative action coordinator of the Nova Scotia Human Rights Commission has put it, goals are necessary to determine "whether a company is living up to its commitment."[11]

A more radical way of supporting the contention that numerical underachievement is usually due to undiscovered or unremedied discriminatory causes is simply to deny the existence of non-discriminatory causes of underrepresentation. This is precisely what is done in CEIC's *Training Manual*, not many pages after it asserts that underutilization in itself does not prove discrimination.

> The basic premise of affirmative action is that the operation of discriminatory social, educational and employment practices is the force which causes disproportionate representation of groups of people in the labour force. In the absence of such discrimination, which is interwoven throughout the fabric of our society, women, Natives and disabled people would be distributed throughout the labour force in approximately the same proportion as they are distributed in the population — with rare exceptions reflecting genuine preferences of some women and Native people and actual limitations of some disabled individuals. (CEIC, 1982:60-61)

From this we learn that not only does a measure of underutilization based on "availability" provide sufficient proof of discrimination, but that virtually any variation from demographic random distribution will do. The assumption on which availability analysis rests — that one must control for non-discriminatory causes of underrepresentation — turns out to be unfounded: there are no such causes and "availability analysis" is therefore strictly speaking unnecessary. It is true that the "interest factor" is mentioned in this passage, but it is dismissed as being "rare," too rare, certainly, to affect the long-term objective of random distribution. It would be difficult to contradict more completely the premise on which the "methodology of moderation" is built.

As with so many other aspects of affirmative action, the "random distribution" hypothesis is borrowed from the United States. According to Thomas Sowell, it arises out of the original civil rights movement, which was dedicated almost exclusively to bettering the condition of American blacks. One of the traditional justifications of the inferior position of blacks in American society has been their alleged lack of innate ability. Against this, reformers argued it was due to discrimination. These eventually became the only explanations of black underrepresentation. With time, this explanatory dichotomy was extended (wrongly in Sowell's view) to the disadvantage or underrepresentation of other racial and ethnic groups and women. Although it was not always recognized by those who accepted this analysis, Sowell argues that it leads inevitably to the "result-oriented" emphasis on random distribution typical of affirmative action rhetoric. "If the causes of intergroup differences can be dichotomized into discrimination and innate ability, then non-racists and non-sexists must expect equal results from non-discrimination. Conversely, the persistence of highly disparate results must indicate that discrimination continues to be pervasive...."[12] (Sowell, 1984:37-38)

If this is true then the more limited numerical goals of affirmative action, which are based on figures derived from an availability analysis, cannot possibly be too high. Indeed, these goals are more properly understood as "medium-term" objectives, which fall short of random distribution not because of non-discriminatory determinants of underrepresentations, but because of concessions to practical considerations.

> Clearly, this long-term objective, which represents an ideal standard, is not useful to the individual company in establishing its immediate and medium-term goals. However, a comparison of the company's current workforce status with the ideal of random distribution does provide a

measure of the magnitude of the problem to be overcome.

> The comparison of workforce data with availability data, on the other hand, provides a practical measure of current status and achievable goals, given the present, imperfect state of the labour market. (CEIC, 1982:60-61)

In addition to long- and medium-term goals, there are also "immediate" or "short-term" goals, which are even more modest. These are arrived at by modifying medium-term goals in light of "attrition rates, availability of target group members and the particular situation of the company at the time." Nevertheless, "It should be remembered that the long-term quantitative objective is representativeness of target group participation in the workforce." (CEIC, 1982:102)

Because the "interest factor" is too rare to affect the long-term goal of random distribution, it would be more than adequately taken care of by existing availability analyses and the 20 percent discount. Short- and medium-term goals would never be too high, and the much vaunted flexibility of goals thus turns out to lie in their inevitable upward revision whenever they are achieved. Failure to reach these modest goals would almost always indicate insufficient diligence, or bad faith, on the part of affirmative action managers in designing and implementing their programs, and would justify the negative career evaluations contemplated in the affirmative action literature.

In brief, we have noted two perspectives on statistical imbalance in the affirmative action literature, sometimes within a single work, as CEIC's *Training Manual* attests. According to the first of these, statistical imbalance may be due to factors other than discrimination and does not in itself prove discrimination or warrant an affirmative action remedy. In the *Training Manual*'s formulation this is apparently true even after an availability analysis has controlled for the most obvious non-discriminatory causes of discrimination. It follows from this that the achievement of proportionality is not essential to a successful affirmative action program. Failure to achieve proportionality (even when it is based on availability rather than total demographic representation) may very well be due to non-discriminatory causes such as the interest factor. According to the second view, departures from random distribution (based not on availability but on total population figures) are sufficient proof of discrimination, and the achievement of statistical balance is the chief goal of an affirmative action program. This second view appears to be the more fundamental one.

AFFIRMATIVE ACTION & SOCIETAL DISCRIMINATION

The status of affirmative action as a remedy for discrimination is said to depend on the inclusion of systemic barriers in the definition of discrimination. In fact, the second way of understanding affirmative action — as a remedy for all statistical imbalance — entails a much more radical expansion, or transformation, of the definition of discrimination. Actually, this is no longer a definition of discrimination at all, for it stretches the term beyond its natural limits. In effect, discrimination becomes a code word for whatever causes statistical imbalance. In this sense, affirmative action really has very little to do with remedying discrimination, and everything to do with remaking society according to the ideal of group proportionality. The society described by this ideal is the good society and any cause that prevents its realization must be overcome. Affirmative action insists on calling all such causes discrimination only because it is rhetorically necessary to do so. But the rhetorical utility of the term depends on its common sense meaning, supplemented at most by the addition of "systemic discrimination." Proponents of affirmative action thus rarely refer to everything else that must be included in the term in order to make it bear the burden of statistical imbalance as such. The very broad definition of the term that is required remains largely implicit; certainly it has not been given a name in the manner of "systemic" discrimination. I shall call it "societal discrimination."

The unequal effect, measurable by statistical imbalance, of either direct or systemic discrimination, as we have defined them, flows from a specific action of policy by an identifiable person or institution. Often, however, a similar statistical imbalance exists even in the absence of such barriers. An interesting example of this phenomenon arose in the case of *Offierski v. Peterborough Board of Education*, which arose under Ontario's Human Rights Code. Offierski alleged sexual discrimination by the board as the cause of her failure to attain the level of vice-principal of a secondary school. Part of the evidence entered in support of her claim was a significant statistical underrepresentation of women at that level. The chairman of the board of inquiry ruled, however, that although there may have been a "factual discrimination," it was not one for which the board could be held responsible, at least in the absence of evidence of direct discrimination, because the statistics also revealed that there were "very few female applicants for the positions and the prerequisite principal's course as well."[13]

Another example of this phenomenon was manifest in the response of certain southern American school boards to the 1954 desegregation decision, *Brown v. Board of Education*.[14] The school boards in question administered school systems in rural districts where the black and white populations were not residentially segregated, but where the schools had been legally segregated in the past. When the latter policy was found unconstitutional by the Supreme Court, a typical reaction was to institute a policy of "free choice" under which each child would be free to attend the school of his choosing. The predictable outcome of this policy was that very few black children elected the formerly all-white schools and no white children chose the formerly all-black schools.[15]

According to one school of thought the kind of imbalance found in these examples is not the result of discrimination at all. In this view, the distinction may be stated as one of "forced" and "unforced" segregation, with only the former qualifying as discrimination. Thus women who would have been forcibly excluded from police work had they applied when a height and weight requirement was in effect, or when direct discrimination was being practiced, are not being discriminated against if they do not apply when these conditions no longer obtain; in effect, they are voluntarily excluding themselves, as were the black children in the American south who used their free choice to stay in black school. Such voluntary self-segregation is an example of the interest factor.

From another perspective, there is no such thing as "unforced" segregation. In our example the women who are allegedly excluding themselves are not doing so voluntarily. They have been subject to a long process of socialization in the dominant assumptions concerning the kinds of work appropriate to men and women.[16] These assumptions reflect prevailing power structures, and although their transmissions may be subtle and unconscious, it is not "unforced." Their alleged self-segregation having been forced upon them, it is as much the result of unjust discrimination as are the other forms of segregation. Similarly, one may argue that, given the predictable social pressures, indeed the intimidation, brought to bear on the so-called "free choice" of school children in the rural American South, the choices were free only in the most formal and abstract sense. Moreover, the state can be understood to have anticipated this result and to have encouraged it by doing nothing about it, in effect by not providing "equal protection" of the laws to blacks who wished to attend formerly all-white schools. This was the view of the American Supreme Court. Since the administration of the "free choice" plans was more complicated and more expensive than the familiar neighbourhood attendance plan would have been, and since the latter plan would inevitably, in the context of unsegregated neighbourhoods, have led to greater integration, the Court inferred that the "free choice" plans were a subterfuge on the part of the boards to maintain the old dual school system.[17]

While it is possible to view sexual self-stereotyping, or the "self-segregation" of southern school children under free choice plans, as the negative effect of invidious social forces, there are other kinds of self-segregation that are more difficult to describe in this way. There is, for example, an observable desire on the part of certain ethnic and racial groups to maintain identifiable geographic communities. No doubt direct and systemic discrimination may also contribute to the phenomenon of ethnic and racial neighbourhoods, but the influence of the less blameworthy trait of group identification cannot be discounted. Indeed, in the U.S. it has been recognized that even the black ghetto, which is now largely responsible for the segregated school, is in part maintained by the pull of racial identification. Similarly, black academics in the U.S. show a strong preference for working in black colleges and universities — so much so that the financial inducement required to persuade a black professor to move to a non-black institution, even if it is much more prestigious, is significantly higher that what is needed to persuade a white professor to move to a better university. This is surely one of the causes of the underrepresentation of black academics at leading research universities. (Sowell, 1975) Adherence to the position that all imbalance is due to discrimination is difficult to maintain in the face of such phenomena unless one claims that there is no innate preference for "one's own," and that such preferences are themselves forms of discrimination. Precisely this conclusion seems to have animated the judicial opinion in a Detroit school desegregation case.

> In the most realistic sense, if fault or blame is to be found it is that of the community as a whole, including of course the black components. We need not minimize the effect of the actions of federal, state, and local governmental officers and agencies ... to observe that blacks, like ethnic groups in the past, have tended to separate from the larger group and associate together. The ghetto is a place of confinement and a place of refuge. There is enough blame for everyone to share. (Quoted in Glazer, 1975:106)

In this view, statistical imbalance is transformed from a symptom of direct or "systemic" discrimination to an alternative definition of discrimination, and nothing more than its presence need be shown. Alternatively, imbalance itself is seen as an unjustifiable inequity, whatever its cause. To put it still differently, the term "systemic" in the phrase "systemic discrimination" comes to refer to the whole "system" of forces contributing to imbalance. These forces include direct and "adverse effect" discrimination, of course, but they also include the more subtle influences that underlie allegedly "private self-segregation," such as group consciousness, patterns of socialization in what was traditionally considered to be the private sphere, and such social institutions as the family. Thus, critics of affirmative action who argue that much of the underutilization of women has to do not with employer discrimination but with the disproportionate share of domestic responsibilities assumed by women upon marriage can be said to be missing the point: they are using too narrow a conception of discrimination, which in this case inheres in the traditional family structure itself. (Hoffman and Reed, 1981; Sowell, 1984: ch.5) According to a Labour Canada report:

> The broadest definition (of discrimination) would include differences in productive attributes resulting from such factors as the traditionally unequal division of household responsibilities between married couples, and conditioning to sex roles in the family and educational institutions. Under this definition, virtually all the observed female-male wage differential would be labelled sex discrimination. (Gunderson and Reid, 1981:31)

For those who take this broad definition of discrimination seriously, individual interests are not really voluntary but socially, or "systemically" produced, which helps to explain the depreciation of the interest factor in the more radical formulations of affirmative action. In order to avoid terminological confusion, I have chosen to call the broader form of discrimination "societal discrimination," retaining the term "systemic discrimination" as the label for neutral rules having an unequal impact.

Societal discrimination produces the group occupational affinities, which affirmative action wishes to overcome, through role-modelling. Far from rejecting the formative power of such role-modelling, affirmative action proposes to harness it for its own purposes. Indeed, the stated objective of many affirmative action programs is to provide non-traditional role models in order to re-socialize the groups to which the models belong. Inasmuch as affirmative action aims to overcome the results of group socialization, it operates by replacing one kind of role-modelling with another: the unregulated role-modelling of "society" (which seems inevitably to lead to imbalance and which is therefore defined as discriminatory) with state-supervised role-modelling designed to break down the occupational affinities of various groups.

RHETORICAL IMPERATIVES

It is only when social forces such as the traditional family and the phenomenon of group identification are included in the definition of discrimination that a policy oriented to the achievement of random distribution can be considered a remedy for discrimination. But to stretch the concept to such an extent renders it meaningless and obfuscates the issues. By using the same term to describe such preferential phenomena as the overt differential treatment of women by an employer and the effect of the traditional family on the female application rate for certain jobs, affirmative action blurs the distinction between them, and clouds the fact that its true purpose is not to redress blatant intentional discrimination, or even systemic barriers, but to restructure society as such.

After reading an earlier version of this essay, an advocate of affirmative action responded "Yes, but so what" to this charge of obfuscation. He was quite content to admit that affirmative action had little to do with discrimination in any meaningful sense of the word and dismissed the tendency so to justify it as a regrettable semantic confusion. A more straightforward formulation, he conceded, would be that affirmative action was not primarily concerned with redressing discrimination, but with achieving equality — "equality of result." My disagreement with this man turns not on our common evaluation of the purpose of affirmative action, but on whether the near universal obfuscation of this purpose by describing it as a remedy for discrimination is merely a poor choice of words. I contend that it is not, that it is in fact based on a shrewd assessment of rhetorical necessity.

This rhetorical necessity is governed, in part, by the fact that the justice of equality of result is not immediately apparent to most people. Furthermore, its achievement requires the overcoming of causes — such as group consciousness and group occupational affinities — that are not generally viewed as intrinsically blameworthy phenomena, or as identical to negative prejudice. On the other hand, there does seem to be widespread disapproval of blatant discrimination and a willingness to contemplate its legal prohibition. By describing itself as a remedy for discrimination, affirmative action cashes in on the latter sentiment while hiding its disagreement with the former. For this strategy to work, of course, the most radical expansion of the definition of discrimination on which it depends — the inclusion of what I have called "societal discrimination" — must remain largely implicit. It is blatant discrimination, and to a lesser extent systemic barriers, that are generally considered to be unjust, and the rhetorical success of affirmative action depends on the association of its enemy with these forms of discrimination.

Affirmative action needs the enemy of traditional discrimination in yet another, deeper sense. The central claim of affirmative action is that an "equal opportunity response" is not enough and must be supplemented by special measures, including remedial programs, and by numerical goals. Remedial programs and goals are necessary because their beneficiaries cannot be expected to succeed without them. But this means that these beneficiaries are in some sense less capable than those who can do well without affirmative action. The typical response is that this "inferiority" is not natural but the result of social disadvantage, historically produced. This response is inadequate, however, because disadvantaged individuals both within and without the target group can and do overcome social disadvantage on their own. Expecting disadvantaged non-target group individuals to do so while giving special help to similarly situated target group members implies that the latter are inferior to the former. To avoid this unpalatable conclusion, affirmative action needs the fall-back claim of continuing present discrimination against target-group members. This extra burden, not inferiority, allegedly justifies the extra help given to target-group members. As Harvey Mansfield puts it: "The unprotected must admit their guilt so that the protected do not have to admit their incapacity." (Mansfield, 1984:28) The unprotected, of course, are white males, at least those who do not support affirmative action. "Not that those guilty white males *do* anything discriminatory," continues Mansfield, for

> any overt action to discriminate would be illegal without affirmative action. Rather, it is their bad attitudes. Those white males glare balefully at the protected groups, wounding and disabling them with negative vibrations and looking out for any chance to do them in by wishing them ill.

Discriminatory actions are necessarily excluded from the continuing present discrimination that justifies preferential treatment because such actions would close off opportunities, and "If opportunities were not open, we would not know that affirmative action beyond opening opportunities was needed." (Mansfield, 1984:28) The present discrimination that justifies affirmative action thus amounts to the wishful thinking of white males that they could release the door of opportunity they so resolutely hold open. The absurdity of this position underlines both the fact that affirmative action has little to do with traditional discrimination and its desperate need of this sort of discrimination as a rhetorical cover.

FOOTNOTES

[1] Treasury Board of Canada, News Release, June 27, 1983. 1.
[2] Human Rights Commissions generally have the power only to approve affirmative action programs, not to impose them. A possible exception is the Saskatchewan commission, which, under section 47 of its Act, appears to have the power to order such programs. In some cases boards of inquiry or tribunals engaged in the quasi-judicial resolution of cases that cannot be settled by the commission have the power to order an affirmative action remedy.
[3] In 1982, Ontario's Divisional Court interpreted these words in the province's Code as limiting the prohibition to intentional discrimination. *Theresa O'Malley v. Simpson-Sears Ltd.* III C.H.R.R. D/796 at D/799. At the time of writing this case is before the Supreme Court of Canada.
[4] News Release, 3; Annex A, 9.
[5] Interview with the author.
[6] Confidential interview.
[7] News Release, Annex A, 1.
[8] News Release, Annex A, 2. Emphasis added.
[9] A voluntary affirmative action program by an employer may also counteract the effect of a systemic barrier. See *Connecticut v. Teal*, 102 S.Ct. 2525 (1982).
[10] News Release, 2.
[11] Caroline Thomas, "Commentary," Canadian Broadcasting Corporation, April 3, 1984.

[12] Sowell contends that "The early leaders and supporters of the civil rights movement did not advocate such corollaries, and many explicitly repudiate them, especially during the congressional debates that preceded passage of the Civil Rights Act of 1964. But the corollaries were implicit in the vision — and in the long run that proved to be more decisive than the positions taken by the original leaders in the cause of civil rights. In the face of crying injustices, many Americans accepted a vision that promised to further a noble cause, without quibbling over its assumptions or verbal formulations. But visions have a momentum of their own, and those who accept their assumptions have entailed their corollaries, however surprised they may be when these corollaries emerge historically" (1984:38).
[13] (1980), I C.H.R.R. D/33 at D/39.
[14] 347 U.S. 483 (1954).
[15] *Green v. Country School Board*, 391 U.S. 430 (1968).
[16] *Offierski*, D/38.
[17] *Green*.

REFERENCES

Bruce, Mary. Equal Opportunity, Affirmative Action — the Toronto Experience. *Affirmation*, 4:3, (1983).

CEIC. *Affirmative Action: Definitions and Terms*, 1979.

CEIC. *Affirmative Action Technical Training Manual*, 1982.

Daudlin, Bob, chairman. Special Committee on Visible Minorities in Canadian Society. *Equality Now*, Ottawa: Queen's Printer, 1984.

Frum, David. "Equal Opportunity?" *Saturday Night*, January, 1984.

Glazer, Nathan. *Affirmative Discrimination: Ethnic Inequality and Public Policy*. New York: Basic Books, 1975.

Gunderson, Morely and Frank Reid. "Sex Discrimination in the Canadian Labour Market: Theories, Data and Evidence." Labour Canada, Women's Bureau. Discussion Series A: No. 3, 1981.

Hoffman, Carl and John Reed. "When Is Imbalance Not Discrimination," in W.E. Block and M.A. Walker (eds.), *Discrimination, Affirmative Action, and Equal Opportunity*. Vancouver: The Fraser Institute, 1981.

Juriansz, Russell. "Systemic Discrimination and Special Programs, in Law Society of Upper Canada, Continuing Legal Education." *Human Rights*, 1983.

Mansfield, Harvey C., Jr. "The Underhandedness of Affirmative Action." *National Review*, May 4, 1984.

Manzer, Ronald. *Canada: A Sociological Report*. Toronto: McGraw-Hill Ryerson, 1974.

Ontario Human Rights Commission. *Life Together: A Report on Human Rights in Ontario*, 1977.

Phillips, Rhys D. "Affirmative Action as an Effective Labour Market Planning Tool of the 1980s." Labour Market Development Task Force Technical Studies Series, No. 29. 1981.

Robertson, Peter C. "Some Thoughts About Affirmative Action in Canada in the 1980s," CEIC, 1980.

Roche, George. "The Balancing Act: Quota Hiring in Higher Education," in Willem A. Veenhoven (ed.), *Case Studies on Human Rights and Fundamental Freedom*, The Hague: Martinus Nijhoff, 1976.

Sowell, Thomas. *Affirmative Action Reconsidered: Was It Necessary in Academia?* Washington, D.C.: American Enterprise Institute, 1975.

----------. *Civil Rights: Rhetoric or Reality?* New York: William Morrow, 1984.

6

THE MANUFACTURE OF MINORITIES

THOMAS FLANAGAN

INTRODUCTION

The title "The Manufacture of Minorities" was inspired by Thomas Szasz' book *The Manufacture of Madness* (Szasz, 1970). Szasz showed how the forms of insanity have been multiplied in connection with the growth of psychiatry as an organized branch of medicine. The central point is that insanity is not an objective fact but is constituted by social definitions in which the power and interests of organized groups play a part. I see certain parallels in the current evolution of human rights legislation in Canada as new minorities in need of equal opportunity are discovered each year. I will search in this paper for the relationship between the legal manufacture of minorities and the institutional embodiment of anti-discrimination policy, namely the eleven human rights commissions in Canada.

WHAT IS A MINORITY?

The word "minority" is derived from the Latin *minor*, meaning "smaller" or "fewer." It can refer to a purely quantitative or statistical relationship, as in the sentence "Only a minority of votes was cast for the proposal." It can also refer to a condition of inferior status or power, as in the expression "age of minority." The dimensions of quantity and power are often so intertwined that meaning can be unravelled only through a specific analysis of usage in social context.

When John Stuart Mill borrowed the phrase "tyranny of the majority" from Alexis de Tocqueville, he had in mind the danger to the "instructed minority." (Mill, 1962:161) Mill believed that, at least under present conditions, people of critical intelligence and cultivated sensibility would be few in number and thus exposed to danger in a democratic age where numbers amounted to power.

Certain crucial aspects of Mill's view were reversed, while others were retained, when "minority" became a common term of political discourse in twentieth-century North America. The social context was the massive immigration around the turn of the century which brought so many Eastern and Southern Europeans to both the United States and Canada, and which was accompanied by the debate over nature and nurture which took place in the first two decades of this century. (Freeman, 1983:3-61) The hereditarians, reading Darwin and Mendel in a certain way, saw the newcomers as inferior races who threatened the genetic purity of the dominant "great race" in North America. Advocates of cultural determinism, on the other hand, saw the immigrants as culturally distinct groups which could readily be assimilated if society was tolerant enough to accept them.

The term "minority" was proposed in 1932 by Donald Young as a way of transcending the hereditarian implications of the word "race," which at that time was in popular as well as scientific use to refer to what today would be called ethnic groups:

> There is, unfortunately, no word in the English language which can with philological propriety be applied to all ... groups which are distinguished by biological features, alien national cultures, or a combination of both. For this reason, the phrases, "minorities of racial or national origin," "American minorities," or "minority peoples" are here used as synonyms for the popular usage of the word race. (Dworkin & Dworkin, 1976:14)

This was a brilliant innovation for the cultural determinists. "Minority" purported to be a neutral, scientific term without the obnoxious connotations of race, but it had its own connotations derived from the liberalism of thinkers such as Mill. A minority was a group which, through no fault of its own, was put in jeopardy by the politics of democracy. Mill's paradigm of a minority jeopardized by an intolerant majority survived, but now the minority was not a cultivated elite but a congeries of low-status immigrant groups of different cultures.

Once these fundamentals were established, studies proliferated under the rubric of minority relations in conjunction with ethnicity, prejudice, and discrimination. Definitions of "minority" multiplied within this framework. Louis Wirth wrote:

> We may define a minority as a group of people who, because of their physical or cultural characteristics, are singled out from others in the society in which they live for differential and unequal treatment and who therefore regard themselves as objects of collective discrimination. (Linton, 1945:347)

(Note that this definition does not even raise the question of numbers.) In 1958 Charles Wagley and Marvin Harris constructed a more elaborate ideal type of minority:

> 1. Minorities are subordinate segments of complex state societies; 2. minorities have special physical or cultural traits which are held in low esteem by the dominant segments of the society; 3. minorities are self-conscious units bound together by the special traits which their members share and by the special disabilities which these bring; 4. membership in a minority is transmitted by a rule of descent which is capable of affiliating succeeding generations even in the absence of readily apparent special cultural or physical traits; 5. minority peoples, by choice or necessity, tend to marry within the group. (Wagley & Harris, 1958:10)

Wagley and Harris went farther than Wirth in including in their definition what was tacitly assumed by all writers on the subject, that minorities were ethnic groups. This linkage still survives in the literature of sociology; introductory textbooks routinely treat minorities in a larger chapter on ethnicity, employing some version of the definitions of Wirth or of Wagley and Harris.

The intellectual ascendancy of this perspective helped to justify the American civil rights movement of the 1950s and 1960s. However, the very success of this movement in removing the legal disabilities of racial and ethnic groups has undermined the consensus about what a minority is. Inspired by the dramatic gains of blacks in the United States and Francophones in Canada, non-ethnic groups also have begun to portray themselves as victimized minorities, the targets of stereotyping, prejudice, and discrimination.

The decisive breakthrough was made by the women's movement, as illustrated by the publication in 1976 of *The Minority Report: An Introduction to Racial, Ethnic, and Gender Relations* by A.G. and R.J. Dworkin. Treating women alongside traditional ethnic minorities, the authors deliberately constructed a more comprehensive definition of a minority as a "group characterized by four qualities: identifiability, differential power, differential and pejorative treatment, and group awareness. (Dworkin & Dworkin, 1976:17) Mere statistical categories, such as left-handed people, can become genuine minority groups if they become aware of their powerlessness and mistreatment at the hands of the statistical majority, and if they can gain a degree of public recognition of their group trait. The Dworkins explicitly raised the possibility of an infinity of other minority groups, such as homosexuals, Communists, or prison inmates. Their approach accurately reflects the politics of the 1970s and 1980s, which have seen the multiplication of *soi-disant* minorities claiming redress for discrimination. Women and the aged have had particular success, as witnessed by the entry of "sexism" and "ageism" into the English language. Homosexuals, welfare recipients, the handicapped, and many others are not far behind in travelling the same path.

HUMAN RIGHTS COMMISSIONS

In 1962, Ontario created the first Human Rights Commission and charged it with enforcing a comprehensive code of anti-discrimination legislation. All other provinces as well as the federal government had followed suit by 1977. By the same date, the two territories had also passed anti-discrimination ordinances without, however, creating commissions for education and enforcement.

There has been a striking tendency to enlarge the mandate of these commissions. Human Rights legislation was initially passed to protect ethnic minorities which bore the weight of overt discrimination. The few prohibited criteria of discrimination were easy to comprehend and were stated in familiar terms such as "race, creed, colour, nationality, ancestry, or place of origin."[1] Currently, there are 30 prohibited grounds of discrimination in Canadian jurisdictions taken together. Of course, no single human rights act mentions all 30. The Ontario Human Rights Code is the most comprehensive in listing 15. The average is 12.3, with a minimum of 9 in Alberta and the Yukon.

In Table 6.1, the 30 existing criteria are listed together with the number of jurisdictions in which each has been adopted. The criteria are also divided into three categories: "stigmata," "life cycle," and "life style."[2]

In simplest terms, stigmata are group characteristics that are regularly passed from one generation to another through genetic inheritance or through some form of predictable social learning. They characterize minority ethnic groups as discussed in the preceding section. These persistent traits, discernible both to the group members and outside observers, mark off or "stigmatize" the group. Under normal conditions, it is not within the power of the group members to divest themselves of their stigmata. These traits are furthermore disadvantageous because they define unfavourable stereotypes in the minds of outsiders, and such prejudices will often lead to harmful discrimination.

Table 6.1
Prohibited Grounds of Discrimination in Canada*

(Numbers in parentheses refer to the total of jurisdictions—federal, provincial, and territorial—which have prohibited that particular ground)

Stigmata	Life Cycle	Life Style
Race (13)	Sex (13)	Pardoned offence (3)
Colour (13)	Marital status (13)	Criminal record (3)
Nationality (3)	Family status (4)	Sexual orientation (1)
National/ethnic origin (9)	Etat civil (1) civil (1)	Drug/alcohol dependence (1)
Ancestry (7)	Pregnancy (3)	Political belief (5)
Place of origin (6)	Age (12)	Source of income (2)
Religion (11)	Physical handicap (12)	Public assistance (1)
Creed (8)	Mental handicap (5)	Attachment of pay (1)
Citizenship (1)		Social origin (1)
Language (1)		Social condition (1)
		Place of residence (1)

"Without reasonable cause" (2)

* This table covers all areas such as employment, tenancy, contracts, access to public facilities. If a criterion is prohibited in any jurisdiction in any of these areas, it is included in the table. The document "Prohibited grounds of discrimination in employment," which is published and periodically updated by the Canadian Human Rights Commission, was very useful in compiling the table but is not entirely accurate. My reading of the thirteen statutes was also checked against the Appendices in Berlin, 1983: 219-231.

Life cycle criteria are biologically based but are not transmitted or distributed in the same way as stigmata. Women do not give birth solely to women, whereas Indians give birth to Indians. Age denotes a series of conditions through which we all pass at different times if we continue to survive. Physical and mental handicaps are conditions produced by a number of biological causes, including genetic inheritance, disease, accident, or aging. They are not transmitted in a direct way like race or national origin. Most deaf children are born to hearing adults, and most deaf adults have hearing children. Nevertheless, life cycle traits resemble stigmata to the extent that they are rarely within the power of the individual to alter.

Life style criteria are the result of personal choice. To be a homosexual, to be convicted of a crime, to receive public assistance, all result from personal decisions. There may indeed be genetically predisposing factors in the human organism, as has been suggested for homosexuals, criminals, and the poor, but then the same must be true for heterosexuals, the law-abiding, and the rich. However, it seems obvious that one has much more personal control over being homosexual or criminal than over being, say, black or female. One can through voluntary action give up a life style characteristic, although there can be severe physical difficulties (e.g., alcoholism or drug dependency) or man-made legal impediments (criminal record).

This threefold classification is burdened with items which seem to straddle categories. Let me therefore discuss the typology at greater length and deal with borderline cases, as well as with the omnibus category of discrimination "without reasonable cause," which has appeared in two jurisdictions.

1. STIGMATA

All thirteen Canadian jurisdictions forbid discrimination based on race or colour. Beyond that, all add some combination of the terms ancestry, national or ethnic origin, place of origin, or nationality. Taken together, they prohibit discrimination based on ethnicity broadly understood, including racial differences as a biologist would define them, as well as the social differences that constitute ethnic identity.

Citizenship does not fit as well into the stigmata. It is naturally acquired, either through inheritance from parents or location at birth; but it can be voluntarily renounced or be taken away by an act of state authority. An individual can also acquire a new citizenship through legal procedures. It can be, therefore, as much a matter of personal choice as of inheritance.

Citizenship is clearly mentioned only in the current Ontario Human Rights Code, and probably would not even be there except for confusion over the word "nationality." This term appeared in the original Ontario Human Rights Code, and was later adopted in three other jurisdictions, instead of the more prevalent "national or ethnic origin." The word "nationality" is ambiguous, meaning either national origin or citizenship. After three Ontario tribunal decisions interpreted nationality as encompassing citizenship, (Tarnopolsky, 1982:175-176) the legislature dropped "nationality" from the Act and replaced it with both "ethnic origin" and "citizenship."[3] The prohibition of discrimination based on citizenship is greatly weakened by a broad exemption legitimating many sorts of preferences for Canadian citizens in employment and other matters.[4] The exemption accords with the common sense observation that citizenship may be a legitimate requirement for many kinds of public employment and that citizenship, or at least permanent residence, may be a reasonable precondition for sharing in certain benefits paid for by the Canadian taxpayers.

There is less difficulty in seeing language, if that means mother tongue, as one of the group stigmata. One's mother tongue is acquired unconsciously in early childhood; it cannot be deliberately forgotten, and one hardly ever acquires another language with equal facility. However, language in this sense is so intimately tied to ancestry or ethnic origin that a complaint could usually be made under those grounds. Only Quebec has seen fit to incorporate language into its human rights legislation. In spite of the many language conflicts in that province, no grievances based on language have yet come to adjudication, perhaps because the B.N.A. Act and the Charter of Rights provide more powerful means of redress.

Religion is a true borderline case. If we think of religion as something inculcated in childhood, it appears rather similar to ethnic origin. It is acquired without a conscious decision being made. This is particularly true of Judaism, which is inextricably intertwined with the cultural traditions of the Jewish people. This relationship is important because the human rights movement in Canada was closely involved with the fight against anti-Semitism. When the first prohibitions of religious discrimination were passed they were primarily conceived as blows against anti-Semitism. Yet religion also has a voluntary aspect. The faith learned in childhood can be rejected and a new one adopted. In this respect, religion resembles life style variables such as political opinion and sexual preference, which may involve as great a commitment as does religious belief.

In practice today, complaints based on religion have more to do with life style than with group stigmata. Gone are the days of signs reading "No Jews need apply." The typical complaint today involves a Sikh who will not wear a hard hat at a construction site, a Seventh Day Adventist who will not work on Saturday, or a member of the Worldwide Church of God who wants time off to attend his annual convention. Under the emerging doctrine of "reasonable accommodation," employers may be required to adjust to these requests as long as the costs are *de minimis* in the eyes of human rights tribunals.

This tendency towards transforming religion into a life style criterion will be accelerated if the word "creed" ever comes into its own. Ontario and the Northwest Territories specify creed rather than religion in their human rights statutes, while several provinces mention "creed" or "religious creed" in addition to religion. Until now, creed has been interpreted as meaning "religious creed" only, as is spelled out in the Saskatchewan statute.[5] But one authority predicts that under the heading of creed in the new Ontario Human Rights Code "protection will almost certainly extend to deistic religions and, probably, to atheistic or agnostic beliefs." (Keene, 1983:63) Thus movements such as Scientology or Ethical Humanism may be able to claim protection under legislation which mentions "creed" as a prohibited ground of discrimination. Personal convictions unconnected to organized groups may also claim protection some day.

2. LIFE CYCLE

The life cycle category includes a number of biological criteria related to the maturation of individuals and the reproduction of the species. As with stigmata, there are some borderline cases which need careful consideration.

Sex, understood as biological gender rather than sexual preferences, has been incorporated into all Canadian human rights legislation. Although occasionally invoked by male complainants, it generally has worked to the advantage of females. It also has spawned a series of related criteria, as experience has shown that simply prohibiting discrimination based on sex leaves women still exposed to certain disadvantages. For example, a financial institution may refuse credit to a married woman without her husband's co-signature. To deal with such situations, all jurisdictions have now outlawed discrimination based on marital status. Three have explicitly brought pregnancy into the definition of sexual discrimination, and four have resorted to the concept of "family status" (*situation de famille*), which includes a variety of relationships such as marriage, divorce, pregnancy, parenthood, consanguinity, cohabitation, and perhaps others. Finally, Quebec uses the technical civil law term *état civil*, which is of somewhat uncertain reach but certainly includes elements of marital and family status as well as aspects of age. (Tarnopolsky, 1982:301-304)

The escalation of the campaign against sexual discrimination borders on invoking life style criteria. Under contemporary conditions, getting married and having children are more akin to voluntary decisions than to natural inevitabilities. Putting marital or family status into legislation may be defended in terms of protecting the family, but in fact it works just as much in the other direction by hindering employers, landlords, and merchants from showing preference to conventional families. Pushed to the limit, such legislation tends to promote individualism rather than family cohesiveness. Cohabitation becomes as respectable as legal marriage, childlessness as important as parenthood. All become matters of personal choice or life style.

Age is the criterion that best fits the concept of life cycle. Its introduction into human rights legislation initially reflected concern for the employment opportunities of older persons, those in the range of 40 or 45 to 65. Three jurisdictions still define age in this way. Five others have lowered the minimum threshold of concern to 18 or 19, thereby opening up new questions such as the leasing of apartments to young tenants. The absence of boundaries of any sort on age in the Manitoba Human Rights Act has led to successful challenges to mandatory retirement. The future tendency may be to "uncap" age as a human rights variable because the Canadian Charter of Rights and Freedoms, which will override all other legislation — at least with application to the public sector — mentions age in an unlimited way.

Physical and mental handicaps are also related to the individual life cycle. They can be thought of as the failure to attain, or the premature loss of, certain capacities characterizing the normal adult. They are organically caused and not generally the result of personal choice, except by reckless exposure to risk. One cannot ordinarily divest oneself of them, though a person may be able to mitigate their effects through medication, rehabilitation, or use of mechanical aids. All jurisdictions except the Yukon now have accepted physical handicaps into their legislation, but mental disability is accepted only in Canada, the Northwest Territories, Ontario, Quebec, Manitoba, and British Columbia.

A look at the definitions of mental disability in the Ontario Human Rights Code helps explain the hesitation:

> (ii) a condition of mental retardation or impairment,
>
> (iii) a learning disability, or a dysfunction in one or more of the processes involved in understanding or using symbols of spoken language, or
>
> (iv) a mental disorder.[6]

Learning dysfunctions are poorly understood conditions which are not always easy to distinguish from low general intelligence, personality disorder, lack of application, or bad teaching. Mental disorder is an equally imprecise term. It surely must include major psychosis, but will it also comprehend neurotic character traits and sociopathic belligerence?

3. LIFE STYLE

Without too much distorting, life style criteria representing conscious, personal choices can be subdivided into two classes, moral and economic. Moral criteria are those in which a person's choices involve serious conflict with commonly held views of right and wrong. These are political opinion, criminal record and/or pardoned offence, alcohol and drug dependency, and sexual orientation. Economic criteria may also have some moral overtones, but they generally apply to situations in which an employer, landlord, or merchant sees a threat to his own pocketbook more than to the moral fabric of society.

Political belief, mentioned in the legislation of five jurisdictions, is the most commonly adopted moral criterion. It generates some old-fashioned, patronage-style complaints where moral issues are not of primary concern. It also leads to contentious cases involving radical or revolutionary ideologies and alleged risks to national security. The most interesting cases come from the highly politicized environment of Quebec. (Tarnopolsky, 1982:320-322) The dimension of moral conflict is obvious in the case of criminal record and sexual orientation. In each instance, inclusion in human rights legislation is an attempt to shield individuals from the social disapprobation attached to violations of law or of deeply ingrained rules of conduct. Alcohol and drug dependency is a more complicated case. The federal government has recently introduced this criterion into its act under the heading of disability:

> "disability" means any previous or existing mental or physical disability and includes disfigurement and previous or existing dependence on alcohol or a drug.[7]

However, in my view, it strains credibility to lump alcoholism and drug dependency in with mental and physical handicaps. Abuse of alcohol and drugs is a behaviour pattern. As Alcoholics Anonymous long ago discovered, these are "diseases" whose remedy is spiritual rather than physical.

The economic criteria are somewhat heterogeneous in character. Place of residence is a prohibited ground of discrimination only in the Northwest Territories and there only with respect to employment. It has not been interpreted in reported decisions. Attachment of pay and social origin are unique to the Newfoundland Human Rights Act. Neither has led to reported cases. The words "social origin," appearing in the phrase "... ethnic, national or social origin of such person or class of person,"[8] may have been intended merely as a fulsome statement of group stigmata, but they clearly have the potential for economic interpretation. Better understood are the concepts of source of income, found in Manitoba and Nova Scotia, and receipt of public assistance, found in the new Ontario Human Rights Code in respect of tenants only. Both criteria function chiefly to prevent landlords from refusing to rent to welfare recipients as a category. Finally there is the omnibus term "social condition" (*condition sociale*) in the Quebec legislation. Without much success, complainants have raised under it issues such as pregnancy, single parenthood, receipt of public assistance, and criminal record (most recently, a man with a conviction for car theft who wanted to work as a parking lot attendant).[9]

4. REASONABLE CAUSE

Amendments to the British Columbia Human Rights Code in 1973 produced a striking innovation with respect to employment and access to public facilities. Discrimination or denial of access was prohibited "unless reasonable cause exists for the denial or discrimination."[10] By 1982, 37 percent of complaints laid under the Code were attributable to this provision. (Simpson, 1983:23) In practice, reasonable cause became an open door through which tribunals introduced life cycle and life style criteria unmentioned in the act. Physical handicap, pregnancy, family status, sexual preference, and linguistic competence have all surfaced in this way. However, the government abolished the reasonable cause provision in amendments introduced in 1983 and passed in 1984.

Manitoba has similar reasonable cause provisions regarding tenancy and public facilities as well as a somewhat weaker formulation for employment, by which stipulated forms of discrimination are prohibited "without limiting the generality of the foregoing."[11] The Manitoba Human Rights Commission has taken assorted complaints to the stage of conciliation under this "residual clause," but has pushed only one case, involving sexual preference, to a board of adjudication.[12] Having lost the adjudication, the Commission decided against an appeal to the courts, for fear of receiving a ruling that would weaken the residual clause even further.[13]

"Reasonable cause" is thus temporarily stymied in Canada, but its long-term outlook may be bright. Section 15(1) of the Canadian Charter of Rights and Freedoms, which comes into effect April 17, 1985, and which will override all existing human rights legislation, reads as follows:

> Every individual is equal before and under the law and has the right to the equal protection and equal benefit of the law *without discrimination and, in particular,* without discrimination based on race.... (italics added)

This clause could become very much like a "reasonable cause" provision in the hands of an activist judiciary. Such a development would probably be welcomed by those to whom "it is generally accepted that the protected classes under human rights law ought to be constantly updated and expanded so as to provide the widest possible protection to the greatest number of persons." (Berlin, 1983:72) Other observers, however, view "reasonable causes" provisions as "dangerously open-ended" (Hunter, 1976:21) because they circumvent the wording of the statute as well as the need to recur to the legislature for amendment.

HISTORICAL DEVELOPMENT

The initial impetus for human rights legislation in Canada was provided by the overt racism and disregard for individual dignity exhibited by the Nazis and other fascist parties. (Bruner, 1979:236-253) Apart from a few special purpose statutes, the Saskatchewan Bill of Rights, 1947, was the first comprehensive attack on discrimination, although it relied on criminal-law methods of enforcement. The grounds of discrimination prohibited by it were pure stigmata: race, colour, ethnic and national origin, creed and religion. The Ontario Human Rights Code of 1962, which served as the prototype for subsequent legislation in this field, had a similarly restricted list: race, colour, ancestry, nationality, place of origin, and creed. This model was followed with little variation by Nova Scotia and the Yukon (1963), Alberta (1966), New Brunswick (1967), and Prince Edward Island (1968).

The tendency toward mention of life cycle criteria began in 1966 when the Northwest Territories listed both sex and marital status in its Fair Practices Act. In the same year Ontario legislated against some forms of age discrimination in a separate statute to be enforced by the Human Rights Commission. The British Columbia Human Rights Code, adopted in 1969, listed sex and age along with the standard stigmata. Thereafter, those jurisdictions creating human rights commissions for the first time usually included the basic life cycle variables of sex, marital status, and age together with the stigmata. Those provinces which had been pioneers in the human rights field introduced life cycle variables by amendment. Sex and marital status were largely taken care of in the first half of the 1970s and pregnancy and family status have been earning acceptance since then. Physical handicap also was an issue of the late 1970s, whereas mental handicap is gaining ground now. The universal acceptance of age was more gradual but is now accomplished for all practical purposes with the 1982 amendments to Quebec's Charter of Human Rights and Freedoms.

The acceptance of life style criteria has been much more erratic and less smoothly progressive. The Northwest Territories listed place of residence as early as 1966. Newfoundland mentioned political belief and social origin in 1970. The latter has found no acceptance elsewhere except possibly for Quebec's "social condition" (1975), but four other provinces added political belief to their legislation in the years 1973-75. However, that criterion has made no further progress since then. Reference to criminal record was introduced by British Columbia in 1973 and was adopted in varying ways in Canada in 1977, and by Ontario and the Northwest Territories in 1981. Manitoba pioneered source of income in 1974; Nova Scotia adopted the same term in 1982; and Ontario added receipt of public assistance in 1981. The high-profile criteria of sexual preference and drug dependency were adopted, respectively, by Quebec in 1977 and Canada in 1983.

Now that so many experiments have been tried (nine jurisdictions have adopted at least one life style criterion), and now that the three leading jurisdictions of Canada, Ontario, and Quebec have committed themselves decisively, it seems reasonable to expect further advances in this field. Indeed, various commissions already are publicly committed to supporting legislative action on life style criteria such as sexual preference; the Alberta and Manitoba commissions made such recommendations in 1984.

While life style grounds of discrimination have been added to legislation, the stigmatic and life cycle grounds have been broadened through adjudication or conciliation to include many life style elements. Thus religion has been interpreted to cover working on Sunday or wearing a hard hat, and physical handicap has on occasion been stretched to include alcoholism, even in jurisdictions where the legislation does not authorize that interpretation. Overall, trends in adjudication and legislation have combined to move "human rights" far from their original purpose.

The progressive incorporation of life cycle and life style criteria into human rights codes is changing the function of the commissions. They were initially established to promote "equality of opportunity" for disadvantaged ethnic groups. That meant combatting prejudice through public education and discrimination through enforcement of fair practices in employment, housing, and so on. This initial mandate could be justified with reference to Gordon Allport's classic study *The Nature of Prejudice*, which was in fact concerned almost entirely with ethnic prejudice. For Allport, all thinking is conceptual:

> The human mind must think with the aid of categories.... Once formed, categories are the basis for normal prejudgement. We cannot possibly avoid this process. (Allport, 1954:20)

Prejudgements are not bad unless they become prejudices, that is, "only if they are not reversible when exposed to new knowledge." (Allport, 1954:9) Thus "ethnic prejudice is an antipathy based upon a faulty and inflexible generalization." (Allport, 1954:9) Such faulty stereotypes do not arise merely from cognitive failure. According to Allport, "Perhaps the most momentous discovery of psychological research in the field of prejudice" is that "the cognitive processes of prejudiced people are *in general* different from the cognitive processes of tolerant people." (Allport, 1954:174-175) The "prejudiced personality" tends to dichotomize "when he thinks of nature, of law, of morals, of men and women, as well as when he thinks of ethnic groups." (Allport, 1954:175) Such persons resort to stereotypical thinking because of insufficient ego strength; they feel threatened by the complexity of experience. Ethnic affiliations inevitably become a way of supporting the ego. Love of one's own and distrust of those who are different reinforce the individual's threatened sense of himself. Thus the inflexible overgeneralizations known as prejudices readily attach themselves to ethnic identities. Since cognitive short cuts fill important emotional needs and are not readily corrected by the test of experience, special educational and legislative efforts may be required to combat their effects.

Discrimination is abhorrent in a liberal society because it treats persons as abstractions rather than as individuals. Personal qualities are lost in the group stereotype. The stereotypes may not be wholly inaccurate descriptors of behaviour; there are indeed many Jewish lawyers and black athletes. However, a public policy of combatting ethnic discrimination is a statement that such stereotypes have no intrinsic validity insofar as the character of ethnic groups is concerned. A much better prediction of behaviour can be gained by looking at individual qualities rather than ethnic derivation. We are better off practically as well as morally if the law requires us to focus our attention on individuals instead of on ethnic labels. Efforts against ethnic discrimination are consonant with the *mores* of liberal society in which we wish to be judged as individuals for "what we do, not who we are."

The creation of human rights commissions rested on a broad and enlightened consensus that ethnic stereotypes were morally demeaning, had no intrinsic validity, were only slightly reliable at best, and could be readily replaced with much better predictors of individual performance. Legislative suppression of discrimination was practically all gain and no loss.

However, the status of categorical thinking related to life cycle and life style factors is markedly different. It may be true that men derive an important part of their identity from dominating women and that this gives rise to sexual stereotypes and prejudices just as inflexible as ethnic stereotypes and prejudices. However, it is doubtful that this sort of comparison can be extended to the relationship between the married and unmarried, the old and the young, the normal and the handicapped, or the gay and the straight. Conceptions held by the majority about the minority may be inaccurate, but there is no *a priori* reason why such views should be inflexibly resistant to improvement or change through experience. In these circumstances, we may suspect that images of such "minorities" will contain an element of truth. To give some examples almost at random: is it blind prejudice to believe that young unmarried men are more dangerous behind the wheel of a car than are most other categories of drivers? that a fifty-year-old candidate for an expensive apprenticeship program will probably have fewer years of productive work to justify the employer's investment than will a twenty-five year old candidate? that a member of the Communist party probably has certain reservations in his loyalty to the constitution of any bourgeois democracy? that one convicted of a criminal offense is more likely to commit another criminal offense than is a person without any criminal record? and, that a Sikh who will not wear a hard hat may expose himself to higher than normal risks of industrial accident? Such opinions may be exaggerated or inapplicable to particular cases, but they are not irrational. They are similar in principle to beliefs such as that it is not necessary to carry an umbrella on a sunny morning unless rain is forecast for the afternoon. One is occasionally caught in an unexpected shower, but the prejudgement is nonetheless a reasonably good guide to reality.

The practical utility of basing judgements on life cycle and life style criteria is shown by the consequences of trying to prohibit such discrimination. Whereas it is possible to prohibit stigmatic discrimination almost absolutely, with only the rarest of qualifications (e.g., exemptions for non-profit ethnic societies or religious schools), such qualifications become commonplace for life cycle and life style criteria. The two chief doctrines in this context are reasonable accommodation and *bona fide* occupational qualification (bfoq). (Berlin, 1983:34) Under the former doctrine, an employer might be required to hire a physically handicapped applicant as long as he could do the job with a "reasonable accommodation" by the employer (e.g., providing wheelchair ramps or washroom facilities). The bfoq doctrine can be conveniently illustrated with respect to criminal conviction. Where employees need to be bonded, an employer might be allowed to demand a clean record. In case of dispute, a human rights tribunal would decide whether the employer had to provide the new facilities or could take criminal record into account.

Both doctrines, bfoq and reasonable accommodation, tacitly admit that the prohibited criteria are not absolutely irrelevant, as race and ethnic origin are deemed to be. Human rights legislation in such cases does not so much outlaw discrimination as set up an external review process to judge the applicability of the contentious criteria in particular cases. From a purely practical point of view this means that an increasing number of business decisions will be made by lawyers or judges with no financial stake in the outcome and possibly little understanding of the concrete difficulties of managing a particular enterprise.

Underlying the expansion of human rights legislation is the demand to treat persons as individuals rather than as members of categories. But this goal requires further consideration. How often is it possible, in a normal business context, to treat persons truly as individuals? Decisions to hire, sign a contract, or lease premises are usually based on limited information. They involve invocation of certain categories or criteria which enable an imperfect but useful prediction. For example, when a landlord rents an apartment, he considers a few variables — stability of employment, references from past rentals, credit checks, age and family status (where the law still permits) — and makes the best decision he can. Prohibition of traditional criteria like age, family status, and source of income does not and cannot lead him to treat applicants as individuals. Rather, it forces him to develop and refine other categories of judgement which remain legal: ability to pay a higher deposit, to survive extended credit checks, to sign a long-term lease. These may be effective predictors of tenant behaviour, but they are costly for the landlord to discover and may also impose burdens on the tenants.

With such life cycle and life style criteria, we are far beyond the attractive rationality and moral simplicity of prohibiting discrimination based on group stigmata. We enter complicated grey areas where the "right" answers are elusive. Should airline pilots have to retire at age sixty? Should Sikhs have to wear hard hats where other workers wear them? Should young, unmarried men pay higher auto insurance rates? These are all complex questions on which reasonable people may differ even if they are equally devoted to the dignity of the individual. Bringing such matters within the scope of anti-discrimination legislation amounts to setting up a second level of decision making to review the decisions made in the market. Market decisions are not necessarily perfect, but they have the great advantage of being made by those who are close to the problem and who have to live with the outcome of the decision. To the extent that a rationale exists for a human rights overlay in life cycle and life style matters, it is couched in terms which were developed for group stigmata and do not apply to these other situations.

POLITICAL DYNAMICS

Why has the purview of anti-discrimination legislation expanded so rapidly, even at the risk of changing its character?

First, the creation of human rights commissions with permanent staff members establishes regulatory agencies with a vested interest in expansion. In the absence of a criterion of profitability, success in the bureaucratic world means to deliver bigger programmes, provide more services, spend larger budgets, and supervise more employees. There is no reason to think that human rights professionals are less motivated by self-interest or ambition than the rest of us, and their self-interest is served by amplifying their mandate. (Niskanen, 1971:36-42)

Of course, they do not think of themselves that way. They experience their ability to help people as hindered by confining legislation. This experience leads the professionals to recommend to their commission ideas for legislative amendments. Commissions then transmit these ideas to the responsible cabinet minister. They may also take steps to promote such amendments in their annual reports or other public statements.

In short, the commissions are not neutral agencies of enforcement. They are active centres for promoting human rights, which has meant adding ever more criteria to the legislation. They continue to lobby in this direction even though, probably without exception, they feel themselves to be without adequate resources to enforce anti-discrimination law in its present restricted form.

Second, the existence of many jurisdictions in a federal system is an important factor contributing to this additive model of legislative change. The commissions keep in touch with what the others are doing, a task made much easier by foundation of the *Human Rights Reporter* in 1980. They meet regularly in the Canadian Association of Statutory Human Rights Agencies (CASHRA). An amendment in one jurisdiction is soon likely to be imitated elsewhere — a process which Jack Walker, commenting on the policy process in American states, has termed "diffusion." (Walker, 1969) Apparently, to professionals in other jurisdictions, each addition to a human rights code is an advance to be incorporated as soon as possible into their own code. It may not be accomplished immediately because of political resistance in the cabinet or among the politically appointed commissioners. Sooner or later, however, the opportunity is likely to come for legislative amendment.

Third, the existence of commissions provides a target for lobbying by organized pressure groups who feel they can advance their cause if they can get it accepted as a human rights issue. For example, incorporation of physical characteristics into the Alberta Individual Rights Protection Act was preceded by long consultation with organizations representing the handicapped. Similarly, when the Manitoba Human Rights Commission held public hearings on a new code in 1983, the gay community attempted to apply pressure through public statements and an organized letter-writing campaign.

However, the importance of such pressure group activity should not be overstated. It is by no means always successful. Further, the majority of amendments to legislation are generated through spontaneous recommendations of the commission to the cabinet, and pressure politics may well only reinforce what would have happened anyway.[14]

Fourth, politicians themselves sometimes inject human rights issues into campaigns. Thus the Alberta Conservatives promised the Individual Rights Protection Act as part of their 1971 campaign against the governing Social Credit party. In 1979, Joe Clark promised to amend the Canadian Human Rights Act so as to prohibit mandatory retirement, although his government was not in power long enough to accomplish this objective. Again, the importance of this factor should not be overestimated since discrimination does not have the electoral weight of great economic issues like inflation, unemployment, and interest rates.

Only in the four Western provinces, where politics is competitive and ideologically polarized between the N.D.P. on the left and the Conservatives or Social Credit on the right, does human rights legislation have an identifiable relationship to party politics. The N.D.P. has almost always been the party in power which expands the mandate of human rights commissions.[15]

This pattern does not exist in the absence of competitive, ideologically polarized provincial politics. In the Maritimes, both Conservative and Liberal governments have created commissions and expanded their purview. The Quebec Commission was created by the Liberals in 1975, and its powers have several times been enlarged by the government of Rene Levesque. And in Ontario, which now has the most comprehensive act of all, the entire history of the Human Rights Commission has been passed under Conservative governments.

Human rights is, after all, an adaptable issue. It can be couched in the socialist rhetoric of equality, the liberal rhetoric of freedom, or the conservative rhetoric of paternalism (looking after the less fortunate). Thus it is not surprising that human rights commissions have been created and have seen their purview enlarged in all sorts of party systems: in two-party competitive and ideologically polarized systems (British Columbia, Saskatchewan, Manitoba, Quebec), in a two-party competitive but not polarized system (Maritimes); and in one-party dominant systems (Alberta, Ontario). This suggests that party competition may foster "the manufacture of minorities" in some circumstances but is neither a necessity nor a sufficient condition for this purpose. Rather, the expansionist tendencies of bureaucratic agencies, once established, seem able to work in almost any political environment and appear to be a more important explanatory factor.

However, the self-interest of public servants cannot be invoked as a fully satisfying cause. Sustained enlargement of the regulatory mandate can be sold to the cabinet and the legislature only if it is broadly acceptable to the current state of public opinion. The political acceptability of human rights expansion is related to what Yair Aharoni has termed the "no-risk society." In his words:

> The state has become a huge insurance agency seemingly trying to guarantee a no-risk society. Government insurance covers not only natural disasters but risks stemming from political or technological changes, lack of information, and even individual folly. (Aharoni, 1981:4)

Anti-discrimination policy approaches this description as it progressively embraces life cycle and life style criteria. It seeks to protect individuals from some of the risks of getting married, having children, growing old, embracing unconventional moral, religious or political ideas, or relying on public assistance.

More precisely, it seeks to control the reactions of employers, landlords, and businessmen towards those whose life cycle or life style traits connote risk. However, the risk itself continues to exist. Pregnant women do require time off, the handicapped may be less efficient at their work, single mothers on welfare may have difficulty in controlling their children in rented housing. What happens, then, is the socialization or dispersal of risk. The costs of "reasonable accommodation" by employers show up in final prices. Rents or insurance rates will ultimately be higher to the extent that landlords are impeded in protecting themselves against the riskiest tenants and insurance companies are forced to accept dangerous drivers on equal terms with others.

Such effects are impossible to trace in particular cases, but economic analysis suggests they must exist. It is necessary to think of "equality of opportunity" not as a costless manna from heaven but as a way of collectivizing risk, which involves considerable costs as well as benefits. In the case of ethnic group stigmata, there is good reason to think the costs are low and the benefits high, but that is far from obvious for the life cycle and life style criteria now in vogue. Human rights professionals, who think almost exclusively in moral and legal terms, naturally underestimate the costs of equal opportunity, since those costs are imposed on other people. Since their bureaucratic self-interest coincides with fulfilment of their moral goals, and since they find it easy to ignore the costs they create for others, it is not surprising that the professionals consistently favour expansion of their own powers.

FOOTNOTES

1. Ontario Human Rights Code, S.O. 1961-62, c. 93, s. 2.
2. These terms are used here with my own stipulated definitions. I am aware that other authors have used them differently.
3. The Human Rights Code, 1981, S.O. 1981, c. 53, s. 4(1).
4. *Ibid.*, s. 15.
5. Saskatchewan Human Rights Code, R.S.S., 1979, c.S. 24-1, s. 2(d).
6. The Human Rights Code, 1981, S.O. 1981, c. 53, s. 9(b)(ii-iv).
7. Canadian Human Rights Act, s. 20; S.C., 1980-81-82-83, c. 143, s. 12.
8. Newfoundland Human Rights Code, R.S.N. 1970, c. 262, s. 7(1).
9. *La Commission des Droits de la Personne du Québec agissant en faveur de Michel Wilkinson v. La Ville de Montréal*, 4 C.H.R.R. D/1444 (1983).
10. B.C. Human Rights Code, R.S.B.C. 1979, c. 186, s. 3(1).
11. Manitoba Human Rights Act, S.M., c. 65, s. 6(1).
12. *Chris Vogel v. Government of Manitoba*, 4 C.H.H.R. D/1654 (1983).
13. Interview with Darlene Germscheid, Executive Director of Manitoba Human Rights Commission, December 13, 1983.
14. Interview with Dale Gibson, Chairperson of Manitoba Human Rights Commission, December 14, 1983.
15. A few examples: N.D.P. governments introduced "reasonable cause" into the British Columbia legislation in 1973 along with other new proscribed grounds of discrimination, created the Human Rights Commission in Saskatchewan in 1971 and expanded its powers in 1978, created the Human Rights Commission in Manitoba in 1969 and repeatedly increased its powers. In contrast, Conservative or Social Credit governments in the West have often held commissions in check by tactics such as appointment of less activist commissioners or even leaving appointments vacant, refusing to appoint tribunals to hear complaints, and rejecting proposed amendments. Premier Bennett's attack in 1983 on the British Columbia commission and enforcement apparatus was the strongest measure so far. In Alberta, a Conservative government created a commission but its powers remain the most restricted in Canada.

REFERENCES

Aharoni, Yair. *The No-Risk Society*. Chatham, N.J.: Chatham House Publishers, 1981.

Allport, Gordon W. *The Nature of Prejudice*. Reading, Mass.: Addison-Wesley Publishing, 1954.

Berlin, Mark L. *New Proscribed Grounds of Discrimination and Emerging Human Rights in Canada*. Ottawa: Department of the Secretary of State, 1983.

Bruner, A. "The Genesis of Ontario's Human Rights Legislation: A Study in Law Reform." *University of Toronto Faculty Law Review*, 37, (1979) 236-253.

Dworkin, Anthony Gary & Rosalind J. Dworkin. *The Minority Report*. New York: Praeger, 1976.

Freeman, Derek. *Margaret Mead and Samoa*. Cambridge: Harvard University Press, 1983.

Hunter, Ian A. "Human Rights Leghislation in Canada: Its Origin, Development and Interpretation." *Western Ontario Law Review*, 1976, 15, 21-58.

Keene, Judith. *Human Rights in Ontario*. Toronto: Carswell, 1983.

Linton, Ralph. *The Science of Man in the World Crisis*. New York: Columbia University Press, 1945.

Mill, John Stuart. *Considerations on Representative Government*. Chicago: Henry Regnery, 1962.

Niskanen, William A., Jr. *Bureaucracy and Representative Government*. Chicago: Aldine-Atherton, 1971.

Simpson, John H. "Law, Politics & Human Rights: A Critical Analysis of Bill 27." Xerox: December 15, 1983.

Szasz, Thomas. *The Manufacture of Madness*. New York: Harper & Row, 1970.

Tarnopolsky, Walter Surma. *Discrimination and the Law in Canada*. Toronto: Richard De Boo, 1982.

Wagley, Charles & Marvin Harris. *Minorities in the New World*. New York: Columbia University Press, 1958.

Walker, Jack. "The Diffusion of Innovations Among the American States." *American Political Science Review*, 63, 1969, 880-899.

7
STEREOTYPES, STATISTICS AND SLIPPERY SLOPES: A REPLY TO PROFESSORS FLANAGAN & KNOPFF AND OTHER CRITICS OF HUMAN RIGHTS LEGISLATION

DALE GIBSON

INTRODUCTION

There are three principal methods by which the problem of unequal opportunity for members of minorities is addressed by governments:

a) prohibition of discrimination based on group stereotypes;
b) affirmative action in the form of special treatment or consideration to members of disadvantaged minorities; and
c) education programs.

All three approaches are currently under siege in Canada, and the first two have been criticized in this collection of essays.

Professor Flanagan's paper deals with aspects of the prohibitory approach, and Professor Knopff's with fallacies he perceives in the affirmative action technique. My remarks will deal with their papers in turn and will then offer some thoughts about what seems to me to underlie the concerns of critics like Flanagan and Knopff: undue fear of government intervention in private and business affairs.

PROHIBITING DISCRIMINATION

It is now more than twenty years since the Ontario Legislature, following American prototypes and building on earlier, less comprehensive legislation, enacted Canada's first modern human rights statute. Every Canadian jurisdiction — federal, provincial and territorial — now has similar legislation. These statutes are all primarily prohibitory in nature: they prohibit unwarranted discrimination in the provision of employment or certain accommodations and services if the discrimination is based on group factors such as race, religion or sex, rather than on individuals' personal merits. (Tarnopolsky 1982).

Two important characteristics of this approach are that it is: (a) individualized and (b) fault oriented. By "individualized" I mean two things. First, the law requires decisions about hiring or the provision of accommodations or services to be founded on the applicants' individual qualifications, rather than on statistical expectations or stereotypes about minority groups to which the applicants may belong. Second, enforcement of the law focuses on individual cases of alleged discrimination, and seeks redress for the individuals affected, rather than general improvement of conditions for members of the minority in question. By "fault oriented," I mean that this type of law prohibits only discrimination that is intended, or is negligently allowed to occur.

As Professor Flanagan's paper notes, early versions of human rights legislation were more limited in their scope than current statutes, to say nothing of proposals for amendment that are being advanced by some human rights advocates. The first prohibited ground of discrimination was race. Other grounds that Flanagan labels "stigmatic" — religion and national or ethnic origin — were added at a fairly early stage.

Although he supports the prohibition of discrimination on these original grounds, and opposes only its extension to non-"stigmatic" criteria, many of Professor Flanagan's arguments against the newer grounds apply to all forms of prohibited discrimination. The question of the cost to the business community of complying with the legislation, which seems to be his root concern, is at least as significant with respect to the original grounds as to the later ones, and some of the examples he offers of cost and inconvenience (such as accommodating the special needs of Sikhs and Seventh Day Adventists) involve the "stigmatic" criterion of religion. A general defence of all anti-discrimination legislation seems therefore to be in order.

The rationale for anti-discrimination legislation is, to use Flanagan's own words, that:

> Discrimination is abhorrent in a liberal society because it treats persons as abstractions rather than as individuals. Personal qualities are lost in the group stereotype.

This is so whether the stereotype is statistically false or accurate. The unfairness is obvious in the case of inaccurate generalizations (that blacks are less intelligent than whites, for instance). But even stereotypes based on statistically valid generalizations (e.g., that there is a higher incidence of alcoholism among Canadian Indians than among the general Canadian population; that women are, on average, physically weaker than men; that older people tend to be less agile than younger people) may be fallacious when applied to any individual member of the groups identified. The particular job applicant might well be a teetotalling native, a female weightlifter, or an elderly mountain climber; and to assume otherwise without further personal information about the individual would be unfair. Statistically sound stereotypes are the more dangerous ones, in fact, because they are more likely to be given wide credence, and to be acted upon when decisions are being made.

Professor Flanagan asserts that: "the stereotype is ... a reasonably good guide to reality." This is true (of statistically accurate stereotypes), only where a statistical approach is appropriate. In the world of scholarly research — Professor Flanagan's world — statistics and stereotypes are helpful for organizing knowledge and for identifying trends. They can also be useful guides to action in certain practical situations, such as the one he cites in support of the above statement: deciding whether to take an umbrella when the weather forecast calls for sunny conditions. In those circumstances the fact that the stereotype will not hold true in a particular case does not carry serious consequences. One's clothes may occasionally get wet, but that is a minor inconvenience compared to the advantage of not carrying an umbrella in fair weather. And it is, after all, one's *own* clothing that will be affected; one's reliance on the statistical method in those circumstances does not affect other people. The employment of statistics and stereotypes is not usually appropriate, however, where it would create a risk of serious and unfair detriment to other persons in matters as basic as their employment or their access to important accommodations or services.

Human rights legislation recognizes that even in the latter types of situation it is sometimes justifiable to employ stereotypes. It is reasonable to assume that a woman would be more appropriate than a man to work as caretaker in the women's dressing and shower areas of a sports facility; that a black actor would be more suitable than a white one to portray the title role in *Uncle Tom's Cabin*; or that a paraplegic might be especially well qualified to act as rehabilitation counsellor for other paraplegics. The legislation permits discrimination based on such reasonable and *bona fide* qualifications for employment, accommodation or service.

But these instances of legitimate discrimination are highly particularized; one cannot generalize from them that women are better caretakers, blacks are better entertainers, or paraplegics are better counsellors. Professor Flanagan falls into the error of such generalization in some of the illustrations he provides of stereotypes which, although perhaps "exaggerated," are not "irrational," and are therefore (he implies) justifiable bases for decision making.

In criticizing the extension of human rights legislation to prohibit discrimination on the basis of political belief, for example, he comments that: "a member of the Communist party probably has certain reservations in his loyalty to the constitution of any bourgeois democracy." Assuming that to be a statistically supportable conclusion, it would certainly justify discrimination in some situations. The fact that a person is a Communist might well be relevant to his or her suitability as an intelligence officer investigating alleged Soviet espionage; and the *bona fide* qualification principle that is integral to all human rights legislation would ensure that a prohibition of political discrimination would not prevent the exclusion of Communists from such work. But what has a Communist's constitutional loyalty got to do with his or her ability to drive a truck or his or her suitability to lease an apartment or purchase a meal? Communists have as much right to employment, shelter and services as anyone else. If human rights legislation entirely excluded political belief as a proscribed ground of discrimination, they could be denied those rights.

In support of his opposition to prohibiting discrimination based on criminal record, Professor Flanagan states that "one convicted of a criminal offense is more likely to commit another criminal offense than is a person without a criminal record." Again assuming the accuracy of the observation for the sake of discussion, one wonders how it justifies a complete rejection of the criminal record criterion. Human rights legislation that prohibited discrimination on that basis would permit an employer to refuse to hire a convicted embezzler as cashier or accountant, or a convicted child molester as day-care worker. But legislation that entirely overlooked that form of discrimination would permit a refusal to hire a factory worker because he or she had once been convicted of some completely irrelevant offense, such as marijuana possession or careless driving.

In short, the *bona fide* qualification principle, which is already built into all human rights legislation, offers a fairer and more realistic method of dealing with justifiable differential treatment than does the arbitrary exclusion of certain grounds of discrimination from the legislation. Professor Flanagan acknowledges the existence of the *bona fide* qualification principle, but he gives rather short shrift to its impact, and criticizes it on the ground that:

> ... an increasing number of business decisions will be made by lawyers or judges with no financial stake in the outcome and possibly little understanding of the concrete difficulties of managing a particular enterprise.

This criticism is misleading. The *bona fide* qualification principle is, for the most part, self-administered. If an employer believes that a job requires a man, or a person free of disabilities, or someone with no relevant criminal convictions, the employer will call for and select applicants on the basis of those restrictions. Only if that decision were challenged, and a human rights agency believed it to be questionable, would anyone external to the employer's business be asked to rule on the reasonableness of the required qualifications. In practice, that is a very rare event. In Manitoba in 1983, for example, the provincial Human Rights Commission received 539 formal complaints (out of a total of 5165 inquiries).

During the same year only seven cases were disposed of by external adjudication. (Manitoba Human Rights Commission, 1983) If one bears in mind that hundreds of thousands of business decisions about employment, accommodations and services must have been made during that period, it becomes obvious that the degree of external intervention into the private decision-making process through the *bona fide* qualification principle is negligible. Even in the handful of situations where it does occur, the operator of the business in question has a full opportunity to explain the practicalities of the situation to the adjudicator.

Business convenience must not be dismissed, of course; it is one of the factors to be taken into account when determining whether a discriminatory qualification is *bona fide* and reasonable. But it is not the sole relevant factor. Against the alleged convenience of basing business decisions on statistically supportable stereotypes must be weighed the fact that some applicants will have been deprived of an equal opportunity to compete for the job or benefit on their individual merits.

Convenience arguments do not always ring true. A large Manitoba company refused to continue the employment of a shift worker whose religious beliefs, as a Seventh Day Adventist, prevented his working Friday nights and Saturdays. When approached by the Human Rights Commission, the company's response was that it would be prohibitively inconvenient to make special shift arrangements for that employee. Subsequent evidence disclosed that the company was nonetheless willing to cope with much more complex shift re-arrangements in order to accommodate the playing schedule of the company hockey team!

It is sometimes also the case that the apparent convenience of stereotype is deceptive. In another recent Manitoba case a printer refused to consider female applicants for a job that involved handling heavy rolls of newsprint. His reason was that men were more likely to possess the physical strength the job required, and he did not have the time to test each applicant's strength. An investigating officer from the Human Rights Commission interviewed male employees who were already doing the work, and discovered that even they were experiencing difficulty with the heavy rolls. Back injuries were common, and considerable time had been lost from work as a consequence. When the employer, at the suggestion of the human rights officer, acquired a mechanical lifting device, the workplace was made safer for both men and women, with resulting reduction of expense and inconvenience for the employer.

Professor Flanagan's division of proscribed grounds of discrimination into the categories "stigmatic," "life cycle," and "life style" is not very helpful. With a few exceptions (some of which he acknowledges and discusses), his classification system does identify *differences* among the various major groups of criteria, but he fails to explain satisfactorily why the prohibition of discrimination is justified in one category, but not in the others. Several reasons for reaching that conclusion are either stated or suggested in his paper, but they are unconvincing, either individually or cumulatively.

The fact that the pioneering legislation was restricted to the discrimination listed in Flanagan's first category is no reason why modern legislation should be so restricted. If one bears in mind that virtually every significant social reform of the past has begun on a small, often experimental, basis, and has grown gradually to its full potential as experience, resources and acceptability permitted, this fact is not a persuasive argument for resisting expansion. It is true that the onus is initially on those who desire expansion to show a need for it, especially where it involves government intervention in the private sector. That deed has been demonstrated, however. The evidence of discrimination against women, against the handicapped, and against members of many other minorities identified by the criteria Professor Flanagan labels "life cycle" and "life style," is knee deep around us. Legislatures in every Canadian jurisdiction have recognized the fact by extending the prohibition on discrimination well beyond the original areas of racial, ethnic and religious bigotry. The Canadian Charter of Rights and Freedoms has now added constitutional authorization to that development by including in its equality guarantee under Section 15 protection against discrimination on many more grounds than those in Professor Flanagan's first category. Flanagan himself recognizes the beneficial impact of those expanded projections:

> Benefits are easy to demonstrate. One can point to a specific number of, say, handicapped people hired through a commission's conciliatory and adjudicatory activities.

Having acknowledged that extension of the legislation has met the need, the onus is now on him to prove that the extension was nonetheless undesirable. Let us examine the arguments he advances in support of that contention.

One possible justification for limiting the prohibition of discrimination to Professor Flanagan's first category is implicit in his terminology, although he never articulates it openly. By referring to the criteria in the first category as "stigmata," he implies that they carry a pejorative sting not associated with the more innocuous "life cycle" and "life style" factors. Webster's *New Collegiate Dictionary* defines stigmata as marks "of infamy or disgrace," or signs of "blemish" or "taint." Flanagan may be suggesting that racial, religious, national and ethnic discrimination, which comprises his first group, is more offensive, and more deserving of legal proscription than other forms of discrimination, because they are more likely to be accompanied by, and to perpetuate, hatred, ridicule or contempt for the discriminated group. If this is his view, I find it difficult to accept. All discrimination is stigmatic. While hatred is not commonly associated with discrimination based on all "life cycle" criteria, it certainly is with some, such as political belief and sexual orientation. Contempt, ridicule, condescension and other denigrating and stigmatizing sentiments accompany discrimination based on every one of the factors Professor Flanagan has listed under those headings. To be refused employment because one uses a wheelchair, or to be denied promotion or harassed because one is female, is stigmatizing. One is labelled as unworthy. The experience is as demeaning, as painful, and as unjustifiable as discrimination based on race, religion or ethnicity.

Another possible reason for excluding the "life style" criteria from protection is that they represent, in Professor Flanagan's words, "conscious personal choices." Some of the factors he includes or excludes from the list raise interesting questions. How can one realistically classify "social origin," "social condition," or "receipt of public assistance" as matters of personal choice, for example? And why treat "sexual orientation" as a matter of choice, but "marital status" as not?

But apart altogether from classification problems, why should it be more acceptable to discriminate against someone who has chosen to be associated with a particular group than one who had no choice in the matter? Flanagan offers no such explanation. The cultural and political pluralism that characterizes Canadian society is not just a question of individual rights; it is also, I believe, a source of vitality for the community as a whole. And that applies as much to differences one freely selects as to those one inherits or unavoidably encounters. I have the same right to my democratic-socialist political associations as I do to my half-Icelandic, half-British heritage. Each is important, both to me and to the community. In fact, one of the chief reasons that tolerance of one's inherited characteristics is important is that it permits a wide range of informed opinions to be available when making decisions about matters over which we do have individual control. It assists me to make an intelligent choice about which political party I should support if I have had the benefit of knowing people with diverse national backgrounds (and accordingly varied political experience) and people brought up with diverse religio-philosophical values and approaches. It would make little sense for a community to say: "You must not discriminate on the basis of race, religion or ethnicity, because we want Canadians to have a wealth of data to draw upon when making social and political decisions; however, you may discriminate against them on the basis of the decisions they make." To do so would mean not only that the majority view dominates public decision making (fair enough in a democracy) but that those who choose to associate with minorities may be discriminated against for that reason (fatal to the preservation of a pluralistic society).

The argument I have just been making does not apply to factors like criminal record or alcoholism, which reflect choices of which the community does not approve. Yet it is in the public interest to prohibit even discrimination on those grounds, because such discrimination inhibits rehabilitation, which is as important to the community as it is to the individual.

Another reason Professor Flanagan believes human rights legislation should be restricted to race, religion, nationality and ethnicity is that those factors are "easy to comprehend" and discrimination based on them is "possible to prohibit ... almost absolutely," whereas the "life cycle" and "life style" criteria are more difficult to understand and apply. Given the inconclusive debates that have raged for decades about the meaning of these notions, this is a surprising position to take. Opinions about the meaning of "race" range, for example, from those who speak of the "British race" and the "French race" to those who recognize only one: the human race. Suppose a Quebecker seeking to work in British Columbia is denied a job because he or she speaks English with a French accent. Plausible legal arguments could be made to the effect that this is discrimination based on race, on nationality (Canada being said by some to be a partnership of "deux nations"), or on ethnicity. Equally plausible arguments could be made that none of those factors is involved. "Religion" or "creed" are similarly imprecise notions. As to their ease of application, I believe that Flanagan is also wide of the mark. While he is correct in saying that the *"bona fide* qualification" exception comes into play infrequently for the factors he calls "stigmatic," discrimination of this type is often much more difficult to identify and to deal with than discrimination based on a factor like handicap, where the exception is invoked frequently. Discrimination is much more sophisticated and less overt than it once was. As Professor Flanagan himself notes: "Gone are the days of signs reading 'No Jews need apply.'" For that reason, correspondingly sophisticated and difficult investigation techniques are required, even for the "traditional" forms of discrimination. On the other hand, discrimination based on handicap, sex, criminal record, source of income, and other newer proscribed forms of discrimination, is more often "up front" and easier to prove. "Traditional" discrimination cannot be distinguished as to either comprehensibility or ease of regulation from "life cycle" or "life style" discrimination.

The final reason for opposing broadened human rights protections is cost and inconvenience. Flanagan is simply wrong in stating that as a result of prohibiting stereotype-based discrimination "landlords are impeded in protecting themselves against the riskiest tenants and insurance companies are forced to accept dangerous drivers on equal terms with others." The real effect of the prohibition is to require landlords, insurance companies and others to make use of more individualized — and therefore more reliable — predictors, such as the tenant's actual credit record or the driver's actual accident record. In many circumstances there is undoubtedly a cost associated with more personalized investigation. The cost is seldom great, however (bearing in mind that accurate individualized data can help to avoid costly errors based on stereotypes), and it is almost always capable of being distributed widely in the form of slight price increases or rearrangements of the risk pool.

Professor Flanagan summarized the situation well:

> It is necessary to think of 'equality of opportunity' not as a costless manna from heaven, but as a way of collectivizing risk, which involves considerable costs as well as benefits.

He admits that in the case of traditional forms of discrimination "the costs are low and the benefits are high," but he asserts that the opposite is true of "life cycle" and "life style" discrimination. He has failed, however, to demonstrate any real difference in cost or, indeed, any other convincing distinction sufficient to justify prohibiting discrimination by race, religion, nationality or ethnicity, but permitting other forms.

We know the costs — individually and collectively devastating — of unwarranted discrimination based on sex, age, marital status, social condition and so on. Professor Flanagan and others who believe that prohibiting such forms of discrimination is even more costly have an obligation to prove their claim. Flanagan has not done so.

AFFIRMATIVE ACTION

The second major approach to the problem of unequal opportunities for minorities — affirmative action — is a "no-fault" technique. Members of certain disadvantaged minorities (usually a relatively few "target groups") are given special treatment in order to help them catch up to average Canadian standards, whether or not their disadvantage can be proved to have been caused by someone's discrimination. This approach is analogous, in one sense, to workers' compensation, no-fault automobile insurance, disability insurance, and other schemes to assist victims of misfortune without regard to whether someone can be legally blamed for the misfortune. It is a remedy that focuses on need, rather than on causation.

Most of the reasons for using no-fault techniques in other areas are also applicable to the problem of inequality. Causation and fault are often exceedingly difficult to prove, and the legal procedures involved in doing so are cumbersome and costly. Frequently the only ones who benefit from employing legal processes are the lawyers. Moreover, hardship often exists independently of blame. The fact that an industrial accident was no one's fault doesn't make the worker's injuries any less painful or debilitating. The disadvantages experienced by native or handicapped persons are no less destructive because they are rooted in history or in circumstances or attitudes (even those of the disadvantaged groups themselves) for which no individual can fairly be held responsible. Fault-based approaches don't assist in those circumstances.

Nor is it sufficient merely to ensure that the members of disadvantaged groups will not be discriminated against in the future. If some runners in a footrace are unable to start until after the other competitors are well along the track, their disadvantage cannot be erased by merely treating all runners with scrupulous equality thereafter. Catch-up measures are needed if real equality is to be achieved. Affirmative action is a catch-up device.

It is not just the no-fault aspect of affirmative action that distinguishes it from anti-discrimination laws. It also differs from them in that it employs the very statistical methods that anti-discrimination laws condemn. Rather than treating individuals on their own personal merits, affirmative action seeks to provide special consideration or benefits on the basis of association with groups that can be shown statistically to be disadvantaged.

In this respect, the footrace metaphor breaks down to some extent, since it would be a rare event for *every* member of the disadvantaged group to have started late, or for *every* member of the majority to have started on time. Affirmative action plans that operated on an absolutely statistical basis, with no account being taken of individual differences, would be unfair for that reason. They would also be unfeasible in employment or educational contexts, since they would exclude consideration of even minimum qualifications of individuals to do the work or to complete the studies in question. Fortunately, few affirmative action plans are absolute. Most of the successful schemes treat the group association factor as only one of several criteria to be considered together with individual characteristics. For example, entrance to the university faculty with which the author is associated is based entirely upon the individual merit of applicants (determined by results of an entrance examination and past academic performance) for 90 percent of the students. The remaining 10 percent are chosen, after personal interviews, on the basis of all those factors *plus* any "special considerations," such as the fact that they are handicapped or native Indians. Not all affirmative action programs are as modest as that one, of course, but most of them take similar account of individual factors while giving special consideration to members of minority target groups.

It cannot be denied, however, that all affirmative action programs, by definition, involve at least some degree of favoritism based on group affiliation apart from individual merit. The apparent inconsistency between this collective approach and the individualized treatment upon which the anti-discrimination laws insist has resulted in much criticism of affirmative action. In my view the criticism is not merited.

The primary reason for instituting group-based affirmative action is that it is sometimes necessary to "fight fire with fire." Since much of the disadvantage that members of minorities suffer can be traced to their group affiliations, it is appropriate that group approaches should be employed to redress the balance. Professor Knopff's paper takes issue with this rationale, but I find his criticism unpersuasive.

Knopff begins by acknowledging that early advocates of affirmative action saw it as something additional to the arsenal against discrimination. He then points out that more recently some supporters have been claiming that, in the words of the *C.E.I.C. Training Manual*, a belief that "the operation of discriminating social, educational and employment practices is the force which causes disproportionate representation of groups of people in the labour force" is the "basic premise of affirmative action." He explains, very effectively, that this could only be true if the term "discriminatory" were used in the broadest sense, to include "systemic" and "societal" discrimination, for which no one can be directly blamed. Such causes, he points out, "are not generally viewed as intrinsically blameworthy phenomena, or as identical to negative prejudice."

That is true, but irrelevant. Affirmative action is not aimed primarily at prejudice or discussion. Affirmative action is a supplement to anti-discrimination laws which attempts to advance equality of opportunity by positive, *no-fault* means. Section 15(2) of the Canadian Charter of Rights and Freedoms, which gives constitutional recognition to affirmative action, says nothing about discrimination or prejudice. Instead, it describes the "object" of affirmative action as "the amelioration of conditions of disadvantaged individuals or groups."

Statements like those in the *C.E.I.C. Training Manual* create a risk of confusion by linking the need for affirmative action to "discrimination" rather than to the more fundamental notion of "equal opportunity," and Professor Knopff is right to criticize some of the "discrimination rhetoric" used by some affirmative action advocates. His criticism glosses over two points, however. First, *some* of the imbalance which affirmative action is intended to redress *is* the result of discrimination. Second, it is no refutation of the substance of affirmative action merely to attack its rhetoric, as much of his essay does.

Turning to matters of substance rather than rhetoric, we find two basic lines of argument against affirmative action. The first is a bald assertion that "the justice of equality of result is not immediately apparent to most people." Why the rights of minorities should depend upon the perceptions of "most people" (i.e., the majority) is not explained. Nor is any empirical support offered for Knopff's view of what "most people" regard as just. In the absence of such evidence, one might be excused for thinking that Section 15(2) of the Canadian Charter of Rights and Freedoms, which approves affirmative action programs, and was agreed to by Canada's political leaders after lengthy public debate, is a more reliable indicator of the public's sense of justice than Professor Knopff's assertion.

The second line of attack involves a lengthy critique of the statistical approaches Knopff associates with affirmative action. While the critique contains some useful observations, it suffers from the fundamental flaw of attributing to affirmative action programs the goal of complete or excessive proportionality. Affirmative action is seen, Knopff says, as "a remedy for all statistical imbalance." This misrepresents the purpose of affirmative action in Canada. Section 15(2) of the Charter refers to the "amelioration" (i.e., *improvement*) of the condition of the disadvantaged, not the achievement of perfect proportionality. No existing or foreseeable program aims for the elimination of "all statistical imbalance." Rather, they attempt, in a few areas where the imbalance is demonstrably gross, to provide partial, gradual improvement in minority representation, with due regard for individual merit and special circumstances. Nothing current or contemplated in Canadian affirmative action schemes exhibits the "statistical mania" to which Professor Knopff directs much of his attack.

To the extent that statistical methods are employed merely for the purposes of monitoring — to identify groups in need of assistance and areas of under-representation — there would appear to be little justifiable objection to their use, unless they involve undue expenditures of time and effort or unreasonable invasions of privacy. To the extent that they are used to define the "quotas" or "goals" of an affirmative action program, there is an undeniable cost in terms of reduced individual consideration for members of the majority. The question that must be answered before a conclusion can be reached as to the desirability of a particular program is whether that cost is outweighed by the benefits of improving the situation of the minority group. While carrying out that exercise in "hedonistic calculus," one should bear in mind that the cost to the majority will be spread over a much broader population than the benefit to the minority, and will therefore have a greater *individualized* impact for good than for evil.

Affirmative action is, in short, a social mechanism for hardship sharing similar in purpose and operation to unemployment compensation or social assistance. Like the other schemes, it is open to both abuse and administrative asininity. Wisely administered, with due regard for unusual individual circumstances and as little compulsion as possible, affirmative action is as wholesome and as useful as those other forms of community benevolence. In fact, to the extent that it succeeds in its aims, it will reduce the need for other types of social assistance.

THE SPECTER OF GOVERNMENT INTERVENTION

Professor Flanagan opposes the expansion of anti-discrimination laws. Professor Knopff, while less forthright in his opposition, appears to deny, or at least to doubt, the desirability of affirmative action. Having attempted to show that the major arguments advanced by Flanagan and Knopff do not support their respective conclusions, one is left with the uncomfortable feeling of not having addressed the real issue.

I believe that something more fundamental than their formal reasoning underlies the Flanagan-Knopff hostility to human rights initiatives. That factor is suspicion of governmental intrusion into the activities of the private sector.

Both papers bristle with comments and asides expressing concern about the role of government in human rights activities. Professor Flanagan, for example, attributes the thrust for expanded protections to two undesirable influences: "the self-interest of public servants," and a public desire for, in Aharow's words, "a no-risk society" in which the State is a "huge insurance agency." Professor Knopff expresses a desire "to maintain a healthy private sphere, free from excessive government intervention and regulation," and asserts that if affirmative action programs seek to redress what he has labelled "societal discrimination," then "the degree of government intervention will have to increase dramatically."

Similar concerns appear to animate much of the criticism to which the work of human rights commissions has been subjected recently. The advent of 1984, with its Orwellian associations, made it easier to conjure up the bogeyman of Big Government.

An example is found in the December 30, 1983 issue of the *Winnipeg Sun*. A Winnipeg eating place used the word "squaw" to designate certain of its hot dogs. Upon receiving complaints from native Indian women, the Manitoba Human Rights Commission explained to the merchant that although he had not violated any law his use of "squaw" was offensive to some people, and it tried to persuade him to change the designation. The merchant declined, relying on his freedom of expression, and the Commission responded in kind by means of a public statement explaining the pain that can be caused by racially stereotyped terms like "nigger," "kike," and "squaw."

This modest educational exercise provoked two editorials and a cartoon from the *Sun*. The cartoon, in the New Year's issue, portrayed the chairperson of the Commission as the 1984 New Year's baby, staring officiously at passersby from wall posters proclaiming "Little Brother is Watching You!" The accompanying editorial concluded:

> ... well-meaning but thoughtless governments are falling into Orwellian lockstep, re-ordering our environment and our behaviour in a humourless attempt to discourage any deviation, no matter how small, from the state-inspired Plan For Us All.
>
> Brave little soldiers, we ... go forth into 1984 thinking only those thoughts deemed correct by the Human Rights Commission (another Orwellian joke).

Although it was not highlighted in the Flanagan and Knopff papers, the fear that human rights commissions are somehow greasing the slopes leading to the totalitarian abyss seems so important to both authors, as well as to many other critics of the human rights movement, that it deserves to be addressed frontally.

The first point that must be made is that many human rights initiatives involve absolutely no compulsion or intrusion into private decision making. The hysterical editorials in the *Winnipeg Sun* were provoked by a mere press release in which the Manitoba Commission exercised its freedom to comment on the anguish caused, often unintentionally, by racial slurs. The Commission's statement involved neither compulsion nor the threat of compulsion. The affirmative action programs to which Professor Knopff takes exception are, in Canada, almost completely voluntary. Most Canadian commissions will assist entrepreneurs in both the public and private sectors to design affirmative action plans when requested to do so by the entrepreneurs, and they will also monitor plans to ensure that they do not deviate unreasonably from anti-discrimination laws, but there is absolutely no compulsion involved. It is true that some human rights advocates are calling for compulsory affirmative action in some circumstances, but their prospects for success in the foreseeable future are slim. The specter of officially imposed hiring quotas is largely imaginary, so far as Canada is concerned, and it will probably remain so for a long time to come.

The anti-discrimination aspects of human rights protection do involve compulsion and legal enforcement, of course, but they are not necessarily objectionable for that reason. Not every governmental activity is inherently evil. Professors Flanagan and Knopff both acknowledge financial support for their papers from the Social Sciences Research Council of Canada, for example, and they undoubtedly make use without complaint of publicly funded roads and police services. Both would probably agree that new public-sector activities are justifiable if they are: (a) intended to achieve important social goals; (b) more likely than private actions to be effective; and (c) accompanied by satisfactory safeguards against abuse. They would be hard-pressed to deny that equality of opportunity is a goal that Canadian accept as important, especially in light of the equality rights section (15) of the Canadian Charter of Rights and Freedoms. They would find it impossible to persuade anyone familiar with the history and present condition of Canadian Indians or the treatment of Canadian women in the workplace that private benevolence or initiative has served that goal effectively in the past. Rather than questioning the propriety of public authorities stepping in where others have failed, Flanagan and Knopff would have been better advised to concentrate on the third factor, and suggest measures for ensuring that the opportunities for abuse and carelessness by those who carry out that function are kept to a bare minimum. The procedures of every Canadian human rights agency could be improved in that regard; but to contend that such shortcomings disprove the need for the agencies makes no more sense than saying that democracy should be replaced because of its various flaws.

The clinching response to the "Big Brother" line of attack against human rights commissions is that commissions serve, in part, *to control* governmental excesses; weakening the commissions would make things easier for Big Brother. Governmental departments and agencies are often the subject of complaints to commissions. Most Canadian commissions are still sufficiently independent from government, in practice though usually not in law, to carry out as effective investigations and adjudications of those complaints as of complaints against private entrepreneurs. There have admittedly been some glaring exceptions. In 1983-84 the British Columbia Commission and Human Rights Branch, both noted for their independent approaches, were abolished and replaced by a council having no power to act contrary to the wishes of the Minister of Labour. In the summer of 1984 the Saskatchewan Commission dismissed its director, a renowned human rights professional, who had resisted pressure from the Attorney-General not to renew a member of the Commission staff because of his political affiliation. As these exceptions demonstrate, Big Brother is uncomfortable with strong human rights commissions. What is ironic is that the British Columbia government was able to use vague popular fears of government intervention by human rights workers as one of its justifications for effectively removing itself from the Commission's scrutiny. Now that is double-think!

CONCLUSION

Canadian minorities have been reasonably well served by human rights legislation and the commissions that administer it. There are undeniable limits to the degree of equality that can be achieved by such means, but those limits have not yet been reached, or even approached. Working co-operatively with government and industry, and using an intelligent blend of legal enforcement, affirmative action and public education, commissions are capable of placing minority members on a much more equal footing in Canadian society than is yet the case.

Until recently, a steady progression in that direction could be observed; but in the past year or two that progression has slowed or halted, and in some quarters a change of direction is evident. While the disbanding of the British Columbia agencies and the disembowelling of the province's human rights legislation provide the most dramatic illustrations of this reversal, disturbing developments have occurred in other jurisdictions as well. The firing of the Saskatchewan Commission's director has already been mentioned, and that event had been preceded by replacement of the Commission's talented, dedicated and independent chief commissioner. The Québec government has also chosen to replace the head of its Commission, a president who had established a reputation for both integrity and independence. In Manitoba, a government that enthusiastically requested its Commission to develop a model human rights code two years ago now appears unwilling to consider any legislative improvements at all, and has refused for two years running to provide a penny for the Commission's education budget.

There is a pattern to some of the regressive developments that can also be seen in the Flanagan and Knopff papers. Arguments against human rights initiatives are advanced which, on close analysis, fail to support the conclusions drawn while, by subtle asides, the message is conveyed that strong human rights commissions constitute a serious threat of governmental intrusion into personal life. Paradoxically, the success of this approach has enabled governments in British Columbia, and to a lesser extent in some other jurisdictions, to increase their potential for intrusiveness by weakening the power of their commissions to scrutinize their behaviour.

REFERENCES

Manitoba Human Rights Commission: *Annual Report*. Winnipeg: Government of Manitoba, 1983.
Merriam, G. & C. Co., *Webster's New Collegiate Dictionary*. Toronto and Springfield, Mass., 1953.
Tarnopolsky, W.L.: *Discrimination and the Law*. Toronto: DeBoo, 1982.

8
THE RESOLUTION OF COMPLAINTS BASED ON RACE AND ORIGIN: THE CANADIAN HUMAN RIGHTS COMMISSIONS

WILLIAM REEVES
J.S. FRIDERES

INTRODUCTION

The Canadian Human Rights Commission, while carrying out a routine internal evaluation of their programs, noted that complaints based upon race or colour appear to be dismissed at higher rates than are complaints involving grounds such as gender, marital status, and physical disabilities. This paper employs a content analysis of 49 actual case files for the period 1979-83 in an investigation of possible reasons for the outcomes noted by the Commission. The Commission was established by the Canadian Human Rights Act passed by Parliament in 1977 and proclaimed on March 1, 1978. Although major changes were made to the original Act in 1983, its basic structure remains unchanged. The legislation empowers the Commission to receive and investigate complaints of discrimination, settle or resolve cases where discrimination has occurred, and, finally, to develop and promote an educational program to combat discriminating practices. The Commission is independent of a current government and reports to Parliament rather than to a particular minister.[1]

As just noted, the Commission deals with complaints falling into one or more proscribed grounds — race, colour, national or ethnic origin, religion, age, sex, marital status, family status, disability, or conviction for which a pardon has been granted. Its jurisdiction extends to all matters coming within the legislative authority of Parliament, with some exceptions (e.g., departments, crown corporations and the Royal Canadian Mounted Police. The Act also applies to private sector areas subject to federal regulations such as chartered banks, grain elevators, radio and television stations, airlines and some railways and trucking companies.

Six regional offices (plus headquarters) throughout Canada are authorized to receive and investigate complaints. Generally, complaints received within a region are dealt with by personnel from that region, although exceptions may be made when, for example, a heavy case load in one region necessitates the transfer of cases from one region to another. Also, because many of the large employers with whom the Commission deals have decentralized operations — even though policy decisions are made at their head offices — the Commission has established coordinators (depending on the region where the respondent's head office is situated) for processing complaints against major employers.[2]

With respect to employment, the Act affects approximately 11 percent of the Canadian work force, with about 700 employers falling under its jurisdiction. The Act permits and encourages the adoption of special programs to improve opportunities for certain groups as a legitimate mechanism to remedy

Figure 8.1

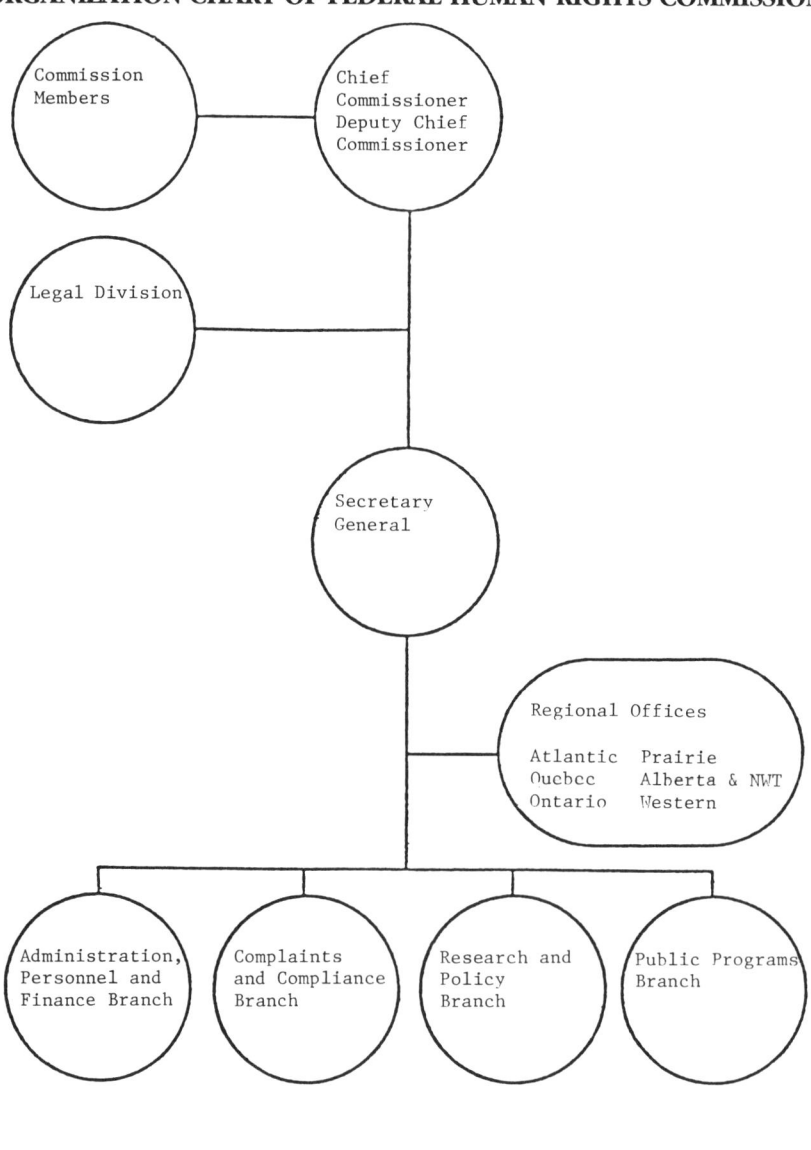

ORGANIZATION CHART OF FEDERAL HUMAN RIGHTS COMMISSION

- Commission Members
- Chief Commissioner / Deputy Chief Commissioner
- Legal Division
- Secretary General
- Regional Offices: Atlantic, Prairie, Quebec, Alberta & NWT, Ontario, Western
- Administration, Personnel and Finance Branch
- Complaints and Compliance Branch
- Research and Policy Branch
- Public Programs Branch

SOURCE: Canadian Human Rights Commission, Annual Report, 1983, p. 47.

discrimination. In addition, section 19 of the Act requires organizations to comply with any terms and conditions relating to anti-discrimination that are included in federal contracts, grants, or licenses. Thus, organizations doing business with the federal government must meet federal standards of anti-discrimination, a practice that differs somewhat from the contract compliance procedure used in the U.S.A.[3]

The organization structure of the Canadian Human Rights Commission is depicted in Figure 8.1. Three major branches, in addition to Personnel, Administration and Finance, comprise the Commission.[4] The Complaints and Compliance Branch deals with all formal complaints lodged with the Commission. The Public Program Branch has recently been reorganized into three subdivisions. The first of these, Program Analysis and Development, undertakes long-term planning and development of services and resources. A second, Information and Production, provides the Commission with public affairs advice and informs the general public about human rights. Finally, Program Delivery provides services such as workshops and seminars for various organizations. The third major branch of the Commission, Research and Policy, was established in 1983. It carries out basic research pertinent to the Commission's concerns and makes representations to Parliament on behalf of the Commission.

PROCEDURE

Once a Human Rights office is contacted, a determination is made as to whether the complaint (a) falls within federal jurisdiction and (b) involves discrimination as defined in the Act. Assuming these two conditions have been met, an investigator collects data from the complainant and respondent, and may augment this with information from other witnesses and sources. The investigator's report and recommendations are then presented to the Commissioners for a final decision. Decisions as to whether the complaint is substantiated, whether a settlement will be proposed, and, if so, what its content will be, then are made by the Commissioners. If the parties do not agree to a settlement, the Commissioners can appoint a conciliator to negotiate one. Finally, if neither the investigator nor the conciliator are able to reconcile the parties, a Human Rights Tribunal can be appointed to conduct a public inquiry into the complaint. All parties involved in cases of discrimination have, as a final recourse, the right to take their case to a court of law.

PROCESSING A COMPLAINT

From its inception to 1980, the Commission processed over 20,000 inquiries. The number of inquiries has continued to increase so that in 1983 alone almost 30,000 were received. However, most of these did not involve a formal complaint. For example, of the nearly 30,000 inquiries made in 1983 only 312 were actually formal complaints (see table 8.1). Table 8.1 also provides data on the distribution of inquiries by type and region.

The processing of formal complaints usually begins in a regional office and is forwarded to the Commission at the end of the investigation.[5] Table 8.2 provides information on the complaints accepted by region for the years 1979-1983.

Table 8.1
Enquiries by regions and selected subjects for 1983 (percentage)

Region	Sexual Harassment	Hate Propaganda	Physical Disability	Charter of Rights	Mental Disability	Equal Pay	Mandatory Retirement	Discriminatory Legislation	Others	Total
Headquarters	75(21)	2(6)	103(15)	29(12)	11(18)	30(24)	25(13)	20(18)	5703(20)	599
Atlantic	36(10)	3(9)	58(9)	7(3)	9(15)	19(15)	16(8)	18(16)	2678(10)	284
Quebec	88(25)	6(18)	192(29)	60(25)	14(23)	38(30)	70(36)	25(22)	8499(30)	899
Ontario	83(23)	8(24)	198(30)	88(37)	14(23)	23(18)	38(20)	28(25)	4982(18)	546
Prairie	10(3)	6(18)	36(5)	22(9)	2(3)	2(2)	9(5)	6(5)	1860(7)	195
Alberta NWT	25(7)	4(12)	41(6)	9(4)	1(2)	6(5)	8(4)	12(11)	1974(7)	208
Western	39(11)	4(12)	37(6)	24(10)	9(15)	8(6)	27(14)	4(4)	2278(8)	243
Total	356	33	665	239	60	126	193	113	27974	2975

SOURCE, CHRC., Annual Report, 1983, p. 39.

RESOLUTION OF COMPLAINTS

Table 8.2 — Complaints accepted by regions by grounds, 1983 (percentage)[1]

Region \ Grounds	Race/ Colour	National/ Ethnic Origin	Religion	Age	Sex	Marital Fam. Status	Disabilities	Pardon/ Retaliation	Total 1983	1982	1981	1980	1979	Total 1979/83
Headquarters	(12)[2] [14][3]	(25) [13]	(40) [4]	(15) [11]	(23) [32]	(5) [2]	(13) [16]	(100) [9]	56(18)	75(19)	109(22)	101(24)	103(26)	444(22)
Atlantic	(17) [26]	(4) [2]	(20) [2]	(10) [9]	(14) [26]	(15) [7]	(17) [28]		43(14)	45(11)	52(11)	65(16)	39(10)	244(12)
Quebec	(3) [6]	(11) [9]	(20) [3]	(27) [31]	(9) [20]	(10) [6]	(13) [26]		35(11)	65(16)	54(11)	52(13)	47(12)	253(13)
Ontario	(29) [28]	(21) [9]	(20) [1]	(34) [20]	(14) [16]	(20) [6]	(20) [20]		69(22)	54(14)	82(17)	45(11)	44(11)	294(15)
Prairie	(12) [19]	(11) [7]		(2) [2]	(11) [21]	(40) [19]	(19) [31]	5[2]	42(13)	56(14)	102(21)	85(21)	78(20)	363(18)
Alberta & NWT	(11) [26]	(11) [11]		(2) [4]	(11) [33]	(5) [4]	(9) [22]	5[2]	27(9)	51(13)	19(4)			97(5)
Western	(15) [25]	(18) [13]		(10) [10]	(18) [35]	(5) [3]	(9) [15]	3[1]	40(13)	51(13)	68(14)	67(16)	84(21)	310(15)
TOTAL 1983	65[21]	28[9]	5[2]	41[13]	79[25]	20[6]	69[22]	5[2]	312[4]					
1982	81[20]	32[8]	6[2]	44[11]	102[26]	24[6]	103[26]	3[1]		397				
1981	102[21]	20[4]	13[3]	61[13]	145[30]	33[7]	112[23]				486			
1980	66[16]	28[7]	9[2]	49[12]	126[30]	42[10]	92[22]					415		
1979	71[18]	28[7]	11[3]	50[13]	114[29]	33[8]	85[22]						395	
Total 1979/83	385[19]	136[7]	44[2]	245[12]	566[28]	152[8]	461[23]	16[1]						2005

SOURCE, CHRC., Annual Report, 1983, pg. 41.

[1] Percentages may not add to 100 percent due to rounding error.
[2] Parentheses refer to column percentages.
[3] Brackets refer to row percentages.
[4] The number of cases accepted in 1983 does not equal the number of cases submitted for decision in 1983 (Table 8.4). Many cases accepted in one year are not submitted for a decision in the same year.

Table 8.2 indicates that about 26 percent of the cases concerned discrimination based on race/colour and national/ethnic origins. An additional 28 percent of the cases were based on gender discrimination and 23 percent on grounds of disability. Complaints made because of age discrimination accounted for approximately 12 percent, with family status and "others" contributing about 10 percent of the cases.

Data on the disposition of the cases submitted to the Commission are presented in tables 8.3 and 8.4. Table 8.3, which presents data on cases submitted since 1979, indicates that the percentage of cases dismissed[6] has increased substantially for the period — from 38 percent to 61 percent. On the other hand, the settled rate has remained relatively constant. Those discontinued showed a small increase, with the overall trend being toward a greater number of closed cases at the year-end — from 72 percent in 1979 to 88 percent in 1983. Cases not closed were sent to Conciliation or Tribunal. The percentage of cases sent to the former remained constant until 1983 when it decreased sharply. Those sent to tribunal decreased steadily over the period.

Regarding dismissals, table 8.4 indicates that, in 1983, 80 percent of the cases involving race/colour were dismissed as were 91 percent of those in which national/ethnic origins were factors. Less frequently dismissed were cases involving age discrimination (60 percent), disabilities (52 percent), and gender (44 percent). Twenty percent of the latter went to either Conciliation or Tribunal as opposed to 16 percent and 4 percent, respectively, of cases involving disability and age discrimination.

As noted above, cases involving complaints about discrimination based on race, colour, and origins were more often dismissed than were those in which factors such as age or gender were the bases for complaints. We may ask whether these observed differences were functions of the types of people who bring complaints to the Commission, whether there were differences in the types of data collected for inclusion in files, or whether the data collected were analyzed differently. In an exploratory study we tried to address these questions utilizing a non-random sample of 49 cases investigated by the Commission during the period 1979-1983. The sample, although it may not be fully representative of the universe of cases from which it was drawn, does provide us with a base from which some observations can be made.

Each case file was read initially, a codebook was developed, and each case file was resubjected to a more detailed and systematic content analysis. Over 50 variables were identified and coded, although subsequent analysis of the data revealed that some of the factors did not exhibit much variability. Because of the nature of the data we were working with[7] and the relatively small number of cases, many of the variables coded were of the "present/absent" variety.

FINDINGS

Our content analysis indicated that substantial variation existed in the ways in which the cases were investigated and reported. The content of files for complaints that were dismissed differed markedly from those involving complaints that were not dismissed. However, almost all of the case files emphasized documentation of evidence. In addition, investigators collected "other" types of evidence; each file also included a narrative process regarding

RESOLUTION OF COMPLAINTS

Table 8.3
Results of cases submitted for decision by year (including percentage of total)[1]

Year	Results	Dismissed		Settled		Discontinued		Sub-Total Closed		To Conciliation		To Tribunal		Total Submitted	
1983		295	61%	110	23%	18	4%	423	88%	34	7%	24	5%	481	100%
1982		213	48%	96	22%	61	13%	370	83%	65	15%	9	2%	444	100%
1981		280	58%	77	16%	57	12%	414	86%	48	10%	18	4%	480	100%
1980		167	47%	79	22%	38	11%	284	80%	48	14%	20	6%	352	100%
1979		93	38%	61	24%	25	10%	179	72%	35	14%	34	14%	248	100%
Total 1979-83		1048		423		199		1670		230		105		2005	

SOURCE: CHRC., Annual Report, 1983, p. 39.

[1] Totals for results of cases submitted for decision each year do not match yearly totals in Table 8.2 because some cases are accepted in one year but not submitted for decision the same year.

Table 8.4
Results of cases submitted for decision in 1983 (percentages)[1]

Grounds	Results Dismissed	Settled	Discontinued	Sub-Total Closed	To Conciliation	To Tribunal	Total Submitted
Race/Colour	(25)[2] [82][3]	(10) [12]	(6) [1]	(20) [93]	(15) [5]	(4) [1]	91
National Ethnic Origin	(10) [91]	(1) [3]	(6) [3]	(8) [97]	(3) [3]		33
Religion	(4) [85]	(2) [15]		(3) [100]			13
Age	(10) [60]	(13) [29]	(17) [6]	(11) [96]	(6) [4]		48
Sex	(22) [44]	(45) [33]	(28) [3]	(28) [81]	(38) [9]	(67) [11]	149
Marital/ Family Status	(10) [78]	(5) [14]	(6) [3]	(8) [95]	(6) [5]		37
Pardon	(0) [100]			(0) [100]			1
Disabilities	(19) [52]	(25) [25]	(39) [6]	(21) [83]	(32) [10]	(29) [6]	108
Retaliation		(1) [100]		(0) [100]			1
	295	110	18	423	34	24	481

SOURCE, CHRC., Annual Report, 1983, p. 38.

[1] Percentages may not add to 100 percent because of rounding error.
[2] Column percentages.
[3] Row percentages.

the disposition of the case that went beyond mere documentation evidence. Grounds for complaint were divided into three categories: those involving national or ethnic origins, those involving race or colour but not origins, and those involving all complaints *other* than national/ethnic origins or race/colour. An analysis of covariance that correlated the resolution of cases (i.e., dismissed vs. non-dismissed) with a number of explanatory factors was carried out for each of the above three categories of complaints. This analysis revealed that differences in the content of files of dismissed and non-dismissed cases tended to vary with the grounds of complaint. Alerted by the very high correlation coefficients between grounds of complaint and dismissal vs. non-dismissal,[8] we reread the files and found the cases involving complaints based on race/colour and national/ethnic origins tended to be resolved in a rather *ad hoc* fashion. Conclusions as to whether discrimination had occurred were avoided, and dismissals of complaints typically were justified by references to the particulars of interpersonal relationships centering on the complainants. Complaints that were not dismissed generally were settled informally, with Commission investigators encouraging the parties to negotiate a resolution of their differences. Commissioners tended to endorse such private agreements.

Cases not involving race/colour or national/ethnic origins tended to hinge on the "facts." If the facts were disputed by the parties, Commission investigators tended to withdraw, recommending dismissal of the complaint. If the facts were not disputed, investigators were more likely to pursue a complaint, establish the nature of discrimination involved, and seek some remedial action that would reduce similar discrimination in the future.

IMPORTANCE OF DOCUMENTATION

Virtually all complaints of discrimination were raised in an organizational context. Most were registered by employees or job applicants, although a few involved clients or customers. Routine organizational documents (usually obtained from the respondents to the complaint) provided one of the prime sources of evidence and were regarded as both factual and objective by Commission investigators.

Zimmerman (1967) has argued that the formal organization typical of large public and private corporations enhances the semblance of objectivity and factualness of the documents they submit. Events in these organizations generally are recorded using standard operating procedures that apply to all individuals and situations. As such, these documents have the authority of independent and impartial testimonials as to the "facts" of any particular case.

For all types of cases, documentation had an important bearing on their resolution. Generally, documents were used by investigators to substantiate the claims of the complainants rather than those of the respondents. The exceptions to this general practice were complaints alleging discrimination on the basis of national/ethnic origins. Documentation in such cases tended to be used by investigators to establish the *reasonableness* of the actions of the respondent. As a result — and unlike all other grounds of discrimination — documentation for complaints based on national/ethnic origins tended to be associated more often with dismissals.

In contrast to well-documented cases, incompletely documented cases —

those with improperly or irregularly processed records — or testimony assembled only for a particular case lack a sense of objectivity and factualness. (Latour and Woolgar, 1979:43-90; Zimmerman, 1967:329-334) These kinds of data are assumed to be open to manipulation by interested parties and they tend to be greeted with a degree of skepticism by Commission investigators. For example, there is suspicion that respondents have been documenting complainants and creating special dossiers in order to discredit them. Indeed, the reports of Commission investigators themselves are inspected for signs that they may have an axe to grind or a special interest in generating a particular outcome.

Inconsistencies and contradictions trigger a review of the sources of information to ascertain whether they have been documented. To repeat, when documents are incomplete, or not processed by procedures and interpreted in the context of generally accepted organizational conventions, they tend to be regarded with skepticism by Commission investigators. Under such conditions the latter are reluctant to draw conclusions regarding the presence or absence of discrimination.

We have argued that the ability successfully to document complaints of discrimination varies with the grounds on which these are based. The latter, in turn, are affected by both historical changes in officially legitimated forms of discrimination and the relative size and structure of organizations in which complaints arise. With respect to changes in discriminatory practices, some forms of discrimination that currently are regarded as illegitimate have been accepted as legitimate and useful distinctions in the past. For example, variations in privileges, rights, and responsibilities that in the past were based on differences in gender, family status, age, disability, and even religion, now are grounds of discrimination that are officially recognized by the Commission. (Kallen, 1982; Tarnopolsky, 1979) Investigators have little difficulty documenting complaints based on such grounds and labelling these practices discriminatory because they have been incorporated in the past into the standard operating procedures, records, and conventional reasoning of both public and private corporations. (Status of Women in Canada, 1970)

However, discrimination on the basis of race/colour or national/ethnic origin have not been institutionalized in Canada to nearly the same extent (Hawkins, 1972) and very few standard operating procedures or formal systems of records have emerged that refer explicitly to them. Consequently, complaints based on race/colour/ethnic/national grounds are more difficult to document. As previously noted, in the absence of complete documentation, and/or when documentation is not based on standard operating procedure, Commission investigators are more likely to avoid drawing conclusions regarding the presence or absence of discrimination.

The importance of documentation has a significant and nonobvious implication. We have noted that the CHRC's ability to investigate and take action is most effective when complaints can be documented. Our review of the history of Canadian political and corporate culture suggests that documentation tends explicitly to acknowledge gender, physical disability, marital status, and age, but is less likely to refer to colour, race, or origin. As a consequence the CHRC is more effective in dealing with complaints based on gender or physical disability than it is in dealing with those involving colour, race, or origin. Our content analysis of CHRC files supports this conclusion.

That the CHRC seems less effective when dealing with discrimination against members of "visible" minority groups seems paradoxical since it is generally believed — and everyday events seem to confirm — that discrimination has been most persistent against "visible" minority groups.

We often presume that the visibility that sustains such discrimination should also make it more susceptible to remedial action from such agencies as the CHRC. The belief seems to be that governmental regulation will be and should be more effective against the more visible and trenchant forms of discrimination. The premises and argumentation advanced in Flanagan's paper in this volume appear to support this view. It is against this backdrop — commonsensical observations about discrimination, the sociological concept of "visible" minority groups, and the arguments of Flanagan — that our findings seem somewhat nonobvious. The "visibility" of race, colour, or origin is a characteristic of *informal* social relations. Irrespective of whether age, marital status, religion, gender, or physical disability are less visible, they are characteristics that are more likely to be *formally* documented in Canadian institutions. Because they are, the effectiveness of the CHRC is more contingent upon the *formal* ability to document discrimination than it is on the visibility of the complainants.

A second factor affecting ability to document discrimination, we contend, is the nature of organizations and the type of people they employ. Organizations vary systematically in the degree to which their procedures and practices are formalized. Correlational studies of organizational structures have consistently found that more formalized organizations tend to be larger corporations that dominate their sector of society, employ a wide variety of technical and professional experts, and have a decentralized pattern of participation in routine decision making. (Child, 1973; Hage, 1980; Perrow, 1979; Zey-Ferrell, 1979) Less formalized organizations, in contrast, tend to have fewer employees, fewer formally trained experts, and a more personal and hence consolidated command. This relationship between the degree of formal organization and size has also been identified by institutional economists. More recently, labour economists and sociologists have shown that it is useful to distinguish between primary and secondary labour markets. (Doeringer and Piore, 1971; Edwards, 1979:162-183) Employees of larger, more formally organized corporations belong to primary labour markets, whereas those of smaller, less formally organized ones belong to secondary markets.

Women and members of visible minority groups tend to be disproportionately represented in the secondary labour markets and, hence, to be employees of smaller, nonunionized firms. (Edwards, 1979:177, 194-197) These data are consistent with our findings that complaints of race/colour discrimination also tended to originate in secondary labour market type organizations. (The few cases involving customers or clients, as opposed to employees or job applicants, tended to involve these types of organizations as well.) The relative concentration in such settings of cases involving race/colour complaints may explain the distinctively *ad hoc* manner in which complaints of these kinds were investigated and reported. Informal organizational contexts appeared to frustrate attempts by Commission investigators to document claims of discrimination based on race or colour. Unable to document such complaints, investigators tended to ascribe them to complainants' personalities and to their difficulty in getting along with others.

Unlike cases involving race or colour, complaints based on national/ethnic origins ranged over primary as well as secondary labour market situations. In part, this can be explained by Canada's immigration policy which has explicitly given priority to those with superior educational and occupational qualifications.[9] As a result, large numbers of highly qualified landed immigrants and first generation Canadians are found in both the primary and secondary sectors of the Canadian economy. While less qualified individuals tended to complain that they were denied opportunities to get a job (typically the case for most race/colour complainants as well), more highly qualified complainants have generally succeeded in securing employment somewhat commensurate with their qualifications. The complaints they raised tended to involve being denied a normal timetable or opportunity for promotion. Unlike less qualified race/colour or national/ethnic origins complainants, the more qualified "origins" complainants were located in formal organizational settings in which Commission investigators seemingly have less difficulty documenting the facts of a case.

Indeed, documentation did typically appear in the text of Commission files on such cases. However, unlike all other grounds for complaint, documentation generally was used by investigators to *dismiss* claims by highly qualified individuals that they were being discriminated against because of their national/ethnic origins. Documentation in such cases instead tended to be used to substantiate the claims of respondents that their procedures were non-discriminatory. Essentially, respondents were able to document their actions towards the complainant, and Commission investigators tended to accept these documented accounts as plausible, if not entirely reasonable. Accordingly, rather than drawing any conclusions, investigators tended to recommend dismissal of the complaint, while noting any residual suspicions they might have for the attention of the Commissioners.

This finding is perplexing. We have no independent way to assess the documents or the nature of the investigation actually carried out. There is no systematic evidence across cases that either the respondents to or investigators of complaints based on national/ethnic origins were manipulating or were being manipulated (e.g., by the respondent "documenting" the complainant or by the investigators being coopted by the respondents). Indeed, it is conceivable that simple non-discrimination might *still* provoke complaints from highly qualified minorities, and that only affirmative action, giving a decided preference to those previously excluded from advancement into higher positions, would satisfy them.

SUMMARY AND CONCLUSIONS

An examination of the disposition of the files of 49 cases of complaints of discrimination investigated by the Canadian Human Rights Commission during the period 1979-83 indicated that cases involving race/colour and national/ethnic origins were dismissed substantially more frequently than were complaints based on other grounds. Complaints based on race/colour and national/ethnic origins grounds tended to be resolved in a more *ad hoc* fashion. Investigators tended to avoid making judgements about whether complainants had actually experienced discrimination and justified dismissing their complaints by referring to problems they had in interpersonal relations.

We also found that the disposition of cases not involving race or origins grounds tended to hinge on the "facts." If these were disputed, the investigators tended to withdraw and recommend dismissal of the complaints. When they were not disputed, however, investigators were more likely to pursue complaints, establish the character of any discriminatory acts involved and seek a remedy for them.

Since the ability of investigators to assemble undisputed facts was a principal determinant of the disposition of cases, documenting these facts was an important part of their work. Complete documentation of the facts — especially if they were assembled by employing standard operating procedures — generally was used by investigators both to substantiate the claims of the complainants and to justify remedial action by the Commission. Exceptions to this general practice were complaints alleging discrimination on national/ethnic origins grounds. In those instances, documentation tended to be used by investigators to establish the reasonableness of the persons or organizations that were the objects of the complaint.

The ability of investigators to document complaints varied with the grounds on which these were based, as well as with the relative size and structure of organizations in which complaints had their origins. Complaints based on differences such as gender, age, or religion not only are proscribed by the Commission, but they also have been incorporated in the standard operating procedures and record keeping of larger, more formally organized public and private corporations in primary labour markets. However, when complaints based on national/ethnic and race/colour origins originated in those organizational environments, documentation tended to be used to support the claims of respondents against the allegations of complainants.

The suspicion — following arguments advanced by institutional economists — is that larger, more formalized corporations may be taking advantage of their dominant position in the political economy to negotiate favourable interpretations from Commission investigators. Complaints of discrimination pose threats to the legitimacy of such organizations. However, these still may be managed by the use of documentation, especially if there are few official references condoning past instances of national/ethnic and race/colour discrimination. Irrespective of whether Commission investigators fully endorse the internal operating procedures of these corporations, the doubt created by documentation appears to be sufficient to avoid Commission findings of discriminatory practices.

We have no evidence to suggest that the above findings are the product of some conscious plan or objective of the Commission. Nor are they the products of some generally understood and/or covert state of affairs. None of the personnel with the Commission was aware of the patterns identified above. Indeed, it was the Commission itself which initially drew the attention of others to the possibility of differential dispositions of cases on the basis of different grounds of complaints. Notwithstanding this fact, systematic differences — however unintended or unconscious — in the disposition of Commission cases are a matter of serious concern meriting additional and more intensive investigation.

FOOTNOTES

1. The Commission consists of a Chief Commissioner, Deputy Chief Commissioner and not fewer than three or more than six other members, to be appointed by the Governor-General in Council. Full-time appointees' terms are for a maximum of seven years, while part-time appointees' terms are three years (renewable).
2. Some respondents also have named coordinators to deal with the Commission so that more uniformity and continuity can be obtained.
3. In the U.S.A., organizations wishing to enter into contracts with the federal government must first show proof that they have implemented an affirmative action program.
4. The budget for the Commission had increased substantially over time. It began operations with a 1978 budget of $2.5 million. This increased to $4.3 million in 1980 and to nearly $6 million in 1983.
5. There are some exceptions. For example, if a regional office has more cases than it can normally process, some of these cases will be shifted to another regional office or headquarters. Other cases originating in a regional office might require the services of a special investigator and will be sent on to headquarters.
6. There are over twenty different decisions that the Commissioners can make for each case, ranging from "no jurisdiction" to "Tribunal." However, for present purposes, we dichotomized the final disposition. Complaints either are "dismissed" or "not dismissed" (substantiated).
7. We were unable to interview either the investigator or the Commissioners. This places additional constraints on our interpretation of the data.
8. Because of the small sample, we required correlations to have a value of plus or minus .6 or mor before they were considered important enough to enter into our statistical analysis of the data.
9. The major exception to this government policy is Canada's open-door policy towards specially designated refugees.

REFERENCES

Child, J. "Predicting and understanding organizational structure." *Administrative Science Quarterly*. 18 (1973): 168-185.

Doeringer, P. and M. Piore. *Internal Labor Markets and Manpower Analysis*. Lexington, Mass.: D.C. Heath, Lexington Books, 1971.

Edwards, R. *Contested Terrain*. New York: Basic Books, 1979.

Galbraith, J.K. *The New Industrial State*. Boston: Houghton Mifflin, 1967.

Hage, J. *Theories of Organization*. New York: Wiley, 1980.

Hawkins, F. *Canada and Immigration: Public Policy and Public Concern*. Montreal: McGill-Queens Press, 1972.

Hirsch, P.M. "Organizational Effectiveness and the Institutional Environment." *Administrative Science Quarterly*. 20 (1975): 327-344.

Kallen, E. *Ethnicity and Human Rights in Canada*. Toronto: Gage, 1982.

Latour, B. and S. Woolgar. *Laboratory Life: The Social Construction of Scientific Facts.* Beverly Hills, Calif.: Sage, 1979.

McNeil, K. "Understanding Organizational Power: Building on the Weberian Legacy." *Administrative Science Quarterly.* 23 (1978): 65-90.

Perrow, C. *Complex Organizations: A Critical Essay* (2d edition). Glenview, Ill.: Scott, Foresman, 1979.

Report of the Royal Commission on the Status of Women in Canada. Ottawa: Information Canada, 1970.

Scott, W.R. *Organizations: Rational, Natural, and Open Systems.* Englewood Cliffs, N.J.: Prentice-Hall, 1981.

Stone, W.R. *Where the Law Ends: The Social Control of Corporate Behavior.* New York: Harper and Row, 1975.

Sudnow, D. "Normal Crimes: Sociological Features of the Penal Code in the Public Defender Office." *Social Problems.* 12 (1965): 255-277.

Tarnopolsky, W. "The Control of Racial Discrimination." In R. Macdonald and J. Humphrey (eds.), *The Practice of Freedom.* Toronto: Butterworth, 1979.

Zey-Ferrell, M. *Readings on Dimensions in Organization.* Santa Monica, Calif.: Goodyear, 1979.

Zimmerman, D. "Record-Keeping and the Intake Process in a Public Welfare Agency." In S. Wheeler (ed.). *On Record.* New York: Russell Sage, 1967.

PART II
MINORITIES IN CANADIAN SOCIETY: PROBLEMS, PROSPECTS, PERSPECTIVES

9

CONFORMITY vs. PLURALISM: MINORITY IDENTITIES AND INEQUALITIES

LEO DRIEDGER

INTRODUCTION

Although two models, which we term "Assimilationist" and "Pluralist," have been developed to describe relationships between the majority (Anglo-Celtic) and minority groups in Canada (and the U.S.A.), in fact, numerous other variants of these "pure" types have emerged, and need to be examined. There are also important conditions essential to the existence of these polarities. Maintenance of an ethnic identity — a form of voluntary separation from the majority society, promoted by groups such as the Hutterites, the Jews, Ukrainians, and others — tends to promote pluralism (resistance to assimilation). Territorial segregation, maintenance of ethnic institutions, ethnic culture, historical symbols, ideology, and charismatic leaderships are all among the techniques that minorities may adopt to maintain pluralist identities. On the other hand, the majority society may be reluctant to allow all groups to enter into full participation. To prevent this they may create social distance between themselves and some minorities by stereotyping, prejudice, and discrimination. Such forced separation encourages involuntary pluralism (blocked assimilation) by excluding racial (Indians) or religious (Jews) minorities.

I. COMPETING NATIONAL MINORITY PERSPECTIVES

ANGLO-CONFORMITY: ASSIMILATION OF MINORITIES INTO THE DOMINANT GROUP

The theory of assimilation has influenced North American thinking greatly during the half-century since the 1920s. The product of an evolutionary perspective, it assumes that ethnic groups are constantly changing from their present minority cultural and structural state to a majority culture, which in Canada and the United States is represented by the British. The theory tends to be deterministic in the sense that it assumes that the seduction of the majority will be too much for any minority group to resist and, therefore, that they will assimilate into the majority milieu.

A classic formulation of this process is identified with Robert Park who suggested that immigrants, when they came into contact with American society, either took the route of least resistance (contact, accommodation, assimilation) or a more circuitous route (contact, conflict, competition, accommodation, fusion), (Hughes et al, 1950). Whereas the latter route would take longer, and entail considerable resistance on the part of the immigrant, the end result would be the same — assimilation and a loss of a distinctive ethnic identity. The dominant language and culture would prevail.

There is a great deal of evidence in Canadian history that many British leaders and influentials had the Anglo-conformity model in mind when they thought of native people, the French, and other immigrants. Lord Durham assumed that others would assimilate to a British legal, political, economic, and cultural system (Stanley, 1960). Many seem to have hoped that somehow even the French would finally assimilate, although via the circuitous route of conflict and competition.

Although the Anglo-conformity and assimilationist perspectives have become less prevalent and appealing in Canada, they continue to be espoused. For example, the late John Porter (1979) held what may be termed modified Anglo-conformity views. Porter referred to ethnicity and multiculturalism as "primordial identity" in analyzing the differentiation he perceived, and emphasized the overwhelming influence of technology and urbanization as major forces that sweep away all of its ethnically based forms. Frank Vallee (1981:641) says "that there is no doubt that Porter would have rejoiced had ethnic differentiation disappeared altogether…. If the choice had to be made between the ideology of the melting pot and the mosaic, he made it clear he would choose the melting pot…. What bothered Porter more than anything was that these group or collective rights were ascriptive, that is, determined by the categories into which one was born." In his *Vertical Mosaic* (1965) Porter argued that ethnicity was an impediment to upward social mobility; he was concerned that all should have the greatest possible opportunity to improve both their social and economic statuses.

MULTICULTURAL PLURALISM: THE ETHNIC MOSAIC

The pluralist view is that many groups will retain a separate identity and not assimilate. Cultural pluralism is often viewed as an arrangement where distinct groups live side by side in relatively harmonious coexistence. Horace Kallen, who first formulated it, espoused pluralism for three main reasons (Newman, 1973): (1) although many kinds of social relationships and identities can be chosen voluntarily, no one may choose his ancestry; (2) each minority group has something of value to contribute to a country; and (3) the American Constitution carries the implicit assumption that all are created equal even though there are many distinct differences. Kallen wished to refute the ideas of assimilation and the melting pot which, in his day, had gained considerable influence.

Whereas the assimilationist view emphasizes the overwhelming influence of technology and urbanization in sweeping away all forms of ethnic differentiation, cultural pluralists tend to focus on countervailing forces such as democracy and human justice which implicitly presume that all people are of equal worth and should have the freedom to choose their own quality and way of life. Assimilation implies the disappearance of immigrant and racial groups, but pluralism suggests that there may be great resistance to assimilate and amalgamate. In fact, the trend toward permissive differentiation seems to be set in Canada. We have accepted pluralist religious expressions, and the same is now true of the political scene, where a diversity of political parties and ideologies exist. Indeed, multiculturalism in Canada is now recognized federally.

The large French population, concentrated as it is in Québec, always has been a very substantial tile in the mosaic. Pluralists would say the native peoples of Canada, isolated in Canada's northlands, represent additional tiles. Canada's blacks, Jews, Hutterites, Doukhobors, Italians, Ukrainians, and Germans in homogenous prairie settlements are more like patches in a highly differentiated quilt than a homogeneous ethnic blend.

II. PRECONDITIONS FOR PLURALISM AND ASSIMILATION

What preconditions or requirements are essential to the existence of the separate and racial minorities that keep Canada a multi-cultural and multi-ethnic plural society? What factors and processes (e.g., discrimination) impede acceptance into the majority society? Let us consider voluntary and involuntary separation in turn.

ETHNIC IDENTITY: VOLUNTARY SEPARATION

In Canada the two charter groups, the British and the French, are by far the largest ethnic group in Canada. From the outset the British have been dominant demographically. English language use is dominant outside Québec, and British economic, political, and legal influences upon the nation are and always have been strong. The French are highly segregated in Québec where, given the authority traditionally exercised by the provinces over education and matters pertinent to culture, they have been able to maintain their linguistic and cultural distinctiveness.

The dominant industrial and political Anglo environment acts as a magnet for ethnic minorities. Access to jobs, economic enterprise, and influence are appealing. But how do the Hutterites, the Jews, the native Indians, the French, and others retain a separate identity, when they wish neither to assimilate nor amalgamate? Dashefsky (1976) has reviewed some of the literature on identity and identification that illustrates the many dimensions attributed to this concept:

> Rosen (1965:17) has ... argued that an individual may identify ... with others on three levels: First, one may identify oneself with some important person in one's life, e.g., parent or a friend (i.e., significant other). Second, one may identify oneself with a group from which one draws one's values, e.g., family or coworkers (i.e., reference group). Last, one may identify oneself with a broad category of persons, e.g., an ethnic group or occupational group (i.e., a social category). It is on the third level that ethnic identification occurs.

Our discussion of ethnic identification touches on six conditions for its maintenance: ecological territory, ethnic institutions, ethnic culture, historical symbols, ideology, and charismatic leadership. These are some of the basic components of an ethnic community. Taken together, according to Gordon (1964), they provide a group of individuals with a shared sense of peoplehood.

Ecological Territory

Successful maintenance of a separate language and culture is difficult and unlikely without a sufficiently large ethnic concentration in a given area. Minorities need territory which they control and within which their offspring may perpetuate their heritage. This can best be done in a tightly knit community. Community space becomes an arena in which ethnic activities occur and are shared.

Joy (1972) demonstrates how, in Québec, the French retain control of the provincial territory, where they perpetuate their language and culture through religious, educational, and political institutions. French scholars such as Rioux

(1971) have shown how, historically, the French were the first Europeans to settle along the St. Lawrence River; Miner (1939) describes beautifully the community life of St. Denis in the 1930s; Gold (1975), who studied St. Pascal, describes how the modern rural French parish has changed, yet how the territory remains very important for maintaining rural French culture.

The Hutterites provide a good example of a rural ethnic community with extensive boundary maintenance and controlled exposure to outsiders. Indian reserves also represent examples of ethnic territorial segregation. Chinatowns are urban examples. Most minorities cannot maintain such exclusive control over a territory; it is a goal, however, to which many minority groups seems to aspire.

Ethnic block settlements are common. The Germans are heavily concentrated in the Kitchener-Waterloo area of Ontario; and the Ukrainians settled in the Aspen Belt of the Prairies. Richmond (1972) found extensive residential segregation in Toronto; Kalbach (1981) found historical Jewish and Italian settlement patterns in Toronto.

Ethnic Institutions

Forces of attraction are generated by the social organization of ethnic communities within their established social boundaries. Integration into one's own ethnic community, supported by the institutional completeness of the group, reinforces solidarity. (Breton, 1964) Institutional completeness is important because the extent to which a minority can develop its own social system with control over its own institutions is the extent to which the group's social actions will take place within the system. Religious, educational, and welfare institutions are crucial. Driedger and Church (1974), for example, found that in Winnipeg, as compared to other ethnic groups, the French and Jews maintained the most complete set of religious, educational, and welfare institutions. These two groups were also the most segregated, in St. Boniface and the North End respectively, where they had established their institutions. The French and the Jews identified with both territory and ethnic institutions. Residential segregation and ethnic institutional completeness tended to reinforce one another.

Ethnic Culture

Kurt Lewin (1948) proposed that the individual needs to achieve a firm, clear sense of identification with the heritage and culture of the group in order to find a secure ground for a sense of well-being. Territory becomes a crucible within which solid ethnic institutions can be built and within which ethnic culture should be protected.

Factors that influence ethnic cultural identity have been studied by numerous scholars. Driedger (1975), for example, found at least six factors that tended to influence group adherence to culture: language use, endogamy (marriage within the group), choice of friends, membership in religious and voluntary organizations, and parochial school attendance. French and Jews in Winnipeg, who were more residentially segregated and who maintained their ethnic institutions to a greater degree than comparable ethnic groups, also ranked high on attendance at parochial schools, endogamy, and choice of in-group friends. Isajiw (1983) found similar cultural maintenance in Toronto.

CONFORMITY Vs. PLURALISM

Examination of territorial, institutional, and cultural identity factors suggests that they tend to reinforce each other.

Historical Symbols

Villagers may perpetuate their ethnic social structure and community as an end in itself, without much reference to their past and future. Among ethnic urbanites, however, a knowledge of origins and pride in heritage would seem to be a necessary underpinning for sustaining a sense of ethnic purpose and direction. Without such pride and knowledge the desire to perpetuate tradition rapidly diminishes. Jewish children experience a ritualized version of their ethnic history expressed in such symbols as festivals, fast days, candles, food habits, and other commemorative observances. Such historical symbols create a sense of belonging, purpose, and a continuing tradition that is important and worth perpetuating.

A comparison of identity among members of seven ethnic groups in Winnipeg indicated strong French and Jewish in-group affirmation and low in-group denial. (Driedger, 1976) Jewish and French students were proud of their in-groups, felt strongly bound to them, wished to remember them, and contributed to them. Ukrainian, Polish, and German students felt less positively about their ethnic groups and also were more inclined to deny their ethnicity.

Ideology

For many members of the younger generation of ethnics, territory, culture, and ethnic institutions seem less intrinsically valuable than for their elders. A political or religious ideology, however, can supply purpose and impetus. It can promote values considered more important than cultural and institutional ones. Identification with religious beliefs or a political philosophy adds force and point to the question: What is the meaning of this territory, these institutions, and this ethnic culture, and why should they be perpetuated or changed?

Charismatic Leadership

The importance of charisma is demonstrated in a variety of minority movements: Martin Luther King Jr. and Malcolm X among American blacks, René Lévesque among the Québecois, Harold Cardinal among Alberta Indians, to name a few. Individuals with a sense of mission often adapt an ideology to a current situation, linking it symbolically with the past, and using the media effectively to transform the present into a vision of the future. Such charismatic leaders ordinarily use emotional non-rational means to gain a following. Designed to create trust, these methods forge a cohesive loyalty to both leader and in-group. The leader's commitment is passed on to the followers, resulting in new potential for change. In the beginning, the group may not be particularly oriented to territory, institutions, culture, and heritage. But slowly, as the movement ages, such structural features become more important.

Although there may be many more dimensions with which ethnic minorities identify, we have noted that territory, institutions, culture, heritage, ideology, and leaders are crucial. Different ethnic groups identify more with some of these dimensions than others, and some are more successful than others in maintaining a distinct community. The Hutterites have successfully survived in a rural setting, for example, and the Jews have for centuries done so effectively in the city. Any study of ethnic identity needs to explore such dimensions and foci of ethnic identification.

DISCRIMINATION: FORCED SEPARATION

This discussion of ethnic identity has illustrated mechanisms of ethnic maintenance. There also are negative variations that include social distance, stereotypes, prejudice, and discrimination, all of which impede assimilation into the larger society and result in involuntary separation.

Social Distance

When Simmel (1950) introduced the concept of *social distance*, he posited, among other relationships, the existence of an inverse association between in-group solidarity and social distance from out-groups. The closer one feels to the group, the farther one feels from others. Simmel's discussion of "the stranger" includes both the nearness and farness dimensions. Consider these minority Canadians: immigrants coming as strangers to a new land; French Canadians visiting other parts of Canada and feeling like strangers; native Indians segregated on reserves away from the urban industrial mainstream; Jewish Canadians who feel they are practicing their religion among a strange and seemingly alien majority. How can these strangers who strongly identify with their in-group culture and tradition retain their own social world, or "ground of identification" as Lewin (1948) would put it, and at the same time relate securely to others? Minority strangers entering the environment of others can only be expected to be secure if grounded in an ethnic reference group, or if socially and psychologically motivated by the norms of such an in-group. Hence "distance" and "security" are linked.

Levine et al. (1976:835) contend that "Simmel's utilization of the metaphor 'distance' was by no means restricted to his pages on the 'stranger.' It constitutes a pervasive and distinctive feature of his sociology as a whole." They summarize Simmel's meanings attached to distance as:

1. ecological attachment and mobility
2. emotional involvement and detachment
3. the extent to which persons share similar qualities and sentiments.

Simmel himself also thought that distance could be expressed in many ways. While recent work has attempted to sort out these meanings, Bogardus (1959:12) chose to use "the degree of sympathetic understanding that functions between person and person, between person and group, and between group and group" as his measure of social distance. Although distance as exemplified here may be imposed by dominant majorities, it also has long been a tactic that minorities may adopt to preserve their identity by preventing the assimilating and acculturating effects of contact from occurring.

Stereotyping

Allport (1954:187) says that a stereotype differs from a category in that it is a fixed idea that accompanies a category and carries additional judgements or "pictures" about a category or group. A stereotype may be either positive or negative, and is often used to justify behaviour toward a specific group. Negative stereotypes of racial and ethnic groups have been and are widespread. Jews are "shrewd and ambitious"; Italians are "heavily involved in crime"; Irishmen are "drunkards"; native Indians are "lazy and undependable"; Germans are "aggressive and boorish" — all stereotypes, all negative. Positive stereotypes are also numerous: Asiatics "stress family loyalty"; Hutterites are "very religious"; the British are "efficient." (Driedger and Clifton, 1984)

Mackie (1974) examined a group of 590 adults selected from organizations in Edmonton and found that they had an overwhelming negative image of Canadian Indians as sharing neither the work nor success values of the surrounding Canadian society. Stereotypes of Hutterites, in contrast, were mostly positive: clean-living people, religious, hardworking, thrifty, rural, law abiding, pacifistic, sexually moral, sober; but also exclusive, opposed to higher education, old-fashioned, disliked. Mackie's sample members also expressed flattering images of Ukrainians. On the other hand, Berry et al. (1977) found that in Québec images of Ukrainians were not nearly so positive, reflecting the fact that stereotypes are relative to group, time, and place.

Prejudice

Words change over time, and *prejudice* has come to mean thinking ill of others without sufficient warrant. While biases can be both positive and negative, we usually think of ethnic prejudice today as mostly negative. Allport (1954), however, suggests that such prejudgements are prejudice only if they are not reversible in light of new facts.

Although social distance from others may be the result of a desire to maintain a separate ethnic identity, it can also, as we have observed, stem from negative attitudes. Berry, et al (1977) found that those who favoured multiculturalism in Canada also tended to have more positive attitudes toward others. Canadians of British and French origin, however, although they tended to have fairly positive attitudes toward each other, were less positive about out-group association. Those who were more ethnocentric still, such as French Quebeckers and British Maritimers, tended to be more negative toward new immigrants and multiculturalism. The 11 percent of Driedger and Mezoff's (1980) respondents who wished to have the Jews only as visitors to Canada, or to bar them entirely from the country, certainly showed prejudicial attitudes. Indeed, in that same study a majority of the Jewish student respondents reported that they had experienced prejudice in Winnipeg. Similarly, Cardinal (1969) claims that prejudice against Canadian Indians is common and occasionally reflected in the media. Tienhaara (1974) found in her analysis of post-war Canadian Gallup polls that polls taken in 1943, during the war, showed that a majority of Canadians thought the Japanese living on the Pacific Coast of Canada during World War II should be sent inland involuntarily. A national poll in 1961 showed that over one-half of the Canadians questioned thought we should continue to restrict non-whites. These polls indicate that, depending on historical situations and social events, there are attitudes of prejudice among many Canadians.

Discrimination

Allport (1954:50) argues that "discrimination comes about only when we deny to individuals or groups of people the equality of treatment which they wish."

Hagan (1977) suggests that in this connection four distinctions are important: differential treatment, prejudicial treatment, denial of desire, and disadvantaging treatment. Obviously, we cannot treat everyone equally; distinctions must be made. This constitutes differential treatment. Prejudicial treatment will likely lead to unfair teatment. Denial of desire involves placing restrictions on the aspirations of some members of society, such as their desire to belong to any club they can afford. Disadvantageous treatment is a clear form of discrimination which may take a variety of forms. (Allport, 1954)

Anti-locution, or verbal expressions such as jokes and name calling, would be the mildest form. Avoidance is more severe in that prejudiced persons restrict their own movements so that they do not come into contact with undesirables. Discrimination is still more intense in that now acts of inequality, of disadvantage, extend to the ethnic or minority victim, including disadvantages in citizenship, employment, education, housing, or public accommodation. Physical attack, such as ejection from a community, lynchings, massacres, and genocide would be the severest forms. Until recently blacks were still lynched in the United States, massacres of native Indians occurred in Canada, and the Jewish holocaust is still fresh in our memories. Religious and political persecution are constants in Northern Ireland, the Middle East, and elsewhere.

Driedger and Mezoff (1980) found in their sample of 2520 high school students in Winnipeg that perception of discrimination varied by ethnic groups. About one-third of the students reported discrimination. Jews, Italians, and Poles perceived the greatest discrimination in the classroom and in textbooks. The Jews reported vandalism, and physical attacks as well. Blacks and Asians often report discrimination.

During World War II the Canadian government forcibly evacuated Japanese Canadians from the west coast and sent them inland because of a perceived threat to national security. The Chinese were legally restricted from voting and denied access to public places. Laws were passed in Alberta to restrict the expansion of Hutterite colonies. Racism is increasingly reported in urban centers such as Toronto and Montréal. Nova Scotia has discriminated against blacks. Many who are able to gain control of the political and economic institutions use such power to their own advantage and often forget about the rights and aspirations of the weak. This denies many members of minorities equal access to opportunities of the majority.

III. THE ASSIMILATIONIST-PLURALIST CONTINUUM

Having explained the ideal assimilationist and pluralist polarities and reviewed various processes for either maintaining voluntary minority identity or keeping minorities at a social distance, we now consider how these polarities have been modified in practice. In figure 9.1 we have placed the two opposing perspectives at opposite ends, and have plotted six intermediate variables between them, three on the assimilationist and three on the pluralist sides. We propose that in Canadian society all these varied processes have operated, but which ones come to the fore depend on region, time, ideology, and ethnicity. We shall begin with modified assimilationist and move toward modified pluralist modes of thought. This exercise should provide further insights into how rights, justice, and the welfare of minorities are affected by differential perspectives.

CONFORMITY Vs. PLURALISM

**Figure 9.1
The Assimilationist-Pluralist Continuum**

CONFORMITY
(Assimilation)

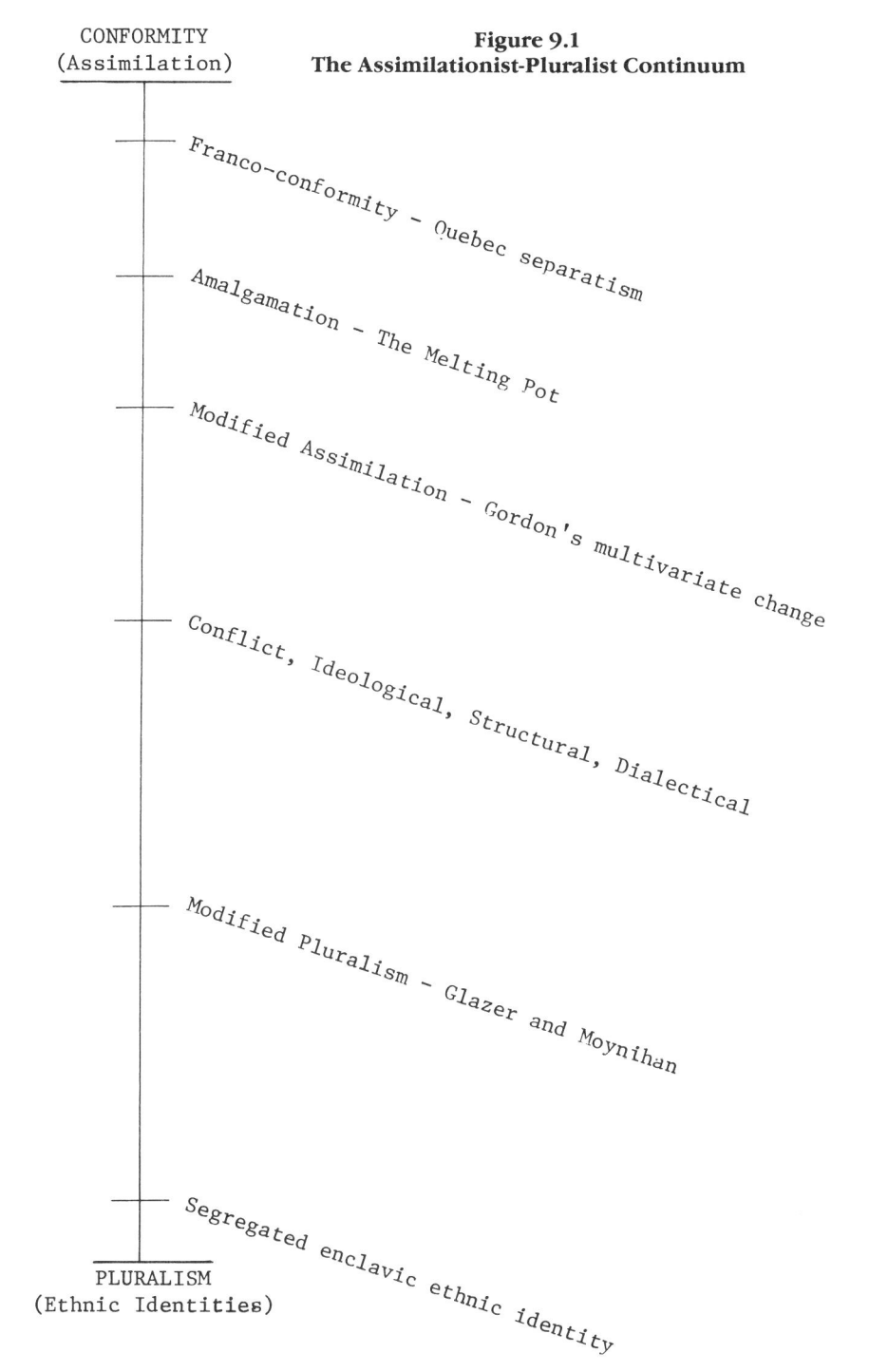

- Franco-conformity – Quebec separatism
- Amalgamation – The Melting Pot
- Modified Assimilation – Gordon's multivariate change
- Conflict, Ideological, Structural, Dialectical
- Modified Pluralism – Glazer and Moynihan
- Segregated enclavic ethnic identity

PLURALISM
(Ethnic Identities)

FRANCO-CONFORMITY: QUÉBECOIS SEPARATISM

The separatist goal for Québec emphasizes conformist thinking and comes as close as possible to exemplifying the assimilationist pole. Franco-conformity is based on the same premises as Anglo-conformity with a few nuances to fit French Canadian survival. If they were a majority in Canada, Franco-conformists would assume assimilation of others into the French milieu just as Anglo-conformists do. However, since they are a minority everywhere except in Québec, they seek to promote a "French Nation" in the province of Québec. The early French elite and clergy made arrangements with Ottawa to maintain their rural French parishes; Québec federalists seek to influence federal politics in ways which will benefit a French Québec; and Québec separatists want to take Québec out of confederation so that they have sovereign control over a new "French Nation."

The basic assumption of sociologists such as Rioux (1971) is that the French people, language, culture, organizations, and history must be dominant in one territory if it is to transform the whole into a French fact. This can best be done by creating a new sovereign nation to promote the aspirations of 80 percent who are already of French origin. Indeed, the Parti Québecois have already legislated Bill 101 which will perpetuate the dominance of the French language and force immigrants to comform increasingly to the goal of a French identity. These actions of French Québec are very similar to those of the Anglo-Celtic segment who hold similar perspectives on conformity and who are dominant in the rest of Canada.

The French emphasis on an alternative culture opens the door to multiculturalism. Logically, if the British and French may perpetuate their heritage, why then should not others be able to do so? If the British and French claim a "right" to special privilege through "charter status," because they were the first Europeans in the confederation, why should not native Indians who were here much earlier also enjoy such a right? Our democratic sense of equality helps make these kinds of questions appropriate ones to raise.

French Canadian concern for enhancing Franco-conformity is also reflected in their negative views on multiculturalism. (Berry, Kalin and Taylor, 1977:74, 147, 269) Comparing five regions of Canada (Atlantic, Québec, Ontario, Prairies, British Columbia), Berry et al found that Quebeckers were less accepting of immigrants and least interested in multiculturalism. They support multicultural programs the least. (Berry, Kalin and Taylor, 1976:149, 150, 152, 156) These views suggest that French Canadians perceive their own privileges as a "right," which others may not enjoy to the same extent. Multiculturalism appears to pose a threat to their own French aspirations. So we argue here that the Québecois separatist movement is a form of Franco-conformity which is seeking to establish a separate nation so that the French can gain political power over the area, and if necessary, force the "French fact" upon all other minorities in the province. This perspective is very similar to the Anglo-conformity pole presented in the beginning of this paper, where assimilation of others to the major core is a desired goal.

AMALGAMATION: THE MELTING POT

Amalgamation scenarios differ from those of assimilation by positing that immigrant groups will be synthesized into a new group. The evolutionary process is the same as that of assimilation, but the end result is a melting pot amalgam different from any of the groups involved. This concept is frequently taken by Americans to be typical of their society.

Herberg (1955) contends, however, that in America the Protestants, Catholics, and Jews never have "melted." Nor have they in Canada. The racial component, well represented in Canada by native peoples and in America by 25 million blacks, seems not to be melting very noticeably either. Certainly the French in Quebec are a bulwark against amalgamation. The prophesied synthesis is slow in coming in Canada. And, in the United States, where the melting pot theory is often applied, more and more scholars are having doubts about its usefulness. (Kallen, 1924; Herberg, 1955; Newman, 1973) Canada's relatively open immigration policy has provided the potential opportunity for many peoples to contribute to a melting pot. The synthesis of British, French, Germans, Ukrainians, Italians, Canadian Indians, and others into a recognizable national character has been a long time coming.

Berry and associates (1977:36-38) note that 80.5 percent of their national sample of respondents who were of British origin preferred the identification of "Canadian." They also found that "Canadian" was most popular in the most easterly Atlantic provinces where the population is mainly of British origin, suggesting that respondents of British origin chose to relabel their loyalties by adopting the "Canadian" label. As the largest and most powerful group, the British can afford the "ethnic" label, hoping that others will join them under a new national label strongly influenced by British history, culture, and language. This is an interesting modification of Anglo-conformity, which begins to move toward a modified centre.

MODIFIED ASSIMILATION

In his *Assimilation in American Life*, Milton Gordon (1964) suggests that assimilation is not a single social process but a number of subprocesses which he groups under the headings "cultural" and "structural." Cultural assimilation refers to acceptance by the incoming group of modes of dress, language, and other cultural characteristics of the host society. Structural assimilation depends upon the degree to which immigrants enter the social institutions of the society and the degree to which they are accepted into them by the majority. Gordon argues that assimilation may occur more in the economic, political, and educational arenas, whereas assimilation may be resisted more in the areas of religion, family, and recreation. It would seem, therefore, that assimilation and pluralism may occur simultaneously, depending on the dimension of activity examined. But, as Newman (1973:43) points out: "Gordon contends (that) once structural assimilation is far advanced, all other types of assimilation will naturally follow."

Gordon's multivariate approach forces scholars out of a unilinear rut. However, each of the seven stages or types of assimilation he identifies tended to be oriented toward either an assimilationist or an amalgamationist target. Cultural, structural, marital, identificational, civic, attitudinal, and behavioural reception are viewed as seven distinctive forms of assimilation, and different ethnic groups represent variations in the process of decline.

Gordon's major contribution is in this complex, multilinear, multidimensional view of the assimilation process. It is regarded as a considerable improvement on Park's assimilation cycle. Although Gordon was concerned with assimilation as such, and though he did not dwell on pluralism, he did admit to the existence of many manifestations of pluralism in such areas as religion, the family, and recreation. Hutterites emphasize religion, for example, and Jews, the family.

CONFLICT: DIALECTIC OF INCOMPATIBLES

Scenarios of assimilation and amalgamation assume an ordered society, for the most part in a state of equilibrium, within which social change and group conflict are but temporary dislocations. By contrast, the scenarios of pluralism and modified pluralism allow for a great measure of inherent conflict in the social system. But Georg Simmel (1950) contends that conflict and consensus are present in every society and that all social phenomena reflect a combination of opposed tendencies. Informed by these contrasting perspectives, we have placed conflict in the middle of the continuum.

The conflict focus, although concerned with structure and institutions, emphasizes processes of ethnic group relations. Since conflict implies the meeting of people with dissimilar or opposite values and norms, it includes competition, confrontation, and argumentation. Following Dahrendorf (1959: 206-207), we define social conflict as "all relations between sets of individuals that involve an incompatible difference of objectives (with regard to positions, resources, or values)."

One way to view conflict is as Marx did in *The Communist Manifesto*: The history of all hitherto existing society is the history of class struggles. Marx saw the relationship between the bourgeoisie and proletariat as a class struggle between opposites. Marx viewed this struggle as much more serious than ethnic territorial squabbles. (Bottomore and Rubel, 1963) Most ethnic groups in Canada do not aspire to such an extensive power struggle, although the Front de Libération du Québec movement in Québec exemplified one that did. And the Parti Québecois may be regarded as a milder form of conflict-oriented institution seeking control of Québec's economic, political, and social institutions via a referendum to secede.

Although conflict occasionally may take the form of revolution and secession, it most often is present in less extreme forms. When many subgroups and a multitude of cultures exist side by side they will maintain distinct identities, which provides a potential for conflicts of values, territorial interests, and power relationships. John Jackson (1975) studied French-English relations in the Windsor, Ontario area and found considerable competition and conflict. By the same token, Québec's "Quiet Revolution," the native peoples' quest for equal rights, and the relations between adjacent ethnic prairie communities all demonstrate a constant potential for conflict. Hutterite expansion into more of the Alberta farmlands and subsequent restrictive legislation, the conflict of French and other ethnic groups over language rights and education during the Manitoba School question, Bill 101, and the conflicts of Italians and recent immigrants with the Québec government over English education in Montréal all exemplify ethnic countercultural conflicts. (Hostetler and Huntington, 1967; Richmond, 1972)

MODIFIED PLURALISM

Glazer and Moynihan (1963) distinguished four major events in New York history which they felt structured a series of ethnic patterns in that city. The first was the shaping of the Jewish community under the impact of the Nazi persecution of Jews in Europe and the establishment of the state of Israel. The second was a parallel, if less marked, shaping of a Catholic community by the reemergence of the Catholic school controversy. The third was the migration of southern blacks to New York following World War I and continuing through the 1950s. The fourth was the influx of Puerto Ricans during the fifteen years following World War II. Their point was that the melting pot did not function in New York. Further, although throughout American history the merging of various streams of population, differentiated from one another in origin, religion, and outlook, seemed always to lie just ahead, the expected comingling has yet to occur.

Glazer and Moynihan suggest that blacks are often discriminated against and their assimilation has been resisted by the majority. In contrast, the Jews, with their distinct religion, generally have no wish to assimilate, whereas the Puerto Ricans and Irish Catholics exemplify combinations of these variations. Thus, over time they change but remain distinct ethnic groups. Modified pluralism takes account of change, as does assimilation and amalgamation, but it also provides for degrees of pluralism often experienced by such Canadian groups as native Indians, Italians, French Canadians, Jews, Asiatics, and many others.

SEGREGATED ENCLAVIC ETHNIC IDENTITY

The pluralist end of ethnic identity is perhaps best illustrated by the Hutterites, Québecois, and Indians on reserves in rural areas, and the Chinatowns, Jews, and blacks in urban ghettoes. But how do Hutterites, Jews, native Indians, French, and others retain a separate identity when they wish neither to assimilate nor amalgamate? Contrariwise, are there other racial and ethnic groups that may wish to assimilate into Canadian society but are not permitted to do so? These are the two sides of the identity coin: voluntary and involuntary maintenance of ethnic identity.

Consideration of the assimilationist-pluralist continuum reveals that the two opposite ideal poles are seldom, if ever, present in reality. The major situations and experiences of ethnic minorities are between these two extremes.

IV. FINDING A CONCEPTUAL MODEL

The discussion so far reflects the great complexity of the whole process. Indeed, ordering the forms on one continuum implies a unidimensionality that may be oversimplified. Therefore, we suggest that a voluntary-involuntary axis be added in describing the process of minority group status. The degree of voluntarism involved in either wanting to assimilate and to become a part of the majority (blacks in the U.S.A.) or wanting to remain apart and separate (the Hutterites) is important. Although Hutterites could have assimilated relatively easily, they set up plural identity barriers so that this would not happen. On the other hand, many blacks in the United States have wanted to become a more integrated part

Figure 9.2 — A Conformity-Pluralist Conceptual Model

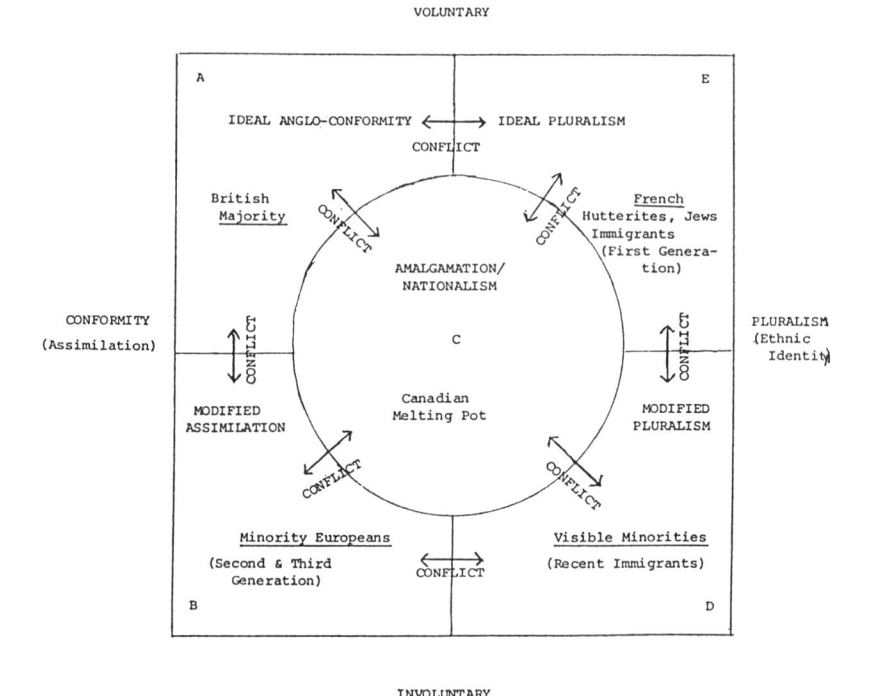

```
                              VOLUNTARY

        A                                                    E
              IDEAL ANGLO-CONFORMITY ←——→ IDEAL PLURALISM
                              CONFLICT

            British                              French
            Majority                             Hutterites, Jews
                                                 Immigrants
                                                 (First Genera-
                          AMALGAMATION/          tion)
                          NATIONALISM

CONFORMITY                       C                        PLURALISM
(Assimilation)                                            (Ethnic
                          Canadian                        Identity)
                          Melting Pot
            MODIFIED                             MODIFIED
            ASSIMILATION                         PLURALISM


            Minority Europeans                   Visible Minorities
            (Second & Third         ←——→         (Recent Immigrants)
             Generation)            CONFLICT
        B                                                    D

                              INVOLUNTARY
```

of society but often have been rejected because of their race and prevented through prejudice and discrimination from doing so. Figure 9.2 depicts the two axes in one model.

When we plot the two axes in figure 9.2, we arrive at five (A, B, C, D, E) cells which summarize some of the discussion which has gone before. Cell A represents the ideal Anglo-conformity pole. Assimilationists assume that most or all other non-British groups eventually will assimilate to the majority or plurality Anglo-Celtic core without too much conflict. They will be attracted to the British way of life, and will conform to this linguistic, cultural, and ideological ethnic core.

Cell B represents the condition of older, mostly north European groups such as the Germans, Dutch, and Scandinavians who have lived in Canada for a number of generations. They have adopted the English language (often involuntarily in the beginning) and are now beginning to conform and accommodate to either an assimilationist (moving toward Cell A) or amalgamationist (Cell C) goal, increasingly leaving their own ethnic identity behind.

Cell C represents the middle of the assimilationist-pluralist continuum where the battle for identity takes place. This sphere seeks to attract the majority (Cell A) as well as other minorities (Cells B, D, E) alike, to an amalgamation, where the outcome will be a melting pot (A + B + D + E — C) in which all groups A, B, D, and E will become a new entity, different from any individual ethnic contributor. Such an outcome will not occur without considerable struggle and conflict.

The visible minorities, especially recent immigrants, are in Cell D, because it is the opposite of A with respect to both conformity and volition. These non-caucasian minorities may wish to join the Canadian society or assimilate into the majority British stream, but are often prevented from doing so by the other groups because of prejudice and discrimination. Potential for conflict is great. Thus they are often forced to remain in a separate pluralist position involuntarily. Native Indians, Asians, blacks, and Indopakistanis are often a part of this cell.

Finally, Cell E represents the pluralist end of the axis, and groups such as the French, Hutterites, Jews, and, often, first-generation immigrants, fall into this category. These groups wish to maintain a separate identity voluntarily, and resist conformity to the majority group and assimilation into it. They also resist amalgamation with Canadian society, seeking to retain a separate linguistic, cultural, ideological, and/or regional identity.

The model just presented is an attempt to combine all the perspectives and theories of assimilation and pluralism into one model. Some of the major ethnic groups in Canada also have been placed into this frame. It suggests that while the Anglo-conformity (Cell A) and pluralist (Cell E) magnets seek to attract recruits to their respective poles, a great deal of conflict occurs in the middle, where the battle for identities takes place. Those who move toward this central fray (Cell C) are liable to come out of it changed in many respects, although with modified forms of identity, amalgamation, and assimilation (as found in Cells B and D).

CONCLUSION

We began by saying that "Assimilationist" and "Pluralist" models have been developed to describe relationships between the majority (Anglo-Celtic) and minority groups in Canada. Many early leaders assumed that the core of Canada would be Anglo-Celtic, and that other immigrants would assimilate into a British Canada.

During the 1960s, the Royal Commission on Bilingualism and Biculturalism increasingly recognized two ethnic solitudes (British and French), and recommendations were made to promote these two European languages and cultures in Canada. However, in the first volume, which was devoted to languages, there already was a minority report by one of the commissioners, Rudnyckyj, recommending recognition of minority languages in Canada. The eventual volume four, *Other Ethnic Groups*, had not been foreseen when the Commission was formed. By the 1970s Trudeau pronounced Canada a multicultural nation with a bilingual framework.

These events illustrate that considerable change is taking place between the assimilationist and pluralist polarities, and that it is necessary to think of these changes more in terms of an assimilationist-pluralist continuum where different groups, under varied conditions, are attracted to one or the other of two ideal poles. Franco-conformity, amalgamation, modified assimilation, conflict, modified pluralism, and segregated enclavic identity exemplify various intermediate alternatives along with an assimilationist-pluralist continuum.

We discussed the preconditions necessary for the existence of the separate minorities needed for a plural society. Both voluntary and involuntary conditions for pluralism were explored. A segregated territory, separate ethnic institutions, and ethnic culture were considered essential conditions in rural areas. We suggested that urban ethnics needed to add historical symbols, a religious or political ideology, and charismatic leadership to make pluralism work in the city.

On the other hand, a majority society often forces a plural existence upon some minorities by creating social distance through stereotypes, prejudice, and discrimination. Racial minorities especially seem to suffer inequities which force them into separate ghettoes, creating involuntary pluralism.

We suggested that voluntary and involuntary conditions could be included with the assimilationist-pluralist continuum to form a five-cell conformity-pluralist conceptual model. We proposed three outcomes or ends (assimilation, amalgamation and pluralism). In the case of assimilation, minorities lose their separate identities and become like the majority group. In the case of amalgamation, all melt into one pot, with no one remaining distinct. In the case of pluralism, each group has a right to maintain a distinct identity if it has the will and can maintain a distinctive structure. There will be conflict when any of the groups are expected to change into something else. To maintain a separate identity also involves considerable conflict, because remaining separate when others beckon is not easy. Visible minorities, who wish to join the majority stream but are not permitted to do so fully, will create further conflict.

Americans stress individual rights for all and guarantee such rights legally. The new Canadian Charter of Rights, in addition to providing for individual rights, also provides some group rights for the two charter groups and Canada's Indians. Assimilationists find it difficult to grant minorities the right to remain distinctive; pluralists tend to assume that any group in Canada has a right to a distinctive identity if it so chooses.

REFERENCES

Allport, Gordon W. *The Nature of Prejudice.* New York: Doubleday, 1954.

Berry, John W., Rudolf Kalin and Donald W. Taylor. *Multiculturalism and Ethnic Attitudes in Canada.* Ottawa: Supply and Services Canada, 1977.

Bogardus, Emory S. *Social Distances.* Los Angeles: Antioch Press, 1959.

Bottomore, T.B. and Maximilian Rubel. *Karl Marx.* Middlesex, England: Pelican Books, 1963.

Breton, Raymond, "Institutional Completeness of Ethnic Communities and Personal Relations to Immigrants." *American Journal of Sociology.* 1964, 70:193-205.

Cardinal, Harold. *The Unjust Society: The Tragedy of Canada's Indians.* Edmonton: M.G. Hurtig, 1969.

Dahrendorf, Rolf. *Class and Class Conflict in Industrial Society.* Palo Alto, California: Stanford University Press, 1959.

Dashefsky, Arnold. *Ethnic Identity in Society.* Chicago: Rand McNally, 1976.

Dawson, C.A. *Group Settlement: Ethnic Communities in Canada.* Toronto: Macmillan of Canada, 1936.

Driedger, Leo. "In Search of Cultural Identity Factors: A Comparison of Ethnic Students." *Canadian Review of Sociology and Anthropology.* 1975, 12:150-162.

Driedger, Leo. "Ethnic Self Identity: A Comparison of Ingroup Evaluations." *Sociometry.* 1976, 39:131-141.

Driedger, Leo and Glenn Church. "Residential Segregation and Institutional Completeness: A Comparison of Ethnic Minorities." *Canadian Review of Sociology and Anthropology* 1974, 11:30-52.

Driedger, Leo and Rodney A. Clifton. "Ethnic Stereotypes: Images of Ethnocentrism, Reciprocity or Dissimilarity?" *Canadian Review of Sociology and Anthropology.* 1984, 21:287-301.

Driedger, Leo and Richard Mezoff. "Ethnic Prejudice and Discrimination in Winnipeg High Schools." *Canadian Journal of Sociology.* 1980, 6:1-17.

Glazer, Nathan and Daniel P. Moynihan. *Beyond the Melting Pot.* Cambridge, Massachusetts: M.I.T. Press, 1963.

Gold, Gerald. *St. Pascal.* Montréal: Holt, Rinehart and Winston, 1975.

Gordon, Milton M. *Assimilation in American Life.* New York: Oxford University Press, 1964.

Hagan, John. "Finding Discrimination: A Question of Meaning." *Ethnicity.* 1977, 4:167-176.

Herberg, Will. *Protestant, Catholic, Jew.* New York: Doubleday, 1955.

Hostetler, John A. and Gertrude Enders Huntington. *The Hutterites in North America.* New York: Holt, Rinehart and Winston, 1967.

Hughes, Everett C., et al., eds. *Race and Culture.* Volume 1, *The Collected Papers of Robert Ezra Park.* Glencoe, Illinois: Free Press, 1950.

Isajiw, Wsevolod W. *Ethnic Identity Retention.* Research Paper 125. Toronto: Centre for Urban and Community Studies, University of Toronto, 1983.

Jackson, John D. *Community and Conflict: A Study of French-English Relations in Ontario.* Montreal: Holt, Rinehart and Winston, 1975.

Joy, Richard J. *Languages in Conflict.* Toronto: McClelland and Stewart, 1972.

Kalbach, Warren E. "Continental Shift: Emergence of the New West." Paper presented at the annual meeting of the Western Association of Sociology and Anthropology, Winnipeg, 1981.

Kallen, Horce M. *Culture and Democracy in the United States.* New York: Liverright, 1924.

Levine, Donald N., Ellwood B. Carter and Eleanor M. Gorman. "Simmel's Influence on American Sociology." *American Journal of Sociology.* 1976, 81:813-845.

Lewin, Kurt. *Resolving Social Conflicts.* New York: Harper, 1948.

Mackie, Marlene. "Ethnic Stereotypes and Prejudices: Alberta Indians, Hutterites and Ukrainians." *Canadian Ethnic Studies.* 1974, 6:39:52.

Miner, Horace. *St. Denis: A French-Canadian Parish.* Chicago: University of Chicago Press, 1939.

Newman, William M. *American Pluralism.* New York: Harper and Row, 1973.

Porter, John. *The Vertical Mosaic.* Toronto: University of Toronto Press, 1965.

----------. *The Measure of Canadian Society: Education Equality and Opportunity.* Toronto: Gage Publishing, 1979.

Richmond, Anthony H. *Ethnic Residential Segregation in Metropolitan Toronto*. Toronto: Survey Research Centre, York University, 1972.

Rioux, Marcel. *Quebec in Question*. Toronto: James Lewis and Samuel, 1971.

Rosen, B.C. *Adolescence and Religion*. Cambridge, Mass.: Schenkman, 1965.

Simmel, Georg. *The Sociology of Georg Simmel*. Ed. Kurt Wolff. Glencoe, Illinois: Free Press, 1950.

Stanley, F.G. *The Birth of Western Canada: A History of the Riel Rebellions*. Toronto: University of Toronto Press, 1960.

Tienhaara, Nancy. *Canadian Views on Immigration and Population: An Analysis of Post-War Gallup Polls*. Ottawa: Manpower and Immigration, 1974.

Vallee, Frank G. "The Sociology of John Porter: Ethnicity as Anachronism." *Canadian Review of Sociology*. 1981, 18:636-650.

10

MINORITIES AND THE CANADIAN VISUAL MEDIA

RONALD S. DICK

INTRODUCTION

Concern among minority groups over what is conceived as a salient media power, variously appraised in terms of past delinquency, present inadequacy, and future potential, and a corresponding responsiveness — enthusiastic or reluctant as the case may be — on the part of the media are facts that can be readily documented. However, many aspects of the interactions between media and minorities and their real effects, positive or negative, are not easily assessed. This is due in part to a certain amount of rhetoric — accusatory, hortatory, inspirational — in both camps, which sometimes confounds aspiration with achievement. It also is due to the troubling ambiguities that continue to obscure actual media effects. "For researchers," one critic has noted, "television's chief significance as a medium has resided in its sheer mass, in its rapid infiltration of everyday ... life, and in the fact that its images, for all their transience, smallness and mediocrity, have been transmitted year after year into the consciousness of viewers." (Kalisch, 1983, VIII). Unfortunately, this understandable awe of a size and availability of audience hitherto unparalleled has not always been followed up by meaningful research to help us decide who may be achieving just what, if anything.[1] Finally, it should be noted that any assessment of media performance with respect to minorities, however broad and tentative, cannot be entirely divorced from a basic favourable or unfavourable attitude to the whole multicultural enterprise. Clearly, if one agrees with the late John Porter that the instruments of "ethnic revival" could easily constitute a radical departure from a society organized on the principle of individual achievement and universalistic judgement, (Porter, 1975, 296) one would probably evaluate media efforts in this area rather differently than if one agreed with T.B.H. Symons, for whom multiculturalism could be the saving grace for a society faced with the ultimate horror of homogenization "à la américaine." (Symons, 1982, 226) And of course it is possible that the media role and contribution might best be judged in a different context altogether than that of simply the advancement of a "multiculturalism policy."

These cautions duly noted, this paper is concerned in rather broad terms with how the media, past and present, have looked to "ethnicity" and how "ethnicity" has looked, in turn, to the media. More specifically, we begin with an overview of the minority complaints against the media. We next consider some aspects of what the media have done by way of response. Lastly, we review some of the ways in which the results have been adjudged by the parties involved.

MINORITIES AND THE MEDIA

It is hardly possible to put a date on the "ethnic revival" if we mean by that term the prolonged period of self-discovery and increasing articulateness on the part of a broad spectrum of visible and ethnic minorities. It is generally agreed that this process owed much to the Civil Rights Movement in the United States and the not-so-Quiet Revolution in Québec. As the "unmeltable ethnics" revived, the long muted voices of minorities began to make themselves heard. One major subject of their comment was the mass media which, during the sixties and seventies, were subjected to a great deal of criticism. That those who felt disinherited by the authorized "charter mythology" should be so concerned with the media was hardly surprising when one considers the awesome power increasingly attributed to these media by the community at large. That power has not lacked for tribunes. Daniel Boorstin, in his *America: The Democratic Experience*, has described television watching as "an addiction comparable only to life itself." Given the statistics about the amount of time the average North American devotes to television watching alone, it is not surprising that popular opinion — and indeed common sense — should attribute a pervasive and perhaps decisive influence to the media as a moulder of attitude and opinion, and not least of bias and prejudice. Nor does the self-image of the media discourage this view. Popular works dealing with the media by their very titles [e.g. *Media, the Second God* (1981); *Movie-Made America* (1979); *The Gods of Antennae* (1976); *Mediacracy* (1975); *Creating Reality: How Television News Distorts Events* (1976); *Mediaworld: Programming the Public* (1977)] cause one to wonder whether almost any problem in social interaction might not be caused or cured by manipulation of the media.

"Manipulation" has been the object of concern and criticism.[2] Has not a tough-minded journalist, Mike Wallace, confessed that the same television news material could, through selection and editing, be made to say exactly opposing things? Has not a respected critic found the potential of the mass media for the control of human beings and nations "greater than the threat of the atomic bomb or any weapon yet devised." (Diamond, 1975, 14) Has not Robert Sklar, in his *Movie-Made America: A Cultural History of the American Movies* (Sklar, 1975), contended that twentieth-century North American life-styles, morality, and even class consciousness largely are "movie-made"? Has not *U.S. News and World Report* ranked media as the third power in the U.S. after the President and the business establishment? As for Canada, has not a Special Committee on the Mass Media undertaken a "massive investigation" of the media in Canada and reported that they have a "pervasive influence" on Canadians. To be on the outs with the media, it might well seem, is to be an outsider indeed.

MINORITY AWARENESS OF MEDIA ROLE

Protagonists of minority groups, who at times have felt penalized by media misrepresentation, bias, or sheer neglect, have readily accepted the media's high estimate of their own potency.[3] Many of the briefs from ethnic groups to the federal or provincial authorities have emphasized that in Canada any real awareness of the reality, as distinct from the concept of multiculturalism, can come for most people only through the media. Those who speak for Canada's expanding visible minorities — soon to number two million — are even more emphatic. "Let's be clear about it," says the black Canadian actress, Salome Bey, "television is our genie of entertainment and our most powerful means of persuasion. The media is the one institution at the epicentre of all our institutions, for it touches them all." (Bey, 1982, 35) In the most recent *Report of the Parliamentary Committee on Visible Minorities* we hear that with respect to the changing racial composition of Canadian cities that "only the media can create an awareness of that change." This view of a critical media role is constant, and is aptly summed up in a brief from the Toronto-based Ad Hoc Committee on Media and Race Relations (1983) to the Special Committee on the Participation of Visible Minorities in Canadian Society which states flatly on its first page "that the media create and perpetuate the images and information that shape our attitudes is a truism."[4]

The real problem, perhaps, is that the study of the actual *effects* of the media remains disconcertingly unproductive of well-anchored conclusions. An early, almost instinctive, uneasiness about the latent power of the media was modified by a considerable body of careful research which suggested that mass communications, including television, functioned far more often than not as an agent of reinforcement. Joseph Klapper has been an articulate proponent of the view that media reinforce existing attitudes, values, and so forth, but do not create them *de novo*.[5] Although the reinforcement concept is still influential,[6] continuing research has supported a concept of the media as a nexus of mediation. This less pessimistic view of the media's capacities is now held rather widely. Thus, Richard Adler has noted that: "Television is not a medium but a mediator between fact and fantasy, between our desire to escape and our need to deal with real problems, between our old values and our new ideas, between our individual lives and the life of the nation and the world." (Adler, 1976, 13)

As just noted Klapper has argued that the principal role of media is to reinforce rather than to create public values and tastes. Of course, he did not mean to imply that the media were either impotent or harmless and was careful to note that "the media's reinforcement effect is politically and socially important, and it reinforces with fine impartiality both socially desirable and socially undesirable predispositions." (Klapper, 1963, 75) Irrespective of whether they create values and attitudes or merely reflect them, or whether they influence singly or in concert with other societal elements, it is clear that media *can* perpetuate both "socially desirable and socially undesirable predispositions." What is constantly reinforced and repeated is strengthened and made more resistant to easy alteration. The result is the phenomenon known as the stereotype. Since negative stereotyping frequently heads the list of minority complaints about the media, a brief glance at this important phenomenon is useful, as is a quick look at the media's unhappy past record in this regard.

STEREOTYPING

Stereotypes have been technically defined as "consensual folk beliefs about the characteristics of social categories." (Mackie, 1974, 39) In terms of ethnic groups, Gardner, Taylor, and Feenstra note "that most studies of ethnic stereotypes operationally define an ethnic stereotype in terms of agreement among members of one group concerning attributes ascribed to some other ethnic group." (Gardner, Taylor, Feenstra, 1970, 321). Why is *negative* stereotyping a danger to society and anathema to minorities? According to John Phelan: "Stereotypes ... are opinions which have become permanent rather than provisional substitutes for knowledge. They act as a barrier against future experience and the assimilation of new evidence. They are fixed and rigid. Being fixed and permanent, stereotypical opinions militate against the knowledge function which is dynamic and adaptive." (Phelan, 1977, 69) Thus, Phelan concludes that although stereotypes may help in the efficient functioning of a group, they can be extremely harmful to a society, delaying, if not preventing progress and adjustment to new majority-minority relations. For Rosemary Gordon, stereotyping is "an analgesic devised by the mind to protect itself against anxiety caused by internal or external threat." (Gordon, 1962, 88-95) Of course, stereotyping can be positive as well as negative. It can glamorize as well as denigrate, make heroes as well as villains. Unfortunately, minorities rarely have been the media's heroes. In the past their stereotypes have been mainly negative, and when the "awakened" minorities looked at the past record of the media, they could hardly be other than appalled.

NEGATIVE STEREOTYPING OF MINORITIES

One beneficial and instructive result of the "ethnic awakening" was the publication of a number of scholarly works casting a critical eye at the media's attitudes to visible and ethnic minorities [See, *inter alia*: Randall Miller's *The Kaleidoscope Lens: Ethnic Images in American Film* (1979); Donald Bogle's *Toms, Coons, Mulattoes, Mammies and Bucks: An Interpretive History of Blacks in American Films* (1973); Thomas Cripps' *Slow Fade to Black: The Negro in American Film, 1900-1942* (1977); Allen L. Woll's *The Latin Image in American Film* (1977); Ralph E. and Natasha A. Friar's *The Only Good Indian ... The Hollywood Gospel* (1972); and Eugene Franklin Wong's *On Visual Media Racism: Asians in the American Motion Pictures* (1977).] Critics like Robert Sklar have shown that from its inception, film on the whole was a liberating force for the majority, acting as an agent of innovation and change, a broadener of horizons, and a solvent for the moral inhibitions and strictures of the past. (Sklar, 1975) But, as the works just cited reveal in devastating detail, over the long half-century when it was by far the most influential medium, the motion picture relentlessly stereotyped, when it didn't ignore, visible and ethnic minorities in extremely negative terms. For example, Eugene F. Wong's comprehensive work, based on a filmography of some 375 titles, shows how an endless stream of films depicted Asians as incorrigibly cunning, sinister, devious, cowardly, sexually immoral, careless of life, given to an especial ruthlessness towards one another, and possessed of a natural gift for complicated crime.[7] Other minorities were equally the victims of negative stereotyping, ranging from the malevolently racist to the offensively paternalistic. For several generations of audiences these stereotypes generated images of the backward, shuffling, inferior (though occasionally amusing) black, of the vindictive and treacherous Indian, of the "folksy" ethnic simpleton, and of the across-the-tracks immigrant — heavily virtuous, eager to put the past away, and forever emitting hosannas to the Statue of Liberty.

The films which these studies analyze were American, but since until very recently the Canadian film market was almost entirely an extension of the American, Canadian audiences were equally exposed to their depiction of minorities. And in fact a large number of these films contained representations of Canadian minorities, Métis, French Canadians, and Indians.[8] Although a few homely virtues were occasionally permitted these groups, by and large they revealed predominantly negative traits: irresponsibility, unreliability, laziness, child-like behaviour, gullibility, the amorality of "children of nature," a marked susceptibility to deception and crime, and a tendency to violent and uncontrollable fits of passion. When one recalls that this pattern of negative stereotypes was persisted in unrelentingly and almost without challenge for fifty years, one can only speculate at the strength of the structure of bias and prejudice left for a later generation to dismantle.[9]

It is all too easy to forget how universal race thinking was until very recently.[10] However, as the potentially lethal consequences of uninhibited racism slowly penetrated the general consciousness, its overt expression became less and less acceptable.[11] In the media there was a steady reduction in the production of the most blatant types of misrepresentation. The type of film described in Pierre Berton's *Hollywood Canada* died, as the author notes, a natural death in the fifties. Clearly there was progress, and there was even, with films like "Crossfire" and "Gentleman's Agreement," the beginnings of a long overdue counter-attack on more subtle aspects of discrimination.

Those who thought that minority groups, because of a relative decline in the more outrageous forms of overt racism, were satisfied with their representation in the visual media were quickly disabused. In the late sixties and through the seventies certain consistent complaints emerged from the many statements, briefs, and hearings which characterized the efforts of minorities to improve their situation in relation to the media. The complaints principally concern the persistence of negative stereotyping, residual racism, ignorance (especially of positive factors about minorities), "invisibility" (i.e., lack of representation both on and in the media), and the misuse or non-use of minority resources in advertising.

Regarding negative stereotyping, one critic noted that "the media in general, and the movie industry in particular ... with an able assist from TV broadcasts (particularly of old Hollywood movies) constantly portray racial and ethnic minorities in the most base and distorted characterizations. It is difficult to combat past stereotypes if the most influential and pervasive medium of them all continues to feature movies which orginated these stereotypes." [Guides to Non-Discriminatory Communication. *Currents*: 1 no. 2, (1983):38-41 No author given.] The persistence of negative stereotypes was further reflected in the limitation put on minority performers in the media. Whereas whites and "anglo-celts" were free to range over the whole spectrum of human character and activity, members of visible and ethnic minorities were apt to find themselves playing "minority roles," with even these hemmed in by preconceived and inaccurate notions. Thus, Wong complained that the media, rather than viewing Asians or blacks as they view majority groups, "have stagnated on race-specific and culture conscious characterizations of people whose assumed racial and cultural affinities are based on descent lines only." (Wong, 1977, 269) And the black Canadian actor, Jeff Henry, observed that "stereotypical images are all caricatures of people who intrinsically lack something — who are only half-human. For non-whites it breeds a sense of inferiority, shame in one's heritage, and lower expectations of achievement." (Henry, 1983, 10)

Minority spokesmen have also pointed to the persistence of residual racism, which has expressed itself in selectivity, attitudes of implicit superiority, paternalism and sentimentality, ethnocentrism, and so forth. With regard to selectivity, for example, it was noted that newspaper headlines and TV news often make it appear that *only* blacks riot. Attitudes of implicit superiority tend to be reflected in news stories in which members of visible minorities are depicted as "welfare consumers," "always in trouble with the police," and "unable to make it even when they get a chance."[12] Ethnic groups also suffer from well-meaning but sometimes embarrassing efforts at counter-stereotyping. The flood of American material — on television, in feature films, daytime serials, and especially situation comedies — now often stand negative stereotypes on their heads and lapse into a demeaning sentimentality, frequently disguised as humour. As a consequence, even today, few representations of visible and ethnic minorities have a natural, genuinely human ring.[13] Many members of minorities feel that decision makers, especially the controllers of job opportunity, are consciously or unconsciously influenced by stereotypes the media have done little to dispel.

Stereotypes and residual racism represent, in the long run, the fruits of a fundamental ignorance of real people, actual situations, and simple facts. In their criticism of the visual media, minority groups have stressed that one of the reasons negative attitudes flourish is that — periodic counter-stereotyping notwithstanding — there is usually little of a positive nature shown to counterbalance them. In the U.S. the Kerner Commission severely criticized the visual media for not having given any real sense of what it is like to be a member of a visible minority, and for having neglected minority culture and history generally. Minority groups in Canada, especially the older ethnic groups, have criticized the Canadian media in much the same terms. Their criticism surfaced in both the Bilingualism and Biculturalism Commission and the Special Senate Committee on the Mass Media. Most groups felt the media had done little to help them retain their threatened sense of cultural identity, to make ethnic cultures more aware of one another, or to make ethnic cultures more familiar to the majority culture. For most Canadians, they complained, the media had failed to provide enough of the substantive detail that would enable them either to better understand minorities or to make the endless and all-too-often ritual references to ethnic groups' "rich cultural heritage" very meaningful. Spokesmen for these groups have expressed the opinion that the visual media can help remedy this situation by making more — substantially more — solid, positive factual material available to the general viewing public.

Yet another charge made by minority leaders concerns their minimal representation in the visual media. For example, a cartoon in *Currents*, a magazine published by the Toronto-based Urban Alliance on Race Relations, shows a young black looking in a mirror and seeing a white face looking back. The caption reads:

> "Mirror, mirror on the wall
> Tell me, do I exist at all?"

This particular cartoon illustrates an article by Henry Gomez entitled, "The Invisible Visibles: Minorities in the Media." (Gomez, 1983, 12) "Invisibility" is a term used to describe either the total absence or token presence of visible minorities in the visual media. Invisibility is so dreaded that one black Canadian actor who preferred not to be quoted told this writer rather wryly that even a negative stereotype was better than complete silence. Given the critical importance ascribed by minority groups to the visual media as perhaps *the* decisive influence in contemporary society, it is not surprising that the actress Salome Bey believes that what is not on TV is not perceived at all. Similarly, Tim Rees, the editor of *Currents*, observed that: "Mass media confer status on those individuals and groups they select for placement in the public eye, telling the viewer or reader who or what is important to know about, think about, or have feelings about. Those who are made visible through the media become worthy of attention and concern; those whom the media ignore remain invisible." (Rees, 1983, 2) Other frequent complaints from minorities regarding their lack of visibility include: (a) a lack of representation among decision makers and holders of the high ground in public and private media organizations; (b) a lack of representation among the "gate keepers" of the media and the production, news-gathering, and writing staffs who control what "goes on" and what does not; (c) an underrepresentation among the technical staffs of the media and the lack of training opportunities to help remedy this situation; and (d) a lack of access to the media as a public forum and an inability to use the media to further minority goals.

Finally, with respect to advertising, most minority criticism has not arisen from hostility to the commercial system as such, but from an uneasy awareness that advertising functions willy-nilly as a pacesetter and seller of attitudes in Canadian society. Among minorities there is a feeling of being left out as actors and consumers alike, of being considered bystanders at the great capitalist barbecue. Further criticisms in this regard have been: that advertisers are dominated by the middle-class affluent white market; that when they use minority actors, they stereotype them (e.g., Indians sell canoes, Chinese sell tea, and blacks sell basketballs); and that although not supported by adequate research, advertisers play a sort of shell game in which the blame for these conditions is passed back and forth among media officials, the public, and themselves.

"MASS CULTURE" VERSUS "CULTURAL PLURALISM"

Minority criticisms of the media have been scarcely flattering to a profession which is by no means indifferent to its "progressive" image, particularly in matters of tolerance and understanding. The same steady liberalizing of attitudes which nourished the "ethnic revival" guaranteed that much of the minority feelings about the media which had accumulated by the early seventies would be found valid, both by the media and the government. The question then became: "What should be done to correct the situation?" As with many issues, two solutions have suggested themselves, one radical, the other "reformist." The first owes much of its ultimate inspiration to the well-known "Frankfurt School" of Adorno and Horkheimer, and makes use of the concept of mass society. Briefly, the argument is that the working classes, instead of opting for socialism, have allowed themselves to be co-opted by capitalism's funfair, the "consumer society." As a result, the structured society with its potential for revolutionary change through class warfare has collapsed into a mass society of frantic consumers dominated from above by business forces. The villains of the piece are the mass media — implacable salesmen of capitalism's goods and manufacturers of opinions that buttress the society and integrate the population into the culture of capitalism. Only radical restructuring, perhaps under a "humanistic socialism" could make the media truly responsive to people's needs. (Swingewood, 1977)

Although a view of society as the prisoner of an omnipotent mass media and its manipulators is too deterministic and pessimistic for the traditional meliorist strain in Anglo-American thought, the anti-capitalist bias remains influential. In Canada, scholars like Wallace Clement (1975:177), and others have made much of the "overlap" between economic and media elites. Although Clement has demonstrated this overlap to his own satisfaction, the omission of the publicly owned media organizations from his calculations has been sharply criticized. (Baldwin, 1977) It is partly because of this omission that he can maintain that since the economic and media elites (as he has defined them) share the same social class and interaction patterns, this suffices to show their ideological affinity as well as the upper-class control (in the interests of corporate capitalism) that is characteristic of the Canadian media. (Clement, 1975, 342) No doubt, if we were to identify the media with our happy hucksters, this radical critique of the media might seem uncomfortably close to the mark.[14] And clearly, the greater the possibility that a monolithic structure exists at the elite level, the less chance for the weaker elements in society, such as visible and ethnic minorities, to get alternative views and interests heard. But is this really the case? Is discrimination really built into the very structure of the society, with media representation a means — conscious or unconscious — of preserving the "status quo"? Or can discriminatory situations be corrected with the help of the media themselves?

The second solution to the problems minorities have experienced with media may be labeled "cultural pluralism." Cultural pluralists take their lead from social theorists such as Edward Shils and Daniel Bell. These theorists reject the idea of mass society as simplistic and argue that the social bases for a genuine pluralism, rather than being weakened by industrialization and technology, have been strengthened by them.[15] The cultural pluralist position would deny that the media (as Clement suggests) present an ideologically uniform message supporting the interests of an economic elite and would argue that John Porter's plural elite model more accurately reflects Canadian reality. In such a society, and in Canada particularly, the possibilities inherent in the highly developed and largely autonomous publicly owned media for qualifying the supposed intellectual hegemony of commercial interests are both substantial and capable of being realized. Most of the problems of minorities, it is argued, including those relating to the media, can be corrected within present structures.

MULTICULTURAL POLICY AND THE MEDIA: RECOMMENDATIONS

Clearly, for a liberal democracy such as Canada, cultural pluralism was and remains the preferred model of social interaction. In the context of the ethnic awakening, the specific expression of this underlying pluralistic commitment, as far as minority issues were concerned, was the federal government's Multicultural Policy. The framers of this policy were certainly aware of media problems and potential, in part because these had been rather forcibly brought to their attention in volume IV of the Report of the Royal Commission on Bilingualism and Biculturalism. The Commission made a number of recommendations. These included expanding the National Film Board's foreign version program and orientating it to Canadian as well as foreign audiences; increasing the program by the Board and by other filmmakers of films dealing with minority groups and multicultural issues; a reconsideration by the CBC of its negative attitude to broadcasting in languages other than English and French; a recognition by its program planners that multiculturalism was now considered to be a policy essential to the preservation of national unity and identity; a loosening by the Canadian Radio-Television Telecommunications Commission of its regulations on non-official languages broadcasting; and the undertaking by the CRTC of research into aspects of minority relations with the media. In time, and from various official quarters (provincial and local as well as federal), there were further recommendations concerning technical training for minority recruits to the media, access to the media for minority groups, a more adequate recognition by advertisers of the existence of minorities, and a number of other matters. In considering the response made to these recommendations, I will focus mainly on the production of visual materials related to aspects of multiculturalism.

VISUAL MEDIA RESPONSE

Since "cultural pluralism" and "multiculturalism" joined "mosaic" in the charter mythology of Canada, there has indeed been an impressive upswing, lasting throughout the seventies and continuing unabated into the eighties, in the production of audiovisual materials related to the multicultural idea. The *Multicultural Film and Video Catalogue* of the Canadian Film Institute lists, down to 1982, some 800 audio-visual items, a very high percentage of them Canadian, and the great majority produced in the seventies. Even this impressive total omits a large number of important items dealing with native peoples, on the grounds that they had already been separately catalogued. TV Ontario's *Multiculturalism Catalogue*, which highlights its own work, lists some 350 items. More specialized listings by groups such as the Cross-Cultural Communications Centre in Toronto include items from an international and radical perspective. And, of course, much relevant audiovisual material was produced before "multiculturalism" became an umbrella term. The National Film Board, in particular, had an excellent record in what was thought of simply as the fight against discrimination [e.g. *A Day in the Night of Jonathan Mole* (1959), *Memorandum* (1965), *Everybody's Prejudiced* (1961)]. To all this must be added a vast array of ephemera — interviews, discussions, debates, news stories, and so forth — which are available on tape. All in all, these constitute a rich variety of materials, perhaps unequalled anywhere, dealing with almost every aspect of multiculturalism, of visible and ethnic minorities, as well as of discrimination and racism.

Limitations of space make it impossible to detail more than a fraction of this torrent of visual materials. Therefore, I will content myself with dipping into the stream here and there to sample the direction and quality of the flow. Accordingly, it should be noted first that there have been a number of TV and film tributes which suggest with unflinching honesty and sympathy just what immigrants to Canada really sacrificed in leaving the old home and what they endured in the new. Outstanding in this respect are a number of the NFB's films in its *Adventures in History Series*. *First Winter* (1981) tells in stark terms the story of an Irish immigrant family in the Ottawa Valley, barely surviving a first winter beyond their worst imaginings and almost beyond their endurance. *Strangers at the Door* (1977) is set early in this century and reminds us how bewildered and homesick immigrants could be preyed upon by their own countrymen, and also how unfeeling were the rigidly applied immigration laws that sometimes broke up families.

A majority can frequently be aided towards a more sympathetic understanding of the character and attitudes of minorities by being given some sense of their history as a group. A number of films have tried to provide such an historical perspective on various groups. For example, *Ukrainians in Quebec (1890 to 1945): The Formative Years* (Ministry of State for Multiculturalism, 1980) stresses the problems of an immigrant group wrestling with two dominant cultures, slow and difficult economic progress, and hostile attitudes during World War I. *A Sense of Family* (NFB-OECA, 1980) outlines the history of East Indian immigration to Canada; and the little-known and badly neglected history of blacks in Canada has finally received some much-needed attention. For example, *Voice of the Fugitive* (NFB-CBC, 1978) looks at the U.S. Fugitive Slave law of the 1850s and the "underground railway" which brought the forebearers of part of today's black community to Canada. *Born Black* (Lenny Little White, 1972) utilizes black communities throughout Canada to document black history in Canada, suggesting that there is much in it for blacks to be proud of.

Perhaps the most universal and often most crippling problem faced by immigrants of any ethnic origin is the problem of imperfect acculturation, of a sometimes prolonged period of transition between an old culture not yet fully abandoned, and a new one not yet fully accepted. The Multicultural Policy has stimulated and supported an impressive number of films that have tried to illuminate complex problems to which earlier "celebratory" films on immigration were largely oblivious. By way of illustration, *This is a Photograph* (NFB, 1971) is a sometimes humorous, sometimes melancholy record of an immigrant's strangeness and uncertainty in a new land. *The Newcomers: 1978* (Nielsen-Ferns, 1979) shows an Italian immigrant achieving a modest success as a grocer who nevertheless wonders whether coming to Canada was right for him after all. *The Visit* (NFB, 1966), on the other hand, shows an immigrant yielding to his apparently incurable homesickness and going back to Italy. He finds it is not always as he remembered it and willingly returns to Canada. *Nikkolina Learning to be Human Series*. Cineflics, 1978) shows the influence on the young of peer pressure and the resulting determination of a young Greek girl to choose new ways over embarrassing old ways. In *Older Sister* (Bortnick, 1981) a Chinese girl is often irritated by her parents' determination to be both Chinese and Canadian, but comes eventually to appreciate their efforts to blend the traditional and the new. Finally, David Suzuki discusses the continuing evolution of minority groups and the sometimes unexpected differences between the assimilation-minded second generation and the more complex outlook of the third. (Nisei-Sansei, OECA, 1973)[17]

The problems that immigrants as individuals can face over the long haul have also received gratifying attention. *Rosanna: Portrait of an Immigrant Woman* (NFB, 1980) shows how slow and hazardous the road to integration can be when personal problems are complicated by the immigrant situation. In *The Newcomers: 1927* (Nielsen-Ferns, 1978) shyness because of language problems causes an elderly Ukrainian to have difficulties with a not unfriendly bureaucracy. And, in *Jobs: How the Brother Feels* (Ontario Ministry of Culture and Recreation, n.d.) visible minority members describe why they feel alienation, scepticism, powerlessness and even fear in their attempts to compete in the job market. Immigration itself has also been treated rather critically in presentations such as *The Sometime Samaritan* (CTV, 1976) and *Conduct Undesirable* (CTV, 1976), where policy is criticized as erratic, opportunistic, and sometimes unjust.

Particularly impressive and useful have been films dealing directly with discrimination, prejudice, and racism. By way of illustration, the history of anti-Semitism in Canada is outlined in *Irving Abella* (TVO — *The Real Story Series*, n.d.). In *Emigrants* (Sec. of State, NFB, 1979) individuals from various visible and ethnic minorities recount first-hand experiences of flagrant discrimination. *Teach Me To Dance* (NFB, 1979) dramatizes anti-Ukrainian prejudices on the Prairies during and after the period of their major influx. *CTV Reports: Racism* CTV, 1977) looks at racism abroad and its disturbing echoes in Canada. *Prejudice and Racism Series* (CTV, 1973-74) examines the mechanics of prejudice in great detail. *Religious Discrimination in Canada* (CTV, 1978-79) is a series dealing with the beliefs of Doukhobors, Mennonites, Hutterites, and Jehovah's Witnesses and the persistent popular and even official attacks on them. The problem of prejudice in the schools is covered from various angles in *Message From a Classroom* (Toronto Board of Education, 1980), a student's view of racism in the public schools, and in *Race Is a Four-Letter Word* (OECA, n.d.). And, in *Canadian Class Structure* (Can., n.d.), Wallace Clement presents his views on the relation between social stratification as a whole and the position of minorities in Canadian society.

CONCLUSION: A MIXED REVIEW

Even on the basis of a limited sampling, it is clear that the visual media response to the multicultural idea may be called, without prejudice, a considerable achievement. In terms of both quality and sophistication of content the contrast with earlier work in this field is especially revealing. The folklore and festival connotation once evoked by the word "ethnic" has been replaced by a genuine empathy and, for the first time, the many-sided story of immigration has been told without being reduced to a patriotic celebration.[18] It was a step forward too that in many of these works minority groups were not simply talked about, but did some of the talking. This feature was particularly effective in a large and important body of work dealing with the native people of Canada.[19]

There have been other encouraging responses by the media to the criticisms made of them by minorities. For those who feel that language retention is fundamental to ethnic minority survival, the relaxation of restrictions on multilingual broadcasting has been gratifying, as has been the remarkable expansion in this area which, by 1981, saw 102 licenses (almost all in the private sector) broadcasting some 881 hours a week in non-official languages. Although the CBC has remained aloof from any non-official language broadcasting (except for its longstanding programs to native people), a modest amount has been done by both CBC and NFB about minority training for employment opportunities in the media. In addition, the principal public visual media organizations have recognized multiculturalism as a continuing concern. The CBC, NFB, and TVO, for example, all have standing internal policies which require program producers and writers to remember the multicultural character of Canada and to support and enhance it where appropriate in their work. In the fields of the feature film and the TV drama series, where dubious stereotypes grow thickest, some respectable efforts at showing Canada's ethnic and cultural diversity in a fairly natural way have been made.[20] Finally, in the important area of advertising, a great deal of meeting, talking, and researching have taken place to confirm that there is indeed a problem. More adequate research seems to have finally convinced advertisers that visible minority actors do not necessarily limit the effectiveness of a commercial. The Advertising Council has communicated this fact to its advertisers, apparently with some success, since some consciously non-stereotypical use of visible minority actors has been initiated by a number of advertisers. The Federal Government in its *Guidelines for the Depiction of Visible and Ethnic Minorities* in *Government Advertising and Commercials* also has tried to see that government materials reflect the country's multicultural character more fairly, and provincial governments are doing the same.

These are signs of progress, and there was even a multicultural clause (No. 27) included in the 1982 Charter of Rights. Yet the tone of statements by a minister of state recently responsible for multiculturalism has been one of continuing concern rather than complacency, especially with regard to the visual media.[21] In addition, representatives of the minorities continue to believe that the causes for criticism of the media persist.[22] How justified, we may ask, are these continuing complaints? A recent study by Gary Granzberg, who analyzed 360 hours of prime time (7-11 p.m.) dramas, documentaries, situation comedies and commercials shown on the CBC, CTV, and CBS networks, appears to support their complaints. Granzberg concluded that minority members generally had a "weak image." They were represented as people who were younger, less gainfully employed, less maritally stable, less important, and less heroic than members of the mainstream groups. In addition, romantic stereotypes tend to blur the value systems of ethnic groups and avoid the real difficulties and complexities of minority life. (Granzberg, 1983)

The films I have noted have for the most part been widely distributed, and a majority have had television showing. What then may the media have actually achieved? Uncertainties about media effects do not permit any precise judgement. John Kehoe has reviewed some very careful research on attitude changes in young people which used the NFB's *Gurdeep Singh Bains*, a film about a young Sikh, which has been widely praised. The researchers did not find it effective at the school level at which it was aimed, but it *was* found to be quite effective at another level. The results, Kehoe notes, are confusing and contradictory. (Kehoe, 1979, 96-97) Conflicting assessments are clearly possible, and both cultural pluralists and radicals might claim support for their arguments. The wide-ranging response to the multicultural challenge in the publicly supported mass media agencies especially — but in the private sector as well — would seem to confirm the claim of cultural pluralists that there are elements available in the media elite which are not simply identifiable with the economic establishment, elements which are liberal reformist by conviction, and which can work successfully in that context. On the other hand, continuing criticism of the media from minority groups and even official quarters suggests that the radical critique has some validity.[23]

While giving good marks to the Canadian visual media's support of the multicultural idea, we would be wise to keep in mind the larger context within which they work. In peak times on Canadian television (7-11 p.m.) three-quarters of all the programs are of foreign origin, accounting for 80 percent of all viewing. Just 4 percent of the dramatic shows are of Canadian origin. In assessing media effects in relation to minorities we must never forget the powerful homogenizing force of the mass media *totality* — an unrelenting flood which tends to put minority traditions and languages at an almost hopeless disadvantage. The main complaints against the multicultural policy by ethnic groups other than the visible minorities have concerned what is felt as inadequate support for language maintenance in the educational system and the media. The concern is well placed. Considerable research into language erosion among Canadian ethnic groups shows that they differ only in degree and speed of language loss. Without a linguistic basis can ethnic groups continue for long to cohere? Nahirny and Fishman have emphasized how difficult it is to persuade children of the value of ethnicity unless the larger environment (as well as the parents) is supportive. (Nahirny and Fishman, 1965, 311-36) The most influential part of that environment frequently becomes for young people the visual media, especially television, where the majority language is devastatingly dominant.

In *Kaszuby* (NFB, 1975), an interesting film dealing with the Polish community in Barrie's Bay, a skeptic and a believer argue over the chances for the success of multiculturalism. The result is inconclusive. Opinions do differ. To Charles Lynch, the journalist, the launching of multiculturalism was "one huge ethnic howler." To the Canadian Consultative Council on Multiculturalism, it is national salvation: "If we accept our multiculturalism, then we assure our cultural identity." No doubt the truth lies somewhere between these extremes. There *has* been progress, as we are reminded in the film *Bamboo, Lions and Dragons* (NFB, 1979), which contrasts two generations of Chinese in Vancouver. One of these, arriving early in the century, never integrated because of the racism that fostered the Asiatic Exclusion Act. The other, born in Chinatown, is now totally acculturated in suburbia. But whatever comes of the more sanguine goals of multiculturalism's promoters, and despite the continuing problems revealed by studies such as Granzberg's, I would argue that the visual media in their efforts to support multiculturalism at least have made and will continue to make a major contribution to the most fundamental problem of all — prejudice arising from simple ignorance.

Perhaps the "mass society" will get us all in the end; perhaps that is even what we want. But whatever the form the future takes in Canada, thanks to the concern with minorities stirred by the ideal of cultural pluralism, I believe that the "people with the funny names" and the "odd looks" will be less ill at ease, perhaps no more so than the McTavishes and the Poiriers. As a result we will all have come at least to like, understand, and even enjoy one another a bit more. If so, that will be a gain indeed.

FOOTNOTES

[1] In Canada, thanks to the enterprise of, among others, the Secretary of State, this lack is being slowly made up by undertakings such as Granzberg's investigation into the persistence of visible minority stereotypes in the media. (1983)

[2] Representative of a considerable polemical literature are *Don't Blame the People: How the Media Use Bias, Distortion and Censorship to Manipulate Public Opinion*, Cirino (1971); and from a different camp, *The Left-Leaning Antennae: Political Bias in Television*, Keeley (1971).

[3] Bahu Abu-Laban maintains that "television, more than any other medium,

provides a unifying force that can hold people together, enforce and sometimes create social norms, and transmit a social and cultural heritage from one generation to the next." (Bahu Abu-Laban, 1981:3) This is almost a definition of what Canadian minority groups hope for from multiculturalism.

4 The media indeed perpetuate, but do they create? The veteran media journalist, Daniel Schorr, argues against critics of the media that the media do not lead, they follow. They are a mirror, and if what is in the mirror changes, it is because the society has changed. Society, not the media, sets the pace. What does seem to happen is that certain leadership groups (to be part of which the media aspire) set the agenda and seek to use the media to persuade others to follow.

5 In his influential paper, "The Social Effects of Mass Communication," Joseph Klapper wrote: "In general, mass communication reinforces the existing attitudes, tastes, predispositions and behavioral tendencies of its audience members, including tendencies toward change. Rarely if ever does it serve alone to create metamorphoses." (Klapper, 1963:75)

6 For example, Paul Rutherford, in a recent history of the Canadian media asserts confidently that "communications are more likely to confirm an existing opinion than change an opinion." (Rutherford, 1978:119)

7 A few titles may be suggestive, viz: *Shanghai Madman, Hatchet Man, Yellow-Cargo, Shanghai Cobra, G. Men versus the Black Dragon,* etc.

8 Pierre Berton, in his *Hollywood's Canada,* analyzes the themes and attitudes which characterized some 600 (!) movies Hollywood made about Canada between 1907 and 1956. Berton's subtitles suggest how stereotypical was the approach: "The Old Fashioned Red Blooded Look; Happy-Go-Lucky Rogues in Tuques; The Volatile Blood of the French, and the Crafty Daring of the Indians; Savage Tribes ... Ready to Explode." Berton's description of the result as a "celluloid mountain of misconception" is not overstated. (Berton, 1975, 205)

9 The heroes, mostly policemen, described in *Hollywood's Canada* had names of a consistently anglo-celtic cast — Renfrew, Mason, Glenister, Clancy, Moran, McKenna, O'Malley, McGuire, O'Neil. Clearly, these anglo-celts were a masterful breed; they were just as clearly carrying the White Man's Burden.

10 Memories can be refreshed by a reading of: Michael Biddiss, *Images of Race.* N.Y. Holmes and Meier, 1979, and Hugh A. McDougall, *Racial Myth in English History: Trojans, Teutons and Anglo-Saxons.* Montreal: Harvest House/Hanover University Press of New England, 1982.

11 It has been said that anglo-conformity was the last casualty of World War II, that "notions of white superiority over other races and Anglo-Saxon superiority over other whites could not survive the crematoria and death camps of Nazi Germany." (Troper, 1979:41)

12 It is also a very real cause for resentment that media news coverage of the countries that were "home" for many among the visible minorities in Canada often highlights the negative; positive achievements are rarely noted. Other Canadians, it is felt, may well ask, "What *can* you expect from those who have come from such benighted regions?"

13 People who for too long have been treated as half-human or flawed don't want suddenly to become super-human or flawless. Another media habit which causes irritation among minorities is a tendency to labour racial

identification where not really necessary. "Race need not," an anti-discrimination guide notes, "be the hidden subject of every piece that happens to include a representation of or reference to a person of minority heritage."

[14] In a presentation to the Special Senate Committee on Mass Media (1970), the president of a Toronto advertising agency stated: "The nature of editorial acceptability becomes: how does it fit? or will it interest the affluent? As a consequence, the mass media increasingly reflect the attitudes and deal with the concerns of the affluent. We don't have mass media, we have class media — media for the middle and upper classes. The poor, the old, the young, the Indian, the Eskimo, the Blacks are virtually ignored." (Head, 1981:6)

[15] Cultural pluralism conceives society as based on an equilibrium of forces where independent groups can exercise some measure of democratic control through access to the major elites, and where peoples' attitudes and opinions can have some bearing upon the policies of their governments.

[16] Also worth noting are: *And When Their Time Had Come* (E. Mina Associates, 1972) which traces Russian Mennonite history from the peaceful pre-revolutionary Ukraine to homesteads in northern Alberta. Different in approach are *Kurelek* (NFB, 1967) and *Kurelek: Les pionniers ukrainiens* (Film Arts, 1975) which show aspects of Ukrainian immigration and survival on the prairies through the paintings of this well-known Ukrainian artist.

[17] In this group should be mentioned also three of the NFB's fine *Children of Canada Series* which show young people dealing with problems of integration and adaptation. Thirteen-year-old *Gurdeep Singh Bains* (1976) wears his turban, attends a Sikh temple, but manages to be quite happily integrated with his schoolmates. In *My Name Is Susan Yee* (1975) an eleven-year-old Chinese girl faces dislocation due to urban renewal. In *Veronica* (1977) a nine-year-old Polish Canadian girl bridges two cultures very successfully.

[18] The ethnic culture approach, if no longer predominant, continues improved in quality and content: for example, *The People of the Book* (NFB, 1973), which looks at the role of religion in Jewish life; *Be a Good Boy Now* (OECA, n.d.), concerning cultural life in Jamaica; *I've Never Walked the Steppes* (NFB, 1975), about Ukrainian customs and cultural memories; and *The Sikhs* (Sakha Films, 1980), the first serious effort to see this remarkable group as a whole in all its cultural and religious aspects.

[19] Probably the most outspoken films dealing with any ethnic group are: *The Other Side of the Ledger* (NFB, 1972), an uninhibited Indian view of the Hudson's Bay Company; *You Are On Indian Land* (NFB, 1969), about Mohawk protests over border regulations; and *Who Were the Ones* (NFB, 1972), in which are expressed bitter Indian memories of exploitation and trust betrayed. A small library of visual material now exists on Indian and Inuit art, music, and customs, extensive enough to form a valuable resource for scholars.

[20] The CBC's *King of Kensington* has been one of its best efforts at dramatic comedy and has won a wide audience. Most successful, perhaps, because it manages to show Canada's ethnic and cultural diversity in a fairly natural way, is *The Beachcombers*, which includes Pat Johns, an effective representation of an Indian character. In the NFB feature film *Cold Journey* (1972), the tragic hero is a young Indian lost between two cultures.

[21] At a Conference on the Visible Minorities and the Media in late 1982, he could

still say: "as our research indicates, the Blacks, the Chinese, the Japanese, the Asians ... and our native peoples are still almost invisible on the screen." (Fleming, 12) While granting that "the media are trying," he noted that "the overwhelming image presented on our TV screens remains seriously out of whack with reality." (Fleming, 13) Minorities, he concluded, are still "plagued by stereotypes" and "stereotyping is still an even more insidious problem for minorities than getting that first big break." (Fleming, 14)

[22] Salome Bey thinks that visible minorities are still oddities, victims or aggressors and complains that not a single visible minority representative sits on the boards of the CBC, CRTC, or Canada Council. In the Spring of 1983 the black actor Jeff Henry could say: "Blacks are still playing the foot-shuffling negro servant, the loveable but incompetent sidekick, the buffoon." (Henry, 1983) Dennis Strong, another black actor, announced he would not play one more pimp, baggage porter, or junkie, and has managed to get roles as a doctor, a police sergeant, and an orchestra conductor. What is new and encouraging is the marked unwillingness of ethnic groups to tolerate slights and misrepresentations that once were considered par for the course. A new alertness in this respect was shown by the well-organized protest of the Toronto Chinese community over an inadequately researched program about Chinese students in Canada, a protest which brought a retraction and apology from its makers, and by the fierce reaction to an incident at station CKFM in Toronto, involving a racial slur over the air.

[23] Granzberg's rejection of any regulations aimed at governing the depiction of minority groups on TV disappointed minority leaders, but it didn't displease the local director of the CBC. "Networks would be courting financial disaster if their programming was so regulated," he said in an interview, "because advertisers won't buy commercial spots unless people watch the shows, and people won't watch something they don't like." (*Winnipeg Free Press*, Jan. 19, 1983:3) The advertiser is always with us. His influence will always bear watching.

REFERENCES

Abu-Laban, Bahu. "Multiculturalism and Canada Television: A Critical View." *Multiculturalism* 1981, 5(1), 3-7.

Adler, Richard and Douglass Cater. *Television as a Cultural Force*. New York: Praeger Publishers, 1976.

Altheide, Richard. *Creating Reality: How Television News Distorts Events*. Beverly Hills: Sage Publications, 1976.

Baldwin, Elizabeth. "The Mass Media and the Corporate Elite: A Re-analysis of the Overlap Between the Media and the Economic Elites" *Canadian Journal of Sociology*. 1977, 2(1), 1-27.

Berton, Pierre. *Hollywood's Canada*. Toronto: McClelland and Stewart, 1975.

Bey, Salome. "Visible Minorities and the Media." *Conference Report*. Ottawa: Multiculturalism Canada, 1982, 30-37.

Bogle, Donald. *Toms, Coons, Mulattoes, Mammies and Bucks: An Interpretive History of Blacks in American Films*. New York: Viking Press, 1973.

Cirino, Robert. *Don't Blame the People: How the Media Use Bias, Distortion and Censorship to Manipulate Public Opinion.* New York: Random House, 1971.

Clement, Wallace. *The Canadian Corporate Elite.* Toronto: McClelland and Stewart, 1975.

----------. "Overlap of the Media and Economic Elites," *Canadian Journal of Sociology.* 1977, 2(2): 205-214.

Cripps, Thomas. *Slow Fade to Black: The Negro in American Films, 1900-1942.* New York: New York University Press, 1977.

Diamond, Edwin. *The Tin Kazoo: Television, Politics and the Media.* Cambridge, Mass.: MIT Press, 1975.

Fleming, Hon. James. "Opening Address." *Conference Report.* Ottawa: Multiculturalism Canada, 1982, 12-17.

Friar, Ralph E. and Natasha A. Friar. *The Only Good Indian: The Hollywood Gospel.* New York: Drama Book Specialists, 1970.

Gardner, R.C., D.M. Taylor and H.J. Feenstra. "Ethnic Attitudes: Attitudes or Beliefs. *Canadian Journal of Psychology.* 1970, 24(5), 321-324.

Gomez, Henry. "The Invisible Minorities: Minorities in the Media." *Currents.* 1983, 1(2), 12-13.

Gordon, Rosemary. "Stereotypes of Imagery and Belief as Ego Defense." *British Journal of Psychology,* Monograph Supplements XXXIV. Cambridge: Cambridge University Press, 1962, 88-95.

Granzberg, Gary. *The Portrayal of Minorities by Canadian Television During the 1982 Prime Time Season.* Winnipeg: Secretary of State, 1983.

Head, Wilson A. "A Critical Examination of Visible Minority Groups in Canadian Mass Media." *Multiculturalism,* 1981, 5(1), 8-12.

Henry, Jeff. "Typecasting." *Currents,* 1983, 1(2), 10-11.

Kalisch, Philip O., Beatrice J. Kalisch, and Margaret Scobey. *Images of Nurses on Television.* New York: Springer Publishing Co., 1983.

Keeley, Joseph. *The Left-Leaning Antenna: Political Bias in Television.* New Rochelle, N.Y.: Arlington House, 1971.

Kehoe, John. "Multiculturalism: The Difficulty of Unpredictable Strategies." *Immigration and Multiculturalism: A Decade to Review.* Toronto: Ministry of Culture and Recreation, 1979, 91-99.

Klapper, Joseph T. "The Social Effects of Mass Communication." Schramm, Wilber (ed.), *The Science of Human Communication.* New York: Basic Books, 1963, 65-76.

Mackie, Marlene. "Ethnic Stereotypes and Prejudice — Alberta Indians,- Hutterites and Ukrainians." *Canadian Ethnic Studies,* 1974, 4(1-2).

Miller, M. Randall. ed. *The Kaleidoscope Lens: Ethnic Images in American Film.* Englewood, N.J.: Jerome S. Ozer, 1979.

Nahirny, Vladimir C. and Hoshua A. Fishman. "American Immigrant Groups: Ethnic Identification and the Problem of Generations." *Sociological Review,* 1965, 13:311-326.

Phelan, John M. *Mediaworld: Programming the Public.* New York: The Seabury Press, 1977.

Porter, John. "Ethnic Pluralism in Canadian Perspective." Nathan Glazer and Daniel Moynihan (eds.) *Ethnicity: Theory and Experience.* Cambridge, Mass.: Harvard University Press, 1975, 266-304.

Rees, Tim. "Editorial." *Current*, 1983, 1(2), 2.
Rutherford, Paul. *The Making of the Canadian Media.* Toronto: McGraw Hill Ryerson, 1978.
Sklar, Robert. *Movie-Made America: A Cultural History of American Movies.* New York: Random House, 1975.

11

WHEN "RIGHTS" ARE WRONG: WITH EXAMPLES FROM ATLANTIC CANADA

FRANK MacKINNON

Among the principal rights of man and his groups is protection from the more selfish advocates of rights and promoters of fanaticism. It is easy, however, to overlook this right in the emotional enthusiasm of crusaders, the blare of fashionable bandwagons, the vague wording of a charter of rights, or the high hopes of the citizenry. Rights and minority identities sound splendid in the abstract. But each one needs to be defined and discussed in relation to how it actually works in a group or location, and what side effects may appear. I use the Atlantic provinces to present illustrations which are both local and national in significance.

There are urgent reasons for the general precautionary right. One is an increasing tendency to enhance groups by calling them minorities and conjuring up privileges disguised as rights. Another is conflict of rights, often aggravated by trivial pretensions and egotism. These phenomena may lead people to lose their identities, control of their affairs, ability to think, even their lives, by overidentifying with causes and other people. Still another reason is a danger to democratic thought — a one-sided discriminatory morality that many activists welcome because fashion dictates it; and that provokes virtuous high dudgeon over a small raise for the Governor of the Bank of Canada but not millions paid in advance for a hockey player; over Chile but not Angola; over the Shah but not the Ayatollah; over doctors' salaries but not the high pay of TV anchormen; and over the rights of arrested activists in Québec 1970 but not the rights of the Laportes, Crosses, and other victims. We protest so much we do not seem to consider the validity of the issues, or to question those who are in charge of our protests and who select our victims. Even the universities, which promote the search for truth through freedom of speech, and the churches, which advocate charity and good will, tolerate the ideas and advocates that suit them, and boycott and shout down the rest. And they will sign petitions and approve resolutions by the bushel without understanding the subjects or the motives behind them.

A depressing atmosphere of alleged high virtue undermines our country today with the exaggeration of rights and minorities. There is a persistent nudging of desirable pluralism into such a multiplication of splintered identities and contesting actions that minorities and rights may come to mean nothing, when what they do and stand for is not worth the effort and ill will they involve. They can be relentless burdens, like the storied albatross and old man of the sea.

If I, for example, got into the minority business, I could flaunt complaints and be fashionably alienated. I could lament injustice suffered by paternal Highland ancestors displaced by the Highland clearances or slain while fighting *not* to be English, and at the same time mourn the troubles my maternal Loyalist ancestors endured to *be* English. I could be infuriated over the tragic loss of rights inflicted by France on my Huguenot connections. And my Irish roots should be good for righteous indignation if someone labels me "anglo" or calls the Scots a founding race of Ireland. But I would not want these "roots" organized for status or politicized for crusades because they would clash with one another and with those of everyone else. All of us honour our traditions, but they denote no special virtue or status on our part. With the rarest exceptions, our language is accidental, our religion is inherited unquestioned, and our looks result from biological roulette. Our background includes fine forebears, like the cast of Grey's *Elegy*, but we keep the black sheep of the families well hidden. As for place of origin, I for one have not thought of my home province and its neighbours as minorities — just small places providing the good life in a big country.

I suggest, therefore, that we should just respect our personal minorities and get our status on our own efforts. And we must redefine the right of free speech to permit two-way dialogue so we can have minds of our own and discuss public questions with less emotion and more sense. As for rights, real rights that is, I believe in them, not because they are fashionable, but because they are good. Indeed I worry about them *because* they are fashionable, and might be washed away with the social tides or embalmed by enshrinement.

I can therefore agree with many of my co-authors and leave the good things for them to explain. But since a devil's advocate is obligatory at a canonization, I might claim that role, while expressing respect for the effective minorities and real rights. I can also affirm my devotion to the Atlantic provinces while using them to illustrate the subject. The reason for this approach is not negative, but positive. In this field, as in all public policy, it is easy to advocate the benefits of rights. But definition of terms, cost in money, effort, and good will, disadvantages to others, and the inevitable side effects are difficult to state, discuss, and admit. To assess only one side of a cause is to undermine it — which is one reason why the chief destroyers of rights are usually those of their possessors who misuse or overdo them. I therefore present this paper as a companion piece to the papers of my colleagues, one which agrees that this field is of first importance, but urges that we must till it properly.

ILLUMINATED HALOS

Accordingly, we should have some assessments to balance hosannas. We say Canada must thrive on unity and strength in diversity. It will, if the unity is developed, not forced, and the diversity is respected, not exaggerated. Emphasized diversity can become snobbish; and it requires massive apparatus, PR, and maintenance which weaken both the unity and strength, indeed the diversity itself. Too many minority halos are illuminated unnecessarily, and worn so tightly they shut off circulation to too many brains. The resulting complaints are often the fault of the people who tout them, but that cannot be said out loud. As for rights, we promote far more than we can handle. We permit social salesmen to peddle them and tell us what is non-negotiable, and we allow many intense people to use them to make gurus of themselves. I question the common association of the words "minority" and "rights." Rights as inflated privileges are used to enhance status and control people. The urge to be recognized as special or unique is strong, especially when a reputation for being virtuous or deserving is hard to establish. Entrenching sounds splendid, but it is often an exercise in face-saving, in which society and effective minorities are slowed down by entrenched mediocrity and frustrated by entrenched evil. Establishing a "right" because of certain conditions, for example — and refusing to give it up when the conditions change — is a nasty, inefficient practice. And so is the rigid rotation of officeholders among interest groups, which limits the available candidates to a quarter or less of the prospects, and lets an appointee cry discrimination if he proves incompetent. If a minority has a problem of its own making it can either remedy its mistake, which it will rarely admit, or, what is easier, blame the majority which, unable to point out where the fault lies, has to accept the blame and perhaps pay for it. Militancy is trendy, but it is rarely judged on whether it involves mere rivalry, old feuds brought to Canada by immigrants, or indeed anything worth being militant about.

Minorities have as bad a history of violating rights as majorities do, and they can neglect rights altogether should they become majorities. The public needs protection against unscrupulous minorities whose claims often illustrate Martin Luther King's words on "thin rationalization to clothe an obvious wrong in the beautiful garments of righteousness." (King, 1968,48) It also needs to be protected against groups that must promote organized loyalty as a psychological crutch to keep and control their membership; against ideological and dogmatic gurus who train members to admit no mistakes and compromise no "principles"; and against the fact that promoting minorities and rights always involves hunting for villains, and going too far makes prospective villains of everyone. While emphasizing our rights we will readily deny those of others. Promoters of minorities and rights include men and women of honour and integrity. But to their own enormous disadvantage, perhaps ultimate failure, they also include moralistic social butterflies that flit from cause to cause in uninformed self-satisfaction, as well as intense authoritarians who, with malice toward all and charity for none, act like piranhas posing as guppies.

Before we examine the subject in the Atlantic provinces there is a distinction to be made between myths and facts. Our constitutional issues, for example, are almost all mistakes painted over and garnished with myths. But no one can say such things in public with illustrations, without spurious dignity being offended. Then excruciating duty banishes the happiness that should be associated with minorities and rights, and, in the revolutionary and ecclesiastical traditions so evident today, a pursed-lipped carping identity flops down in nattering negativity. It becomes easy to play at martyrdom, act like underdogs, develop a siege mentality, seek scapegoats, justify inaction and mistakes, avoid responsibility, assume divine patronage, claim discrimination when the going gets rough, pamper undeserving and oversensitive sacred cows, and use strong words, like alienation, to drive wedges between friends. Indeed, every over-organized and politicized minority allegiance limits the freedom and identity of its possessor the more it is inflated, and erects obstacles to his relations with others in both his own and other affiliations. Many citizens find their more demanding loyalties hard to bear, and may prefer some assurance that being human and Canadian is enough to cope with.

We should assess the use of "minority" and "rights" as **buzz words.** They have tremendous impact in little places and are often invoked in Atlantic Canada for just that reason. Many people glamorize minority as the courageous defender of a "way of life" rallying against a predatory majority. It can be more sensibly defined in statistical terms as a group of less than half, with no suggestion of special status, and in strategic terms as such a group that endures some discrimination for no other reason than that it is less then half. Beyond that, arguments can scatter. For example, is every little group of less than half to be a minority entitled to the emotions that go with the word? Can a minority or majority in one area use its majority or minority status in another area for social and political purposes? And is every tiny sect to enjoy, in whatever way its leaders wish, the awesome responsibilities of freedom of religion?

Recognition and power certainly cannot be limited to groups described as "mainline" and minorities that are pluralities. They will play the minority game and seek rights, whatever their size. But politics does present an obvious need for freedom from the fetters which some minorities want to fasten, using the old divide-and-rule strategy. The already-small Atlantic provinces indicate an amoeba-like dividing tendency that is fine for amoebas but not citizens. As for defining rights, legislatures and courts have not had enough success in doing it precisely, and at times it gets left to those who shout the loudest and most often and thereby get their views established as fashion. Contemporary Canadian literature on the subject is on the whole trendy and weak.[1] Some very frank writing and discussion are necessary to even ask questions without being labeled bigoted, "not with it," or anti-something; to seek the dividing lines between mere privileges and real rights; to clarify conflict of rights; to determine what responsibilities must go with rights; and to discourage people who destroy rights by overdoing or abusing them.

And what about the interests of the majority in democracy when it has to adopt an artificial *mea culpa* attitude to keep the peace — like "anglos" blamed for the consequences of governmental and ecclesiastical isolationist neglect of the industrial age in Québec, men and women cowed by Amazonian tendencies in some women's movements, and those who do not remind Indians that much of their trouble was caused by tribal warfare? Sooner or later *mea culpa* will prove forced, and wrong, and expensive, and frustrated patience will run out. Real discussion is therefore necessary instead of pusillanimous one-sided exchanges. Surely Canadians have been kept undeservedly long at the social confessional and the political penitent bench.

We should therefore question some fashionable views, not to oppose minorities and rights, but to safeguard them in their true places in our society and allow us to enjoy them. Unfortunately the very words "minority" and "rights" now have an adversary connotation in Canada encouraged by the pouts and moues of querulous factions, and an implication of suspicion, as excessive villain-hunting labels us all as dangerous innocents lurking under one another's troubled beds. What is going on is weakening our country. The many causes once had an aura of attractive morality and service. But we have often become so intense, so boring, so untruthful about the causes, that we are creating too many chips for shrugging shoulders, while the morality has disappeared and the action is not fun any more. And all this in a country that has given us so much to cheer and be thankful about, and so much with which to respect one another!

I suggest, therefore, that we respect thinking minorities and promote deserved rights, but, for their sakes and Canada's, dissociate the two and tone them down — and firmly argue the pretentions of *all* organized politicized minorities and the advocacy of privileges disguised as rights with a view to putting some strength in our politics and an end to one-sided shilly shallying in our scholarship. The Atlantic region is as good a place as any to begin.

STATUS ATLANTIC

Neither the Atlantic region nor any of its provinces can be properly described as a minority. And each province is not a collection of minorities, but a pluralistic society that has been splintered too much in a politicized scramble for local status and power. Minorities in the statistical, unpoliticized meaning of the word are effective in the community life of the small provinces. But the over-politicized ones hold it back. And they are undemocratic when their personnel are identified less as citizens and more as minority members looking to gurus for leadership rather than politicians. Nevertheless, Easterners, like most Canadians, have by world standards no idea of the significance in their lives of "minorities" and "rights," and the more they inflate and overuse them the more confused they become.

Some Canadians think Atlantic society moves in the "slow lane." On the contrary, for those who care to live fully, the pace can be very fast and dangerous, with varied and fascinating experiences in a splendid and challenging environment. While the standard of living as a statistical indicator is low, the standard of life can be very high. The society is so pluralistic there are endless opportunities for those who like to manage and enjoy community activities and participate in politics. Many hobbies and sports that are costly in big cities are within easy reach of practically everyone. And the people can combine the best of rural and urban worlds without many of their troubles. In all walks of life are many "fine people," as they say in old communities, some who mistakenly view themselves as "the salt of the earth," and enough "characters" to avoid the commonplace.

This existence has its dark side, however. It encourages some to be too satisfied, and too undisturbed by initiative, hard work, and responsibility, often too critical and jealous of the enterprise of others. They do live in the slow lane. The pluralism can inflate small matters and groups far beyond their importance; cherished localism disguised as a "way of life" can obscure the real world, and perpetuate what may be weak or wrong in that way of life and prevent improvement; and rivalry among politicized groups can become more and more vicious and less and less significant as they take their organized allegiances too seriously and their responsibilities as citizens not seriously enough. And that furtive question "what's in it for us?" can destroy the service that groups are supposed to perform. Small is beautiful, but for it to be more than a cliché, the standard of life has to be fortified by a standard of initiative and action.

Atlantic politics reflect the physical and psychological results of geography, and illustrate Canada's politics on a small scale. The little provinces have enormous political status per person, per square mile, and per dollar earned and spent. They know macro politics for micro events, and permit political associations to pervade their societies and minority affiliations to dominate their politics. Government combines business and sport — sometimes with doubts about which is which. Political tragedy is unknown and the political fatality rate is zero.[2] In Gilbert and Sullivan's words,

> ... the duties are delightful, and the privileges great;
> But the privilege and pleasure
> That we treasure beyond measure
> Is to run on little errands for the Ministers of State.

The ministers may disagree, however, and prefer another description of what happens:

> This pluralist societee!
> To be an active somebodee
> You tout for your minoritee,
> And keep the pots a-boiling and all those fellows toiling,
> Those busy errand-runners, the Ministers of State.

Having big establishments in four such small separate land masses is not necessarily inefficient. It is easily defended with the demands of geography, the capriciousness of history, comparisons with advantages given to other provinces, and the fact that the happiness of man does not depend on the size of his habitat. But whether it can be respected depends on how the biggest problem in the region is handled. The status and politics may be inflated with excessive tradition and privilege without maintaining the productive effort needed to keep up so large an overhead. It is easy to seek outside help. But to justify status, and reinforce it with respect, the help can only supplement local action, not replace or smother it. Pump priming is a popular phrase down East, but it is useless unless followed by vigorous pumping.

There is too little pumping for the amount of priming. This is the first lesson from Atlantic minorities and rights when people emphasize getting over doing, politicization over productivity, membership over citizenship, "taking in one another's washing" over industrial innovation. Its impact is easily seen when magnified in small areas. Activists may spend so much time competing for minority recognition and rights that they cannot handle or enjoy them when they do get them. Here is a major reason for Atlantic regional disparities. People can devote so much effort to maintaining the status that they have little energy left to do the things they thought the status necessary for in the first place. Being a member of an organized minority involves obligations; every right has responsibilities. Thus several allegiances at any one time may turn a person into little more than a professional minority member and status maintenance man disguised as a devotee of community service. It is this situation, to be found in national as well as provincial affairs, that prompts me to emphasize pumping as well as pump priming, and to indicate the debilitating efforts of status seekers and privilege gatherers who give excessive attention to priming.

Let me be clear on this comment. I do not mean the effective organizations and members who go about the useful and enjoyable activities they were intended to do, and do not inflate themselves by posing as minorities and touting rights. I do mean the politicized status ones, the social or political freeloaders who know a good thing when they see it and present their minority activity as real work, and those content to live off priming who will not pump. In the prevailing fashion, they generally can count on others to accept them at their self-proclaimed face value, lest they throw a tantrum about how miserably treated they are at the hands of the majority or some alleged Mephistophel in Ottawa. I also mean complainers who cannot let problems be settled when they have no emotional sustenance to fall back on. This is how problems become chronic and how a mere viewpoint becomes a myth, the myth accepted as fact, and the fact accorded the status of enshrined holy writ. The sheer numbers of groups in tiny areas limit their value the moment they become politicized, and restrict severely the productivity of the area. There is just so much community work to do and time and patience to do it, so much politics needed to get the public business done, so many dollars available, and so many benefits that can result. The workings of Parkinson's Law and the Peter Principle are obvious here.

Numerous commission and other reports have described this situation over the years. The consequences have been frankly stated in the Speech from the Throne in the P.E.I. Legislature in 1981:

> Many of the unrealistic assumptions and expectations of the past few decades must be discarded. A new view of society, and of ourselves, is required. We must become more self-reliant ... make more efficient use of resources ... tailor our expectations to the actual productivity of our economy ... recognize that our well-being depends on our own initiative and resourcefulness, rather than on the largess of government.... The future well-being of our province is not a right which can be guaranteed; rather it is a challenging task for which all Islanders must be willing to bear their share of responsibility.[3]

Another problem of personnel in the Atlantic provinces began in earliest colonial times when French and English governments sent to small possessions many civil servants, clergy, and land and business administrators who were unsatisfactory at home. There were minor functionaries to whom some small patronage had to be given. The problem has continued. Although countless excellent officers of governments and organizations have been appointed to the Atlantic provinces, many others who have failed elsewhere have been sent, or foisted on careless local employers, for a comfortable life without increased responsibility.[4] These people do much harm because, local incompetence having already been compensated for over time, imported incompetence has sharp and sudden impact. They want respectability and acceptance quickly, and are among the most enthusiastic joiners of groups and espousers of causes.[5] Such people are to be found anywhere, of course, but when over-politicized minority activity is emphasized in small places they gambol off with any trendy will-o-the-wisp. Fortunately the disadvantage of their presence is partially offset by able junior personnel sent for a short while to small places for experience and promotion not possible for tactical reasons in larger places. By and large their group identity and personal affiliations are not displayed or used as steps to preference; and they take on and do well only one or two activities at a time, rather than a scatteration of ineffective busyness.

These matters are illustrated in Eastern economic enterprise. Some barriers to it are difficult to surmount in any event. But one is very high — the careless ease with which outside authorities are asked to provide, build, pay for, and run enterprise by way of branch plants, military establishments, public service buildings, and the like, which give handfuls of jobs and revenue, or politically popular consumer benefits. Too often communities stop there, and become so dependent on them they have to be continued after their usefulness ceases. They also crowd out economic investment of lasting value when people become accustomed to being sustained rather than to being creative, and to relying on the errands of excessive pluralism to occupy their time rather than productive activities. It is not the enterprises that are wrong, but the dependence on them.

The situation is compounded as citizens demand that enterprises be divided among tiny constituencies and districts a few miles apart, rather than placed in efficient concentrations in a few locations. This kind of sterile planning becomes the very stuff of minority activities as little groups manoeuvre to get things for, or "save," a community. They do not study the redundant or uneconomic facility, or listen to argument about long-run benefits and employment with meaning. Boondoggle or not, they want it. But they rarely unite in productive enterprises of their own: it has long been well known that the first opposition to Maritime projects comes from within the region itself. Meanwhile those who live off forced patronage, which they will call their "rights," do not have to improve their efforts and products to meet real competition, and this further weakens enterprises and prices services and products out of the markets.

The alternative is difficult at the start, but is much more efficient and productive for all. Local people need to go beyond status and rights designed to get things, to assume full responsibility for planning, financing, constructing, and managing their own enterprises so they will not be dependent one-interest communities. There has to be no group identity whatever that will clash with other group identities to prevent or compromise a project, or boost the cost through recognitions and patronage. Successful examples show what can be done. Their individual entrepreneurs and one or two associates found out beforehand what was involved and how to do it themselves, and then did it. Although chronic critics and alleged experts tallied up the reasons why the projects would not work, and minority activists snorted that something was being done without them, or that there was "nothing in it for us," the most unlikely projects have succeeded in what seemed most unlikely communities. A brush factory in Saint John, a stove foundry in Sackville, a food-processing plant in East Florenceville, and an airline in Charlottetown, which were the laughing stock of the region when they started, were turned into enormously successful businesses of national and world status.[6]

What are needed in the Atlantic provinces are not status studies of minorities, rights, and what the provinces have not got. Difficulties have been voiced, dissected, royal commissioned, and task forced without let-up. It is the answers to two frank questions which have not been asked that are now needed. What are the personal resources to be found in the area, and how can they be tapped and increased from within and without? Where has the initiative come from to create what successes there have been, and what initiative has been contributed or obstructed by politicized minorities? But whether the numerous interests and those dependent on them for votes can tolerate such questioning is now an indication of how limited and one-sided is the right of enquiry and free speech in contemporary issues.

Governments make many of the mistakes, but it is not right to blame everything on them. Groups make a large share of them, but the public is not permitted to hear of them. This is true elsewhere too, but in the Eastern provinces governments that become heavily involved may leave little scope for non-governmental initiative. Then the minorities force the governments into doing or not doing things, and they do not hesitate to hamstring or bribe in small places where every vote counts. It is a local condensed version of the one-interest group problem that bedevils the U.S. Congress and the Canadian Parliament.

WHEN "RIGHTS" ARE WRONG

Minorities and rights have to be paid for and the cost is staggering. Must the taxpayers in the Eastern or any provinces cut down on essential duties and expenditures in order to pay for status for favoured groups, losses from mistakes and privileges, extras to all grants to take care of patronage and boondoggles, deficits involved in scattering enterprises around, losses incurred by token but not working representatives of minorities on boards and committees, and the expenses of creating more "rights" than an area can stand in an ever-splintering society? What kind of handicap is the total of all these costs in the over-all enterprise of a province or the nation? And what real independence and sovereignty are left to governments that on local insistence become in effect committees for the distribution of funds with inadequate time and resources for governing?

We are not a new country any more, but an old one for which an inferiority complex cannot be an excuse in this demanding age. If we think it is, then history may judge our problems to be of our own creation, or figments of our own imagination, or results of normal hard luck that we could have overcome with less whining and more work and good will. The problems and the inferiority complex may also be ascribed to our crusades against one another, our villain-hunting, in the name of so many factions and rights. Herein is tragedy; although we have little to complain about by world standards, we must find villains among ourselves to blame for sad problems, and defy Canada's spirit to find sad solutions.

I would suggest a project for some group. Secure funds for the printing and distribution of a large poster. On it would be a picture of Sir John A. Macdonald drawn with sharp eye and pointed finger, like the famous one of Kitchener. On the top would be the words "Is your politicized minority *really* necessary?" and, below the picture, "Have *you* earned your rights today?" They should be placed where they are most needed: in legislative smoking rooms, court antechambers, church vestibules, university and school halls, and other places where Canadians may take their pretensions too seriously. At the bottom of the poster might also be a small sketch of the Founding Father saying with a smile, "Why not enjoy Canada? She has much to offer!"

FOOTNOTES

[1] See frank appraisals by Prime Minister Trudeau and an editor of the *Canadian Historical Review* in *Maclean's*, October 20, 1975.

[2] The Canadian political fatality rate of two in 117 years (D'Arcy McGee and Pierre Laporte) is surely the lowest in the world.

[3] The *Guardian*, Charlottetown, February 20, 1981.

[4] *Macleans*, for example, described the perpetuation of "a colonial industrial structure by attracting lameduck companies to backward regions (*Macleans*, June 13, 1977). While an M.P., Premier Angus MacLean of P.E.I. described the Island's federal-provincial development plan as a "hare-brained one which was dreamed up by formerly unemployed economists" (*Canadian Annual Review* 1969, 155, and 1977, 201). It might be, admitted one Newfoundland professor, that his province "failed to maximize its potential through incompetence." David G. Alexander, in Sager, Fischer, and Pierson, eds., *Atlantic Canada and Confederation: Essays in Canadian Political*

Economy. Toronto, University of Toronto Press, 1983, 105 and 111.
5. For an example from one of the most intense of all Maritime issues, see Sir Richard Cartwright's description of the "shibboleth of adherence to the cause of temperance" which was exploited by "not a few of the greatest scoundrels I have known" in an atmosphere of "zeal without knowledge." Sir Richard Cartwright, *Reminiscences.* Toronto, Briggs, 1912, 170.
6. Sims Brush Co., Enterprise Foundry, McCain Foods, and Maritime Central Airways.

REFERENCES

Martin Luther King, Jr. "The Future of Integration." In W.W. Boyer, ed. *Issues 1968*, Lawrence: University Press of Kansas, 1968, 48.

12

THE WEST: A POLITICAL MINORITY

BARRY COOPER

> Do not forget that the people of the prairie economic area have always been and by present prospects, always will be, politically a minority in such vital matters as the tariff, freight rates, and fiscal policy, all controlled by a federal Parliament in which we of the prairie provinces only at long intervals can hope to hold even a balance of power.
>
> Stuart Garson
> Premier of Manitoba, 1947

> Then the snow melted, swiftly unveiling a sky perfectly healed, perfectly blue.
>
> And leaving behind great towers of glass, of silver and copper and steel, where the city had once stood. Towers that glittered like ice.
>
> A fantastic new city of towers ablaze in the bright autumn day.
>
> And machines, floating out of the sky, brought people to fill up the towers.
>
> Geoffrey Ursell,
> *Perdue: Or How the West was Lost*
> (1984)

A recent collection of essays, with the declared objective of "coming to terms with the nature and significance of the recent struggle over constitutional reform and its results embodied in the Constitutional Act, 1982" bore the sobering title: *And No One Cheered.* (Banting and Simeon, 1983, xi) Roger Gibbins (1983, 126) observed, quite rightly, that "April 17 is unlikely to occupy a place in the Canadian political culture comparable to that of May Day, Bastille Day or the Fourth of July." Indeed, one of the significant features of the ceremonies on Parliament Hill was that they were apparently scheduled to end so that the important participants might enjoy a fine luncheon, at 9 a.m., Pacific Standard Time.

In the document itself, recognition is given to minority language groups and to aboriginal peoples. An implicit recognition is extended to non-French, non-English minorities insofar as the Charter is to be interpreted in a manner consistent with the preservation and enhancement of the multicultural heritage of Canadians. Part III of the Constitution Act, which dealt with regional disparities, could also be read as an implicit recognition that territory is a category that conveyed minority status; certain aspects of the amending procedure may also be interpreted in that way.

Most of the discourse dealing with minorities in Canada, however, and many of the papers in this volume deal with what might be termed the pre-political or social constituent elements of minority status. These pre-political realities include such familiar items as age, gender, culture, religion, and ethnicity, to which more colourful and recondite matters of sexual preference and orientation have recently been added. In large measure they constitute the social substance that lies behind the constitutional forms and the multicultural guidelines as well as various human rights regulations. Moreover, they form the basis in reality for the intellectual justification of one of Canada's important growth industries, servicing the complaints of citizens who consider themselves minorities. Accordingly, these pre-political things have become important for Canadian politics.

In addition, however, region or, more conceptually, territory, has operated as an explicit political (and not as an implicit, social, or pre-political) criterion for majority/minority cleavages. In this paper, I would like to consider the West as a political (not social, ethnic, cultural, etc.) minority. Regarding the inhabitants of the region as a political minority means that the usual methods for identifying minority status, namely social indicators or legal instruments, are, for methodological reasons, inappropriate. Since aggregate social facts and the particularist or discriminatory contents of laws may simply reflect the expression of pre-political factors, the correct analytical approach must also consider: (1) the differential impact of uniformly administered laws, that is, the different historical impact resulting from common public policies; (2) competing or coordinate spheres of legal competence, which is to say, the institutional environment; and (3) the variety of Canadian patriotism in the West that endows those institutions, laws, and policies with local meaning.

The first two points have been widely discussed by a generation of Canadianists who cut their teeth, as it were, on the Rowell-Sirois Report. Multifarious accounts of co-operative federalism, of province building, of executive federalism, of federal-provincial diplomacy, and the like may be collapsed under the heading, "patterns of policy." This topic is considered in section one. To provide an initial context for these historical facts, section two considers the most important theoretical argument concerning the nature of federalism. The purpose here is to suggest that federalism is not simply a matter of Dominion-provincial relations, of bureaucratic competition, of federal "societies," of regional disparities, economic exploitation, and so forth, though these matters are not unimportant. Federalism is first of all politics, and politics is first of all conflict, chiefly conflict over what is right or just, which often appear as the defence of one's own interest and second, politics is the conciliation of conflicting interests.

Politics is not just these things, however. It is also controversy, that is, speech among and within groups struggling for power and for what is right within the political community. A second context, then, is one of inwardness, of meaning that appears as speech, eventually as the highest kind of political speech, namely law making. Policy and federal theory are important for citizens insofar as they are seen to express a, or perhaps the, meaning of their common life. The privileged discursive form for the communication of meaning is the story or the myth. In Canada, however, there is no story common to both the West and the East, to say nothing of the North or of other places. Consequently, the combination of a federal regime and contrasting accounts of the meaning of common life in the country has made the political consciousness of Westerners difficult to express comprehensively and accurately, which is why such fundamentally misleading terms as "Western alienation" are so often employed. Section three, then, indicates the major dimension of a conflict of meaning, of a mythic conflict rather than of a conflict of interest, within the Canadian body politic.

In the concluding section there are a few tentative remarks to suggest the kinds of transformations of Western and Canadian consciousness, that is, of meanings, and of our political institutions and conflicts that have followed from the advent of what Ellul (1964) called the technological society. These changes constitute the most comprehensive, as well as the most recent context, and indicate the ambiguous significance not only of the West as a political minority, but also of the pre-political minorities discussed elsewhere in this volume.

1. PATTERNS OF POLICY

The American colonists prior to their war of independence from Great Britain drew up a declaration and gave voice to a long train of abuses that, in their view, justified breaking implicit or explicit oaths of loyalty to the monarch. Retrospective Westerners can enumerate a long train of abuses as well, though few of them would draw the conclusions of the eighteenth-century colonists. Unlike the American West, where inhabitants of the territories of Texas, Oregon, and California actively sought admission to the Union, the North-West began its political association with Canada by resisting military occupation. From the National Policy to the National Energy Program, there has existed a fissure, narrow but bottomless, between Westerners and non-Westerners regarding the meaning of the term "national" and the emotional valence attached to it. The facts of the policies of the Dominion government regarding the West and the ambivalence of Westerners in the face of those policies can hardly be in dispute. Westerners all know that the CPR existed following the realization of the "national dream," when the last spike was pounded. And what we know of the CPR is summed up not in the poetry of E.J. Pratt nor in the prose of Pierre Berton, but by phrases all too familiar to Western ears: the monopoly clause and freight rates. J.F. Conway was surely correct to observe that the great defect of Canadian scholarship lay not in a failure to unearth the facts: "Indeed, the facts have been repeated with a regularity that has become tiresome." (Conway, 1978, 124) The problem is that these facts have not been placed and understood in a sufficiently comprehensive context. That is, the meaning of the facts, the story into which they have been cast, has been insufficiently discussed.

This is not to say that political scientists have ignored the connections between policies and political institutions. On the contrary, it was nearly twenty years ago that Black and Cairns (1966) essayed a different perspective on Canadian federalism that emphasized the importance of institutions in "province-building." At the top of provincial societies, a redistribution of administrative skills effectively ended a paternalism on the part of the central government that had been based upon superior knowledge. Nowadays, there may be more mandarins in Ottawa than in Victoria or Edmonton, but they are not necessarily more competent. Moreover, throughout provincial societies, "mechanisms set in motion by the creation of political institutions permit provinces such as Saskatchewan and Alberta, which possessed little sociological legitimacy at their birth, to acquire it with the passage of time and creation of a unique provincial history." (Black and Cairns, 1966, 40) Later analyses have exposed the effects of governments and of the electoral and the party systems in fostering regionalism. The decline or eclipse of intra-state federal institutions, such as the Senate, House Committees, political parties drawing their electoral strength from the entire country, and of regional representation in cabinet, has been discussed (and usually deplored) at great length. Moreover, there have been extensive analyses of economic, demographic, attitudinal, and voting data. All of this work is useful; no one who wishes to understand the West can afford to ignore it.

Something more is needed because there is more to the minority status of being a Westerner than appears through recounting the historical patterns of "national" policies or through an analysis of the majoritarian inclinations of central institutions and the twin consequences of those policies and that bias, namely province building and the decline in the representation of territorial interests within the central government. We need not research such important historical questions as the passage of the Manitoba Act or the disallowance of the Bank Employees Civil Rights Act to grasp the connection between majoritarian central institutions and the production of policies that reflect the interests and opinions of central Canadian majorities. This same insight is found daily in the pages of the *Calgary Herald* when the editorial lights of that journal are directed to a consideration of the Senate, energy policy, or the production of hogs. In the following section I would like to reconsider some of this essentially common knowledge in light of the focus provided by political philosophy.

2. A POLITICAL THEORY OF FEDERALISM

The perplexing problem of federal politics concerns the difficulty of combining territorial with numerical representation. Some light can be shed on it by considering a few texts from the most important work in the history of political thought that deals explicitly with federalism. In 1787, after the federal constitutional convention, Alexander Hamilton began the difficult task of securing ratification by New York of the new U.S. Constitution. He proposed a series of essays expounding the virtues of the document, recruited John Jay and James Madison to his purpose, and began publishing in the New York press a series known to us as *The Federalist Papers*. At the same time, the complete text was published as a book prior to the completion of the serialization, and it then was distributed to leading supporters of the Constitution. That is, it was addressed both to a wide audience and to the men who would actually decide on ratification. *The Federalist* was both a piece of propaganda and an attempt to influence how later generations would understand the U.S. Constitution by means of authoritative commentary. One could, through a judicious interpretation of Montesquieu, the English "classical republicans," or even of Machiavelli, extract similar insights. *The Federalist*, however, is especially useful since it does not demand much interpretative ingenuity and so avoids the appearance of arbitrariness. The argument, moreover, applied not only to the political regime established in the United States but also to Canada, at least insofar as Canada is a liberal democracy established more or less in accord with the principles established by John Locke.

The authors, chiefly Hamilton and Madison, published the text under the pseudonym Publius. Publius was named for Publius Valerius Publicola, described by Plutarch as the saviour of the Roman republic. The problem, as originally formulated by Montesquieu, was that large countries need despotic rule as a consequence of their size, whereas small ones could remain "republics." In *The Federalist*, a republic was a mixed regime, with emphasis on the democratic component, equivalent to what we would call representative government. In this respect, the theoretical importance of the distinction between representative government and the Canadian "republican" or "mixed" form, which from the 1830s we have called responsible government, is secondary.

Publius saw a three-fold difficulty in popular government. First, there was the danger that the citizens would lose control of their government; second, there was the danger that majorities would rule oppressively; third, there was the possibility that they would rule not oppressively, but foolishly. The answer to this three-fold danger, Publius said, was in a constitutional separation of powers and in multiplicity of factions. Together they would mitigate the overriding danger of oppressive majorities by ensuring institutional competition and overlapping bases of support. There were, in Publius' view, two reasons why this structure would have the desired result. First, "Ambition must be made to counteract ambition. The interest of the man must be connected with the constitutional rights of the place (i.e., of the office). It may be a reflection on human nature, that such devices should be necessary to control the abuses of government. But what is government itself but the greatest of all reflections of human nature? If men were angels, no government would be necessary." (Fed. 51, 349) That is, incumbents would defend their offices because their ambition (or pride, love of fame, or even love of fortune) would lead them to identify self-interest with the integrity of office; since that integrity would be called into disrepute by laws that sought to oppress or offend the incumbents, they would oppose such laws.

A second problem concerned faction. In *Federalist* No. 10, Publius argued that control of faction was the most important political problem in a free society. Representative or popular government was the regime appropriate to a free society, but there was always the possibility that citizens might abuse their freedom to the detriment of others. A faction existed, Publius said, when a number of citizens combine, "whether amounting to a majority or a minority of the whole, who are united and actuated by some common impulse of passion, or of interest, adverse to the rights of other citizens, or to the permanent and aggregate interests of the community." (Fed. 10, 57) Factions could be dealt with in two ways: by removing the cause, or by controlling the effects. There were two ways to remove the cause, either by abolishing freedom, which was rejected out of hand, or "by giving to every citizen the same opinions, the same passions, and the same interests." This second expedient, which we in Canada would call national unity in its political aspect[1] and conformity in its social aspect, was, however, said to be "impracticable" rather than "unwise." Publius' reasoning regarding its impracticality was straightforward: the fallibility of reason meant that men would hold different opinions and so espouse different interests. Moreover, "the diversity in the faculties of men from which the rights of property originate, is not less an insuperable obstacle to a uniformity of interests." Accordingly, protection of these different faculties was the first objective of government; consequently different and unequal faculties would result in "different degrees and kinds of property ... and from the influence of these on the sentiments and views of the respective proprietors, ensures a division of the society into different interests and parties." (Fed. 10, 58) Factions result from religious, and what we would call ideological, sources as well, and from attachment to ambitious or inspired leaders, "but the most common and durable source of factions, has been the various and unequal distribution of property." (Fed. 10, 59) The causes of factions, "are thus sown in the nature of man." It was, then, in Publius' view, impossible that the cause be removed.

The best that men and governments could hope for was that the effect of faction be controlled. The best way of doing so was to prevent the same passion or interest from arising in a majority, or in modern language, to prevent political unity and social conformity from coming into existence. In a large and geographically dispersed political regime prevention was more likely because of the difficulty of citizens gaining a single interest. They may have the same motive, which was directed at property, but the exclusiveness of property would prevent this same motive from turning into a common interest. Publius had a reasonable or prudential fear that unity or wholeness would bring an end to liberty.

Publius made, in effect, a liberal restatement of Aristotle's discussion of *stasis* in book V of *The Politics*, where, however, the problem was not faction simply, but majority faction. In Aristotle's language, the majority, the many, were the poor or, we might say, the comparatively poor; the few were the comparatively rich. *The* political problem, Publius said, was to avoid those brief "spectacles of turbulence and contention" that lead to "domestic convulsion" when the many and the few contend openly. (Fed. 10, 61) In a large commercial republic, with both different amounts and different kinds of property, the fatal contentions of class struggle would be replaced with struggle between different kinds of propertied interest, with what we could call regional or sectoral competition. In such a regime, "the society itself will be broken into so many parts, interests and classes of citizens, that the rights of individuals or of the minority, will be in little danger from interested combinations of the majority." (Fed. 51, 351)

The political teaching of Publius assumed, much as did Adam Smith, that there was a connection among a large commercial territory, the division of labour, and the propensity of individuals to strive for their own immediate and private gain. Laws must protect property but not bar the poor from opportunity; in this fashion, largely private passions and interests could be turned to the public good. The policy, he said, "of supplying by opposite and rival interests, the defect of better motives, might be traced through the whole system of human affairs, private as well as public. We see it particularly displayed in all the subordinate distributions of power; where the constant aim is to divide and arrange the several offices in such a manner that each may be a check on the other; that the private interest of every individual, may be a sentinel over the public rights." (Fed. 51, 349) Moreover, the "compound republic" comprised of central and state governments which "will control each other" (Fed. 51, 351) by the same operations of interest and ambition as provided internal controls to each branch of government taken separately.

Publius wrote in support of "a more perfect union," and we will consider the relevance of his remarks for Canadian federalism below.[2] Initially, however, we may indicate the limitation of Publius' teaching by pointing to the fact that there may be some emotions that cannot be checked by ambition, some circumstances where private interests cannot watch over public rights. Under these conditions it may be necessary, if a mixed regime is to be maintained, to sacrifice private interests and to sacrifice ambition too. That is to say, while most of the time it is prudent to rely on men's ambition and interests and not on their virtue, it is foolish to think that self-interest is the ultimate guardian of what Publius called republican virtue. Having acknowledged this limitation, it must be stressed again that factors other than ambition and interest only rarely play a part in political life, so that undue attention to questions of virtue or what we might call moralizing is worse than misguided; it is boring.

Politics, including politics in federal regimes, deals with conflicting interests. The teaching of Publius, that opinion and property create and sustain conflicting interests and that interest and office create and sustain political activity, seems to me to be at least partially persuasive. It has been confirmed by contemporary studies such as that undertaken by Black and Cairns, and helps explain why Westerners have adopted such a large number of strategies to promote and defend their interests and, in a broad sense, their property, within the federation. As Davis Smith has said, "for three quarters of a century the region has sought to influence government by working successively in the following ways: first through the dominant party of the period, next through third-party persuasion of the dominant party, then through third-party balance-of-power tactics, and finally through the principal opposition party. No other area of the country has experimented with so many partisan alternatives and has so little apparent satisfaction from the results." (Smith, 1981a, 177; see also Smith 1981b) Considered in light of *The Federalist*, then, the essential feature of majority politics in the West is simply one of resistance to majority faction. For those with a taste for edifying moralism, one might say that this resistance has been the West's greatest service to the country, comparable in this respect to the service rendered by Québec in sustaining bilingualism. Political men in the provinces, especially in the West and in Québec, defend their offices, as Publius counselled, because of their ambitions, interests, and opinions. In this way they defend the integrity of the federation, of what Cartier in the *Confederation Debates* (1963, 50) called the political nation, by defending their self-interest, which is congruent with provincial interest. Dominion servants of the crown do likewise: ambition checks ambition.

3. A REGIONAL MYTH OF IDENTITY
The danger of majority faction, so far as provincial or regional minorities are concerned, is that majorities tend to diminish or even destroy the particular good that minorities cherish as their own. The result is, of course, unwelcome to minorities, but more to the point, the world is diminished in its vitality and variety of meanings. The popular sense of provincial particularism or, more broadly, of regional identity is expressed not simply in applauding the ambitions of political men, but in common stories. It is here we encounter the largely ignored domain of inwardness in Western political life. What began, for example, as a political complaint over land policy or an economic objection to discriminatory freight rates has become the constituent element of a story and the revelation of a meaning. This transformation of fact or narrative into a typical example distinguishes history from myth. The two forms overlap to some degree: myths often contain a great deal of history in the sense of *res gestae*, and historiography is often structured to conform with mythic conventions. Even so, history generally aims at telling what happened, whereas myth aims at telling what happens all the time.

The privileged discursive vehicle for recounting myths is imaginative literature. In Canada, it is fair to say, there is no writer (and no literature) of whom we can say they belong among the classics. This is not, however, to be deplored, at least not by political science. As Northrop Frye observed, "if no Canadian author pulls us away from the Canadian context toward the centre of literary experience itself, then at every point we remain aware of his social and historical setting." (Frye, 1971, 214) Canadian literature records what the Canadian imagination has experienced as meaningful, and it tells readers of those meanings the way that nothing else could do. Whether or not Canadian imaginative writing is good literature is a question that can be answered by reference to formal canons of what literature is, but that question does not concern us. Like Audrey, it may be an ill-favoured thing, but it is our own. (*As You Like It*, V, iv, 60) And being our own, even if graceless, it gives an undistorted voice to our imaginative experience. Chief among the questions literature answers is, as Frye remarked, "where is here?" to which may be added a derivative one, "who are we?" The short answer is: we are those who know where here is; they don't know because they are not from here but from there. The "knowledge" of we and they, of here and there, and of all the subsidiary things that are implied by this strange knowing is not an awareness of a factual array or the conceptual grasp of a deployment of data. It is an imaginative and participatory knowledge, a knowledge of reminiscence and reflection, not of reductive transformation and scientific restatement.[3]

To put this point abruptly: when someone says, "I am a Westerner," he means *something*. Specifically, he is making an imaginative or metaphorical identification of place and meaning. He is answering the question: "where is (my) here?" Properly to understand Western regionalism, it seems to me, one must take into account texts that document the structure of Western imaginative consciousness, because only in such texts does one find questions of meaning presented.

When one reads this literature and the interpretation that critics have made of it, one discovers several important things. First of all, there isn't very much of it. It is possible to read a very large percentage of Canadian literature and every scrap of Canlitcrit with a comparatively small investment of time. If it is true, as Frye said, that literature reflects to the reader a discourse on identity, then the size of the corpus of Canadian literature and its relative neglect suggest that Canadians have not wanted to find out who they were or where is here. For many years, a book by an American man-of-letters (Wilson, 1965) was the most important critical work on Canadian literature. This is what the author said: "In my youth, of the early nineteen-hundreds, we tended to imagine Canada as a kind of vast hunting preserve convenient to the United States." It is the same image of Canada we find in current TV beer ads.

Second, however, are the interpretations of Canadian critics, of whom Northrop Frye is the most eminent. As he said and we agree, literature expresses a sense of identity. "Identity is local and regional, rooted in the imagination and in works of culture; unity is national in reference, international in perspective, and rooted in a political feeling." (Frye, 1971, ii) Later in the same book, however, he summarized his impressions of the *Canadian* imagination as being characterized by "what we may provisionally call a garrison mentality." (Frye, 1971, 225-26) There is a contradiction here. Frye made a useful distinction between unity and identity, which he then surrendered with his evocation of a national identity expressed in a national literature that made articulate the garrison mentality. As

THE WEST: A POLITICAL MINORITY

Dennis Duffy pointed out in his study of the literature of Upper Canada and Ontario, "Canada" as a symbol of identity was centred in the Loyalist heartland, the wedge of land south of the Shield between the valley of the Ottawa River and Lake Huron. Imaginatively, it was indeed filled with garrisons concerned with survival and hanging on — not least of all with hanging on to the West. In that place, the myth of exile (from the American colonies), covenant (loyalty to the crown), and return to a garden (the transformed wilderness) fully expressed the regional identity of "Canada." (Duffy, 1982, 131-32)

Duffy's analysis clarified a crucial but unanalyzed assumption of Frye. Canada, the imaginative reality, belonged to the experience of the Loyalist heartland. Like all such experiences, it was local. Canada, the political reality, what Duffy called the "noblest product Ontario had to offer to the rest of Canada," was "sectionalized, misappropriated, its rhetoric employed to justify the smashing of the alternative Canada that had sprung from the Métis experience." Duffy did not enlarge on what the Métis-inspired alternative might have been. He did, however, identify it with the West, which suggested that an ampler Canada that did not betray itself was somehow linked to the export of the noblest product of Ontario. He did not dwell on what made that "vision of nationhood" noble, nor did he say what he meant by vision. We can, however, make the following tentative conclusion: Canada, the imaginative reality, centred in the Loyalist heartland, became Canada the political reality. By so doing, it betrayed its own regional identity and destroyed the possibility of an alternative political reality that Duffy identified in an unclear way with the Métis experience and in any event was located in the West.

The conclusion to be drawn seems clear: there is an ambiguity in the meaning of the term "Canada." Those who drew their sense of place from the imaginative Canada, the Loyalist heartland, as Frye did, implicitly identified that place with the political unit stretching from sea to sea, and from the river — the St. Lawrence River — to the ends of the earth (cf. Psalm 72:8), which meant not a vague emptiness off towards the North Pole, but the great lone land lying in a northwesterly direction beyond the river and the Bay. To the imaginative Canadians, the ones of the garrison mentality, the ones who drew up the national motto, the West was the end of the earth, a "there" not a "here."

The insights of Duffy and Frye tell us a great deal about the meaning of those two great symbols of Loyalist regional identity, "Canadian nationalism" and "national unity." Both terms exemplify what Duffy called the use of rhetoric and what might be more accurately called propaganda or straightforward lying. That is, national unity and Canadian nationalism are symbols that express the regional identity of imaginative "Canada," the Loyalist heartland. This is why, for example, such "nationalist" policies as the National Energy Program, the "regulation" of foreign investors, or of the importation of well-made foreign automobiles, look to Westerners like moves by the garrison to protect its own interests inside the Eastern industrial fort. Naturally enough, if you dwelt within the fort, if you were an imaginative Canadian as well as a Canadian citizen, things would look quite different, which simply reinforces the importance to be accorded conflicting interests, ambitions, and opinions. The third point is, therefore, obvious: imaginative regional Canada must be distinguished from federal political Canada. To be more pertinent, Western regional identity, to the extent that it is distinct from "Canadian" identity, refers to particular experiences expressed by way of particular symbols and themes.[4]

This substantive point has been made by literary critics who have turned their attention to Western literature. The significance of these studies has been all but overlooked by political scientists.[5] Nearly all Western literature and criticism emphasizes the importance of environment, in particular of the landscape. "All discussion of the literature produced in the Canadian West," Henry Kreisel (1968, 173) announced, "must of necessity begin with the impact of the landscape upon the mind."[6] Donald Stephens (1973, 2) made a more explicit contrast: "The 'garrison mentality' so obvious in the writing of Eastern Canada (in the Maritimes, Quebec, and Ontario) is not prominent in Western Canada (the Prairies and British Columbia)." The reason, he said, was because "the prairie is a landscape that makes them (the inhabitants) greater than (garrison) life; it is an environment that brings out the best, worst in man." This interpretation contrasts starkly with that of a typical Eastern writer such as Margaret Atwood(1972). Finally, the land is not an imaginative threat, as apparently the forests of Ontario and Québec were. The point is plain: the West is not a transplanted imaginative Ontario garrison.

The imaginative prairie landscape had both a spatial and a temporal dimension. Spatially, it extended, as David Carpenter (1975, 17) said, "from the dryland to the Promised Land," that is, from Manitoba and Saskatchewan to Alberta. Imaginatively, Alberta is the quintessential West, the far West, McCourt (1949, vi) called it in his classic study, and B.C. is the near East. However that may be, changes over time are more important for our purposes than changes over space, because it is over time that there has appeared a distinctive Western voice formed in response to the internal landscape, which is not just the response to a geographic environment.

The historical theme of Western identity has consisted in variations in the response of European groups and individuals to a non-European world. The new land did not have an impact on an empty head but on a conscious one filled with the old culture. Right from the beginning, British words such as meadow and snow proved inadequate to the reality experienced. More generally, the experiences of Westerners have had to come to terms with the disjunction between a literary language and culture and the oral language of daily life, between *Maclean's* or the CBC and the Longview bar. (Stegner, 1955)

Only recently have cultural geographers and historians devoted much attention to the problem of how the Western landscape was articulated by the pre-settlement consciousness of explorers and furtraders.[7] After the early explorers, who were more interested in markets than landscape anyhow, descriptions turned technical or fictional; from about the mid-nineteenth century, economics and calculative reason parted company with imagination and emotion. Explorers were supplanted by men on expeditions, hastily scribbled journals of mnemonic doggerel gave way to official reports, scientific accounts and speculations about rainfall, flora, and isotherms. Maps were drawn on grids. From the beginning of the systematic deployment of European knowledge over the region, the West has felt the impact of the most advanced technology of the day, a fact to which we shall return.

But first a preliminary observation. Unlike the great technologies of central Canada, Western ones were concerned directly with resource extraction, not industrial manufacturing. At the same time, however, they were subordinated to these and other central Canadian technologies. Consider, for example, the prairie town. The "hugeness of simple forms" that Wallace Stegner evoked congealed into the mass production of identical elevators, banks, railway stations, a main street called Main Street, and a dirt road beside the tracks called Railway Avenue. It was as if the CPR had but one blueprint and people were made to fit it. Variety was provided, of course, but only by the several names of CPR directors, their families and mistresses; the technology of administrative control was uniform and external to the region.

Not until recently has the balance between landscape and technology shifted decisively in favour of the latter. After two or three generations, technological activity transformed the prairie space into an imaginative void, at least for the most sensitive minds. (Ricou, 1976, 72) Even today, however, it may be doubted that the poetic sensibilities that discover a sense of nothingness in the existence of high-tech, multi-section Saskatchewan wheat farms are shared by the men who operate them. Nor does it necessarily follow that the lives of the men and women who fill the towers of glass that glitter like ice are as cold, transparent, and empty as they appeared to Perdue. In any event, Western identity, such as it is, has been made articulate in the past by imaginative writers who found meaning, not its absence. Indeed, some critics have argued that the dominant spirit even of recent Western literature is comic, the spirit of new beginnings. (Harrison, 1977, 179; Ricou, 1982; Lecker, 1982)

* * *

In the previous section a reading of *The Federalist* suggested an interpretation of federal politics that stressed the benefits of a conflict of interests, opinions, and ambitions. The political activity of the West, in this respect, has been one of resistance. Imaginatively, it has been resistance to the military-administrative rule by members of the central garrison. The comic form of Western identity, which may well derive from the imaginative transformation of the openness of the landscape, of an openness that suggests limitless possibility and an impatience with those who muse gloomily in their garrisons about survival or gaze at length into the fog across the North Atlantic, is what keeps political resistance from turning into rebellion. Western Canadians are every bit as patriotic as their fellow citizens in the East. The difference, perhaps, is that they understand themselves as part of a political order comprised of conflicting political and economic interests. A threat to the garrison may appear to them as an opportunity for heroic or futile action.

4. TECHNOLOGY AND REGION

The most comprehensive context for Western as well as Canadian politics, the context within which the fortunes of Canada, the political unit, as well as the imaginative realities of Canada and the West unfold, is given by technology.[8] The historical reasons for the importance of technology are obvious enough. Even if we discount our intimate connections to the greatest technological centres of the last century and a half, namely Great Britain and the United States, Canadian society has, for much of that time, from necessity been preoccupied with the practical business of a pioneering nation. Energies have been directed towards material rather than spiritual ends; the active not the contemplative life has guided the aspirations of most men. A large continent was settled and developed by pioneers; from the perspective of the world, scientific technique combined with natural resources to produce a society the vast majority of whose members were, by all historical comparisons, very wealthy. What Aristotle thought to be impossible, that the many and the rich could coincide, has largely been achieved.

Moreover, this devotion to technical practicality continued long after it had ceased to be a consequence of necessity. (Grant, 1951, 121) The people who undertook the pioneering task had neither the time nor the concentration to consider what changes they had made to the world, nor how those worldly changes had affected their minds or consciousnesses and the minds of their children. And, in any case, immigrants to this continent were seldom people who had a profound understanding of the spiritual riches of European civilization. Those for whom the Toronto of the 1870s was Eldorado were not unlike those who saw the Calgary of the 1970s in a similar way. Such persons usually have exhibited a modest capacity for contemplation. A concern for practical things and the exhortation to confidence ensured that a basically unphilosophical temperament would be considered normal and good. The arts and thought would be considered a diversion, recreations like hockey and whisky. (Brown, 1971, 42)

What sustained our technological drive beyond the limits of practical necessity, and indeed beyond a concern with survival, was the end product of a certain kind of Protestantism. Under the impact of the pioneering experience, the infinite yearning and moralizing orthodoxy of Puritanism, which also has a certain affinity for the garrison (or at least for Toronto-the-good) has been modified into what might be termed scientific or technological meliorism. A generation ago, this spiritual drive had two typical representatives: the self-made man and the scientist, including the practitioners of administrative science. Today the two types have been fused by a process that reminds one of nothing so much as the recombinant DNA technologies that some of them practice. The ferocious faith of the Puritan still burns brightly in the eyes of those who direct their energies to changing the world through technical activity. And yet, changing the world has been accomplished by a fading of the presence of the infinite from our consciousness. Some have argued that the two experiences are causally connected. However that may be, it would seem that a technological society also generates a demand for motive and meaning that it is imperfectly equipped to fulfil. This larger context of technology bears upon our immediate concern with the West as a political minority because it alters the significance or meaning of both politics and regional identity.

These closing remarks on the current meaning of the West as a political minority are offered as a speculative argument, not a firm conclusion. Some years ago George Grant (1965) showed in *Lament for a Nation* that Canadian independence, in the sense of a particular relation of political existence and culture, had already been lost. What Canadians had inherited from the European traditions of Britain and France had ceased to have any political visibility because those traditions had ceased to animate the souls of Canadians. To see how this is so, consider a simple, familiar, and practical question: why should Westerners support the Ministry of Communications in their attempt to control satellite dishes when Canadians in all parts of the country prefer to watch TV with a universalist flavour for free rather than watch TV with a universalist flavour made expensively in Toronto? If the universalism is as present in a Toronto production as in one made in New York City (and if it is any good it will conform to universal production values), why not take the cheaper product? The benefits of placing universal stories in a Canadian setting are not worth the cost because the benefits are zero. There is no point in trying to save what has lost truth and authority, which is why nationalist, that is imaginatively "Canadian," propaganda is viewed by Westerners with suspicion or contempt. Those who reject the appeal of Ottawa do so, generally speaking, because they wish to live more naturally in the technological empire and to participate more extensively in its local management.

Grant's lament for a nation, for the imaginative reality Canada, may have been the lament for an anachronism as well as a region of the political unit. In Europe, nations developed as bodies politic after the wars of religion had destroyed the older political forms of *Christianitas*. But now even Europe has become an economic association. Just as in the Soviet Union and its neighbours, so too in North America, multi-national economic organizations are the prevailing political form. Again, it is not the fact, but the meaning of this change that is of concern.

Compared to previous medieval forms, national states were the beginning of a reversion to nature. That is, spiritual experiences expressed with great clarity in a political text such as Augustine's *City of God* and imperfectly embodied in the institutions of Church and Empire were eclipsed by experiences of national self-sufficiency in matters of spirituality or, if you like, in matters of meaning. Compared to experiences of participation in the realm of the spirit, experiences of participation in self-sufficient national political bodies amount to a kind of reversion to nature, where nature is considered as origin rather than goal. Economic or technological empires that have begun to succeed national states are a further return to nature, to the mode of existence that Hannah Arendt (1958, chs. 20, 45) called *animal laborans*. The national or political community is no longer considered basic; the economic independence of individuals, their metabolism with nature, and what we call freedom are considered fundamental. This is not to say that the old institutions, the monarchy, for example, or attachment to the traditional language of most of the inhabitants of Québec, have disappeared. On the contrary, we are still attached to these expressions of a vanishing order, but not seriously. We regard them with nostalgia and enjoy the pomp of royal tours (or papal ones) as novel and interesting diversions, as rare entertainment; we take seriously only naturalistic individualism because there lies the source of the state and of our other institutions.

To take two examples, it seems apparent that the *indépendantistes* of Quebec do not wish to isolate themselves from the affluent and productive North American economy any more than do their fellow Canadians. They do not desire an independent state, a sovereign political body in the old style; they do, however, desire to participate in the modern technological society more naturally, that is, in French. This shows their lack of seriousness: they wish to retain what Hegel would say had no truth for them. A second example: there exists a widespread belief that the only limit to freedom is equality. Since this equality is also natural, it can be applied not simply to fellow citizens, which would be a particularist equality before the law, but socially as well, for example, to "non-traditional roles," which we call women's rights, and without restriction to all humanity, which is what we mean by human rights. Indeed, natural equality has also been extended to small seals, medium-sized wolves, and very large whales; other creatures may in the future be similarly favoured with the status of honourary sacred cows. They too would have (modern) natural rights, being part of nature.

The condition for continuing this regime, which James Doull (1983) has called anarchic socialism, and which was founded upon a spiritual stance that Hegel called naturalistic individualism, is coexistence with bureaucratic socialism, the command structure of administrative rule. The difficulty is to think how both coexist. Consider the case of those individuals who wish to save baby seals or the culture of Eskimos. In these examples, it is not proposed to ground rights in the authority of law or in political institutions but rather in nature. Given institutional authority is held to be incompatible with freedom. But this means the protests to save nature and more primitive or more natural peoples are also unserious. Protesters hold to the natural against the technological by means of the technological. Moreover, it is by means, precisely, of the technological that they are free within nature. It would take one with far greater comic talents than I possess to explore fully the significance of saving baby seals by landing on ice floes and growlers with helicopters and green spray paint. That is, the contradictions of technological naturalism are most clearly seen in the love of the primitive and the desire, were it humanly possible, for sheer animality. The same contradiction, I suggest, exists in the example of Western regionalism within a technological empire.

The meaning of the West as a political minority under technological conditions is ambivalent in the extreme. On the one hand, it is clearly allied with the universalism of technology. As we have seen, Westerners have from the beginning of settlement worked out their destiny within the assumptions of pioneer practicality, an attitude or consciousness that easily melts into the technological naturalism of the present, especially with the atrophy of traditional institutional restraints associated with farm life.[9] On the other hand, they have persistently resisted the administrative technologies of rule from Ottawa and have opposed the armed and unarmed functionaries acting on behalf of the Loyalist garrison, without, however, embracing the American notion that sees naturalistic individualism as the end product of revolution. In the early days this was done by means of political life within a federal regime. Historically, that is, Westerners have resisted the demands of the garrison because they have appeared predatory, and they have found some meaning as Westerners in that resistance. More broadly, the political life of Canada as a whole had a meaning that was expressed in myths and stories of the several regions within the political unit. But those stories and meanings were not taken entirely seriously because the country was sheltered from the more strenuous aspects of international politics by its status within the British Empire, and by its rejection of full-blooded, revolutionary American liberalism: we have never fought our own wars, though Canadians have shown courage in fighting in imperial ones. Imaginatively, contemporary Western literature is a dream of origins, a dream of home that may never have been and to which contemporary Westerners can certainly never return. But in the same way that it makes no sense to try to refute a poem, no more than a sense of Eastern alienation can be gained by pointing out the "romantic" nature of this imaginative contemporary Western reality. Its reality, not its reasonableness judged in light of external criteria, carries meaning and political weight.

To this initial political, economic, and imaginative ambivalence must be added another. Under the impact of technology, the particularist demands of

Westerners for political power, for control over natural resources — land in the days of the National Policy, petroleum in the days of the National Energy Program — amount to demands to be as universalist as possible. This is why, for example, the comic assertiveness of Western regional identity commands our admiration even while we may be appalled by the deep resentments that nourish it. It is, accordingly, easy to mistake those particularities, those regional identities, for something else, namely an attempt to defend a particular way of living against the destructive uniformity of technological universalism or, politically speaking, of centralized administration, which Canadians call national unity. In fact, however, those particularities are secondary. Whether Western regionalism and its political appearance — namely conflict of opinion, ambition, and interest within the federation — can subsist not only in the form of modern natural rights (once called the joyless quest for joy — Strauss, 1953: 251) but as something more noble, as forces for political education, none can say.

FOOTNOTES

[1] National unity is, in Canada, an imaginative term. Its meaning is clarified below.

[2] In terms of U.S. political thought, the position in favour of which I argue has a good deal in common with that of the anti-federalists. That the text we are considering here can be put to alternative use is an indication of its comprehensiveness. See Storing (1981) for an account of the anti-federalist position.

[3] For further analysis of this question see Cooper (1979, 1981a, 1981b).

[4] The following political story illustrates the point as well. On March 25, 1983 Joe Clark described William Davis as a regional candidate for the leadership of the Conservative Party. On June 7, four days before the leadership vote, which in the event Davis did not contest, he gave a dinner at the Albany Club in Toronto for 150 people who had helped organize his bid for the leadership. In his remarks to his supporters that night he commented on Clark's earlier statement. "I am not a regional candidate," he said. "I believe in Canada, not a community of communities," a term that Clark had borrowed from Frye. As Martin, Gregg and Perlin (1983, 53) said, "Davis's eyes filled with tears as he spoke of this commitment and his audience was visibly moved."

[5] I have given a more extensive account of the argument in the remainder of this section in Cooper (1984).

[6] Consider the opening sentence of one of the most famous Western novels, W.O. Mitchell's *Who Has Seen the Wind*: "Here was the least common denominator of nature, the skeleton requirements simply, of land and sky — Saskatchewan prairie."

[7] A selection of the early writings is in Warkentin (1964); discussion of several of them is found in: Kaye and Moodie (1973), Dunbar (1973), Moodie (1976) and Francis (1982).

[8] My understanding of technology has been shaped by the work of Jacques Ellul (1964), George Grant (1969), and Leo Strauss (1958). The focus of the writings of these men is upon technology considered as a method, the one best (= most efficient) way of acting in any field of activity so as to overcome chance. Thus, for example, a rifle is a better means to kill a deer than is an

automobile; administrative rule is a more efficient way to run a country than is participatory democracy. Technology, that is, is by no means confined to hardware machinery.

[9] This aspect of Western regionalism has received exhaustive treatment in Gibbins (1980).

REFERENCES

Arendt, H. *The Human Condition.* Chicago: University of Chicago Press, 1958.

Atwood, M. *Survival: A Thematic Guide to Canadian Literature.* Toronto: Anansi, 1972.

Banting, K. and Richard Simeon, eds. *And No One Cheered: Federalism, Democracy and the Constitution Act.* Toronto: Methuen, 1983.

Black, E.R. and Alan Cairns. "A Different Perspective on Canadian Federalism." *Canadian Public Administration*, 1966, 9, 27-44.

Brown, E.K. Canadian Poetry (1943). *Contexts of Canadian Criticism: A Collection of Critical Essays*, Eli Mandel, ed. Chicago: University of Chicago Press, 1971.

Carpenter, D. "Alberta in Fiction: The Emergence of a Provincial Consciousness." *Journal of Canadian Studies*, 1975, 10:4, 12-23.

Confederation Debates. P.B. Waite, ed. Toronto: McClelland and Stewart, 1963.

Conway, J.F. "Populism in the United States, Russia, and Canada: Explaining the Roots of Canada's Third Parties." *Canadian Journal of Political Science*, 1978, 11, 99-124.

Cooper, B. "Reason and Interpretation in Contemporary Political Theory." *Polity*, 1979, 11, 387-99.

----------. "Hermeneutics and Political Science." H.K. Betz, ed. *Recent Approaches to the Social Sciences*, Calgary: Social Sciences Symposium Series, 1979, II, 17-30.

----------. "Reduction, Reminiscence and the Search for Truth." *The Philosophy of Order*, Peter J. Opitz, Gregor Sebba, eds., Stuttgart: Klett-Kotta, 1981, 316-31.

----------. "Western Political Consciousness." *Political Thought in Canada*, Stephen Brooks, ed., Toronto: Irwin, 1984, 213-38.

Doull, J. "Naturalistic Individualism: Quebec Independence and an Independent Canada." *Modernity and Responsibility: Essays for George Grant*, Eugene Coombs, ed., Toronto: University of Toronto Press, 1983, 29-50.

Duffy, D. *Gardens, Covenants and Exiles: Loyalism in the Literature of Upper Canada/Ontario*, Toronto: University of Toronto Press, 1982.

Dunbar, G.S. "Isotherms and Politics: Perception of the Northwest in the 1850s." *Prairie Perspectives 2*, A.W. Rasporitch and H.C. Classen, eds., Toronto: Holt Rinehart and Co., 1973, 80-101.

Ellul, J. *The Technological Society*, J. Wilkinson, tr., New York: Vintage, 1964.

The Federalist Papers, J.E. Cooke, ed., Middletown: Wesleyan University Press, 1961.

Francis, R.D. "Changing Images of the West." *Journal of Canadian Studies*, 1982, 17:3, 5-17.

Frye, N. *The Bush Garden: Essays on the Canadian Imagination.* Toronto: Anansi, 1971.

Gibbins, R. *Prairie Politics and Society: Regionalism in Decline.* Toronto: Butterworths, 1980.

----------. "Constitutional Politics and the West." Banting (1983), 119-132.

Grant, G. "Philosophy." *Royal Commission Studies*, Royal Commission on National Development (The Massey Commission). Ottawa: King's Printer, 1951, 119-35.

----------. *Lament for a Nation: The Defeat of Canadian Nationalism.* Toronto: McClelland and Stewart, 1965.

----------. *Technology and Empire: Perspectives on North America.* Toronto: Anansi, 1969.

Harrison, D. *Unnamed Country: The Struggle for a Canadian Prairie Fiction.* Edmonton: University of Alberta Press, 1977.

Kaye, B. and D.W. Moodie. "Geographic Perspectives on the Canadian Plains," ed., Richard Allen, *A Region of the Mind: Interpreting the Western Canadian Plains*, Canadian Plains Studies, No. 1. Regina: Canadian Plains Research Centre, 1973, 17-46.

Kreisel, H. "The Prairie: A State of Mind." *Transactions of the Royal Society of Canada*, 1968, Series IV, vol. vi, 171-80.

Lecker, R. "Bordering On: Robert Kroetsch's Aesthetic." *Journal of Canadian Studies*, 1982, 17:3, 124-33.

Martin, P., Allan Gregg, G. Perlin. *Contenders: The Tory Quest for Power.* Toronto: Prentice-Hall, 1983.

McCourt, E. *The Canadian West in Fiction.* Toronto: Ryerson, 1949.

Moodie, D.W. "Early Images of Rupert's Land." *Man and Nature on the Prairies.* Richard Allen, ed., Canadian Plains Studies, No. 6. Regina: Canadian Plains Research Centre, 1976, 1-20.

Ricou, L. *Vertical Man/Horizontal World: Man and Landscape in Canadian Prairie Fiction.* Vancouver: University of British Columbia Press, 1973.

----------. "Circumference and Absence: Land and Space in the Poetry of the Canadian Plains." *Man and Nature on the Prairies*, Richard Allen, ed., Canadian Plains Studies, No. 6. Regina: Canadian Plains Research Centre, 1976, 66-76.

----------. "Field Notes and Notes in a Field: Some Forms of the West in Robert Kroetsch and Tom Robbins." *Journal of Canadian Studies.* 1982, 17:3, 117-23.

Smith, D. "Political Culture in the West." *Eastern and Western Perspectives: Papers from the Joint Atlantic Canada/Western Canada Studies Conference.* David Jay Bercuson, Philip A. Buckner, eds. Toronto: University of Toronto Press, 1981, 169-82.

----------. *The Regional Decline of a National Party: Liberals on the Prairies*, Toronto: University of Toronto Press, 1981.

Stegner, W. *Wolf Willow: A History, a Story, and a Memory of the Last Plains Frontier.* Lincoln: University of Nebraska Press, (1955) 1980.

Stephens, D. Introduction. *Writers of the Prairies.* D. Stephens, ed., Vancouver: University of British Columbia Press, 1973.

Storing, H.J. *What the Anti-Federalists Were For.* Chicago: University of Chicago Press, 1981.

Strauss, L. *Natural Right and History*. Chicago: University of Chicago Press, 1953.

──────. *Thoughts on Machiavelli*. Glencoe: The Free Press, 1958.

Warkentin, J. ed. *The Western Interior of Canada: A Record of Geographical Discovery, 1612-1917*. Toronto: McClelland and Stewart, 1964.

Wilson, E. *O Canada: An American's Notes on Canadian Culture*. New York: Farrar, Strauss and Giroux, 1965.

13

THE CHANGING POLITICAL SITUATION OF WOMEN IN CANADA

JOEL SMITH
ALLAN KORNBERG
BETH RUSHING

INTRODUCTION

These past few years we have been heavily involved in research on regime support — the factors and processes that relate to its potential and its manifestation. The vehicle for addressing these issues is a study of the development of people's understandings of the meaning of the Québec Referendum for Canada and of responses to those understandings. The relevant theory implies that events of this type may activate any latent predispositions toward regime support. The actions precipitated by that mobilization, of course, play an important role in a regime's future. This analysis of the changing political status of Canadian women develops directly from our involvement in studying the Referendum.

Our decision to focus on the changing political status of women is more than a matter of convenience. Obviously, even if they are on the decline — and that is an arguable point — there are major gender inequalities in family roles, employment patterns, wages, education, religion, and status generally. However, in the long run the equality of any group in a democratic state is achieved and maintained through participation in the political process. If legislation is necessary and if it is to be enforced effectively, telling demonstrations of political interest and strength by the group concerned are necessary preconditions to state action. Slow change or no change implies weak and ineffective politics by a subordinate group. We focus on political interest, attitudes, and participation because in countries like Canada any gender differences in political effectiveness no longer have a legal basis. Women are not disenfranchised nor are they barred from office. Hence, because men traditionally have dominated politics and are not strongly motivated to change the situation voluntarily, gender differences are more likely to reflect how women relate to the political process rather than whether it is legally possible to do so.

No one who has followed the rise to power of the Parti Québécois and the actualization of its political program by holding the Referendum can fail to be aware of the increasing and changing significance of women in Canadian political affairs. The Parti, of course, worked to involve and secure support from women in its successful drive to concretize the broad social changes that constituted the Quiet Revolution. Nonetheless, perhaps the most dramatic event in the Referendum campaign was the "Yvette" episode triggered by some ill-conceived remarks by the P.Q. official responsible for securing women's support for the "Oui" faction. At the height of the Referendum campaign Lise Bisonette injudiciously commented that women ought to follow their men in supporting the proposition. This sparked a massive rally of Montréal women who objected to what they considered to be evidence that the P.Q. either wished to return to or never really had departed from traditional Québec familism. It is not our intention to analyze these events here. We mention them only to identify some of the stimulus to this present undertaking.

THE STATUS OF WOMEN: RECEIVED WISDOM AND RECENT CHANGE

In this paper we draw primarily upon analyses of data we collected in three community panel studies conducted as part of our Referendum research. As do all representative random samples of adult populations, those panels contain majorities of women. That fact by itself signifies the importance and pertinence of our topic. The issues addressed are shaped by some provocative facets of the literature reviewed for an analysis some eight years earlier of women who held positions in local political party organizations. (Kornberg, Smith, and Clarke, 186-216) In particular, the data gathered for our Referendum study seemed potentially useful for examining Thelma McCormack's analysis of the state of knowledge about women's political roles in her essay "Toward a Nonsexist Perspective on Social and Political Change." (1975) Although we shall not test any of Professor McCormack's ideas directly they motivate and inform this work.

Professor McCormack's thesis is that not enough is known about women and politics to be able to say anything reliable about women's political roles. More specifically, she asserts that there is an absence of depth and richness in social scientists' understanding of women's political participation, that the few generalizations that are widely accepted may well be wrong, and that the reason for this lack of understanding and misunderstanding is a fundamental male bias that has shaped political studies. She argues that male politicians pay little heed to women and their political concerns because the available wisdom from years of research since World War II boils down to three propositions: women participate in politics less than do men in such respects as interest, motivation, intensity, and frequency; women tend to be much more conservative and less willing to risk change than are men; and women participate politically more as a reflection of the family solidarity of male-dominated households than as an expression of either their own interests or those of the other non-family groups with which they personally are identified. She goes on to question the validity of these generalizations because they are based upon gender comparisons of individual attitudes and opinions on matters that primarily concern men and on modes of participation and political expression that are more available and appropriate to men than to women.

Concern with regime support and the particular case of the Referendum sensitizes us to gender differences in politics and, particularly, interests us in the contemporary pertinence of the sorts of propositions and arguments that McCormack develops. In addition, the development of the feminist movement with its relatively different approach to power and politics, tending to rely more on moral suasion than on the power of the ballot, and with its success in achieving symbolic gains for women while at the same time failing to rally their mass support, is additional reason to be sensitive to women's changing position in the political system and to want some basis for assessing the validity of her analysis.

Such manifestations of the changing politics of women — partly as cause and partly as effect in a reciprocal influence loop — are only segments of a much broader pattern of changing status for Canadian women relative to Canadian men. Data series pertinent to the matter are innumerable. Women comprise the larger portion of the Canadian population. This is because women long have had greater life expectancies than men. That differential has been increasing during the last two decades as women have been experiencing larger gains in life expectancy than have men. Perhaps more important, however, are subtler changes in status outside the realm of numbers.

Canadian women, like their counterparts in other Western countries, have been entering the labour force in steadily increasing numbers. In 1921, barely 20 percent of Canadian women were employed outside the home; by 1975 that figure had grown to 41 percent. (Cheki and Hofley, 1980:380) In 1977, 53 percent of Canadian women between the ages of 20 and 64 were in the labour force. Despite these remarkable changes, the difference between women's and men's labour force participation rates is still large; 90 percent of Canadian men aged 20 to 64 were employed in 1977. Additionally, 78 percent of the women who were employed in 1977 were full-time workers, compared with 95 percent of male workers. (Saunders, 1982:238) Although married women remain the least likely of all women to be employed, they too are joining the labour force in record numbers. In 1976 almost a quarter of the Canadian labour force was comprised of married women (44 percent were married men), and 41 percent of them had children. (Statistics Canada, 1979)

Although women do every conceivable type of work, despite equal opportunity programs they remain overwhelmingly concentrated in occupations that have been traditionally filled by women. (McDonald, 1979:340) Approximately 71 percent of all women in the labour force in 1977 were concentrated in just three sectors: finance, insurance, and real estate; trade; and services. In contrast, only 38 percent of males in the labour force were in these three sectors. (Saunders, 1982:239) Levels of pay, unionization, and security for jobs in these sectors typically have been and continue to be low. They are, to use Edwards' terminology (1979), in the "secondary sector" of the economy, requiring low skills, providing little or no control over individual work tasks, lacking opportunities for advancement, and offering few and small rewards. (Edwards, 1979) It is not surprising, therefore, that there is a substantial male-female income gap. That gap also continues because, in addition, women often are paid less than men for equal work. Despite equal opportunity and equal pay programs, the average income for full-time female workers was only 57.8 percent of that of their male counterparts in 1977. (Saunders, 1982:242) The gap is particularly large for women who are or have been married. (Cheki and Hofley, 1980:391) Moreover, from 1955 to 1969, as women increasingly have entered the working world, the gap has doubled, and, by 1973, in absolute dollars it was greater than the average income for women. (McDonald, 1979:340) Data for 1972 and 1977 indicate that for all comparable occupations examined the gap between female and male earnings has increased. (Saunders, 1982:243) McDonald estimates that if current equal pay legislation were successful, women who work full-time would earn an average of approximately 80 percent of their male coworkers' incomes.

Education is another arena in which women's situations are changing. From 1967 to 1977, the number of women enrolled full-time in undergraduate courses almost doubled. (Statistics Canada, 1978:43) Female full-time graduate enrollment in 1977 was nearly triple the level of 1967. During that same period, the number of female part-time undergraduates also tripled and the number of female part-time graduate students increased fourfold. (Statistics Canada, 1978:43) In 1976 almost twice as many women as men received a one- or two-year college diploma, slightly fewer women than men earned a three- or four-year college degree, and virtually equal numbers of women and men earned bachelors or first professional degrees. (Devereaux and Rechnitzer, 1980:32-34) At higher levels, the numbers of men receiving degrees were increasingly greater. Within each level of education, Devereaux and Rechnitzer found that women tended to earn degrees mostly in such female-dominated fields as nursing, secretarial skills, education, the humanities, and community service, suggesting that schools continue to shape women's occupational and educational choices away from traditionally male-dominated fields. (p.175) Thus, although women are entering the Canadian work force in ever-growing numbers, the increase in share of jobs has not resulted in equal pay, equal benefits, equal opportunities, or equal status. Women's income, relative to that of men, is low. With equal education, women still earn less than men do. Indeed, even in a female-dominated field such as nursing women earn less than men with the same education. (Devereaux and Rechnitzer, 1980:191)

In similar fashion, gender differences in overall participation levels generally are small, but women participate in different sorts of activities and organizations than do men. Moreover, although there are no substantial gender differences in participation in voting, variations in office holding both in government and political parties, as well as participation in the more influential types of politics, are substantially to the disadvantage of women. The absence of systematic data series makes it impossible to render any judgement as to change in women's political status. The import of the most obvious observations is mixed. Jeanne Sauve is now Governor General after having been Speaker of the House, but still very few women sit in Parliament. Women generally exercise the franchise as much as men do, but in Québec they were not as supportive of the P.Q. as were men. In our own data women were more likely than men either to be unable to answer or to say "Don't know" to many questions concerning political attitudes, opinions, and behaviour. This mixture of signs of change and no change, of patterns of evidence confirming and contradicting the common wisdom, and of conflicting observations generally might be less confusing if interpreted from the perspective of Professor McCormack's thesis.

Professor McCormack (1975) cites a variety of studies to support her argument. Some of them go back as much as forty years. Hence, it is possible that whatever the situation was with respect to gender differences in politics, it has changed. Even if it hasn't, she has argued that the proposition that women are less interested and participate in politics less than men may be a spurious by-product of the fact that political sociologists study phenomena of less general relevance to women than to men. Moreover, if the issues addressed in research are of little interest to most women, married women simply may defer to the men in their families either by doing as the men would wish or by withdrawing attention. Nonetheless, younger unmarried women may be as interested and as active as men are, and may take different positions even if the issues are not gender-relevant. If the issues are gender-relevant, however, women generally may take positions that differ from those of men. Thus, the passage of time, changes in the differential gender-relevance of issues and in differences in access to political processes, as well as the changing status of women through the life course may interact to produce an overall picture that still supports the common wisdom but remains spurious.

STRATEGY OF ANALYSIS

In this paper we report an effort to untangle these several factors. Although we lack longitudinal data covering many years, we have tried to specify in ways that are testable with these data some implications of the arguments that (1) gender differences are a spurious by-product of a number of other gender-related phenomena, and (2) whatever real differences there may have been, have been decreasing. The data pertain to people's opinions and attitudes, on the one hand, or to their actions, on the other. With respect to opinions and attitudes, they address topics of no apparent special relevance or of apparent special relevance to women (e.g., equal access to jobs, equal salary for equivalent work). It should be noted that the term gender-relevance is used here only to refer to topics that generally are understood to represent values, goals, and achievements for women by proponents of improvements in the general status of women. *The term is not used for matters of special pertinence to men or for matters of no apparent differential relevance for which there nevertheless are gender differences in the distributions of responses.* Responses to items of each type have two dimensions: (1) there are or are not clear opinions and attitudes expressed, and (2) if expressed, they support one of two or more positions on a matter in question. The combination of gender-relevance and aspect of response creates four different conditions within which gender differences may be examined. For each we have somewhat different expectations, and different tests are in order.

The political activities for which we have information do not differ in terms of gender-relevance (e.g., general frequency of voting, participating in non-traditional modes of political activity), but some vary in whether they are equally accessible on a collective basis to all persons without regard to gender. For example, regardless of local norms, everyone is legally eligible to vote; in contrast, only members of the labour force may strike, and more men than women are in the labour force. Or, men are more likely than are women to have higher incomes and to be the dominant persons in spousal pairs on financial matters, thus suggesting that men are more likely than women to be able to make financial contributions to political campaigns. As with opinions and attitudes, somewhat different expectations and different types of tests are in order for the two sorts of activities.

Although we specify a variety of different expectations for these tests, gross comparisons in any single test between all the interviewed men and women would be misleading for several reasons. (1) Even if traditional relations have changed, for structural reasons the communities probably still differ with respect to men-women relations. But even if the communities are not different currently, differences in past conditions certainly would have had a differential impact on the older members of our samples. In particular, more than either Peterborough or Lethbridge, Trois Rivières was marked by a traditional Québecois emphasis on familism with male dominance. Moreover, levels of dissatisfaction and information about the various matters on which the respondents were questioned also varied among the three. For these reasons the community samples always are analyzed individually. A side benefit of not combining communities is that the samples do not have to be weighted to adjust for somewhat different sampling rates. (2) For similar reasons marital status also must be taken into account. Only married persons were subject to the influence of spouses at the time of the interview; widowed and divorced persons, however, might still be under past spousal influence. Moreover, because male mortality at all adult ages is higher, men and women differ in their distribution across the various marital status categories (e.g., there are more widows than widowers). (3) Age also must be taken into account. Unfortunately, in cross-sectional samples individual ages reflect age, period, and cohort effects simultaneously. For various reasons (including research that calls into question the old saw about people becoming increasingly conservative with age), we generally shall interpret age differences as reflections of periods. We assume that with the passage of time during the twentieth century there has been both an opening of opportunities for women and a growing expectation that women will be as politically interested and active as are men.

To illustrate how we would expect these several factors to interact, we start with the case of the absence of clear opinions or attitudes on issues of general rather than gender-relevance. More women than men would be unable to answer these questions or claim not to know about the matter if the generalization about greater interest on the part of men than of women is correct. However, if the feminist movement both has been consciousness-raising and has impacted on socialization so as to decrease differences between boys and girls, we might expect gender differences among older men and women, and among married men and women, but not among men and women who have not married (most of whom would be young). Given that there would be more women than men among those groups where gender differences might be expected, the effect on the total sample would be a higher proportion of ignorance and indifference among women than men. Those differences should disappear, though, when men and women are compared net of the effects of age and marital status. In fact, our tests apply just this logic, i.e., the averages for men and women were compared and tested for significance, then retested net of the direct and interaction effects of age and marital status. With respect to the absence of interest or opinion on issues of gender-relevance, following McCormack's argument, we would expect either no difference or that women would have lower levels than do men. When those levels are equal — consistent with the logic of taking into account age and marital status effects — we would expect rates net of those other factors to show a difference.

With regard to the positions expressed by those *with* opinions on issues, predictions are more difficult because some women may see gender-relevance in matters that do not have such relevance on the face of it (e.g., describing Canada or the U.S. with the phrase "no one goes without"). However, were we able to be precise in classifying gender-relevance, we would expect more women than men to take the positions viewed as enhancing women's status or reflecting their concerns. On non-gender-relevant political issues — and they are in the majority

— the situation is confused. If McCormack is correct that many women are disinterested in these issues, then those with opinions would include a mix of both women who were atypically independent and not in traditional women's status positions and those who acquire (or whose answers would reflect) the opinions of the dominant man in their lives. The consequences of this unknown mix on gross comparisons and the impact of removing the effects of age and marital status are unclear. In addition, local factors also are likely to affect the proportions of these types. For example, in Lethbridge women may be more independent than in the other cities, reflecting the city's relatively "frontier-like" conditions. However, as compared with Peterborough, Lethbridge also has more residents from ethnic groups (e.g., Ukrainians) with strong familistic traditions that tend to subordinate women to men. Such varied community conditions also impair our ability to predict. Nonetheless, if these various unmeasurable factors are randomly distributed, we would expect few differences among the attitudes and opinions professed by both men and women. These same circumstances also may affect the distributions of opinions on issues of gender-relevance, but also the expected majority of women choosing the "women's position" still should appear in the data.

Our predictions for activities in the political arena parallel those for the presence of clear positions on issues. For activities less accessible to women as a group, we would expect gross comparisons to show women not to participate as much as men. However, assuming that younger women would be likelier either to have access or to have the motivation or energy to overcome barriers, and that unmarried women will be less constrained to avoid forms of participation others do not consider appropriate for them, we would expect their levels of participation to be more equal. For equally accessible modes of participation we expect no gender differences in levels of participation. Application of age and marital status controls may actually imply higher levels of participation by women. Again, because factors that contribute to community variation (e.g., local norms, different patterns of ethnicity, different local economies that affect the chances of women to work and become union members) mix in different degrees and cannot be controlled in the analysis, unspecifiable community departures from these predictions are possible.

To test these predictions we selected items of political interest from our three waves of interviews and, to the extent possible, classified their gender-relevance. Opinion items were recoded to estimate the levels of unawareness and disinterest by grouping such standard categories as "don't know," "depends," and "not ascertainable" and taking the total as a percent of those in the group. This is done separately for men and women in each community. Actual opinions held were taken as a percent of those choosing one of the options for a dichotomous item; the percent of those agreeing with any one of a number of selected positions, each treated as a dummy variable, for a non-dichotomous item; or as an average score for items with several levels on an underlying single dimension. All of these measures of type of opinion held were calculated only for respondents who expressed positions on the issue. In addition to gender as the independent variable, respondent's chronological age and marital status were included in the analysis as controls. Marital status was reduced from five standard categories to "never having been married" (i.e., single), "married at the time of the interview," and "formerly married" (i.e., widowed, separated, or divorced).

The three variables are partially related as demonstrated by the data in table 13.1. Only in the two English cities are formerly married men no older than married men.

The analysis employed the options in the General Linear Model (GLM) program of the SAS package, particularly the Type I (gross) and Type III (net) effects of the independent and control variables on each dependent variable. The models estimated for this purpose include the three two-way interactions and three-way interaction among gender, age, and marital status. The program output also provides gross unadjusted means for each and within class regression weights that can be used to estimate the adjusted net means for men and women. Gross and net means and the importance of the differences between them can be exemplified by data on the absence of opinions on either the propriety of a federal governmental role or on the quality of governmental performance in dealing with ten different national problem areas. The established view being criticized by McCormack is that women would give more responses indicating the absence of opinions and, indeed, the gross means of such answers in Trois Rivières for women is 1.302 as compared to .801 for men, a statistically significant difference. Adjusting the means to take account of the relationships among gender, age, marital status, and their interactions produces means of 2.464 for men and 1.80 for women, the differences no longer being statistically significant. That is what we have argued would happen if apparent gender differences were spurious by-products of other relationships. A similar example is provided in Peterborough where approximately equal proportions of men (4.3 percent) and of women (4.7 percent) had no opinion on government's role in assuring everyone's right to work. The net proportions of 33.2 percent for men and 6.5 percent for women, however, are significantly different and are at levels consistent with our interpretation of the impact of gender-relevance on women and men's responses to items. Unfortunately, however, the complex relationships that shape these adjustments from gross to net are such that frequently the computed net values are impossible (e.g., negative percents, means outside the limits of the range provided) or counter intuitive. Because there are many such solutions and because it is inappropriate to report selectively only solutions that support one's thesis, we shall not report shifts from gross to net means or the directions of difference between the estimated values of the net means.

The contrast option of the program permitted tests of gender differences within marital status categories. Gender differences within either age or maital status-age categories were not estimated or tested directly because age was included in the analysis as a continuous rather than categorical variable. This was necessary because the correlations among the three variables resulted in there being insufficient cases for analysis in certain categories (e.g., "young formerly-married," "old never- married" male). In this paper we report counts of outcomes of all these tests in terms of whether they support, do not support, or contradict our various hypotheses. The results of tests on selected individual items sometimes are reported for illustrative purposes.

In view of the numerous uncontrollable factors that can obscure our results and the absence of both longitudinal data and strongly validated classifications of the gender-relevance of issues and forms of political behaviour, nonrandom selection of items is justifiable. For the same sorts of reasons (as well as the fact that we often predict direction of difference) we use .10 rather than .05 levels of significance in interpreting the results.

To recapitulate, we shall argue that regardless of whether McCormack specified her argument correctly and/or whether there have been real shifts in women's status as political actors, our analyses will be consistent with the position that apparent differences are (and, perhaps, always were) spurious by-products of both the issues examined and the impact of their other statuses on women, and that in many respects there no longer are gender differences, if, indeed, there ever were.

GENDER DIFFERENCES IN POLITICAL OPINION AND ACTION

We examine differences in the responses of men and women to a number of items concerning their political activities and their attitudes and beliefs on a large variety of politically relevant issues. Activities that are not likely to be as accessible to women as to men are distinguished from those that usually are equally open to persons of either gender. Two aspects of attitudes and opinions are examined — whether a respondent expresses a clear position on the issue, and, if so, what that position is. For the analysis of whether respondents hold a clear position, issues are classified as to whether they have special relevance to women. The positions actually held by those who commit themselves are classified in terms of whether they also are espoused by groups committed to improving the status of women.

Although large numbers of items could be examined for our purposes, limited resources forced us to be somewhat selective. Since there were unequal numbers of items for each of the six types of tests, we have included as many salient items as possible. Nonetheless, the six types of test items are distributed very unevenly. The test results were highly consistent, however, so we discuss them in summary fashion by type, rather than item by item.

1. THE LACK OF CLEAR POSITIONS ON NON-GENDER-RELEVANT ISSUES

Thirty-seven different issues were examined on which respondents could assert a position. The argument that politics and its study are male-biased asserts that generally women will appear to be politically less interested than men because the issues to which they are asked to respond are not salient to them and, therefore, they indicate disinterest or ignorance. If this is so, or if things have changed, we have argued that such gender differences should disappear when they are examined net of marital status and age. The results of the tests are strongly in accord with this expectation. In Trois Rivières, seventeen of the items showed women to have statistically significant more non-informed or less involved responses than men, but not when retested net of the other factors. Fourteen additional tests showed neither gross nor net significant differences between the genders — the pattern expected if the assertion of gender differences simply is wrong. In only three items are women's levels of no opinion higher than those of men under both test conditions, a number very close to that expected by chance at the .10 level of significance chosen. In Peterborough and Lethbridge, thirty-one and thirty-two of the test outcomes, respectively, were of these two types. However, the number of statistically significant differences in gross rates varied considerably from Trois Rivières. In Peterborough nine were significant and twenty-two not; in Lethbridge the comparable distribution was twelve and twenty. Given the likelihood, at least in the past that women in Québec were more likely than those in Ontario or Alberta to be influenced by the men in their families, this difference is not unexpected. Women's rates of being without opinions were significantly higher than men's in both the gross and net tests only in three cases for Peterborough and two for Lethbridge. It is the pattern that reflects the traditional view of gender differences.

2. THE LACK OF CLEAR POSITIONS ON GENDER-RELEVANT ISSUES

Only six of the items included have particular current interest to women. They include such matters as whether the federal government should have a role in assuring equal rights for all persons regardless of ethnicity or gender, or should have a role in assuring the right to work for anyone who desires to do so. We expected either that fewer women than men would be without opinions on such issues, or that there would be no gender differences. In the latter case, tests net of other factors also might show no differences or might indicate that adjusted women's rates were lower than men's. In Trois Rivières, two of the tests of gross and net rates indicated no difference, as did three of the tests in each of the Anglophone cities. In Trois Rivières, two other tests indicated no difference in gross rates but a significant difference in the rates net of the other factors. One test each in the Anglophone cities had the same pattern. In each city one test also indicated a significantly higher rate of no opinions for women than for men that was no longer significant net of age and marital status. These results are consistent with the general argument of male bias in political research, but they are not as strong as others (e.g., significant gross and net tests of higher men's than women's rates) might have been.

3. POSITIONS ON GENDER-RELEVANT ISSUES

Among persons with opinions on such issues, we expected more women than men to espouse positions being propounded by proponents of improved status for women. In cases of no significant gender difference in gross rates, we might expect the test net of age and marital status to indicate great agreement with the pro-women's position by women. Finally, if the gross difference indicates less agreement with that position by women than by men, we would expect the net test to show no difference or more agreement by women. Of eleven such items tested, ten in Trois Rivières and nine in each of the English cities indicated no gross gender difference. In both Trois Rivières and Peterborough, two were significant when retested net of the other factors. One other test in each of these cities and two in Lethbridge indicate significantly more agreement by women than men, but no apparent real difference after taking account of the role of the other factors. Finally, one test in Peterborough initially indicated more agreement by men than by women, but the net test indicated that this difference was attributable to age, marital status, and the various interactions.

Except for the possibility that the four significant net tests could involve adjusted mean differences in the contrary direction, the twenty-nine other test results are consistent with the argument of male bias in research. The outcomes do not indicate strong male domination of women on issues that might undermine male superiority were women to be successful in achieving the position they espouse. There are two possible reasons for the apparent weakness of this evidence for spuriousness or incorrectness in the argument that women are politically unequal to men because they are inactive and disinterested. One is the possibility that the feminist effort has already succeeded in persuading many men of the need for steps to achieve women's equality. This would not mean universal support of that view, only that differences on the matter would no longer be as visible on gender as on other lines. The other (and it happens to reinforce the first) is that at least eight, and possibly as many as ten, of the thirteen statistically significant contrasts for gender differences within marital status categories indicate that women are more in agreement with the "women's" position than are men.

4. POSITIONS ON NON-GENDER-RELEVANT ISSUES

Most of the tests, by far, are of this type. The argument that because of factors such as the success of the women's movement "things have changed" suggests no differences between genders, gross or net. The argument of spuriousness, in contrast, suggests gender differences in either direction (i.e., men and women disagreeing, with either group being more or less in agreement with a position being considered) that dissipate in the net tests. The argument that male dominance is exercised as influence by men over the women they are close to suggests that there will be no gender differences in gross rates, but that statistically significant differences will be observed when controls are taken into account.

Of the approximately eighty tests of this type, sixty-four for Trois Rivières, sixty-six for Peterborough, and sixty-seven for Lethbridge indicate no net gender differences. However, it cannot be concluded that the remaining tests contradict McCormack's argument simply because they suggest real gender differences net of age and marital status. That conclusion would depend on the combination of the issue involved and the real values of the adjusted means in each such case. Net gender differences occur largely on items that initially showed no gross difference. The few other combinations that occur are scattered. In Lethbridge, however, the number of items that have significant gender differences only in the net test is what would be expected by chance. In Trois Rivières and Peterborough, this type of test result occurs in approximately 20 percent of the cases for which there is an opportunity for such a difference between gross and net. Only in Trois Rivières, however, is there close to a significant probability that this is not due to chance.

Test results were searched for further indications that there might be substantial support for the position of real gender differences in political interest by also examining the number of significant gender differences tested within marital status groups. In none of these cases, however, is there more significant gender differences than might be expected by chance. We conclude, therefore, that the weight of these tests is in the direction of the expectations based upon McCormack's thesis.

5. POLITICAL ACTIVITIES LESS ACCESSIBLE TO WOMEN

The only activity tested in which women clearly were likely in the nature of things to be at a disadvantage to men was the contribution of funds to federal and to provincial political campaigns. These possibilities were examined separately. Only one of the six tests did not conform to the expected pattern of significantly higher gross rates of men than women reporting such participation, and no differences net of the controls. In the one non-conforming case, a surplus of men as contributors in Lethbridge remains significant in the net test. Gender-related unconventional political activities like participation in strikes were not tested separately, but the distributions suggest that they, too, are gender-structured. The data point in the direction of the general argument.

6. EQUALLY ACCESSIBLE POLITICAL ACTIVITIES
Fifteen different activities were tested with the expectation of no net gender differences regardless of whether the gross rates indicate no difference or more activity by men than by women. The latter pattern was predominant, appearing in eight tests for Lethbridge and nine for each of the other two cities. Three Peterborough tests and two in each of the other cities indicated neither gross nor net differences. The remaining tests suggest higher rates of participation for men, but do not occur at a significant frequency. The contrasts for gender controlled for marital status, however, suggest change, for the only cases in which women participate significantly more than men occur in the younger groups that never have been married. This portion of the evidence strongly supports the overall argument.

HAVE GENDER DIFFERENCES RE. POLITICS CHANGED?

The previous analyses primarily are pertinent to McCormack's argument that the widely accepted assertion that men are more politically interested and active than women is spurious and reflects gender-slanting attributable to research that suffers from a combination of issue bias and a failure to adjust for differentials in the status positions and demographic attributes of men and women. The tests largely supported this argument. However, even if that argument had been incorrect, relatively recent data might not reveal the gender differences expected because the feminist movement may have increased the political interests and activities of women and altered norms pertaining to the roles of women. If so, it also is desirable to examine our data for changes over time if there are proxies for this purpose to take the place of more appropriate but unavailable longitudinal data.

Although not ideal, comparisons of the answers of men and women across the three marital status categories can serve this purpose. Unfortunately, a fairly substantial correlation between marital status and age prevents the use of age as a categorical variable for this purpose. However, despite the facts that the "never married" groups include a few older persons, that married persons span the entire adult age range, and that formerly married men in the English cities are of the same average age as married men, the data in table 13.1 indicate that the marital status categories can serve as rough proxies for age as a period phenomenon. Accordingly, we have examined and report aspects of the patterns of means of the items for the "never maried" (youngest), "married" (intermediate), and "previously married" (oldest) categories as they compare for gender. Although change may take various forms, the argument here is that

Table 13.1 — Distribution of Gender, Age, and Marital Status of Respondents in Trois Rivières, Peterborough, and Lethbridge.

CITY		MEN			WOMEN	
Age	Never Married	Married	Formerly Married	Never Married	Married	Formerly Married
Trois Rivieres						
Up to 40	41	45	4	28	33	8
40-54	4	30	1	2	59	7
55 and over	3	28	5	5	26	21
$\bar{x}$ age	27.7	44.6	53.5	30.4	45.7	56.0
Peterborough						
Up to 40	29	24	4	19	59	2
40-54	1	34	7	1	29	5
55 and over	1	35	4	6	30	18
$\bar{x}$ age	25.5	49.6	50.5	34.3	42.4	63.1
Lethbridge						
Up to 40	17	30	2	23	47	10
40-45	3	32	1	–	33	9
55 and over	2	38	2	2	30	14
$\bar{x}$ age	29.4	50.0	48.4	26.1	46.2	52.0

women are more politically interested and active than men at younger ages (the never married level) and that in higher age groups (married, formerly married) increasingly this is less the case. Therefore, for items in which women show more interest or activity in the "never married" group, averages will either invert or converge. For items in which younger women are only as interested and active as men, change would be manifested as divergence toward increasing male interest or activity without an inversion. Any such patterns are taken as indicating temporal changes away from traditional gender differences.

With respect to the positions expressed on issues, our reasoning is similar. If there has been a real change and traditional gender differences obtained only in the past, we would expect older women to taken positions relatively more accepting, nurturing, and less critical than those taken by older men. Contrariwise, younger women would be expected to be relatively more critical, less satisfied, and more politically realistic — perhaps even more radical. When there is little difference between the genders at the younger ages (i.e., in the "never married" group), we would expect the gender groups to diverge in the same directions for the older marital status categories.

These expectations are subject only to very crude tests involving the interpretation of the patterns of difference between the genders at each of the three levels of marital status. There is, of course, initial uncertainty as to whether to consider small differences between the genders as real. Even more ambiguous is the issue of how much of a difference in differences across marital categories should be considered evidence of a changing progression of the sort expected. We had expected to be able to base that conclusion on our tests of "marital status x gender" and "age x gender" interactions, but those tests are more sensitive to simple changes across the category than to orderly progressions. Therefore, we simply count any progression of gender differences in the designated directions as indicative of changes in the political status of the genders. The major uncertainty preventing a stringent test of a formal hypothesis, however, arises from the question of how to judge the significance of the results of these counts. Given the large numbers of different patterns that could have occurred in the data and the constraints of the marginal distributions and parameters involved, it is very difficult to estimate the probability that progressions of gender differences suggestive of change are occurring at more, the same as, or less than a rate that might be expected on the basis of chance.

Fortunately, the results of our counts seem to be sufficiently clear to point to a conclusion even though the data have not been subjected to formal statistical testing. table 13.2 summarizes the number of patterns in each city that suggest change from a traditional women's political position for each type of test item. Aside from types of items with very few tests, it may be seen that in total and for most types of test items in each city approximately 30 percent of the cases indicate such change. In view of all the possible alternative patterns and uncertainties as to the equal relevance of all test items for this purpose, this seems to us to be an unusually high rate. Following are a few examples of the sorts of observations counted in these totals.

In both Trois Rivières and Lethbridge, inversions in the proportions without opinions that would indicate changes in men and women's levels of interest occurred on the question of whether the federal government should assure individuals the right to work, and, if so, how well the government served this role. In Trois Rivières 4.2 percent and in Lethbridge 4.5 percent more of the "never married" men had no position on one or the other aspect of the issue. Taking the cities in the same order, among the "married" members of the samples 5.3 percent and 0.5 percent more of the women than of the men had no position, and among the "formerly married" these differences increased to 8.3 percent and 12.1 percent, respectively. In Peterborough, with respect to the federal government's role in providing welfare, 2.6 percent more "never married" men than women, and 3.5 percent more of the "married" men than women lacked opinions, in contrast to the 16.0 percent more "formerly married" women than men without opinions.

Similar shifts in gender differences were observed in each of the three marital status groups of each city for the average number out of ten such issues on which people lacked opinions. Taking marital status categories in the same order, in Trois Rivières the averages for men were .02 more than for women, and for women .60 and .51 more than for men for the three groups respectively, while in the other two cities the averages for women always were higher than for men, going from differences of .22 to .33 to .41 in Peterborough and from .13 to .40 to .80 in Lethbridge.

In Trois Rivières, among "never marrieds" 2.1 percent more men than women had not heard of the referendum during the first wave of interviewing even after being probed with a statement paraphrasing the proposition. Among "marrieds," however, 1.5 percent more women were ignorant of the

Table 13.2 — Number of Items for Which Response Patterns Indicate Age-Related Changes in Gender Differences

TYPE OF ITEM	PATTERNS OF CHANGE	NO CHANGE PATTERN	TOTAL
Opinions of Non-Gender-Related Issues			
Trois Rivieres	25	55	80
Peterborough	22	58	80
Lethbridge	16	63	79
Opinions on Gender-Related Issues			
Trois Rivieres	7	5	12
Peterborough	5	6	11
Lethbridge	3	8	11
No Opinions on Non-Gender-Related Issues			
Trois Rivieres	8	29	37
Peterborough	9	28	37
Lethbridge	14	23	37
No Opinions on Gender-Related Issues			
Trois Rivieres	3	3	6
Peterborough	1	5	6
Lethbridge	2	3	5
Non-Gender-Related Political Activities			
Trois Rivieres	3	12	15
Peterborough	2	13	15
Lethbridge	7	8	15
Gender-Related Political Activities			
Trois Rivieres	–	2	2
Peterborough	1	1	2
Lethbridge	1	1	2
Total Items			
Trois Rivieres	46	106	152
Peterborough	40	111	151
Lethbridge	43	106	149

Referendum and among "formerly marrieds" the difference was 5.6 percent more women. In Lethbridge the pattern was similar prior to probing, 1.8 percent more of the "never married" women being unaware, in contrast to 10.2 percent of the women who were or who had been married. The same type of pattern was observed in all three cities with regard to the absence of opinions on the government's role in dealing with regional inequalities. Taking the marital status groups in the same order, in Trois Rivières the differences were 5.4 percent more of the men than the women, 6.3 percent more of the women than the men, and 9.4 percent more of the women than the men; in Peterborough the pattern was the same, the differences in proportions without positions being 8.4 percent more men than women, and 1.8 percent and 5.3 percent more women than men respectively; and in Lethbridge, where the proportions of women without opinions were higher than those for men in each marital status group, the differences were 2.4 percent, 5.6 percent, and 18.2 percent.

People also were asked whether they agreed with the pro-social position that everyone was entitled to a basic minimum, or with the position that people were entitled only to what they could provide for themselves. In Trois Rivières, more women than men in each marital status agree that persons were entitled to a minimum, but the difference in proportion declined, going from a high of 14.6 percent among the "never marrieds" to 6.9 percent to 3.5 percent. In Lethbridge 26.3 percent more "never married" women than "never married" men took the pro-social position, the proportion difference then inverting, with 6.9 percent more of the "married" and 10.9 percent more of the "formerly married" men selecting that position. Approval of the Parti Québecois, and, implicitly, its more radical program for the future of both Québec and Canada, was higher among "never married" women than men in both Trois Rivières and Lethbridge, less so but in the same direction among the "married," and higher among "formerly married" men than women in both cities. In Trois Rivières and Peterborough, a comparison of the number of critical and negative images of Canada selected by members of each gender group showed the same progression across marital status, women's averages being higher than men's among the "never married" and men's averages being higher among the "formerly married" with the married between. As a final example, in Lethbridge 12.2 percent more "never married" women than men expressed the view that social classes were bound to conflict, whereas for the two other categories the differences were 5.1 percent and 14.7 percent more for currently and previously married men than women espousing that view.

The tallies first reported in this section indicate that there could be many more examples. We interpret these differences across categories as not reflecting aging. We would not expect younger men and women progressively to become like the older ones. Rather, the patterns are in accord with what one would expect if younger women are more aware of and concerned about their rights, their place in society, and their opportunities to alter reality than older women are. There is no indication that women's interests in their position in Canadian society will be declining in the forseeable future. Thus, we would argue that our data on political interest and activity reflect the general changes toward gender equality that have been transpiring in Canadian society.

DISCUSSION

It has become banal to note that women are not a numerical minority in societies like Canada. The issue of women's status and status change, rather, has to do with subordination, deprivation, and the denial of opportunities to exercise their rights. In this regard, social indicators reveal that in Canadian society women's status is improving but still subordinate to that of men. In this paper we have addressed the question of gender differences with respect to politics both because the established position on gender differences could be interpreted to imply that women necessarily always will be less politically active and involved and because interest and involvement in the political process are perhaps the most effective ways to achieve status change in democratic polities. Essentially, therefore, we have tried to address the related questions of what has been and what is the character of gender differences with respect to political interest and participation in Canada, and, if there is evidence of inequality, is there evidence of movement toward equality.

Despite their apparent formality, our data analyses are subject to limitations that must be acknowledged. We examined samples from three communities rather than from the country as a whole. Moreover, the study for which the data were collected deals with a different matter and so most of the materials are not pointed to the issues raised here. In addition, the values of the adjusted means being tested in the net tests could not be examined systematically. Furthermore, ideally the question of change needs to be addressed with material collected over a fairly long period of time — a condition not met by our three-wave panel study. Perhaps most important is the fact that the gender-relevance of the items being examined is the key factor in analyzing any such material. We do not have information on whether each respondent sees each of the items considered as gender-relevant. Indeed, we do not know the more general relevance of gender to them, or, if it is relevant, how they see the present situations of Canadian men and women.

The emphasis we have placed on contrasts between gross and net tests of the differences between the various measures for the two genders should not be misconstrued. If a gross test is significant and a net test not, that does not mean that the observed difference being assessed is not real. However, the data associated with the gross and net test difference do begin to provide an understanding of why that gross gender difference occurs. The value of that information is scientific. Of course, it also may help with future prognoses for gender differences and, depending on what is being contrasted and what the controls are, provide clues to policies that may hasten the end of these presently real differences.

In view of the limitations of our data and tests, the analyses are impressively convincing in what they do indicate: namely, that any past or present gender differences in political roles are not inevitable. Indeed, they do not suggest that any such differences have a "sex role" basis — that is, that it is generally socially accepted that women will and should be less politically involved and independent than men. Rather, the observed gender differences seem best understood as reflecting "opportunity" differences, inequalities engendered not by gender, per se, but by such related factors as family status and age. We restricted our choice of covariates to only these two, but our data could provide opportunities for a fuller exploration of other factors that also may account for gender differences (e.g., labour force participation, social class).

Our data do suggest change both in women's awareness of issues that bear upon their status in Canadian society and in their willingness to become involved in the sorts of political activities that will provide opportunities for further improvements in position. We started our inquiry out of curiosity as to the validity of Thelma McCormack's thesis of bias in social scientific analyses of gender differences in politics. We found that it had merit even though it also became obvious that her analysis is not so clear that it is easily testable. Nonetheless, to the extent that our analyses support her claims, they suggest that the contribution of the feminist movement to the improving political status of Canadian women is not one of merely providing new opportunities or enhancing interest, but also of redirecting the arena of issues so that it is more pertinent to women's social and economic lot in society. McCormack argued that women always have been interested and willing to participate and our analysis suggests that that is so. Given meaningful opportunities, women make meaningful responses. Of course, equity is not yet at hand. However, even in parts of Canada where women were entrenched in a subordinate social position, differentials in interest and participation are on the wane.

REFERENCES

Cheki, Dan and John Hofley. "Women and inequality: some indicators of change." in J. Harp and J. Hofley, eds. *Structured Inequality in Canada.* Scarborough, Ontario: Prentice-Hall, 1980, 378-400.

Devereaux, M.S. and Edith Rechnitzer. *Higher Education-Hired?* Ottawa: Statistics Canada, 1980.

Edwards, Richard. *Contested Terrain.* New York: Basic Books, 1979.

Kornberg, Allan, Joel Smith, and Harold D. Clarke. *Citizen Politicians — Canada.* Scarborough, Ontario: Prentice-Hall, 1983.

McCormack, Thelma. "Toward a nonsexist perspective on social and political change." Marcia Millman and Rosabeth Moss Kanter, eds. *Another Voice: Feminist Perspectives on Social Life and Social Science.* Garden City, N.J.: Anchor, 1975, 1-33.

McDonald, Lynn. "The gap between women and men in the wages of work." J. Curtis and W. Scott, eds. *Social Stratification: Canada.* 2nd ed. Scarborough, Ontario: Prentice-Hall, 1979, 340-348.

Saunders, Eileen. "Women in Canadian Society." D. Forcese and S. Richer, eds. *Social Issues.* Scarborough, Ontario: Prentice-Hall, 1982, 211-257.

Statistics Canada. *Education in Canada.* Ottawa: Information Canada, 1978.

──────────. *Canada's Families.* Ottawa: Information Canada, 1979.

14

DENE-GOVERNMENT RELATIONS: THE DEVELOPMENT OF A NEW POLITICAL MINORITY

FRANCES ABELE

THE DENE: AN OVERVIEW

The Dene (Indians) are aboriginal people who live in the western half of the Northwest Territories (NWT). Their traditional lands comprise over 450,000 square miles on either side of the Mackenzie River, which flows north from Great Slave Lake at the 61st parallel, to the Arctic Ocean. In 1981, there were about 13,000 Dene and Métis in this region.[1] The Dene and Métis share the area with a slightly smaller number of residents of non-native origin.

The Dene speak five related Athapaskan languages. It is only during the last fifteen years that members of these language groups have come to define themselves as one people — the Dene — and to emphasize the similar rather than different aspects of their traditional cultures. During the 1970s, the Dene achieved national and international prominence in the course of their battle to halt the construction of a major pipeline through their traditional lands. Engaged in this struggle, which was waged in large part before the highly publicized Inquiry into the Construction of a Mackenzie Valley Pipeline (the Berger Inquiry), the Dene developed a common and public interpretation of their own history which formed the basis of a strategy for defending their collective interests and for preserving certain aspects of their traditional culture.

What appeared in the 1970s to be a sudden effluorescence of Dene political activism in fact was only one phase of a much longer development. To understand Dene political objectives, and their approach to constitutional questions in particular, it is necessary to have some appreciation of the nature of Dene societies before European contact, and also of the nature of their relationship with European and southern Canadian institutions during the two centuries which preceded the eruptions of the 1970s. It has been against and through various institutions and policies of the Canadian state that the Dene have developed their political position. A close examination of this process reveals a good deal about the limits and opportunities presented to evolving political minorities by the institutions of the late twentieth century state.

Although the Dene are a statistical minority — in the sense that they comprise only a tiny fraction of the Canadian population — in the western Northwest Territories, the Dene and Métis constitute a scant majority of permanent residents. Moreover, in the NWT as a whole, the aboriginal peoples (the Dene, Métis, Inuit and Inuvialuit) comprise a comfortable majority of the population. This latter fact is reflected in the territorial legislature, which has seen native members in the majority since 1975. Since the Dene exercise majority power in their homeland and regional political jurisdiction, they are unique among native people in Canada, and enjoy a certain amount of extra leverage as a consequence. It must be noted, however, that this leverage is tempered by the fact that the Northwest Territories government exercises a much narrower range of powers than those exercised by the 10 provincial governments. (Drury 1980)

It should be noted also that the Dene, like other native minorities, are in a fundamental way different from ethnic groups and other aggregations (for example, women) in Canada. In their official political statements, the Dene claim a special status as the original and long-term residents of a territory which has known European habitation for only a relatively short time. The most forceful expression of this position is the 1975 Dene Declaration. The Dene Declaration presents the Dene as an oppressed nation of people who "find themselves as part of a country," Canada, and who do not accept the legitimacy of Canadian governing institutions. Although the language used by the Dene to describe their political program has been altered significantly since 1975, one underlying premise has not changed. They do not see themselves as a minority group of Canadians whose collective interests will be served best by special government programs designed to equalize individual group members' opportunities for economic advancement and integration, or programs developed to nurture and preserve aspects of their cultural heritage. Instead, they seek constitutional entrenchment (and thereby recognition in perpetuity) of their special status as aboriginal people, and the establishment of new governing institutions in their region which would guarantee their permanent influence *as a people* in issues of public government. Although there has been a limited *rapprochement* recently, by and large the federal government has been unable to accommodate these objectives. Most government programs and policies have treated the Dene as a minority group who require funding and special programs to equalize their opportunities and to help preserve their cultural heritage. Any proposals for a constitutionally entrenched "ethnic government" have been flatly rejected.

I shall argue that underlying this constitutional impasse are two mutually exclusive versions of the meaning of Dene history since European contact, each rooted in very different life circumstances and experiences. I shall argue further that it has only been when a communications bridge has been established between the two versions of historical reality that any *rapprochement* has been possible. In part this has occurred quite simply because effective communication permitted better mutual understanding and, on this basis, the development of more nuanced statements of the Dene and federal government positions. Other factors, however, also have been at work. In the course of developing their political stance, the Dene increased their own solidarity, their links with other political interests and their own knowledge of the nature of institutional power in Canada. In short, by organizing they entrenched for themselves a position of objectively greater political influence. The evolving federal response to Dene claims, while undoubtedly informed in recent years by a more sophisticated appreciation of Dene objectives, must be seen as a gradual recognition of an alteration of the balance of real political forces in the Northwest Territories and Canada.

To recapitulate, my argument turns on two related claims. First, the emergence of the Dene as a self-defined political minority in Canadian politics required that mechanisms be established for communication between spokespeople for what were until very recently two solitudes. Second, one consequence of the use of such mechanisms has been an adjustment in the relative political power exercised by the Dene in their region and in Canada. In developing this argument, I must acknowledge the limitations of my own situation, which is firmly within one of the two cultural systems. To deal with this difficulty I have relied upon the public statements of both sides, understood from the artificial position of an "outsider" who takes each version of reality seriously. The stratagem of taking an outsider's view is bound to be met by only partial success; I merely scramble away from the more obvious ethnocentrisms and perch on a shaky ledge of detachment where the view of another culture is somewhat improved.

I. THE POLITICAL SIGNIFICANCE OF EARLY RELATIONS BETWEEN THE DENE AND EXOGENOUS INSTITUTIONS

Before European contact, the primary social unit among aboriginal societies in the Mackenzie Valley was what anthropologists call a "local group," a self-sufficient assembly of about twenty to thirty related people who made their living by hunting, fishing and gathering. Local groups were nomadic, often ranging over hundreds of miles in a seasonal pattern adapted to game migration and weather patterns. There was the customary division of labour by age, sex and ability. In societies organized in this way, concepts of ownership, controls of property and of land use are very different from those typical of agricultural or industrial societies; property rights need be neither individual nor exclusive, but tend, instead, to be based upon traditional use and need. Similarly, political institutions emphasize co-operation, flexibility and efficient responsiveness to changing environmental conditions. (Sahlins 1972)

The Dene first encountered non-aboriginals in the late eighteenth century, when European fur traders and missionaries entered the Mackenzie Valley. In the nature of their work, which was the conversion of native people, to Christianity, the missionaries challenged the legitimacy of traditional "religious" ideas which in fact regulated the whole network of social life, including hunting practices, residency patterns and the relations among men and women. The fur trade brought major changes to the nature of productive activity which reinforced the missionaries' influence. As the traders became established in the Mackenzie Valley, the Dene came to depend upon certain food stuffs, steel traps and rifles which they received in exchange for fur. With this dependence came the end of the self-sufficient "total economy" of pre-contact times (Asch 1977:47), and a new vulnerability to world prices for fur and trade goods which brought severe hardships when market conditions were unfavourable or when fur was temporarily unavailable.

In the area of political ideas, it is very likely that significant changes occurred in conceptions of relative social power, both within and between societies. The organization of hunting and gathering societies virtually precludes complex hierarchical organization; the social unit is small, the customary division of labour encourages task-related opportunities for revolving leadership, and disputes between nomadic social units tend to be resolved by relocation. (Sahlins 1972) In contrast, the Europeans encountered by northern native people were virtually all representatives of large, hierarchical organizations whose power over their field representatives was evident from the way trading company policies and church edicts were obeyed. Furthermore, native people themselves felt this distant power directly. The early contact period probably was characterized by mutual dependence. Indeed, European fur traders probably were more dependent upon native people than native people were upon traders.

However, from the heyday of the fur trade through most of the nineteenth and twentieth centuries, northern native people interacted with the fur traders (as with virtually all representatives of European civilization) from a position of power disadvantage. Fur traders controlled the supply of essential commodities — and in hard winters, of food — while the missionaries stood at the gateway to converts' everlasting life.

In the early experience of northern native people with the trading companies and the churches, then, it is possible to identify the roots of new political ideas. To the traditional limits to an individual's discretionary behaviour was added an understanding of another kind of limitation — one imposed by a hierarchical organization controlled from a distant place. And, to traditional methods of interaction with groups and individuals outside the family group, was added the experience of dealing with the locally powerful representatives of much larger organizations. These new political ideas were reinforced by native people's early experiences with the administrative branch of the Canadian state.

Although formal responsibility for the Canadian northwest passed to the Dominion government in 1880, the state presence in the region was slight until the Second World War. Before the war, social welfare services available to native people were delivered by the churches or, occasionally, by the regional representatives of the great trading companies. (Zazlow 1971; Rea 1968) Ottawa's interest in the region waxed and waned with changes in the prospects for development of the North's mineral resources. The Klondike gold rush led to the negotiation of Treaty 8 with Chipeweyan tribes living in what is now northern Alberta and Saskatchewan and the southern Northwest Territories, and to the installation of patrolling Royal North-West Mounted Police detachments. The 1921 discovery of oil at Norman Wells on the Mackenzie River prompted the government to sign another treaty (Treaty 11) with the remaining Indian groups.

Federal presence in the North, however, remained slight until Japan's entry into World War II. With this development, the western continental Arctic became the focus of intense armed forces activity. The Alaska Highway, a winter road from the Mackenzie Valley to Alberta, the Canol pipeline, and an oil refinery in Whitehorse were constructed in short order. These efforts brought thousands of Canadian and American military personnel into the North. Although many left after the war's end, the Cold War again made the North an object of military attention. In addition, the expanding post-war global market for natural resources renewed federal interest in the development of the North's mineral wealth.

A by-product of the unprecedented penetration of the North by southerners during and after the war years was a much greater awareness in southern Canada of the life circumstances of northern native people. On the whole, these are not favourable. Since the Great Depression, falling world fur prices combined with inflation in the price of trade goods had significantly reduced the well-being of most trappers. (Asch, 1977) Although during the war and in isolated pockets of industrial development after the war there were more wage labour jobs in the North than ever before, these jobs were generally not filled by native trappers but by a swelling white migrant labour force.

For decades, the hardships faced by Mackenzie Valley native people were understood in Ottawa to be natural life circumstances of aboriginal people, and their evident reluctance to participate in the wage economy was a matter of little consequence. After World War II, these same conditions became a major "policy problem" for federal officials. The renewed federal interest in northern Canada, based during and after the war on sovereignty and defence considerations and in the economic potential of the North's non-renewable resource base, coincided with the post-war expansion of state social welfare responsibilities. The result was a reinterpretation in Ottawa of the situation of Mackenzie Valley native people — and of northern native people in general — as one in which "poverty" and "unemployment" were major problems requiring major remedial measures. These measures embodied complementary policy objectives of: (1) developing the regional economy principally through the production for export of non-renewable natural resources; and (2) preparing permanent northern residents for work in the new industries which were to be developed.

Consistent with this perspective, a panoply of major new federal programs were introduced during the 1950s and 1960s. A sustained resettlement campaign was begun, aimed at concentrating the native population in government-built houses around the old fur trade posts located at intervals along the major water transportation routes. Efforts also were made to establish institutions of local self-government in the new communities.

Complementing the relocation campaign were a variety of other programs. During the 1950s, a Northwest Territories public school system was established. The old church-run institutions were taken over, and several large schools were built with dormitories to house children from distant settlements. Programs were begun to promote agricultural activity, develop home handicraft industries, as well as industries based upon commercial production of fish and wildlife resources. Hospitals were constructed, nursing stations established, and territorial health services were re-organized as a new division within the Department of National Health and Welfare. Finally, although there was some lag between their provision in southern Canada and their implementation in the North, by the early sixties virtually all native and non-native northerners were receiving both federally supported and shared-cost social welfare benefits — including family allowance, old age security payments and unemployment insurance.

All of these new programs brought major changes to the structure of northern administration in Ottawa and to the way of life of the people of the North. First, the administration of the new programs, together with new national defence commitments, compelled a re-organization of federal northern policy making and program implementation structures. The need for co-ordination of the new responsibilities was recognized in the creation of two new bureaucratic structures: the Advisory Committee on Northern Development (ACND) in 1948, and the Department of Northern Affairs and National Resources (DNANR) in 1953. DNANR was to administer federal northern programs "like a province," whereas ACND's mandate was to provide "the mechanism for interdepartmental planning and co-ordination of federal policies and programs pertaining to the Canadian north." (Abele and Dosman 1981)

In the North, the new federal programs brought changes to virtually every aspect of northern native life — from community size and organization to family relations and the nature of productive activity. Particularly during the 1950s, the populations of most settlements increased steadily, as native people moved from trapline cabins to government-issue settlement houses. In the settlements, they found a new lifestyle. The greater availability of alcohol and other diversions combined with other pressures to disrupt family authority patterns and support systems. Although many people continued to hunt and trap, the importance of these activities diminished as social welfare benefits increasingly supplemented family income.

The number of native people attending school rose rapidly. One reason for the increase was a growth in the absolute number of school-age children, as a result of improved health care services and a declining infant mortality rate. By 1967, just under one-half of the northern native population were under fourteen years old, compared to one-third for the Canadian population as a whole. In addition, for the first time there were sustained federal efforts to send native children to school. As a consequence the proportion of school age children attending school increased dramatically: from 23 percent in 1950-51 to 75 percent by 1961-62. (Rea, 1968) One result of these two changes was the emergence of a new and important fraction of the native population. Its members were young and disproportionately English speaking. They shared at least some of the skills, values, tastes, and aspirations of their southern Canadian peers. These qualities, coupled with their absence from home during most of the time when they would have been learning traditional skills, created a distinct and difficult generation gap. It also created an important new capacity within native communities for understanding and dealing with southern Canadian institutions, a capacity on which the northern native response to the resource and land use debates of the 1970s was based.

II. DENE-STATE RELATIONS IN THE 1970s

From the native point of view, twentieth century northern administration was not a natural process of development with clear direction, but a series of shocking and dislocating experiences. First the fur traders and missionaries and then the Treaty Commissioners and the Mounties developed relationships with aboriginal societies in the Mackenzie Valley which had profound and locally unanticipated consequences. In the post-war period, federal resettlement programs, educational services and social welfare provisions altered central aspects of the Dene way of life. The old norms of native self-government were not replaced by the liberal democratic methods of community self-government, despite federal administration efforts in this direction. Like the traders, the missionaries and the police, government personnel represented a large, hierarchical organization exercising considerable power but which native people found difficult either to influence or resist. This aspect of Dene-state relations changed dramatically in the 1970s, as native people in the Mackenzie Valley formed political organizations and began to be heard.

THE PEOPLE'S MOVEMENT
Father René Fumoleau has described these events as evidence of the rising of a people's movement in the Mackenzie Valley. Fumoleau's judgement is accepted here, if by the term "people's movement" is meant a broadly based and initially uncoordinated increase in the level of political awareness and activism of a homogeneous group faced with a major threat to their accustomed way of life.

The people's movement had its roots in the common historical experience of Mackenzie Valley native people which has just been reviewed, and was sparked by two major developments of the late 1960s. First, as a logical stage in the opening of the North, a decision was made to transfer the effective seat of territorial administration from Ottawa to Yellowknife, and to transform the old territorial administration by stages into a structure closer to the norm of regional government in the provinces. (Carrothers 1966) Within fifteen years, this process of transformation — including the development of a democratically elected legislative branch — was well-advanced. In the early 1970s, however, its principal manifestation appeared to be a sudden and massive increase in the number of civil servants in the Northwest Territories.

The second proximate cause of the Mackenzie Valley people's movement was the 1968 discovery of commercially viable quantities of oil and natural gas at Prudhoe Bay, Alaska. The Prudhoe Bay discovery revived flagging industry and government enthusiasm for the petroleum potential of the northern Canada sedimentary basin, and it led immediately to a dramatic increase in exploration activity in the Mackenzie Delta/Beaufort Sea area. With the increase in seismic exploration came an increase in air, water and ground traffic through many Mackenzie Valley communities. On the land, traplines and game patterns were disrupted. Further, the American discovery prompted the government of Canada to bid for a share in the potential oil bonanza. This bid was a proposal to build a large diameter natural gas pipeline in the Mackenzie Valley that would carry Canadian and American Arctic offshore natural gas through Canada to northeastern U.S. markets.

Together, the oil rush and the increase in the size and activity of territorial administration shattered the relative isolation of Dene communities. In the past the Dene had dealt with similar incursions in one of two ways: by moving out of the contested zone or — where moving was impractical — by seeking to regularize the terms of joint occupancy in a treaty. The oil rush and the expansion of the territorial government were so generalized that relocation was not a viable alternative. Moreover, educational, medical and social welfare services available in the communities tended to hold people there. As a consequence the regularization of joint occupancy alternative was chosen.

In 1969, chiefs assembled at an Indian Affairs Advisory Committee meeting decided to found the Indian Brotherhood of the Northwest Territories. The immediate concerns of the chiefs were similar to those of Indian leaders across Canada. These included the development of a strategy to reverse the 1969 federal Statement on Indian Policy (the 1969 "White Paper"), which in their eyes threatened Indian communities with annihilation by assimilation, and the establishment of a grass roots base for a new organization which would fight for Indian interests. Like their counterparts across Canada, Indian Brotherhood leaders took advantage of federal funding which was becoming available for this purpose. An Indian Brotherhood office was established in Yellowknife, with a small staff and the major task of building support for the new organization in the scattered communities of the Mackenzie Valley. In stages over the next several years, the Indian Brotherhood became the focus of the disquiet felt throughout these communities. In its first two encounters with the federal government — before the courts and before a public inquiry — the new organization enjoyed startling and early successes.

THE ROLE OF THE COURTS
In summer 1972, clearing for a road intended to support construction of the anticipated Mackenzie Valley pipeline was begun beside the Mackenzie River. Faced with this concrete evidence of the imminence of the project, and lacking any means to influence federal government plans, the leadership of the Indian Brotherhood decided to begin legal action that would make a negotiated land claims settlement with the federal government possible. Like native people in Alaska and other parts of Canada, Indian Brotherhood leaders regarded such a settlement as a means of insuring local control over the pace and direction of development in their region.

Because the Indian Brotherhood represented people who had previously signed treaties with the Crown, the necessary first step was to challenge the legitimacy of treaties 8 and 11 in the courts. The Brotherhood did so by seeking a development-freezing *caveat* on over 400,000 square miles of land in the western Northwest Territories, arguing in part that the literal wording of the treaties did not reflect the Indian signatories' understanding of the agreement. Against vociferous resistance from the federal Justice Department, Mr. Justice Morrow of the Supreme Court of the NWT ruled in favour of the caveators. (Morrow 1973)

Although Justice Morrow's decision was reversed in 1976 after appeals to the NWT Court of Appeal and to the Supreme Court of Canada, its immediate political consequences were dramatic. What had begun as a gesture by a small group of activists meeting in Yellowknife became, with news of Morrow's decision, a widely publicized and electrifying demonstration that native political action against the federal state could succeed.

No *caveat* was ever filed, but land development in the Mackenzie Valley was effectively halted. Further, the Indian Brotherhood case, together with native court actions in other parts of the country, had made an important political point and a change in federal policy towards native claims was announced in August 1973. Specifically, the Department of Indian Affairs and Northern Development indicated the government's willingness to negotiate both specific and comprehensive native claims settlements through the Department's new Office of Native Claims. Comprehensive claims could be filed with respect to "any native rights based on traditional land use and occupancy (which) had not been extinguished by treaty or superseded by law." The Indian Brotherhood's land claim was ultimately accepted under this category, a *de facto* abrogation of treaties 8 and 11.

TESTIMONY BEFORE THE BERGER INQUIRY
Limitations of space prohibit reviewing the complex concatenation of circumstances which led cabinet to appoint a social democrat and former native rights lawyer, Mr. Justice Thomas Berger, to conduct a public inquiry into the Mackenzie Valley pipeline project, or to explore the circumstances which led ultimately to the project's deferral. Of crucial importance to the present argument, however, is the nature of native testimony before Berger and the impact it had upon his final report.

At hearings during 1974-76, Berger heard testimony from over one thousand witnesses, approximately seven hundred of whom were northerners living in the thirty-five northern communities affected by the pipeline project. The transcripts of the community hearings richly illustrate the political attitudes of Northwest Territories native people. They reveal that this population almost unanimously opposed construction of a Mackenzie Valley pipeline. In addition, the transcripts provide a unique record of the Dene version of their own history, spoken at the first occasion upon which they were able, as a group, to address the government and the rest of Canada.

Two representative testimonies, given by Charlie Snowshoe, a forty-five-year-old trapper from Fort McPherson, and Frank T'Seleie, the twenty-six-year-old chief of the Fort Good Hope band, are discussed in detail below. Close examination of the testimonies reveals considerable stylistic and substantive congruence, but also a striking dissimilarity in key political attitudes. Snowshoe and T'Seleie spoke as representatives of two generations. The contrast in their testimonies marks the transformation in Dene political thought underway in the 1970s.

Snowshoe's testimony begins:

> I'm sorry to say that I had short notice of coming here. I was walking the street yesterday thinking of getting ready to go out in the bush and I was met by Chief Johnny Charlie in Fort McPherson and he asked me if I would come down here; I had no choice but to come because I'm interested in what's going on....
>
> I was in a residential school in Aklavik until I was fifteen years old. I got kicked out of school — I wasn't a drop-out — for saying "Go to hell" to the supervisor. I came back home and that same spring my Dad got a registered trapping area.... My Dad took me there and showed me a little bit how to trap rats — muskrats. And then I was told I had to go back to school again.
>
> The next fall my Dad took me up the Peel River to a place called Snake River....

There follows a detailed description of the areas in which Snowshoe's father taught his son to trap marten and muskrat and to hunt caribou. He continues:

> Every year around, this was what the old-timers had been doing.... This is how the people at Fort McPherson and some from Aklavik trapped in this area. Until the fifties we did it like this. Then employment started coming in, so my Dad and I worked in the summertime around Fort McPherson and then in the fall we'd go back to hunting.... In 1960 I got married and moved up to Snit Lake.
>
> We lived there year round, and one time between Christmas and New Years I had to go up to visit my lake which is about three days from the cabin. There was a couple of guys coming behind me and about six miles below I seen the smoke up there and there was no trail on the road. I was thinking "What the heck is going on?" as I was going up and pretty soon I was getting puzzled. You know, I was confused. When I got to below that place there was a truck sitting with smoke from the exhaust going up in the air. I never heard of anybody working in that area. So I went up and asked them, "What are you guys doing?" When he said "seismic lines" I didn't know what he meant. And that's the way it has been started. Nobody knew what was going on.

After a few more years in the bush, Snowshoe decided to enter the job market. He attended an adult education class and secured "an office job":

> But when I was trying that, I was getting lonesome for my land. And I was lonesome especially when there was nice sunshine outside and all the rats were swimming around the ducks flying in.
>
> That's when they started coming in with the low rental housing and welfare. The people, the native people of the North, were independent until you brought in that low rental housing, and that's where we first got sucked into that business. They subsidized the oil, the gas, taking our own houses away from us, moving us from where we used to be, where we could cut wood for ourselves in town. We were working every day then, not like today. That's the start of spoiling. I was one of them. Today I'm sorry. I was sorry long ago, but right now if I move out of that house, I don't know where else I have to go. I have six kids at home. But we are thinking of getting our own house and starting to burn wood.
>
> When I first started working in town there was booze, and liquor came free to all of us as long as we had money and I became an alcoholic.... But now I haven't drunk for over a year and I still try to do my best.
>
> Last spring I was working on the Dempster Highway and I didn't like what I saw concerning us natives. From there I went in and worked in the co-op store and then I said, "no way, I'm not going to work, I'm going to go back in the bush and fish." And that's what I did last summer.
>
> In January I got a job working with alcoholics. We got a little centre in Fort McPherson and I'm glad to help....
>
> We are screaming about our land and we don't want the pipeline to come through....
>
> The only thing I can say is the change in life sort of crept upon us and we are realizing now what we got into. At the time, everything was changing, and I used to say we were sleeping the time the government stepped over us. But we weren't sleeping. We were out living in the bush and we didn't know what was going on in the community....
>
> All these new things came upon us — like education and working. We realize now that our way of life was good when we used to stay in the bush. We are trying, we are going back slowly.

Snowshoe's testimony is similar in style and in general content to the testimonies of many of the community witnesses of his generation and older. In several ways, it is "traditional," characteristic of the style of political expression used in the internal deliberations of native communities. Snowshoe began by referring to the short notice he had to prepare his remarks, politely suggesting that these would not be as well-cast as the occasion merited. Then he used the narrative form to display and to argue for the political position he wished to put before the Inquiry. In this case, aspects of his own life story were presented to explain from the native point of view the recent history of contact between native and southern Canadian societies.

The Inquiry learned that residential schools were unnecessarily authoritarian, and that school attendance directly interfered with Snowshoe's education in the traditional ways of his people. The efforts of his father overcame this interference and provided him with a viable way of life. When southern society touched his life again, the effects were either unequivocally damaging (in his experience with alcoholism) or simply not satisfying (in his experience with the training program and office job). These experiences led him to conclude that: (1) the pipeline should not be built, since it would bring more damaging and unsatisfying contacts with southern society; and (2) native people should be left alone to solve their own community problems and to return to a way of life best for them. No blame is assigned in connection with these assertions, and they are offered in a manner intended to persuade rather than to antagonize his audience. The persuasion depends upon the audience coming to see the events he has discussed in a new way, one which incorporates what Snowshoe treats as a formerly unknown perspective, that of the Dene. It is important to notice, too, that while Snowshoe's remarks are indirect, his meaning is not ambiguous. He reveals a firm position, and defends it; as a matter of form, the conclusions are left to his hearers.

Frank T'Seleie makes many of the same points as Snowshoe, but his style is different. He begins:

> Mr. Berger ... I want to welcome you and your party to Fort Good Hope. This is the first time in the history of my people that an important person from your nation has come to listen and learn from us, and not just come to tell us what we should do, or trick us into saying yes to something that in the end is not good for us....
>
> You are here on behalf of your government to ask us our opinions on the plans your people have for our land. Because you are honest and just, I do not believe you would be asking these questions if your nation had already made a decision on these plans. It is not at all inevitable that there will be a pipeline built through the heart of our land. Whether or not your businessmen or your government believes that a pipeline must be built through our great valley, let me tell you, Mr. Berger, and let me tell your nation, that this is Dene land and we the Dene people intend to decide what happens on our land....
>
> Mr. Berger, there will be no pipeline. There will be no pipeline because we have our plans for our land. There will be no pipeline because we no longer intend to allow our land and our future to be taken away from us so that we are destroyed to make someone else rich.

After reading a letter written from his community to the government of Canada in 1928, T'Seleie stated that it proved that the Dene had always objected to intrusions from the South, but that their objections had not been heeded. He called the cumulative effect of federal policy in the North "genocide," and he addressed the representatives of the pipeline construction companies directly. One president, Bob Blair of Foothills, attended the community hearing at which TSeleie spoke.

> Mr. Blair, there is a life and death struggle going on between us, between you and me.... You are coming to destroy a people that have a history of thirty thousand years. Why? For twenty years of gas? Are you really that insane? The original General Custer was exactly that insane. You still have

a chance to learn, a chance to be something other than a fool bent on destroying everything he touched....

It seems to me that the whole point in living is to become as human as possible; to learn to understand the world and to live in it; to be part of it; to learn to understand the animals, for they are our brothers and they have much to teach us. We are a part of this world.

We are like the river that flows and changes, yet is always the same. The river cannot flow too slow and it cannot flow too fast. It is a river and it will always be a river, for that is what it was meant to be.... Our Dene nation is like this great river. It has been flowing before any of us can remember. We take our strength and our wisdom and our ways from the flow and direction that has been established for us by ancestors we never knew, ancestors of a thousand years ago. Their wisdom flows through us to our children and our grandchildren to generations we will never know. We will live out our lives as we must and we will die in peace because we will know that our people and this river will flow on after us.

We know that our grandchildren will speak a language that is their heritage, that has been passed on from before time.... We know they will look after their old people and respect them for their wisdom. We know they will look after this land and protect it and that five hundred years from now someone with skin my colour and moccasins on his feet will climb up the Ramparts and rest and look over the river and feel that he too has a place in the universe; and he will thank the same spirits that I thank, that his ancestors have looked after his land well, and he will be proud to be a Dene.

It is for this unborn child, Mr. Berger, that my nation will stop the pipeline. It is so that this unborn child can know the freedom of this land that I am willing to lay down my life.

Snowshoe and T'Seleie take the same position on the major issue: the pipeline must not be built because it will destroy the basis of a way of life which is important to each of them. For both witnesses, two separate societies exist, their own and that of southern Canada, and both believe that the latter threatens their own. Both, too, speak to the Inquiry without deference, as representatives of a larger group of people with whom they have powerful common interests. Two related themes shape both speakers' explanations of the way of life which they fear is threatened. The first is the theme of generational continuity, expressed most forcefully in T'Seleie's river analogy, but present also in Snowshoe's discussion of the ways in which his father mitigated the effects of the residential school to provide Snowshoe with a way of making a living in the old style, and in his plans for "going back slowly" and building something better for the people who follow him. The second theme concerns the special relationship of the Dene to the natural world. Many other witnesses who spoke at the Inquiry tried in various ways to explain to the Inquiry the nature of this relationship. Very often, the land is called "Mother" — the source of sustenance, security and spiritual support and the object of love and respect from the Dene. These attitudes are traditional in the purest sense, with their origins in the pre-contact period.

Although it is evident that T'Seleie and Snowshoe's testimonies share this common ground, a closer examination reveals interesting differences in their political perspectives. While Snowshoe spoke extemporaneously, T'Seleie read from a prepared text. T'Seleie's remarks were clearly deeply felt, and in this sense personal, but he did not choose to present his analysis in the form of a personal history. Instead, he introduced documentary evidence, and he placed events in the North in a broad social and historical perspective, with allusions to other battles fought by indigenous people against the same expansionary and dangerous foes. T'Seleie chose a much more antagonistic rhetorical position than did Snowshoe, casting the relationship between Dene society and southern Canada as a long confrontation which had reached a decisive moment. Whereas Snowshoe offered a resolution that would involve different policy choices, T'Seleie emphasized the willingness of his people to offer resistance, including, he suggested in his concluding statement, violent resistance.

In Snowshoe's presentation, native people appear as the confused or, at least, unaware victims of a situation with which they are only gradually coming to terms. T'Seleie, instead, suggests that his people have long understood and rejected the negative aspects of this situation. Because the situation is changing — with the prospect of pipeline construction and more intensive interaction with southern institutions — the form of their rejection also is changing. Here he takes an important step. He claims control over the use of "Dene land," including the right both to exclude southerners from its use and to formulate plans for the manner in which it will be used by future occupants.

THE AFTERMATH OF THE PIPELINE INQUIRY

Before proceeding to a consideration of the significance for evolving Dene-government relations of native testimony before the Berger Inquiry, it will be useful to conclude the narrative with a review of some of the major political changes which occurred after the Berger Inquiry left the North. First, the federal cabinet decided in 1977 to defer construction of the Mackenzie Valley pipeline in favour of another route through the Yukon Territory. The recommendations of the Mackenzie Valley Pipeline Inquiry, released just before this decision was reached, exercised some influence in the process through which cabinet reached this decision, but the Inquiry's report was far from the most important determining factor. The Inquiry *process* was important in increasing southern Canadian understanding of the broader pipeline issue and providing a focus for the mobilization of southern groups who lobbied the government on behalf of the Dene. In addition, the fact that the Inquiry was in progress permitted the federal government to postpone a decision on northern hydrocarbon production systems while the very uncertain energy picture of the mid-seventies was clarified.

Whatever the impact of the Inquiry in the South, it is clear that its influence in the Mackenzie Valley was profound. During the course of the Berger hearings, communication among Mackenzie Valley communities increased considerably, both because the hearings received extensive coverage in the northern media and because Indian Brotherhood staff had received funding to visit communities in the course of preparing their submission. In addition, the Brotherhood submitted a proposal for negotiation of a native claims settlement with the federal government, which they argued should precede development of Mackenzie Valley non-renewable resources.

Testimony by native people in Mackenzie Valley communities, and to a lesser extent the testimony of the Indian Brotherhood itself, was reflected clearly in the Berger report. The Brotherhood proposal for the settlement of native claims, however, was rejected by the federal government in 1977. This proposal envisioned the establishment of a new, almost exclusively native territory to be governed through unspecified but innovative institutions; cabinet refused to negotiate on this basis, stating that "ethnic governments" would not be countenanced in Canada, and would not be discussed in any event in a forum at which only some of the residents of the Northwest Territories (i.e., native people) were represented.

The federal rejection of this approach effectively halted claims negotiations, and it placed new pressures on the Indian Brotherhood political strategists. At federal instance, the Métis Association and the Brotherhood were required to submit a joint claim on the grounds that their membership shared a common aboriginal heritage and a common land base. The Métis Association, although initially supportive of the Brotherhood's attempt to negotiate new constitutional arrangements at the claims table, did not place the same priority on the issue. Faced with this differing opinion from their negotiating partners, with the federal refusal to move on the issue, and with severely restricted funding, the Indian Brotherhood developed a new and less confrontational three-pronged strategy. First, federal restrictions upon issues which could be discussed at the claims negotiations table were tacitly if not officially accepted. Second, the Brotherhood sought the support of the non-native population of the Northwest Territories for redesigned governing institutions which would meet Dene concerns. Finally, an earlier Indian Brotherhood position, which discouraged participation in territorial elections on the grounds the territorial government was an imposition of a foreign power, was reversed.

As a result, the territorial election of 1979 brought to office a Legislative Assembly which included Dene (as well as Inuit and Métis) activists, and some non-native representatives who were open to compromise on native demands. The newly-elected legislators quickly worked out a means to promote public discussion of alternative government institutions and they began to take action to meet native concerns in such areas as education and renewable resources management. In addition, in 1981, the Indian Brotherhood and the Métis Association published a new official statement to supplement the Dene Declaration, titled *Public Government for the People of the North*. *Public Government* is identified as a discussion paper, not a manifesto. It outlines a proposed form of government for the Northwest Territories which blends province-like liberal democratic governing forms with certain innovations designed to preserve native control in areas of crucial concern.

Discussion continues in the Northwest Territories of these proposed arrangements. Although a consensus has yet to be reached, it is likely that native participants will continue to lead the debate. Meanwhile, negotiations for a land claim settlement are in progress through the mechanisms of a Joint Negotiating Secretariat (formed by the Dene Nation and the Métis Association of the Northwest Territories) and the federal Office of Native Claims. In addition, with the support of the entire Legislative Assembly, NWT native leaders are participating with national Native groups in the negotiations concerning the entrenchment of aboriginal rights in the Canadian constitution. If negotiators on the native side and leaders of the native organizations are successful territorially and nationally in keeping the claims negotiation process and the wider public discussion of institutional reforms to the NWT government proceedings in tandem, native people in the western Northwest Territories may yet achieve a unique (for Canada) form of self-government which can protect their collective interests, as these were defined during the 1970s. At a minimum, the institutional arrangements now in place guarantee that the passage of the Dene — from a position of "silence" and virtual political powerlessness to one in which their influence over at least regional affairs is assured — will not be reversed.

III. SUMMARY

For decades, Ottawa decision-makers behaved as if the aboriginal residents of the Northwest Territories could be administered without consultation on the basis of an understanding of aboriginal needs developed "by inspection" and at a distance. When native protests began to be registered, avenues of communication with decision makers were opened. Eventually, the entire array of liberal democratic institutions linking citizens to the state were employed — advisory councils, publicly funded organizations for interest aggregation, the court system, a public inquiry, and, finally, electoral politics. Information generated by these institutions affected subsequent public policy. It is important to note, however, that limits to the state's capacity to accommodate Dene objectives also were revealed. No concessions were made on proposals challenging the sovereignty of the federal government. Nor would the federal government consider constitutional proposals that would establish the Dene as a special class of Canadian citizens with unusual rights and privileges, although the 1983 entrenchment of still-undefined aboriginal rights in the Canadian constitution suggests that progress in this direction may now be possible.

Despite federal opposition, the Dene have not abandoned their goal of achieving a "special" constitutional arrangement. The version of Dene history presented to the Berger Commission suggests at least two reasons for the tenacity with which Dene leaders (and, on the whole, the people they represent) have maintained their political direction. One reason, of course, is that the Dene share a distinctive culture which has its roots in a style of life very different from that of non-native Canadians. In addition, the Dene share a common historical experience with non-Dene institutions which until very recently were unresponsive to local needs and aspirations.

A comparison of the statements of Charlie Snowshoe and Frank T'Seleie before the Berger Inquiry suggests that the objectives and values associated with the new Dene politics are similar to those espoused by older generations. The *practice* of the new politics, however, differs significantly from the old. When the Dene began to achieve real influence, through the courts, the Berger Inquiry and in the territorial legislature, they accepted (at least provisionally and implicitly) the institution through which influence was possible. In doing so, they accepted, as well, the legitimacy of the state and its ultimate authority to regulate their relationship to the land. They did so, however, without abandoning their claim to use the land in traditional ways, and to find a means within the Canadian constitutional tradition to maintain their integrity *into the future* as a distinctive and self-determining collectivity.

Earlier in this paper, the institutions which permitted some resolution of the constitutional impasse between the Dene and the state during the polarized 1970s were called "communication bridges" — institutional mechanisms which improved mutual understanding and which also provided a means for an adjustment in the relative political power of the Dene. My suggestion is finally that the usefulness of these institutions is by no means an historical accident, but rather an application in new circumstances of institutional gains won by other disadvantaged groups. (Thompson, 1975) It is this quality of liberal democratic governments which distinguishes them from fascist and authoritarian states, and which makes possible the peaceful resolution of profound social conflicts and the protection of the interests of political minorities. In the case of the Dene, the institutions of liberal democracy have demonstrated profound and seductive integrative power.

[1] Two organizations represent the Dene and Métis of the NWT. Discussion in this paper focusses upon the political development of the Dene, whose organization was named the Indian Brotherhood of the NWT until the late 1970s, and later the Dene Nation. The Métis are represented by the Métis Association of the NWT. People who identify themselves as Métis are typically of mixed native and non-native heritage, but their choice of the designation 'Métis" is often less a matter of ancestry than a statement of political and social perspective. Many self-identified Dene are also of mixed ancestry. Similarly, status under the Indian Act does not determine whether a particular native person will choose to be identified as Dene or Métis.

I acknowledge with gratitude the generous assistance of Sheree Skulmoski, James Ross, Neil Nevitte and Charles Baker who helped in various ways to produce this paper.

FOOTNOTES

[1] A survey of litigation in the past fifty years relating to women's rights in Canadian public law is included in M.E. Atcheson et al. *Women and Legal Action*, Ottawa: Canadian Advisory Council on the Status of Women, 1984.
[2] (The reference is to Tom Flanagan's paper in this volume.)
[3] One early expression of this concern is in the "Summary of Those Resolutions Passed at The Ad Hoc Conference on Women and The Constitution which deal with Required Amendments to the Proposed Charter of Rights and Freedoms, together with commentary on the significance of the amendments for Women and the proposed wording of the Charter as amended, prepared pursuant to the Ad Hoc Conference on Canadian Women and the Constitution held on February 14th and 15th, 1981."
[4] Consider, for example, *Morgentaler v. The Queen* (1975), 20 C.C.C. (2d) 499 (geographical location); *R.v. Burnshine*, (1975) 1 S.C.R. 693 (age and geographical location); *Prata v. Minister of Manpower and Immigration*, (1976) 1 S.C.R. 376 (citizenship and domicile); *MacKay v. The Queen* (1980), 114 D.L.R. (3d) 393 (military).
[5] In *R.v. Drybones*, (1970) S.C.R. 282.

[6] *Re Federal Republic of Germany and Rauca* (1983), 41 O.R. (2d) 225 and *Re Southam and The Queen* (No. 1) (1983), 3 C.C.C. (3d) 515 (Ontario Court of Appeal).
[7] *Operation Dismantle Inc. et al v. Government of Canada et al.* (1983), 49 N.R. 363 (Fed. C.A.).
[8] *Murdoch v. Murdoch*, (1975) 1 S.C.R. 423.
[9] Changes in pregnancy leave were introduced by: *An Act to Amend the Unemployment Insurance Act, 1971*, S.C. 1980-81-82-83, c. 150.
[10] A bill formulating changes to the Indian Act failed to pass the Senate early in 1984: *An Act to Amend the Indian Act*, Bill C-47, Second Session, Thirty-second Parliament, First reading in the Commons June 18, 1984.
[11] See M.E. Atcheson et al. *op. cit.*, note 1, at pp. 27-28.
[12] Some statutes require that consent of the Minister or Attorney-General is necessary before a prosecution for an offence under the Act can be brought, but no consent is required to bring an ordinary civil action.
[13] *Borowski v. Minister of Justice for Canada*, (1982) 1 W.W.R. 97 (S.C.C.).
[14] See the discussion in *The Elimination of Sex Discrimination from the Indian Act* (Ottawa: Indian Affairs and Northern Development, 1982).
[15] Marc Gold, "A Principled Approach to Equality Rights: A Preliminary Inquiry," (1982) 4 *Supreme Court L.R.* 132.
[16] W.S. Tarnopolsky, "The Equality Rights," in W.S. Tarnopolsky and G.A. Beaudoin, eds., *The Canadian Charter of Rights and Freedoms: Commentary* (Toronto: The Carswell Company Limited, 1982), at pp. 421-422.
[17] *Op. cit., supra*, note 16, p. 422.
[18] Douglas Sanders, in an essay to be published in Bayefsky and Eberts, eds., *Equality Rights and the Canadian Charter of Rights and Freedoms*, (Toronto: The Carswell Company, forthcoming).
[19] See, Dale Gibson, *Impact of Canadian Charter of Rights and Freedoms on Manitoba Statutes*, Legal Research Institute of the University of Manitoba, 1982; Mary Eberts, *Preliminary Study: Equality Rights under the Canadian Charter of Rights and Freedoms and the Statutes of Canada* (Ottawa, March 1983); *An Act respecting Compliance of Acts of the Legislature with the Canadian Charter of Rights and Freedoms*, S.N.B. 1984, c.4 (effective date of s. 16 is April 1, 1984; effective date of the balance is June 30, 1983).

REFERENCES

Abele, Frances and E.J. Dosman. "Interdepartmental Co-ordination and Northern Development," *Canadian Public Administration*. 24 no. 3 (1981).

Asch, M. "The Dene Economy." In Mel Watkins, ed. *Dene Nation: The Colony Within*, Toronto: University of Toronto, 1977.

Burch, Ernest S. "The Ethnography of Northern North America: A Guide to Recent Research," *Arctic Anthropology*. 16 no. 1, 1979.

Canada. Advisory Commission on the Development of Government in the Northwest Territories. *Report to the Minister of Northern Affairs and National Resources*. 1966.

Canada. Department of Indian Affairs and Northern Development. *Northern Frontier, Northern Homeland: Report of the Mackenzie Valley Pipeline Inquiry*. Volume 1, 1977.

Canada. Special Representative for Constitutional Development in the Northwest Territories. *Constitutional Development in the Northwest Territories.* 1980.

Carrothers Report. Canada, Advisory Commission on the Development of Government in the Northwest Territories. *Report to the Minister of Northern Affairs and National Resources.* Ottawa, 1966.

Drury, C.M. *Constitutional Development in the Northwest Territories: Report of the Special Representative.* Ottawa: Supply and Services, 1980.

Fumoleau, Rene. Personal interview with the author. August, 1981.

Paulette's Application to file a Caveat, Re. S.C.N.W.T. 6 W.W.R. 97 (1973) (cited as Morrow 1973 in text).

Paulette's Application to file a Caveat, Re. N.W.T.C.A. 2 W.W.R. 193 (1976).

Paulette et al v. The Queen. S.C.C. 1 W.W.R. 321 (1977).

Rea, K.J. *The Political Economy of the Canadian North.* Toronto: University of Toronto Press, 1968.

Sahlins, Marshal. *Stone-Age Economics.* Chicago: Aldine Publishing Company, 1972.

Snowshoe, Charlie. Testimony at the Hearings of the Mackenzie Valley Pipeline Inquiry, Yellowknife. April 28 and 29, 1976. Vol. 147: 22475-22538; Vol. 148: 22539-22626. Reprinted in Watkins (1977).

Thompson, E.P. *Whigs and Hunters: The Origin of the Black Act*, London: Penguin, 1975.

T'Seleie, John.Testimony at the Hearings of the Mackenzie Valley Pipeline Inquiry, Yellowknife. July 23, 1976. Vol. 169: 26211-26367. Reprinted in Watkins (1977).

Weaver, Sally M. *Making Canadian Indian Policy: The Hidden Agenda 1968-1970.* Toronto: University of Toronto Press, 1981.

Zaslow, Morris. *The Opening of the Canadian North 1870-1914.* Toronto: McClelland and Stewart, 1971.

15

MINORITIES AS AN ATTITUDINAL PHENOMENON: A COMPARATIVE ANALYSIS OF YOUTH ELITES

NEIL NEVITTE
ROGER GIBBINS

INTRODUCTION

The efforts of Canadian governments to protect and advance the cause of minorities are not new; as others have pointed out, they can be traced to the 1960s. Those early efforts took place within the broader context of a general North American awakening to the plight of minorities, a context dramatically shaped by the politicization of American blacks, landmark judicial decisions by the United States Supreme Court, and the divisive politics of the American Civil Rights movement. The scope of government intervention on behalf of minorities expanded considerably in both the United States and Canada. Affirmative action, a term which was first used in a racial discrimination context in President Kennedy's Executive Order No. 10925 in 1961 (Sowell, 1984: 39), has become a broad-gauge policy goal of Canadian governments which, like their American counterparts, aim at assisting a wide variety of groups including racial minorities, women, the handicapped and aboriginal Canadians.

In December 1983 the Parliament of Canada charged the Special Committee on the Participation of Visible Minorities with the responsibility of charting a new course for Canada's visible minorities. (Special Committee, 1984) Significantly, the mandate of the Committee was broad. It was asked among other things "to seek positive and constructive ideas and models pertaining explicitly to ameliorating relations within Canada between visible minorities and other Canadians...," "to recommend the development of positive programs that the Committee finds necessary to promote racial understanding..." and, in general, to review federal policies and programs in the area of race relations. (Special Committee, 1984: vi) It is to the appropriate models that should be used, and the parameters of political support for ameliorative public policies, that the present paper is addressed.

In looking at minority relations in Canada, what is clearly apparent is the extent to which Canadian analysis and policies, on the part of both minority groups and governments, have been informed by the American experience. We argue, however, that parallels between the Canadian and American experiences are too readily assumed, and that the temptation to approach Canadian minority relations within an American framework invites a potentially serious distortion of the Canadian reality. In an impressive critical analysis of American policies towards minorities, Thomas Sowell argues that American policy has been dominated by a "civil rights vision." (Sowell, 1984) This vision, he suggests, was the product of a specific history of a specific minority — American blacks — and that the extension of that vision to inform policies which embrace all minorities is both inappropriate and problematic. We argue that the extension of the civil rights vision becomes even more problematic when it is transported outside the United States and used as a framework for minority relations in Canada.

There is no parallel in the Canadian historical record for the experience of American blacks; there has been no history of slavery, no civil war fought in large part on the issue of emancipation, no Reconstruction period, no civil rights movement analogous to that which reshaped the American society over the last thirty years. The pre-eminent minority in Canada has been linguistically rather than racially defined, and the position of Francophones in Canada — who comprise over a quarter of the national population, control the government of Canada's second largest province, and have made major contributions to the political leadership of the nation — bears little resemblance to that of blacks in the United States. To be sure, the Canadian racial relations copybook has been blotted many times; one has only to look at the treatment of Chinese immigrants in British Columbia, the expulsion of Japanese Canadians from the west coast during the Second World War, and the history of blacks in Nova Scotia. But these experiences are hardly comparable to the sustained politicization of racial policies in the United States which historically have simultaneously educated and divided the American public.

It follows, then, that we should expect Canadians to order their attitudinal orientations towards minority relations in a manner somewhat different from Americans. To expect otherwise would be to deny any significant impact from historical experience on public values and attitudes, a position we find untenable. The intent of the discussion that follows, therefore, is to explore the parallels and contrasts between American orientations towards blacks, and Canadian orientations towards racial minorities. In conclusion we will depart from the data somewhat to offer a broader commentary on minorities as an attitudinal phenomenon, and on the significance of Canadian-American differences for an appreciation of minority relations in Canada.

DATA AND METHODOLOGY

Our analysis of Canadian and American orientations towards minority relations is drawn from data derived from two surveys of senior undergraduates in Canada and the United States.[1] The American survey, which provided the benchmark for the Canadian questionnaire and sampling strategy, was administered in 1979. Through a mailed questionnaire, with a 53 percent response rate, 364 respondents were drawn from a random sample of senior undergraduates at ten regionally dispersed universities. The Canadian survey, conducted by the authors in early 1983, drew upon random samples of senior undergraduates from nine universities: Memorial, Dalhousie, Laval, Montréal, Queen's, Toronto, Wilfrid Laurier, Calgary and U.B.C. The response rate of 53 percent to the mailed questionnaire, close to that achieved through in-person survey techniques, yielded 558 Anglophone respondents from the seven non-Québec universities and 221 Francophones from the two Québec campuses. In total, then, we have 1143 respondents who replied to 118 questions common to both the Canadian and American questionnaires. Standard checks show that neither sample is systematically biased with respect to respondent characteristics such as gender and program of study.

We cannot claim that the Canadian and American respondents are representative of their respective national populations or even of the senior university students in the two national communities. Nonetheless, university students provide a particularly useful population for two reasons. First, our interests go beyond a simple isomorphic comparison of the three samples, single issue by single issue. We are more interested in the *pattern* and *coherence* of minority group orientations, in whether orientations towards one minority are linked in some systematic way to orientations to other minorities or to other values within the political culture. Here a substantial body of research has shown that, in general, the beliefs of most people are characterized by little attitudinal constraint and that attitudinal or what might be termed ideological patterns emerge only within a relatively limited segment of the population characterized by high levels of formal education. (Converse, 1964) It is thus easier to identify attitudinal structures through the university samples, structures that may be present to a degree within the larger population but which tend to be masked by the "noise" generated by a lack of constraint and coherency.

The second point to be made is that our respondents essentially constitute an elite segment of the population. Universities are the recruitment ground, if not necessarily the training ground, for tomorrow's elites, and thus we might expect today's students to be at the policy-making command posts in the society of the future, to be opinion leaders within their communities. It is noteworthy also that, in the Canadian sample, we are drawing on the educated elite of the single most significant minority in Canada — Francophones resident within the province of Québec.[2]

The nature of our data prevents any ready generalizations to the national populations within which university students are embedded. Somewhat paradoxically, however, the research design is one that brings national differences into bold relief by eliminating significant differences in education, age, socio-economic position or gender. Because our respondents share so much in common, all being fourth-year students within a North American university, the difference in nationality is highlighted and brought to the fore. We have, then, good reason to believe that the differences in attitudinal structure that do emerge are reflective of underlying differences in national culture. Here it should be noted that the level of formal education has been demonstrated to be the single most important factor affecting levels of tolerance to stigmatized groups in society. By holding education constant through our sampling design, the impact of education has been removed in order to bring national differences into sharper focus. While any inference to the more general population is necessarily compromised, this in itself is not without benefit. Given that our main interest is in both attitudinal structures and national differences across such structures, and that from the perspective of public policy elite opinions are of particular relevance, we regard our focus on informed opinion to be more rather than less illuminating.

DISCUSSION

Our analysis of orientations to minorities in Canada and the United States focuses primarily on a pool of questions which asks American respondents about their views towards blacks, and Canadian respondents about their views towards racial minorities. We realize, of course, that these groups are not precisely the same; blacks are more readily identifiable as a single group, even a single culture, and can be regarded as a subset of the more general category, "racial minority," which can encompass many cultures. Both groups, however, are equivalent in the sense that both are involuntarily stigmatized by skin colour; both are visible minorities. More importantly, the fact that the Canadian and American surveys use the same questions, substituting only "racial minorities" for "blacks" in the Canadian case, lays the foundation for the argument developed in this paper. Simply put, we will argue that this substitution is associated with a very substantive alteration in minority group perceptions, that "racial minorities" in Canada are not equivalent to "blacks" in the United States. Somewhat ironically, this difference is more clearly demonstrated through a set of questions common to the two groups.

The questions listed in table 15.1 include all those common to both the Canadian and American surveys, and in which the only difference in question format lay in the reference group — "blacks" in the American case as opposed to "racial minorities" and, in two cases, "minorities" in the Canadian case. The six questions tap not only perceptions about the status of blacks and racial minorities but also the level of support for a variety of remedies ranging from government intervention to ensure fair treatment in the workplace (question 1) to the use of quotas in school admissions and job hiring (question 5). A comparison of the simple frequencies reported in table 15.1 reveals some important similarities and differences among the three samples.

A majority of all three samples supports the view that white people do not have the right to refuse to sell their home to blacks/racial minorities (question 2) and that the government should see to it that blacks/racial minorities get fair treatment in jobs (question 1). Similarly, between thirty and forty percent of respondents from all three samples believe that black and minority leaders should have more influence in American and Canadian life respectively (question 6). But in this instance more than a third of the English Canadian sample reports the belief that minority leaders should have relatively "little influence" in Canadian life. This finding hints at a pattern of differences among the three samples which is revealed more clearly in responses to the remaining questions.

We might expect that support for solutions or remedies to a variety of social, economic and political inequities would be related to respondents' explanations for the existence of such inequities as well as some assessment of the consequences of those inequities for society. In this vein, it is useful to look at the pattern of response across questions three, four and five. The responses to question 5, which asked respondents whether the inequities facing minorities are due to systemic factors — social conditions — or to the lack of effort on the part of minorities themselves, illustrate significant differences among the three samples. American respondents are the most likely (38 percent) and English Canadian respondents the least likely (18 percent) to blame systemic factors for the relative poverty of visible minorities. Similarly, English Canadians are more likely (43 percent) to endorse the idea that "school admissions and job hiring should be based strictly on merit" than are either the American (26 percent) or Québecois (29 percent) respondents (question 4). At the opposite end of the same scale, less than 10 percent of the English Canadian respondents were prepared to support the use of quotas in these areas compared to nearly 30 percent of the American and 23 percent of the Québecois respondents.

Table 15.1
Comparative Orientations to Visible Minorities

		U.S.	English Canadian	Québeçois
1. If racial minorities/blacks are not getting fair treatment in jobs the government should see to it that they do.	% strongly agree	57.4	53.9	67.7
	% strongly disagree	5.9	3.1	1.8
2. White people have a right to refuse to sell their homes to blacks/racial minorities.	% strongly agree	13.5	6.9	6.0
	% strongly disagree	54.1	67.3	81.7
3. Relative ranking of "achieving equality for blacks/racial minorities" as an important goal for society.	% important goal	28.1	18.2	24.3
	% not important	16.6	48.5	35.3
4. "Quotas in school admissions and job hiring should be used to ensure the representation of minorities" vs. "School admissions and job hiring should be based strictly on merit."	% for quotas	29.9	9.6	23.1
	% for "merit only"	25.6	42.8	28.6
5. "If blacks/racial minorities would try harder they could be just as well off as whites" vs. "Social conditions make it impossible for most blacks/racial minorities to overcome poverty even if they try."	% try harder	5.6	9.8	5.5
	% social conditions make it impossible	38.0	18.8	28.4
6. Relative influence black/minority leaders should have in American/Canadian life.	% very influential	36.6	31.1	39.6
	% little influence	27.0	35.1	25.9
	Sample size	364	558	221

These differences, at least partly, may be due to the generally greater individualistic and non-interventionist orientations found in the English Canadian sample. (Gibbins and Nevitte, 1984) This, however, does not seem to be a compelling explanation for respondents' relative rankings of "achieving equality for blacks/racial minorities" as a more or less important goal for society (question 3). The fact that both Canadian samples are less likely than their American counterparts to view equality for visible minorities as "not important"

Table 15.2

Item Inter-Correlations for Questions on Blacks/ Racial Minorities*

		1	2	3	4	5
1. "If blacks/racial minorities are not getting fair treatment in jobs, the government should see to it that they do." (4-point scale)	EC Que Amer	— — —				
2. "White people have a right to refuse to sell their homes to blacks/racial minorities." (4-point scale)	EC Que Amer	.25 .05 .38				
3. The importance attached, among 11 policy concerns, to "achieving equality for blacks/racial minorities"	EC Que Amer	.34 .36 .37	.26 .05 .34			
4. 7-point scale ranging from "quotas in school admissions and job hiring should be used to ensure black/minority group representation" to "school admissions and job hiring should be based strictly on merit."	EC Que Amer	.16 .08 .41	.11 .12 .43	.17 .24 .53		
5. 7-point scale ranging from "social conditions make it almost impossible for most blacks/members of minority groups to overcome poverty even if they try" to "if blacks/minority groups would try harder, they could be just as well off as whites."	EC Que Amer	.23 .08 .41	.24 .13 .39	.32 .41 .49	.29 .27 .49	
6. On a 7-point scale, "how much influence should black/ minority group leaders have over American/Canadian life."	EC Que Amer	.23 .22 .33	.20 .10 .40	.31 .34 .41	.18 .26 .50	.29 .29 .43

* all correlations are Pearson r's; for ease of interpretation, all variables have been recoded so that low values are associated with a positive orientation towards blacks/minority groups.

MEAN ITEM-INTERCORRELATION: English Canadian respondents = .239
Quebecois respondents = .201
American respondents = .415

points rather to substantially different national experiences in the politicization of racial differences.

The fact that American, English Canadian and Québecois students have similar dispositions towards many minority group issues, and that they also differ in some respects, reveals only one dimension of their attitudinal world. In table 15.2, we present the item-intercorrelations for the six variables discussed in table 15.1. The average item-intercorrelations for the three sets of respondents, obtained by summing the item-intercorrelations in the above table and dividing by the number of such intercorrelations, suggest that opinion in the American sample is more "coherent" or more consistent than in either Canadian case. The difference between the English Canadian and Québecois samples is small but interesting nonetheless, given that students within the majority culture appear to have more consistent predispositions towards racial minorities than do students in the minority culture. As the analysis unfolds below, it will be seen that this divergence between the two Canadian samples is reinforced.

That American respondents have a more coherent orientation towards blacks than Canadians do towards racial minorities should not be surprising. Nonetheless, the Canadian-American difference is important to note for it suggests caution in assuming that Canadians organize their opinions towards racial minorities in a manner analogous to the way in which Americans organize their opinions towards blacks. Canadian opinion appears to be "softer," less sharply defined than its American counterpart. Of even greater interest is that this national difference extends to the manner in which Canadians and Americans link opinion on minority issues to other aspects of their attitudinal domain.

Table 15.3 examines the relationship between attitudes towards racial minorities and blacks, on the one hand, and gender-related issues on the other. In the political arena both racial minorities and women are often portrayed as visible minorities, although in the latter case, of course, minority status stems from economic and social discrimination rather than from a lack of numbers *per se*. In the American sample, the two sets of attitudes are tied together; knowing how a respondent feels towards blacks enables one to make a reasonable prediction as to how he or she feels about the status of women in the American society. There is, in other words, some significant linkage between attitudes towards the dominant American racial minority and attitudes towards the gender "minority." Among English Canadian respondents, however, the linkage is more tenuous; knowledge about respondents predispositions towards racial minorities reveals little about gender predispositions. In the case of Québecois respondents, the linkage is more tenuous yet.

It is interesting to note the correlations between the two quota questions — question 4 in both the gender and minority batteries. As we would expect, the correlations are very high and to a degree are indicative of a general predisposition towards the use of quotas independent of the specific groups involved. At the same time, however, the correlations are not perfect, indicating some willingness or ability on the part of respondents to make their general orientations to the use of quotas conditional on the specific groups to whom quotas are to be applied. Here we should also note the correlations between the two very similar questions addressing the explanation for poverty among

Table 15.3
Attitudinal Linkage Between Minority Relations and Gender Issues*

MINORITY RELATIONS**

		1	2	3	4	5	6
1. "The Equal Rights Amendment, which aims at eliminating distinctions in the treatment of men and women, should be ratified/There should be more laws which aim at eliminating distinctions in the treatment of men and women." (4-point scale)	EC Que Amer	.31 .11 .26	.15 .04 .32	.19 .14 .23	.14 .05 .28	.18 .23 .29	.17 .18 .25
2. The importance attached, among 11 policy concerns, to "achieving equality for women"	EC Que Amer	.20 .07 .22	.19 .02 .21	.44 .22 .58	.19 .20 .33	.25 .20 .28	.21 .10 .33
3. 7-point scale ranging from "discrimination makes it almost impossible for most women to get jobs equal to their ability" to "if women tried harder, they could get jobs equal to their ability."	EC Que Amer	.18 .10 .29	.14 .15 .36	.21 .17 .29	.19 .15 .34	.45 .44 .52	.25 .30 .36
4. 7-point scale ranging from "quotas in job hiring should be used to increase the number of women in good jobs" to "job hiring should be based strictly on merit."	EC Que Amer	.08 .02 .34	.08 .19 .40	.22 .15 .44	.75 .65 .78	.28 .26 .46	.22 .30 .49
5. On a 7-point scale, "how much influence should feminist groups have over Canadian/American life."	EC Que Amer	.13 .14 .26	.13 .07 .33	.20 .28 .31	.27 .30 .37	.24 .23 .36	.46 .42 .67

* all correlations are Pearson r's; for ease of interpretation, all variables have been recoded so that low values are associated with a positive orientation to blacks/minority groups and women.

** see Table 2 for an identification of these variables

MEAN ITEM-INTERCORRELATION: English Canadian respondents = .235
Quebecois respondents = .196
American respondents = .365

minority groups and a lack of good jobs for women — question 5 from the minority battery and question 3 from the gender battery. The correlations are not high enough to demonstrate a general predisposition to blame the individuals involved — "if they only worked harder" — irrespective of the groups involved. Explanations for the conditions faced by women are not transferred holus polus to the conditions faced by racial minorities, or vice versa.

The imposition of gender controls did not alter the basic national difference in table 15.3. As table 15.4 demonstrates, the linkage remained stronger for American men than for Canadian men, and stronger for American women than for Canadian women. There is, however, an important gender difference that emerges from the table. Given that many women consider themselves a minority, we might expect this segment of the population to generalize about their minority condition, extrapolating concerns about their own status to a more global concern about minorities in general. We find, though, that female respondents were less likely than male respondents to link their opinions towards racial minorities and gender issues. To the extent that there was some global disposition towards "minorities" that encompassed both racial minorities and women, this disposition was most evident among male respondents. To stretch the data findings a bit, we might conclude that for women, women are not "another minority" but are *women* with group-specific concerns and interests. Only to men does it make sense, and even then not much sense, to see women as a minority group or at least as a minority group analogous to blacks or racial minorities in Canada.

Table 15.5 expands the discussion by examining the linkages between minority orientations and a series of basic values which might be seen as cornerstones to political culture. Debates over government intervention and the use of the state to redistribute wealth, for example, are not only perennial but can be seen as constituting the "basic stuff" of political life. Table 15.5 presents a great deal of data and warrants detailed examination. The rough correlational pattern, however, is revealed through the mean scores. These simply total the correlations within each set, and for each sample, and divide by the total number of correlations. Thus we can see that across the three government intervention questions, American opinions are more strongly tied to minority orientations than is the case among English Canadian or Québecois respondents. Indeed, for Québecois respondents the linkage is negligible while for English Canadian respondents it is weak. For Americans, then, support for the black minority is associated with a positive orientation towards state intervention, an association that is not surprising given the growing role of state intervention for the protection of minority interests. What is perhaps more surprising is that the English Canadian association is so weak, and that the Québecois association is virtually non-existent.

If we turn to the three questions in table 15.5 dealing with income redistribution, the same national difference emerges. American respondents who are more favourably disposed towards minority groups are also more prone to endorse income redistribution while those who oppose minority groups are also more prone to oppose the redistribution of income. (The *direction* of this relationship is not clear; one could, for example, oppose minority interests because the satisfaction of such interests would entail a redistribution of income, or one could oppose income redistribution because the redistributed income

Table 15.4

Mean Correlation Between Minority Relations and Gender Issues: Controlled for Gender of Respondent

	Males	Females
English Canadian respondents	.265	.174
Quebecois respondents	.214	.156
American respondents	.373	.302

would flow to minority groups which one disliked or saw as undeserving.) While the same relationship exists among Canadian respondents, it is much weaker although in this case there is little to distinguish Francophone and Anglophone respondents. The national difference in table 15.5, we would argue, reflects rather different national experiences. In the United States the black minority has been characterized by relatively low levels of income and socio-economic status. Thus addressing the concerns of this minority necessarily entails some real redistribution of income and economic opportunities. In this sense the American attitudinal linkage reflects a political fact of life; to support minority groups while opposing income redistribution is an untenable position.

In the Canadian case, however, the empirical relationship in the larger society between minority status and economic disadvantage is less clearly established. While it is characteristic of aboriginal Canadians, it is not so clearly the case with other visible minorities such as Chinese and Japanese Canadians. The relatively modest attitudinal linkages that we observed among our Canadian respondents could reflect either a different Canadian reality or that our respondents failed to grasp that many although by no means all minority groups' claims are redistributive in character. If the latter explanation prevails then existing public support for minority claims, premised on the erroneous assumption that such support is cost-free, may be softer than appearances would suggest.

The question in table 15.5 on equality of opportunity reinforces the findings discussed above. Americans are simply more prone to link minority orientations to other fundamental social and political values than are Canadians. The left-right question reveals that for American respondents there is a clear and reasonably powerful relationship between minority orientations and one's location on the ideological spectrum. Those who locate themselves to the political left are much more favourably disposed towards minority groups than are those on the right or, conversely, one's predisposition towards minority groups provides a very good indicator of one's location on the ideological spectrum. For English Canadian respondents the relationship is much weaker, and for Québecois respondents it disappears. Here the differences among the three groups reflect a generally higher level of ideological coherency among American respondents, compared to Canadians, and greater coherency among

English Canadian respondents as opposed to Québec Francophones. (Gibbins and Nevitte, 1984)[5]

Our data analysis concludes with table 15.6, which examines the linkage between minority orientations and a selection of Canadian issues possessing some "minority component." Thus we find that orientations to "racial minorities" or to minorities in general are very weakly linked to the two questions dealing with a specific and important minority, native Canadians. Here it is particularly interesting to note the low correlation between question 4 on the minority battery — the use of quotas in school admissions and job hirings — and the question dealing with university quotas for native students. The weakness of the relationship suggests that respondent opinions are dependent upon the specific group involved, that we cannot assume that a general endorsement of quotas for "minority groups" will extend to an endorsement of quotas for any specific minority or, conversely, that a general opposition to quotas will translate into opposition in any specific case.

The two questions dealing with language demonstrate some linkage between general minority orientations and opinion towards a specific linguistic minority. The strength of the relationship, however, is very modest among Anglophones and all but disappears among Francophone respondents. (For Francophone respondents, the educational question referred to an English-language requirement for university graduation.) Thus, within the attitudinal world of our respondents, minority relations and French-English relations are not seen through a single optic. Our findings suggest that to cast French-English relations as a subset of minority relations more broadly defined would not reflect the reality of Canadian life. Nor would it be correct to assume that Canadian orientations towards the French linguistic minority are shaped to any significant degree by the orientations that Canadians hold towards minority groups in general.

To summarize briefly the data presented above, it is clear that the orientations of American respondents towards blacks are quite different in character than are Canadian orientations towards minority groups more generally defined. American orientations display greater internal coherency or consistency, and are linked to a variety of other values and group interests. Moreover, the magnitude of the difference between the American and English Canadian respondents approximates that between English Canadian and Québecois respondents. While the internal consistency and external linkages of minority orientations among English Canadian respondents are substantially weaker than they are among American respondents, they are weaker yet among Québecois respondents *despite what might be seen as the minority status of such respondents*. Here, however, we must recognize the rather ambivalent minority status of Québec Francophones. While Francophones are a minority within Canada, they are a majority within Québec and, since the Quiet Revolution, there has been a concerted political effort to redefine the relevant *national* majority as Québecois rather than Canadian. Québec Francophones, in other words, have increasingly come to see themselves as part of the national linguistic majority — within Québec — rather than as part of a national linguistic minority — within Canada. To the extent that this redefinition has taken hold among our young, post-Quiet Revolution respondents, it might explain the lack of any coherent or far-reaching minority orientation.

Table 15.5

Ideological Linkages with Minority Relations*

MINORITY RELATIONS*

		1	2	3	4	5	6
GOVERNMENT INTERVENTION							
1. "The country would be better off if business were less regulated." (low=agree strongly)	EC Que Amer	-.25 -.10 -.27	-.25 -.04 -.33	-.25 -.04 -.23	-.20 -.07 -.34	-.25 -.13 -.32	-.27 -.14 -.32
2. The importance attached, among 11 policy concerns, to "reducing the role of government" (low=very important)	EC Que Amer	-.33 -.09 -.27	-.20 +.06 -.32	-.33 -.12 -.23	-.13 +.01 -.21	-.23 +.01 -.25	-.18 -.02 -.26
3. "All except the old and the handicapped should have to take care of themselves without social welfare benefits" (low=agree strongly)	EC Que Amer	-.19 -.14 -.32	-.15 +.02 -.32	-.26 -.18 -.33	-.17 -.22 -.36	-.25 -.16 -.43	-.21 +.04 -.39

Mean value for the 18 correlations: English Canadians = -.24   Quebecois = -.07   Americans = -.31

		1	2	3	4	5	6
INCOME REDISTRIBUTION							
4. 7-point scale ranging from "all people should earn about the same" (low value) to "people with more ability should earn higher salaries" (high value)	EC Que Amer	.14 .08 .29	.20 .05 .31	.23 .31 .38	.35 .41 .48	.23 .29 .41	.23 .28 .36
5. "The government should work to reduce substantially the income gap between rich and poor" (low=agree strongly)	EC Que Amer	.25 .20 .33	.15 .10 .37	.23 .22 .43	.29 .17 .54	.30 .22 .46	.26 .27 .43
6. 7-point scale ranging from "taxing those with high incomes to help the poor is only fair" (low value) to "taxing those with high incomes to help the poor only punishes the people who have worked the hardest" (high value)	EC Que Amer	.18 .17 .45	.17 .10 .40	.16 .20 .43	.22 .12 .56	.25 .23 .57	.21 .10 .44

Mean value for the 18 correlations: English Canadians = +.23   Quebecois = +.20   Americans = +.42

COMPARATIVE ANALYSIS OF YOUTH ELITES

OTHER CORRELATES

MINORITY RELATIONS

		1	2	3	4	5	6
7. "Here are two ways of dealing with inequality: which do you prefer: equality of opportunity -- giving each person an equal chance for a good education and to develop his or her ability -- or equality of result -- giving each person a relatively equal income regardless of his or her education and ability?" 7-point scale, equality of results = high values	EC	-.03	-.07	-.07	-.25	-.13	-.07
	Que	-.04	+.02	-.15	-.24	-.11	+.01
	Amer	-.18	-.27	-.27	-.38	-.32	-.28

Mean value for the six correlations: English Canadians = -.11   Quebecois = -.08   Americans = -.28

8. Respondent self-location on a 7-point left-right scale (low = far left)	EC	.13	.18	.23	.24	.24	.25
	Que	.13	-.05	.13	.04	.09	.16
	Amer	.31	.43	.40	.51	.47	.50

Mean value for the six correlations   English Canadians = .22   Quebecois = .08   Americans = .44

* all correlations are Pearson r's; for ease of interpretation, all of the minority variables have been recoded so that low values are associated with a positive orientation to blacks/minority groups

** see Table 2 for an identification of these variables

Table 15.6

Canadian Issue Linkages to Minority Relations*

MINORITY RELATIONS**

		1	2	3	4	5	6	$\bar{X}$
1. 7-point scale ranging from "Native Canadians should be guaranteed special rights in the Constitution" (low value) to "Native Canadians should have the same rights as other Canadians" (high value)	EC	.05	.10	.09	.26	.19	.19	.15
	Que	.07	.02	.07	.14	.13	.18	.10
2. "There should be special university quotas for Native Canadians". (low = agree strongly)	EC	.10	.03	.01	.25	.13	.15	.11
	Que	-.11	.01	-.16	.16	.18	.02	.02
3. 7-point scale ranging from "the Canadian government has gone too far in helping francophones" (low value) to "the Canadian government hasn't gone far enough in helping francophones (high value)	EC	-.18	-.18	-.23	-.22	-.34	-.24	-.23
	Que	-.02	+.04	-.10	-.12	-.11	-.22	-.09
4. "All students at Canadian universities should be required to pass a French/English language course before graduation" (low = agree strongly)	EC	.07	.17	.14	.12	.16	.16	.14
	Que	-.04	.21	.03	-.03	-.06	.11	.04

* all correlations are Pearson r's; for ease of interpretation, all minority relations variables have been recoded so that low values are associated with a positive orientation to blacks/racial minorities

** see Table 15.2 for an identification of these variables

CONCLUSIONS

In bringing this discussion to a close, we would like to explore the more general implications of this study for an understanding of minority relations in Canada. Perhaps the first point to make is that, in the field of minority relations, the Canadian attitudinal world is quite different in character from the attitudinal world in the United States. Lacking the black experience and confronted by a smaller, more diverse, and less politicized minority population, the Canadian world is characterized by less consistency and by relatively weak linkages to other values which, at least logically, should be closely entwined with minority orientations. There has been no ready Canadian equivalent of the American black experience as an organizer of Canadian thought on minority relations. Our data at least suggest that the American civil rights vision has not been transplanted to Canadian soil.

While it might be thought that French-English relations would be a rough equivalent, that the linguistic cleavage in Canadian life has approximated the racial cleavage in the United States, our data offer little support for this assumption. Certainly our Francophone respondents did not demonstrate a more ordered and wide-ranging set of minority orientations than did their Anglophone counterparts. Indeed, the reverse was the case. It appears, then, that French-English relations cannot be packed into the more general phenomenon of minority relations, that the two occupy quite distinct attitudinal domains.

Canadians appear to make rather sharp distinctions among minority groups. Respondents, for example, did not appear overly constrained by their general predispositions towards minorities when it came to the questions dealing with native Canadians. General predispositions did not organize specific attitudes. This finding is of considerable interest for the general thrust of attitudinal research on minority relations has usually emphasized the importance of more global dispositions. The term ethnocentrism, for example, refers to a general antipathy to any and all minority or foreign groups, regardless of their specific characteristics. There is little evidence in the Canadian data of such a global predisposition as respondents made relatively clear distinctions among groups. There was little evidence of a general predisposition to "minorities" *per se*, be they racial, linguistic or gender-related in character.

At this point it is useful to recall the nature of our respondents, all of whom were senior university students. Among such respondents one is less likely to encounter public expressions of racial prejudice or minority group hostility, if only because such individuals have an acute sense of what sentiments are socially acceptable. Thus one might argue that among such individuals prejudice is likely to be a private rather than public opinion, that it will not be linked to other issues within the public domain such as government intervention and income policies. In order to account for variations in the strength of prejudice, one would have to go more deeply into the psychological characteristics of respondents rather than searching for attitudinal linkages *per se*. Nonetheless, in the United States, and among respondents nearly identical to those surveyed in Canada, orientations towards blacks are public opinions rather than, or in addition to, private opinions. They are linked to the important political and social issues of the day, and form a key component in political ideologies. This reflects in turn the dramatically different impacts of the black and racial minority experiences on the

American and Canadian societies.

In general, it appears that the very term "minority" is not a powerful organizer of Canadian opinion. Our findings suggest that attitudes towards racial minorities, women, native Canadians and French Canadians drift almost independently of one another. The fact that all might be considered to be minority groups in some respect has little relevance to the way in which our respondents make attitudinal sense out of their social and political world. There is little evidence of any general orientation towards minorities that informs, shapes or constrains attitudes towards specific minority groups. Canadians have not appropriated the American civil rights vision as minorities *per se* have not occupied a place in Canadian life analogous to that occupied by American blacks. These findings, in short, seriously call into question the appropriateness of the American model.

By extension, they also challenge the assumption that minority legislation and minority groups in Canada will be able to draw from the same reservoir of ideological support that blacks have been able to tap in the United States. There is a "liberal" ideology in the United States that embraces not only a positive orientation towards the interests and aspirations of blacks but also a positive stance towards feminist issues, towards state intervention and towards a more equitable distribution of wealth and economic opportunity. There is greater potential for the type of minority "rainbow" coalition that Jesse Jackson tried to forge in his pursuit of the Democratic presidential nomination. In Canada, however, there is less evidence of a general liberal ideology that embraces minority group claims. Minority orientations are not anchored to other and basic political values as they are in the United States, and they display little consistency across groups.

A significant consequence of these findings is that there may be less potential for political coalitions across minority groups. To lapse into social science jargon, minority groups may have to pull their own political wagon and beat their own drum. Smaller groups, much to their disadvantage, may not be able to ride on the coattails of larger and more efficacious groups, just as the latter may not have to carry with them smaller and potentially damaging groups. This also suggests that there may be little political capital to be garnered by groups like women presenting themselves as a "minority"; the attachment of this label promises little in the way of broader ideological support or support from specific groups which, in a conceptual manner, might also be seen as minorities.

In short, there may be little political or *conceptual* utility in the concept of "minority." It does not suggest a clear linkage with other political values, and it does not open up opportunities for political support. At the same time, however, the very "unconnectedness" of minority orientations in Canada may turn out to be of considerable value to minority groups and governments in Canada. For numerically small and politically disadvantaged minorities, the lack of linkage may be a blessing as it shields them from more general ideological values in the general population which, if mobilized, could seriously compromise their interests. A Canadian drift towards neo-conservatism, for example, may not have the same adverse implications for Canadian minorities as it appears to be having in the United States. For their part, the lack of connectedness may mean that Canadian governments can be more innovative and flexible in their approach to minority relations. They may be able to strike pragmatic bargains with specific groups without engaging general principles or problems of across-group equity. Governments may be able to address minority issues *per se* without engaging in a broader ideological debate if Canadians do not perceive a linkage between minority group claims and other political values. Policies to address minority issues may not encounter ideological resistance springing from other strongly held values within the body politic. However, whether governments will be able to exploit the policy *adhocery* suggested above in the face of the policy consistency implied in the new Charter remains to be seen.

FOOTNOTES

[1] Both surveys are segments of a larger study, the *Cross National Equality Study*, under the direction of Sidney Verba. This project addresses core political values which are of central concern to the study of political culture, and does so through a common questionnaire and sampling strategy which maximize cross-national comparability.

[2] In the American sample, only 10 respondents (2.7 percent) identified themselves as blacks, and only 15 (4.1 percent) as neither white nor black.

[3] For a detailed analysis of this point, see Gibbins and Nevitte, (1984).

REFERENCES

Converse, Philip E. "The Nature of Belief Systems in Mass Publics." In D. Apter (ed.), *Ideology and Discontent*. New York: The Free Press, 1964.

Gibbins, Roger and Neil Nevitte. "The Canadian Political Culture: A Comparison of English Canadian, Quebecois and American Respondents." Paper presented to the Annual Meeting of the Canadian Political Science Association, Guelph, Ontario, June 1984.

Sowell, Thomas. *Civil Rights: Rhetoric or Reality*. New York: Morrow, 1984.

Special Committee on Visible Minorities in Canadian Society, Ottawa. *Equality Now!* Queen's Printer, 1984.

16

ACTIVE MINORITIES: POLITICAL PARTICIPATION IN CANADIAN DEMOCRACY

HAROLD D. CLARKE
ALLAN KORNBERG
MARIANNE C. STEWART

> "...the notion of political participation is at the center of the concept of the democratic state."
>
> Barnes, Kaase et al., *Political Action*

> "... Canadian politics will remain an elite process tempered by occasional populist anger."
>
> Banting and Simeon, *And No One Cheered*

Canada, like other contemporary liberal democracies, has an open political system, and anyone who wishes to participate in politics and public affairs ostensibly is free to do so. Despite a paucity of formal impediments to political action, twenty years of empirical research have indicated that only a small minority of Canadians do anything other than vote in periodic elections, read about politics, or occasionally discuss politics with their friends and family.[1] Indeed, between two-thirds and nine-tenths of the public never have engaged in even such relatively mundane activities as trying to influence another person's vote or placing a candidate's bumper sticker on their car. Not surprisingly, therefore, Canadian have been depicted as spectators rather than participants in the great game of politics (e.g., Van Loon, 1970), and the Canadian political culture has been described as "quasi-participative." (Presthus, 1973)

Of course, voting and other electorally related activities do not exhaust what Barnes, Kaase, et al. (1979) have termed the "political action repertoire" of advanced democratic states. Since the mid-1960s at least some citizens of those states have resorted to less familiar forms of participation such as protest marches, some peaceful, others less so, picketing, denying entrance to and exit from governmental facilities, boycotting products of corporations and even countries, and "sitting in" public and private buildings. Occasionally violent and frequently disruptive, these activities have been widely publicized by the media, both because of their relative novelty and their seeming ability to achieve dramatic changes in the policies of private organizations and even of governments. For example, in the United States, student activism not only led to significant changes in the operation of colleges and universities, it also was a major factor in generating massive public opposition to the Vietnam War. Because of this, student and other activists have attracted the attention of social scientists who mounted a number of major studies in several countries of them and their various activities in the early and mid-seventies.[2] In Canada, however, many basic questions about the "who" and "why" of what may be termed "unconventional" or "protest" political activities (we will employ these two labels interchangeably) and their relationships to more traditional forms of political action remain unanswered.

In this paper we will address these questions employing data gathered in a national study of the Canadian public conducted in the autumn of 1983. We will demonstrate that unconventional forms of political action, despite their visibility and the frequency with which they seem to occur, are not all of a piece. They fall into "moderate" and "extreme" categories, and the more extreme the actions, the smaller the number of persons who either engage in, approve of, or believe they will be effective. We will argue that political socialization-political cultural, social structural and instrumental factors are important determinants of the extent of both unconventional and conventional political participation. It will be further argued that in a democratic polity such as Canada, people's willingness to engage in more extreme forms of political action is influenced by their levels of support for the national political community and regime, their perceived need to comply with the authoritative edicts of government, and their evaluations of the effectiveness and fairness of government's operations. We begin with a discussion of the theoretical orientations guiding our choices of predictor variables and a description of the data set and measures of political participation that were employed in the several analyses.

PERSPECTIVES ON POLITICAL PARTICIPATION

The selection of variables included in this study was informed by our previous investigations of political participation and political support in Canada. For example, earlier research on participation in local party organizations and more recent work on the bases of national community and regime support have utilized three theoretical orientations which we term "political socialization-political cultural," "social structural," and "instrumental." (Kornberg, Clarke and LeDuc, 1978; Kornberg, Clarke and Stewart, 1979; Kornberg, Smith and Clarke, 1979; Kornberg, Clarke and Stewart, 1980; Clarke, Kornberg and Stewart, 1984) The political socialization orientation implies that a group of people who currently manifest patterns of political behaviour which differ markedly from those of others do so because over time they have been reared in environments and exposed to events and conditions as a consequence of which they have acquired values, attitudes, information, and perspectives which also differ. The cultural orientation is a variant of this approach, asserting that certain of the values, attitudes, and opinions acquired during the political socialization process are so strongly held that they constitute "rules of the game" which constrain and shape the political behaviour of members of a group. The social structural orientation argues that political behaviour is strongly influenced by the statuses, skills, and resources (material and otherwise) which people have accumulated since birth. Moreover, other factors being equal, status begets status. Thus, for example, in advanced industrial societies the better educated generally enjoy more prestigious occupations and higher income than the less educated. They also generally have greater leisure time and/or flexible work schedules so that they can participate more readily in relatively exotic political activities such as working in party organizations.

In contrast, the instrumental orientation assumes that variations in socialization, socioeconomic status, and accumulated resources notwithstanding, people will become politically involved if they conclude it is in their personal interest, or in the interest of individuals and groups they value, to do so. Their calculations about the utility of engaging in political action may be neither precise nor based on perfect information. Indeed, they may deviate widely from the criteria of "strategic rationality" public choice theorists typically employ. "Rough and ready" or even "wrong headed" as they may seem, however, citizens' evaluations of the performance of political authorities and of the structures and processes of government constitute a third basis for political action.

The political socialization and social structural orientations have enabled us to delineate the conditions under which: (a) a small minority of Canadians was willing to accept and retain positions in local party organizations, and (b) a fraction of this minority was able to attain influential positions within their parties or become contenders for or holders of public office positions. The political socialization-political cultural and instrumental orientations have helped guide and organize our aforementioned research on regime support. We have argued that support has two principal sources. One is early or later life socialization experiences which generate affect of varying intensity and duration for political objects. The other is instrumental assessments of the effectiveness and fairness of the political system (or aspects thereof) in allocating societal values generally, and providing for the well-being of the person making judgements in particular.

In previous work on support we also have contended that a triadic relationship exists among the level of people's support for various political objects, the extent of their political participation and the degree to which they feel they should comply with the authoritative edicts of government. More specifically, we have hypothesized that the latter (i.e., degree of compliance) is an intervening variable between levels of national regime and community support on the one hand, and variations in the extent of both conventional and unconventional political participation on the other.

In the present paper the assumptions, propositions, and findings outlined above are used to select independent variables and develop hypotheses that help explain variations in conventional and unconventional political participation. The following explanatory variables are employed: parental political interest and activity, respondents' region of residence, ethnicity, age, political interest, trust in political authorities, extent of formal education, annual family income, levels of national community and regime support, beliefs regarding the need to comply with the edicts of government, evaluations of the responsiveness of Members of Parliament, judgements of the equity and effectiveness of government's operations, evaluations of government's impact on personal well-being and assessments of the effectiveness of unconventional political activities of various kinds.

In the Canadian context, age, region, and ethnicity are assumed to be "proxies" for some of the more important but elusive and temporally distal forces operative in the political socialization process. Their inclusion in the multivariate analyses (region and ethnicity are dummy variables) permits us to consider residual political cultural effects on participation that may not be captured by other variables.[3] The conceptual status of some of the other predictors is more ambiguous. For example, students of political socialization who emphasize the primacy of early life experiences might argue that indices of political interest and trust are measures of the *consequences* of socialization processes, whereas those who feel the process continues over the life space might contend that these indices also reflect people's reactions to current conditions and events. Measures of education and income are also ambiguous. They typically are employed as indicators of social structural factors that bear on political participation, but they also may reflect inter-group (e.g., class-related) variations in socialization that influence the likelihood of engaging in various political activities. Similarly, measures of people's perceptions of MPs' responsiveness, and of governmental performance and its impact on them are designed to tap the instrumental basis of their political involvement. But the criteria they employ in making such evaluations may well reflect specific socialization experiences or more general political cultural orientations. Our previous research (Clarke, Kornberg and Stewart, 1984) further suggests that national regime and community support levels are influenced by public evaluations of salient political authorities and institutions and a complex set of socialization and social structural factors. This likely is true of people's compliance orientations as well.

With regard to the direction of relationships between predictor variables and the extent of *unconventional* political participation, results of previous investigations suggest that younger Francophone residents of Québec, who were socialized in politicized familial milieux, are themselves interested in politics, but do not trust political authorities and will be more likely to engage in protest activities than other Canadians. We further expect that regardless of their ethnicity or province of residence, individuals who believe that unconventional political activities are effective, manifest lower levels of support for the national community and regime, are less compliant, consider MPs unresponsive and ineffective, judge that the operation of government is neither fair nor effective, are dissatisfied with their current economic and more general life situation, and believe government bears responsibility for their unhappy condition, also will be more likely to engage in unconventional modes of political action than people who hold opposite views.

The direction of relationships among education, income, and unconventional political participation is more problematic. On the one hand, higher levels of education and income are indicators of the possession of material and other politically relevant resources, and repeatedly have been found to be positively correlated with conventional participation. Thus, one might anticipate they also will be positively associated with unconventional activity. Consistent with this expectation is the probability that people with high levels of education are likely to have learned that political involvement is important because it can influence government to act in ways they desire. On the other hand, income and education are indicators of socioeconomic status. Given the privileged positions in Canadian society that higher status persons generally enjoy, it seems likely that they also will be relatively satisfied with the status quo and hence less likely to engage in behaviour that might eventually threaten the stability of the political system.

With respect to the determinants of *conventional* participation, we expect that middle-aged Canadians with higher levels of education and income, who were reared in politicized familial environments, are themselves interested in politics, and believe that MPs are responsive[4] to their needs and demands, will manifest the highest levels of political involvement. Additionally, we hypothesize that people who perceive that the political system operates equitably and effectively, and who also are strong supporters of the national political community and regime, are more likely to engage in conventional political activities than people who have opposite feelings and beliefs.

After describing our data set, we will delineate the extent to which Canadians participate in a variety of conventional and unconventional political activities and then demonstrate that there is a bidimensional structure to the latter. Next, we will construct three summary measures of political participation and employ these in a series of multiple regression analyses using the predictor variables discussed above. Then, two typologies of patterns of participation will be constructed and logit analysis will be utilized to delineate the clusters of attributes which distinguish different types of participants. The paper will conclude by discussing the implications of the findings for better comprehending the nature of political involvement in contemporary Canada.

DATA

Data from a recently completed wave of a national panel study are employed to assess the distribution and determinants of conventional and unconventional political participation in Canada.[5] Structured interviews averaging forty-five minutes in length were conducted between October 1983 and January 1984 with 2107 respondents. Weights for province, age and community size are employed to ensure a representative national sample.[6] The weighted sample size is 2117.

DIMENSIONS OF POLITICAL ACTIVITY

Data on the frequency with which Canadians participate in electorally related and other conventional political activities are presented in table 16.1. Consistent with earlier research (e.g., Van Loon, 1970; Burke, Clarke and Leduc, 1978), most respondents report that they confine their involvement to voting in periodic elections and occasionally discussing politics with friends and neighbours — 87 percent of the 1983 sample report "often" voting in federal elections and 64 percent state they "often" or "sometimes" converse with others about political matters. Most people (over 60 percent in each case), however, never try to convince friends how to vote, attend political meetings or rallies, contact public officials or politicians, or work for a political party or candidate. Given the importance of elections in a democracy such as Canada and the crucial roles political parties play in the electoral process, it is noteworthy that only 2 percent report that they "often" engage in party work. These data are consistent with the findings of earlier investigations (e.g., Van Loon, 1970) that have characterized Canadian political participation as a hierarchically structured enterprise in which most citizens play the role of "spectator-participants."

Our study was designed to investigate the extent to which activities that Inglehart (1977, 1981), Barnes, Kaase et al. (1979) and others have labelled "unconventional" appeal to Canadians. Data pertaining to their approval and perceived effectiveness of as well as their involvement in various unconventional forms of political action are displayed in table 16.1.[7] As is the case with conventional participation, levels of public involvement in protest activities vary

Table 16.1
Frequency of Participation in Conventional Political Activities*

Activity	Often	Sometimes	Seldom	Never
Vote in Federal Elections	87	5	1	7
Discuss Politics	24	40	25	11
Convince Friends How to Vote	4	13	14	69
Attend Political Meeting or Rally	2	12	18	68
Contact Public Officials or Politicians	3	16	18	63
Work for Political Party or Candidate	2	8	10	80

*- horizontal percentages, N = 2117 for all items except vote frequency where previously ineligible voters (N=23) have been eliminated.

Table 16.2
Unconventional Political Activities – Approval, Effectiveness, Participation*

A. Approval	Approve	Disapprove	No Opinion/DK
Sign a Petition	85	12	3
March or Rally	53	42	5
Boycott	64	31	5
Wildcat Strike	12	84	4
Sit-in	26	69	5
Demonstration or Protest with Chance of Violence	11	86	3

B. Perceived Effectiveness	Effective	Depends	Ineffective	No Opinion/DK
Sign a Petition	71	11	17	2
March or Rally	52	14	31	2
Boycott	61	9	27	3
Wildcat Strike	33	9	56	3
Sit-in	35	9	53	4
Demonstration or Protest with Chance of Violence	23	6	69	2

C. Participation	Yes	No	DK/NA
Sign a Petition	68	31	1
March or Rally	20	79	1
Boycott	38	62	1
Wildcat Strike	6	93	1
Sit-in	5	95	1
Demonstration or Protest with Chance of Violence	4	95	1

* - horizontal percentages, N = 2117 for all items.

widely. People are more likely to approve than disapprove of, and to find effective rather than ineffective, relatively safe, "mild" activities such as signing a petition, taking part in a march or rally, or joining a boycott. In contrast, they are less likely to approve of and regard as effective the more extreme, risk-taking acts of joining a wildcat or unscheduled strike, sitting in a public or private building, or demonstrating when violence is possible. For example, Canadians more often approve of signing petitions (85 percent) than they do of boycotts (64 percent), marches or rallies (53 percent), or sit-ins (25 percent). They least often sanction wildcat strikes (12 percent) and demonstrations/protests where there might be violence (11 percent). This ordering is repeated for perceived effectiveness; 71 percent report that petitioning is an effective way for people to make their views known, but only 23 percent claim that a possibly violent demonstration of protest is likely to be effective.

Another finding is that regardless of how likely Canadians are to endorse various unconventional political activities or to judge them effective, in most cases the gap between their "words" and "deeds" is a wide one. Thus, whereas 53 percent approve of marches and rallies and 52 percent believe they are effective, only 20 percent actually have engaged in them. Sixty-two percent never have boycotted a particular product or store, 79 percent never have gone on a march or rally, and over 90 percent never have joined a wildcat or unscheduled strike, sit-in, or potentially violent protest. Petitioning is the only activity in which a large number of people (68 percent) state they have participated. For unconventional participation, then, Milbrath and Goel's (1976) well-known "gladiatorial" metaphor of political spectators and combatants seems appropriate. Indeed, given the imagery protest activities evoke, the gladiator metaphor seems singularly appropriate.

Having examined the distribution of unconventional and conventional activities, we next employed principal component factor analyses to determine whether there was an underlying dimensionality to them. In table 16.3, two analyses of conventional participation — one which includes voting, and one without — are presented. Unlike some previous studies (e.g., Verba and Nie, 1972, 1978; Uhlaner, 1982), these analyses generate only one factor. Consistent with previous studies, however, vote frequency has a relatively weak loading (.35) on a factor where other conventional forms of participation such as attending political meetings of rallies or working for a political party of candidate, load heavily (.75 and .69, respectively, in the present instance). The weak loading for the vote frequency item and its highly skewed response distribution (87 percent claimed to vote "often" in federal elections)[8] led us to replicate the analysis omitting this item. The result (table 16.3, Analysis 2) shows that the remaining variables yield a single factor solution that explains 45 percent of their variance, with factor loadings ranging from .59 to .77.

Table 16.3
Factor Analysis of Conventional Political Activities

Activity	Analysis 1 Factor 1	Analysis 2 Factor 1
Vote in Federal Elections	.35	e
Discuss Politics	.61	.60
Convince Friends How to Vote	.57	.59
Attend Political Meeting or Rally	.75	.77
Contact Public Officials or Politicians	.67	.68
Work for Political Party or Candidate	.69	.70
Eigenvalue	2.3	2.3
% of Variance Explained	38.7	45.0

e - item not included in analysis

Table 16.4
Factor Analyses of Approval, Perceived Effectiveness and Participation in Unconventional Political Activities

A. Approval and Perceived Effectiveness

Activity	Approval Factor 1	Approval Factor 2	Effectiveness Factor 1	Effectiveness Factor 2
Sign a Petition	-.02	.73	-.11	.81
March or Rally	.37	.65	.40	.57
Boycott	.04	.72	.23	.62
Wildcat Strike	.74	-.05	.80	.05
Sit-in	.62	.30	.75	.23
Demonstration or Protest with Chance of Violence	.71	.06	.78	.10
Eigenvalue	2.0	1.1	2.4	1.1
% of Variance Explained	33.6	18.8	39.7	18.0

B. Participation

Activity	Factor 1	Factor 2
Sign a Petition	-.06	.78
March or Rally	.51	.46
Boycott	.11	.73
Wildcat Strike	.53	-.12
Sit-in	.65	.12
Demonstration or Protest with Chance of Violence	.70	.10
Eigenvalue	1.8	1.1
% of Variance Explained	30.8	17.9

The factor analyses of unconventional activities are displayed in table 16.4. In every case (i.e., approval, perceived effectiveness and actual participation) two factors are generated that explain a respectable percentage (58.7 percent) of the variance in the original items. The pattern of factor loadings is very similar in every instance, with two of the mild activities — petitioning and boycotting — loading heavily on factor 2 and the three more extreme activities — wildcat strikes, sit-ins, and demonstrations with a risk of violence — loading heavily on factor 1. Perhaps reflecting the diverse character of marches and rallies, the item has a moderate to strong loading on both factors.[9] The results of these principal component analyses provided the information we needed to construct summary indices of the extent of people's involvement in conventional and protest activities.

DETERMINANTS OF POLITICAL ACTIVITY

MEASURES

Three composite variables were constructed that enabled us to conduct reasonably parsimonious analyses of the several forms of conventional and

POLITICALLY ACTIVE MINORITIES

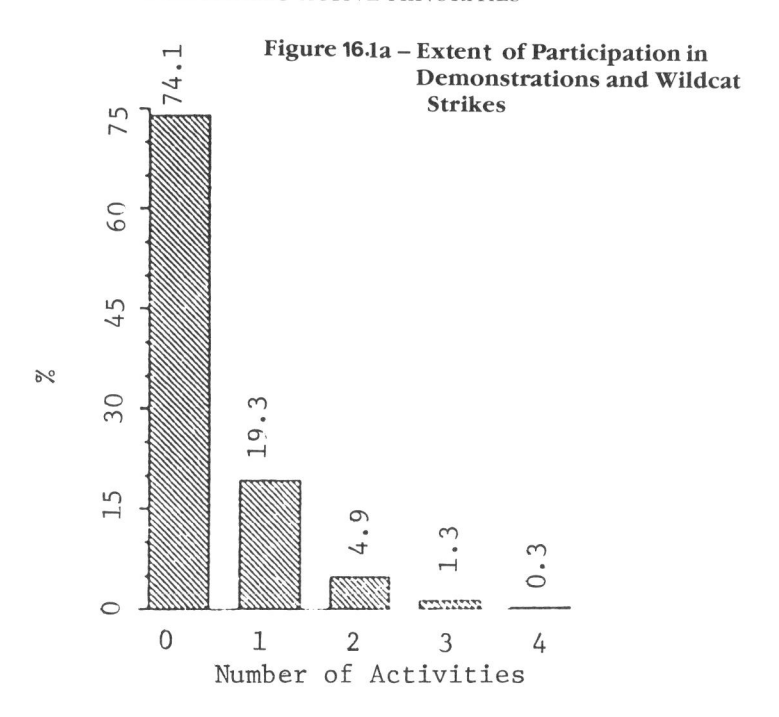

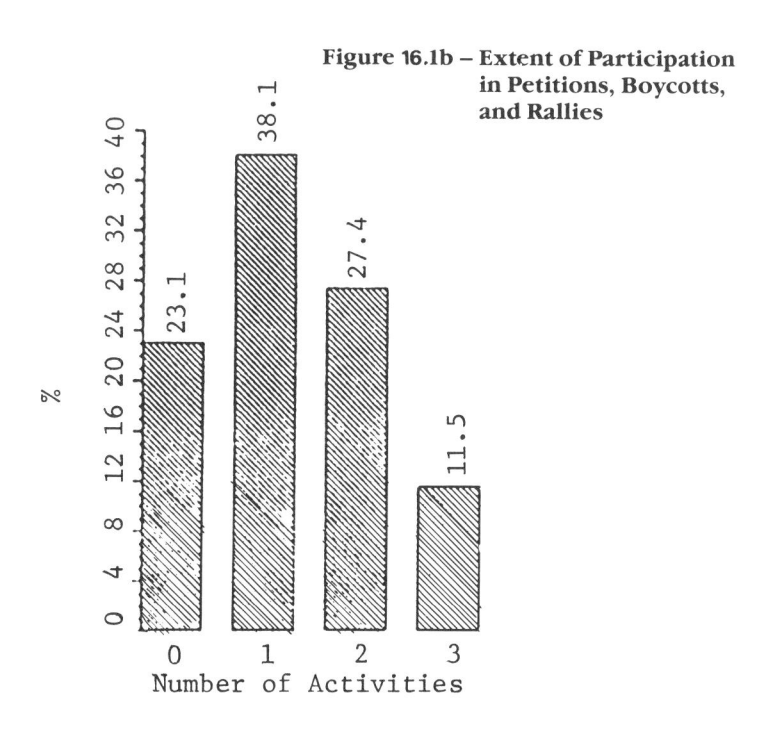

Figure 16.1a – Extent of Participation in Demonstrations and Wildcat Strikes

Number of Activities	%
0	74.1
1	19.3
2	4.9
3	1.3
4	0.3

Figure 16.1b – Extent of Participation in Petitions, Boycotts, and Rallies

Number of Activities	%
0	23.1
1	38.1
2	27.4
3	11.5

unconventional political action. The first of these was a factor-score measure of conventional political action. The variables included "discuss politics with other people," "try to convince friends to vote the same as you," "attend a political meeting or rally," "contact public officials or politicians," and "spend time working for a political party or candidate." (For reasons noted above, the "vote in federal elections" item was not included.) Following standard procedures, the resulting factor-score measure has a mean of 0 and a standard deviation of 1.

Since relatively little still is known about the extent of unconventional participation in Canada, and since factor-score measures based on standardized variables would tend to obscure basic information, we decided to employ two simple additive indices rather than factor-score measures. The first index used variables loading on factor 1 (table 16.4B): namely demonstrations with a risk of violence, sit-ins, wildcat strikes, and marches or rallies. The second included variables loading on factor 2 (i.e., signing a petition, boycotting, and marches or rallies). The decision to include the latter item in both indices reflects its ambiguous status, with loadings of .51 and .46 on the two factors.

It is instructive to note the distribution of respondents on the two indices. We find that fully 74.1 percent of the sample had not engaged in any of the extreme activities; 19.3 percent had engaged in one; and only 4.9 percent, 1.3 percent and 0.3 percent had participated in two, three, and four, respectively. (See figure 16.1a+b) The distribution on the second index was quite different: 23.1 percent had not undertaken any of the milder acts; 38.1 percent had engaged in one; 27.4 percent in two; and 11.5 percent in three. The different distributions on the two indices are consistent with our earlier observation (table 16.2) that participation in each of the unconventional political acts varies widely. Thus, wildcat strikes, sit-ins, and demonstrations in which damages to persons and property are possible continue to be eschewed by an overwhelming majority of Canadians, whereas signing petitions, engaging in marches or rallies, or boycotting selected goods and services are more commonly undertaken.

Given the low level of participation in more extreme protest activities, the summary index on which these are based takes on the properties of a "rare event" variable. As Muller notes: "[r]eliable statistical analysis of relationships between a rare event variable and a set of predictor variables is enhanced if the distribution can be made more symmetric so as to better satisfy certain statistical assumptions, especially the assumption of homoscedasticity or stability of variance." (Muller, 1979: 53) The standard procedure is to convert scores on the skewed variable into logarithms (base e). (Tufte, 1974: 108-128) The procedure was followed for both indices because it was felt that expressing them in logarithmic terms would enhance the comparability of results of the multivariate analyses.

ANALYSIS

Table 16.5 summarizes the multiple regression analyses of the determinants of conventional political activities. Two sets of statistics are presented: one for an analysis employing all predictors, the other for significant predictors only.[10] The results are quite similar and, in some respects, will not surprise students of previous research on electorally related forms of political participation in Canada (e.g., Van Loon, 1970; Burke, Clarke and LeDuc, 1978; Kornberg, Smith and

Clarke, 1979). Thus, political interest emerges as the strongest predictor ($B=.40$) of conventional participation. Other familiar statistically significant predictors include parental political involvement and annual family income. The latter relationships are positive and are another indication of the importance of socialization and social structural factors in facilitating conventional forms of political involvement.

Table 16.5
Multiple Regression Analyses of Conventional Political Activities

Predicators	All Predictors b	B	F	Significant Predictors Only b	B	F
Age	.01	.02	0.45			
Education	.03	.05	4.31[c]			
Income	.07	.09	14.32[a]	.09	.11	23.45[a]
Parental Political Involvement	.20	.12	32.16[a]	.20	.13	34.05[a]
Political Interest	.58	.39	285.32[a]	.60	.40	326.94[a]
Trust in Political Authorities	.02	.02	0.66			
MPs' Responsiveness	.07	.15	36.47[a]	.07	.15	42.11[a]
Federal Government Performance	−.04	−.06	5.51[c]	−.03	−.05	4.90[c]
Federal Government Impact	.01	.03	1.50			
National Regime Support	.00	.01	0.29			
National Community Support	−.00	−.05	3.93[c]	−.00	−.05	4.38[c]
Protest Approval/Effectiveness	.03	.07	10.51[b]	.03	.08	11.86[a]
Compliance-Federal Government	−.03	−.03	2.13			
Compliance-Forces, Police	.06	.06	7.33[b]	.06	.06	7.61[b]
Region/Ethnicity:						
Atlantic	.17	.05	4.03[c]			
Quebec-French	.22	.10	12.39[a]	.16	.07	8.85[b]
Quebec-non-French	−.21	−.03	1.99			
Prairies	.12	.04	3.44			
BC	.07	.02	0.92			
R =		.52			.51	

a − $p \leq .001$
b − $p \leq .01$
c − $p \leq .05$

Other results, however, are less familiar. The significant coefficients for perceived responsiveness of MPs and judgements regarding federal governmental performance suggest that instrumental variables are important predictors of conventional participation. The first of these is positive, indicating that Canadians are more likely to engage in conventional political acts if they believe their elected representatives are attentive to their needs and demands. However, the latter coefficient is negative, suggesting that conventional participation in part is grounded in people's judgements that the government's performance is something less than satisfactory. The coefficient for national community support suggests that variations in the level of that support can have behavioural consequences,[11] whereas the coefficient for protest approval/

effectiveness indicates persons who approve of protest activities and feel they are effective also engage in more traditional forms of political action.

As observed earlier, the inclusion of regional/ethnic dummy variables allows us to investigate the possibility of regional political cultural effects on participation. The positive sign for the significant coefficient "Québec French" signifies that, net of other factors, Québecois are more likely than other Canadians to engage in conventional forms of political activity. It is important to recognize, however, that the Québec/French term is not large. Indeed, an analysis of communities[12] (data not shown) reveals that together all of the region/ethnicity variables increase the total variance explained by only 0.8 percent. There is, then, no evidence of a sizable *direct* impact of regional political culture on conventional political participation. Most of the explanatory power in the analysis is captured by other variables and regional political cultural effects, to the extent they exist, are primarily indirect.

Turning next to protest activities, levels of formal education, annual family income, and political interest all have positive effects of the likelihood of engaging in petitioning, boycotts, and rallies (table 6). The presence of these effects suggests that political socialization and social structural factors play a role in unconventional as well as conventional political actions. Regarding socialization effects, although the probability of participating in protest activities is influenced by the regional/ethnic variables (residents of the Atlantic provinces are less and Québecois and British Columbians more likely to do so) their magnitude should not be exaggerated. Together the five region/ethnicity terms increase the variance explained by only 0.9 percent.

Table 16.6
Multiple Regression Analyses of Unconventional Political Activities: Petitions, Boycotts, Rallies

Predicators	All Predictors b	B	F	Significant Predictors Only b	B	F
Age	-.00	-.01	0.16			
Education	.07	.24	88.05^a	.07	.25	103.47^a
Income	.04	.10	17.02^a	.04	.10	17.09^a
Parental Political Involvement	.02	.03	1.83			
Political Interest	.07	.10	18.89^a	.06	.10	18.14^a
Trust in Political Authorities	.01	.02	0.40			
MPs' Responsiveness	.02	.10	16.70^a	.02	.10	16.42^a
Federal Government Performance	-.05	-.17	42.70^a	-.05	-.18	54.42^a
Federal Government Impact	-.01	-.04	2.54	-.01	-.05	3.85^c
National Regime Support	-.00	-.02	0.94			
National Community Support	-.00	-.04	2.43	-.00	.05	4.10^c
Protest Effectiveness-F2	.12	.27	146.64^a	.12	.27	153.79^a
Compliance-Federal Government	-.02	-.03	1.94			
Compliance-Forces, Police	-.02	-.04	2.71			
Region/Ethnicity:						
Atlantic	-.08	-.05	4.81^c	-.08	-.05	4.71^c
Quebec-French	.06	.06	4.18^c	.06	.06	6.04^c
Quebec-Non-French	.07	.02	1.00			
Prairies	-.01	-.01	0.07			
BC	.07	.05	4.32^c	.07	.05	4.33^c
R =		.49			.49	

a - $p \leq .001$
b - $p \leq .01$
c - $p \leq .05$

It also appears that there is an instrumental basis to unconventional political participation. Specifically, the proclivity to petition, boycott, and rally varies inversely with evaluations of the impact of federal governmental activity on individual well-being and more global assessments of federal governmental performance, and directly with judgements of the effectiveness of protest behaviour and perceptions of the responsiveness of MPs. The latter relationship suggests that Canadians do not petition, boycott, or participate in rallies because they believe politicians are unresponsive. Rather, those doing so more likely feel that political authorities *will listen* to their grievances. Finally, as in the analysis of conventional activities, national community support is negatively related to milder forms of protest activity, suggesting, once more, that variations in politically supportive attitudes have meaningful consequences for political behaviour.

The analyses of other, more extreme, protest activities yield results that are, in certain respects, similar to those for other forms of political participation (table 16.7). Thus, for example, both education and political interests are positively associated with the likelihood of engaging in more extreme acts, as are judgements regarding their probable effectiveness. Again, regional political cultural effects can be detected, with the "Québec-French" and "Prairies" variables having positive and negative effects, respectively. The impact of these region/ethnicity variables is greater than in previous analyses; 27 percent of the variance explained is uniquely attributable to them.[13]

Table 16.7
Multiple Regression Analyses of Unconventional Political Activities: Demonstrations, Strikes

Predicators	All Predictors b	B	F	Significant Predictors Only b	B	F
Age	-.02	-.07	6.21[c]	-.01	-.06	5.28[c]
Education	.03	.11	14.89[a]	.03	.13	24.41[a]
Income	.01	.03	0.99			
Parental Political Involvement	.01	.02	1.05			
Political Interest	.05	.09	12.42[a]	.06	.10	16.13[a]
Trust in Political Authorities	.03	.06	4.70[c]			
MPs' Responsiveness	.01	.04	2.35			
Federal Government Performance	-.02	-.07	6.47[c]			
Federal Government Impact	.00	.01	0.08			
National Regime Support	.00	.01	0.20			
National Community Support	-.00	-.09	10.56[a]	-.00	-.08	9.96[b]
Protest Effectiveness-F1	.07	.19	57.23[a]	.07	.20	62.91[a]
Compliance-Federal Government	-.04	-.11	20.71[a]	-.04	-.11	19.87[a]
Compliance-Forces, Police	-.03	-.07	8.70[b]	-.03	-.07	7.82[b]
Region/Ethnicity:						
Atlantic	-.01	-.00	0.03			
Quebec-French	.16	.18	35.82[a]	.14	.16	37.01[a]
Quebec-Non-French	.10	.04	2.53			
Prairies	-.07	-.07	7.86[b]	-.09	-.09	13.72[a]
BC	.06	.05	3.40			
R =		.38			.37	

a - $p \leq .001$
b - $p \leq .01$
c - $p \leq .05$

Also, unlike previous regressions, age enters the equation predicting more extreme unconventional actions. The age coefficient is negative; more exotic political acts tend to be the preserve of younger Canadians. This finding is not surprising. Over the past two decades scholarly observers and media pundits alike have commented repeatedly on the tendency of younger persons to be in the vanguard of political protest (e.g., Sutherland, 1981, ch. 5). However, the negative association between age and unconventional participation holds only for more extreme activities. Milder forms of unconventional action as well as electorally related activities have curvilinear relationships with age. For example, the likelihood of engaging in actions such as boycotts is strongest among persons in the 36-45 age bracket; for electorally related activities, participation is greatest among those in the 46-55 year-old cohort.

A second noteworthy point about the regressions for more extreme forms of protest activity concerns the effects of the political support and the two compliance variables. All three are negatively associated with variations in involvement. Further evidence regarding the nature of the impact of supportive attitudes on unconventional political participation is the finding that compliance is positively related to both regime and community support (appendix 16 C), suggesting that the support variables have *indirect* effects on unconventional participation that cannot be detected by regression analysis.[14] Additionally, previous research has shown that regime and community support are influenced by early and later-life socialization processes as well as by evaluations of the performance of both the federal government and political authorities. (Clarke, Kornberg and Stewart, 1984) Support, compliance, and more exotic forms of political action, therefore, can be seen as the end products of a lengthy and complex skein of instrumental and affective orientations toward the political system.

PATTERNS OF POLITICAL ACTION

Thus far, we have examined conventional and unconventional political activities and the predictors thereof in isolation. To gain a better understanding of patterns and determinants of political participation in contemporary Canada, it will be useful to study various combinations of the three types of political action considered above. We will confine our attention to the three summary measures of participation and focus on patterns of unconventional and conventional activity revealed by these measures. To facilitate interpretation, selected combinations of different levels of conventional and unconventional activities have been delineated and are displayed in table 16.8a and 16.8b. Table 16.8a shows that there is a modest, positive relationship ($V=.14$, f. .001) between conventional and unconventional participation when the latter is measured by the index of extreme activities. In terms of specific combinations, only 6.5 percent (table 16.8a, cell a) of the 1983 respondents have very low levels of conventional participation and also eschew extreme unconventional activities. For heuristic purposes we label such persons "inactives." Four other theoretically interesting combinations also can be identified. These are: "minimal participants" (cell b, 42.3 percent); "conventional political activists" (cell c, 25.3 percent); "unconventional political activists" (cell d, 12.4 percent); and 20.1 percent are dual activists (cell e).

Table 16.8
Joint Distributions of Unconventional and Conventional Political Activities

A. Demonstrations and Conventional Activity

Conventional Activity Index

Demonstrations No. of activities	Low $\leq -1s$	$-1s - \bar{x}$	$> \bar{x} - +1s$	High $> + 1s$
0	a 6.5	b 42.3	c 16.0	9.3
1	0.9	8.9	5.5	3.9
2	0.2	2.0	1.6	1.2
3	d 0.0	0.3	e 0.1	9.9
4	0.0	0.1	0.1	0.2

/100%
$V = .14$, $p \leq .001$ (N=2075)

B. Petitions, Boycotts, Rallies and Conventional Activity

Conventional Activity Index

Petitions, Boycotts and Rallies No. of activities	Low $\leq -1s$	$-1s - \bar{x}$	$> \bar{x} - +1s$	High $> + s$
0	a 3.6	b 14.1	c 3.5	1.8
1	2.7	21.4	8.5	5.4
2	1.1	13.7	8.0	4.6
3	d 0.2	3.9	e 3.6	3.9

/100%
$V = .17$, $p \leq .001$ (N=2071)

Before determining which predictor variables distinguish among the several types, let us note the distribution of respondents across them. Perhaps most salient is the finding that no single type comprises a majority of the population — patterns of political participation are quite varied. Additionally, regardless of which unconventional activity index is employed, the modal type is the one we have labelled minimal participants. The latter completely avoid extreme forms of unconventional activity, may or may not have performed one of the milder unconventional acts, and engage in no more than an average level of conventional activity. Not completely inert, but very limited in their political involvement, people making up this type conform well to Canadians' "spectator-participant" image. Only one-fifth to one-quarter of the respondents conform to a traditional model of citizen involvement that emphasizes electorally related activities. Equally — or more — common (depending upon which typology is employed) are persons who *combine* conventional and protest activities, or avoid the former and do the latter. By considering various protest as well as more traditional forms of political action, then, one discovers several "active minorities," each of which is large enough to play an important role in Canadian political life.

One must be careful, however, not to overstate the *extent* of citizen political involvement. This is particularly true of their involvement in unconventional activities. To measure them, respondents were asked whether they *ever* had performed a certain act. But, the actual frequency with which they may have done so was not ascertained.[15] This caveat notwithstanding, the findings that few respondents (less than 7 percent) are virtually or totally inactive and that many have engaged in one or more of the milder unconventional activities suggest that political participation in Canada is richer and more variegated than commonly assumed. As Mishler (1979:61) has concluded: "The Canadian citizen does not conform to the classical conception of *homo civicus*. However, it is equally apparent that the structure of participation in Canada deviates significantly from the elitist conception. If not a model democrat, neither is the average citizen the apathetic 'political piltdown man.'"

We would add two points to this characterization. First, it is somewhat misleading to speak of an "average" political participant. A more accurate conception is one which recognizes various combinations of citizen involvement in political life; "minimal participants" may be the modal type, but they are only one of several, each of which constitutes a minority. Second, only by considering what Barnes, Kaase, et al. (1979) have called the "expanding political repertoire" afforded by non-electoral activities can one appreciate the point of Mishler's argument. Moreover, if Barnes and his colleagues are correct and these activities constitute an emergent reality in contemporary liberal democracies, then the potential for diversity in the political activities of Canadians has yet to be realized.

We can learn more about the several types of political participants by considering which of the predictor variables employed earlier best discriminate among them (i.e., the types). To simplify matters we will contrast a number of different pairs of types. Since the dependent variables in these analyses are dichotomies, the multivariate statistical technique that will be employed is logit.[16]

Inspection of the logit results (tables 16.9 and 16.10) reveals that several variables that were strong predictors of the extent of involvement in unconventional and conventional activities considered separately also discriminate effectively among the participant types, the estimated multiple R's varying from a low of .29 to a high of .70 and having an average value of .46. In general, the 14 analyses in tables 16.9 and 16.10 document that both socialization and social structural variables are important discriminators of patterns of political participation; education is significant in 10 of the 14 analyses, and income and parental political involvement appear in 9 and 16 cases respectively. In terms of possible regional political cultural effects, the region/ethnicity dummy variables are significant in several cases, with the Québec-French term appearing in 9 of 14 instances. The signs of the coefficients associated with this term indicate that being a Québecois is associated with enhanced political activism, particularly with movement from passivity or more traditional forms of participation to one of the types involving a degree of protest activity.

Variables that capture evaluative orientations toward the behaviour of political authorities and institutions, such as perceptions of the anticipated responsiveness of MPs, assessments of federal governmental performance, and judgements about the probable effectiveness of protest activities, frequently play significant roles as well. In fact, the first of these variables appears in 10 of 14

Table 16.9
Summary of Logit Analyses of Selected Contrasts of
Conventional Activities v. Petitions, Boycotts and Rallies

Predictors	0/1	MP/ Unc	MP/ Dual	MP/ Conv	Inac/ Unc	Inac/ Dual	Inac/ Conv	Conv/ Unc
Age								
Education		+	+		+	+	+	+
Income			+	+	+	+	+	
Parental Political Involvement			+	+				
Political Interest			+	+	+	+	+	−
Trust in Political Authorities								
MPs' Responsiveness			+	+		+	+	−
Federal Government Performance		−	−	−	−	−	−	−
Federal Government Impact								
National Regime Support						+		−
National Community Support								
Protest Effectiveness-F2		+	+		+	+	+	+
Compliance-Federal Government			−					
Compliance-Forces, Police				+				−
Region/Ethnicity:								
Atlantic				+				−
Quebec-French			+	+				
Quebec-Non-French							−	
Prairies								−
BC		+	+					
R =		.29	.51	.34	.55	.70	.51	.39
Fraction of Concordant								
Pairs =		.69	.83	.73	.89	.93	.86	.76
Rank Correlation =		.40	.67	.48	.78	.89	.73	.53

\+ − positive relationship, $p \leq .05$
− − negative relationship, $p \leq .05$

Inac = Inactives
MP   = Minimal Participants
Conv = Conventional Political Activists
Unc = Unconventional Political Activists
Dual = Dual Political Activists

analyses, whereas the latter two do so 11 times. Perhaps the most interesting finding here is that the signs of the coefficients for the governmental performance variable consistently are negative. That is, critical evaluations of government and politicians tend to be associated with several different combinations of enhanced citizen involvement.

As for variables that reflect both effective and instrumental orientations toward the political system (i.e., political interest, compliance and national regime and community support), the results are mixed. The impact of political interest, for example, is nearly ubiquitous, being significant in 12 of 14 cases. Support and compliance, in contrast, play much more selective roles. When protest activities are extreme, community support serves to distinguish unconventional from conventional activists and the former from minimal

Table 16.10
Summary of Logit Analyses of Selected Contrasts of Conventional Activities v. Demonstrations, Strikes

Predictors	0/1	MP/Unc	MP/Dual	MP/Conv	Inac/Unc	Inac/Dual	Inac/Conv	Conv/Unc
Age			−					
Education		+	+		+	+		
Income				+	+	+	+	
Parental Political Involvement			+	+		+		−
Political Interest			+	+	+	+	+	−
Trust in Political Authorities							+	
MPs' Responsiveness			+	+		+	+	
Federal Government Performance		−		−	−	−		
Federal Government Impact								
National Regime Support				+				
National Community Support		−						−
Protest Effectiveness-F1		+	+		+	+		+
Compliance-Federal Government		−	−					
Compliance-Forces, Police				+				−
Region/Ethnicity:								
Atlantic				+				−
Quebec-French		+	+	+	+	+		+
Quebec-Non-French							−	+
Prairies		−						−
BC			+		+	+		
R =		.29	.45	.35	.41	.64	.51	.47
Fraction of Concordant								
Pairs =		.70	.81	.73	.81	.92	.85	.82
Rank Correlation =		.41	.63	.48	.62	.84	.71	.64

\+ - positive relationship, p ≤ .05
− - negative relationship, p. ≤ .05

Inac = Inactives
MP = Minimal Participants
Conv = Conventional Political Activists
Unc = Unconventional Political Activists
Dual = Dual Political Activists

participants. Regime support and compliance discriminate between some types, both when unconventional activists are mild and when they are more extreme.

In all cases the direction of the support-compliance-participation triad is as anticipated. For example, lower levels of regime and/or community support are associated with being an unconventional activist rather than a minimal participant or a conventional activist. In contrast, people in the latter type, as well as dual activists, are more supportive of the regime than are the inactive or minimal participants. Similarly, compliance is positively associated with being a conventional rather than a minimal participant and negatively associated with being an unconventional or dual rather than an electorally oriented activist. Relationships such as these accord well with the more general argument that orientations towards political support and compliance play meaningful and comprehensible roles in the complex processes that generate diverse patterns of political action in contemporary Canada.

SUMMARY AND CONCLUSIONS

Canada is a liberal democracy in which citizens are entitled to participate in a variety of activities that can influence both "who governs" and the content of public policy. Despite these opportunities, two decades of research on electorally related activities indicate that a large majority of Canadians do little more than make occasional sojourns to the polls. Although electorally related activities do not exhaust the range of participatory opportunities in advanced liberal democracies, in Canada relatively little is known about the scope and character of "unconventional" forms of participation, which some political scientists have termed "protest" activity. (In this paper the two terms have been used interchangeably.) This lack of information and the fact that during the past twenty years protest activities of various kinds periodically have helped generate major changes in the governmental policies of a number of liberal democracies led us to ask respondents in our 1983 national survey whether they approved of or had ever engaged in six such activities. Factor analysis indicated the structure of these activities was bidimensional. One dimension can be labelled "extreme" and included taking part in wildcat strikes, sit-ins, and potentially violent protests. A second, "mild" dimension included signing petitions and joining boycotts. Participating in a march or rally loaded on both factors. The more extreme an activity, the less inclined Canadians were either to engage in or approve of it.

After regressing summary indices of conventional and unconventional participation on several predictor variables, two five-category typologies of political action were created. For the sake of convenience, these types were labelled inactives, minimal participants, conventional activists, unconventional activists, and dual activists. Their distribution reveals that patterns of political action in contemporary Canada are varied and complex. The traditional dichotomy counterposing a large majority of political spectators to a small minority of inveterate political activists fails to capture this complexity. A more accurate characterization is one that juxtaposes several active minorities against a small group of inactives and a modal category of minimal participants. Significantly, however, this latter group is itself a minority.

Limitations in available data do not permit an accurate assessment of the *extent* of political involvement of the various groups that we have labelled "active minorities." However, existing research does suggest that political action of *whatever kind* is episodic rather than continuous for the vast majority of citizens. If, as has been argued, a model democracy is characterized by high and sustained levels of citizen participation in public affairs, it seems clear that contemporary Canada falls short of this ideal. "Active minorities" and "model democratic citizens" are not the same.

An examination of our data indicates that political socialization and social structure variables such as parental political interest and activity, annual income, and degree of political interest are positively associated with conventional participation. Further, political interest, income, and education are positively correlated with unconventional participation. Additional evidence of the stimulus to participate provided by political socialization and social structural factors is contained in the logit analyses. Finally, the effects of political socialization and political culture on participation are captured by the proxy variables (region and ethnicity), which are relatively consistent (if not strong) predictors of variations in both conventional and unconventional participation.

The effects of instrumental factors in accounting for variations in participation also were manifested in the regression and logit analyses. People's evaluations of the federal government's operation, assessments of how government actions affect personal well-being, judgements about the responsiveness of MPs and the effectiveness of protest activities all predict conventional and/or unconventional participation. Finally, national regime and community support, as well as compliance orientations, were significant predictors in several analyses. Previous work, as well as present findings, indicate that support and compliance are governed by relatively concrete instrumental orientations toward the political system and more amorphous socialization processes. Support, compliance, and patterns of political action are grounded in complex sociopolitical processes which our research (of which this paper is a part) is attempting to clarify.

There may be a dynamic in these processes which is expanding the "political action repertoire" in Canada. At least some of the political activities we have classified as unconventional meet with widespread approval. Moreover, in the aggregate there is an almost perfect correlation between the extent of people's participation in and their approval of a particular action. The substantial majority which signs petitions and the even larger majority which approves of such acts suggest that petitioning may be thought of as an *alternative* to rather than a *substitute* for conventional political participation. Although there is less approval of and participation in boycotts, the latter may be similarly viewed. Indeed, more people have participated in a boycott at some time during their lives than have attended a political meeting or tried to influence another person's political opinions.

We may speculate that one reason protest activities such as the ones on which we have focused have achieved varying degrees of social acceptance is the extensive coverage they have received in the media, especially television. Television supposedly has an insatiable appetite for action programming that attracts and retains viewers. Sit-ins, marches and demonstrations of various kinds — particularly those that result or promise to result in violence — are considered excellent raw material for such programming. Not surprisingly, given their newsworthiness, protest activities frequently become "media events." Conversely, protesters invariably not only welcome but solicit the attention of the media (especially television) because of the visibility the latter provide them and their causes. Thus, over the past two decades a symbiotic relationship has developed between protest activities and the media that in one sense has trivialized the former by highlighting them and exaggerating the frequency with which they occur. In another sense, however, their seemingly mundane quality is what has made them increasingly acceptable. If so, why, one may ask, do not *more* people approve of and engage in the kinds of extreme unconventional activities that most frequently attract media attention? Also, why is participation in more extreme protests frequently correlated with youth and, in Canada, with Francophone's residence?

In our judgement there are several reasons. First, and notwithstanding any symbiotic relationship between protest activity and the media, there are very substantial differences in the degree to which people accept and approve of different acts. It is one thing to refuse to shop at a store whose employees are on strike. It is another to sit in that store and prevent others from shopping there. And, it is still another to mount a demonstration that might result in the destruction of store property or physical injury to shoppers or other innocent bystanders.

Second, protest activities, especially of the extreme variety, still carry with them a degree of risk. Most people, especially older, well-established middle — and upper-middle — class people, are reluctant to place themselves at risk. Again, it is one thing to sign a petition or be part of an audience at a rally. It is quite another to scuffle with police, be arrested, or jailed — even if briefly.

Third, and relatedly, many Canadians probably understand that protest activities that result in serious or frequent disruptions of public order eventually threaten political order and stability. Many also understand that in a liberal democracy such as Canada, political leaders are reluctant to make extensive or intensive use of coercive mechanisms to maintain public order because to do so would contravene some of the fundamental values on which a democratic political order and a free society rest. Since many citizens value freedom and democracy in general and the Canadian political system in particular (witness the consistently high level of public support over time for the national political community), they voluntarily refrain from engaging in actions that eventually could require even the most permissive public officials to employ coercive countermeasures. This kind of self-denying behaviour is a public's "quo" for their political leaders' "quid." (Almond and Verba, 1963, ch.15) It enables a democratic political order to be maintained in Canada and elsewhere even as the delicate balance shifts between political stability and governmental effectiveness on the one hand, and enhanced democratization and citizen participation on the other.

Finally, as for the well documented tendency of younger, well-educated and politically interested Québecois to be more involved in and approving of protest activity, it can be argued that they are no less enamoured of democracy and no less self-denying than other Canadians. Unlike the latter, however, a significant number aspire to a democratic political order in a Québec that is *not* part of the Canadian political community. For Québecois, the emergence during the not-so-Quiet Revolution of the sixties of this aspiration, its growth during the seventies, and its more recent retreat constitute a significant example of the very important and exceedingly complex triadic relationship among political support, compliance, and participation that characterizes the political system of Canada and other Western democracies.

The new constitution with its Charter of Human Rights may significantly increase both the complexity and diversity of political activity in Canada. If the United States' experience — especially during the past three decades — is any guide, we may assume that traditionally disadvantaged minorities themselves will undertake (and be encouraged by others) to expand and intensify their efforts to improve markedly their status and position. We may further assume that these attempts will take a variety of forms, including well-publicized protest activities such as those considered here. Whether these actions will encourage others, in turn, to do the same or will have a chilling effect will depend upon many factors. Not the least of these are the responsiveness of public authorities and other societal groups to the claims being advanced, the relative success of minorities in achieving their goals, and the manner in which their goals and tactics are represented by the media and interpreted by the public. In this regard, the eleventh-hour efforts of womens' and native peoples' groups to secure changes in the content of the new constitutional document may well have been interpreted by other minorities as illustrating the kind of policy objectives that can be achieved through unconventional political action. Whether — and the conditions under which — they may test this possibility, of necessity, are topics for future investigation.

FOOTNOTES

[1] See, for example, Van Loon (1970), Burke, Clarke, and LeDuc (1978), and Kornberg, Mishler, and Clarke (1982: ch.4). These studies are typical in that they focus on electorally related activities. Mishler (1979), looking beyond the electoral arena, has argued that participation is somewhat more widespread and varied than much of the available literature suggests, and cautions that more research on non-electoral forms of political actions is needed. With the exception of studies of activity patterns in political party organizations (e.g., Clarke, Kornberg and Lee, 1975; Pammett, 1976; Clarke, Price, Stewart and Krause, 1978; Kornberg, Smith and Clarke, 1979), such research is rare. See, for example, Welch (1975) and Sutherland (1981).

[2] Especially noteworthy is the cross-national research by Verba, Nie, and Kim (1978) and Barnes, Kaase et al (1979). In the first, surveys were conducted in Austria, India, Japan, the Netherlands, Nigeria, the United States, and Yugoslavia. In the second, countries surveyed included Great Britain, West Germany, the Netherlands, Austria, the United States, Italy, Switzerland, and Finland.

[3] Over the past decade Canadian political scientists have expressed a great deal of interest in regional variations in political culture. Some studies, (e.g. Schwartz, 1974; Simeon and Elkins, 1974; Wilson, 1974; Ullman, 1977, 1978, and Bell and Tepperman, 1979) have made strong claims for regional cultural effects on political behaviour. Other research, (e.g., Kornberg, Clarke and Stewart, 1979, 1980; Gibbins, 1980; Ornstein, Stevenson, and Williams, 1980; and Kornberg, Mishler, and Clarke, 1982) has challenged some of these claims and qualified others. On the logic of political cultural explanations in the context of multivariate statistical analysis see Przeworski and Teune (1970) and Elkins and Simeon (1979).

[4] Perceptions of the responsiveness of MPs can be conceptualized as one aspect of what some analysts have labelled "external" political efficacy (e.g., Shingles, 1981). A host of studies has documented positive correlations between efficacy and conventional modes of participation. (Milbrath and Goel, 1976: 57-75) In Canada existing research shows that efficacy-participation relationships, although statistically significant, are not particularly strong (e.g., Van Loon, 1970; Burke, Clarke and LeDuc, 1978).

[5] This study, entitled "Sources, Distribution and Consequences of Political Support in Canada," is funded by the National Science Foundation. The study

consists of two national surveys, one conducted in October, 1983, and the second during the week following the September 4, 1984 federal election. Using a sample design that incorporates respondents participating in the 1979 and 1980 National Election Studies, these surveys include interlocking panels, with subsets of respondents interviewed in 1974, 1979, 1980, 1983, and 1984.

[6] Details concerning the study design and weighting scheme may be obtained from the authors upon request.

[7] There are many different unconventional political activities in which people have engaged at various times and places. For example, people have chained themselves to gates at military bases and laid down on the floors of legislatures and in front of moving traffic to prevent the latter, other people, or commodities from entering or leaving an area. Their variety notwithstanding, we believe that the items included in the present study are representative of the larger universe of unconventional political action.

[8] Similar to the results of surveys in other countries, the percentages of respondents claiming to have voted in previous Canadian federal elections tend to be inflated. On problems associated with recalled voting data see Weir (1975) and Gutek (1978).

[9] Marches and rallies vary enormously in their size, salience, and context. In some cases the resources required for participation and the risks attendant upon doing so are nonexistent or trivial; in others they are substantial.

[10] This type of regression analysis proceeds in a forward stepwise fashion. At each step only the predictor variable with the strongest effect is added, and any previously included predictors whose effects become significant with the inclusion of an additional variable are deleted from the equation. See Kornberg, Clarke, and Leduc (1978).

[11] Critics of the study of political support, conceptualized as a set of psychological orientations toward the political system and aspects thereof, have argued that existing research has failed to document that variations in support have behavioural consequences. For discussions of this point see Easton (1975, 1976); Muller and Jukam (1977); Muller (1979); Rogowski (1983); and Kornberg, Clarke, and Stewart (1984). These works contain extensive citations to other relevant literature on the causes and consequences of regime and community support.

[12] For a brief non-technical description of this technique see Nie, Verba, and Petrocik (1979:303, n.8). On the test of significance used see Pedhazur (1982:63).

[13] These effects, however, are not overwhelming in an absolute sense in that only 3.7 percent of the total variance is explained.

[14] In causal modelling terms multiple regression estimates direct effects only (Pedhazur, 1982:593).

[15] Two recent national surveys conducted as parts of the "Social Change in Canada" project (principal investigators: Tom Atkinson et al., Institute for Behavioural Research, York University) have attempted to measure the extent of participation in two forms of unconventional political activity. In 1981, 60 percent of the respondents stated that they had never petitioned a government agency, 32 percent said they had done so once or twice, 6 percent reported doing so three to five times, and 2 percent indicated six or more. A

second activity investigated was "attendance at protest meetings." Here, the comparable percentages are: never = 83 percent, one or two = 13 percent, three to five = 3 percent, six or more = 2 percent. Participation rates for these activities as measured in an earlier survey (1979) are virtually identical.

[16] On the rationale for using a technique such as logit when analyzing dichotomous variables see Fiorina (1981: appendix 16.A).

REFERENCES

Almond, Gabriel and Sydney Verba. *The Civic Culture*. Princeton: Princeton University Press, 1963.

---------- eds. *The Civic Culture Revisited*. Boston: Little, Brown, 1980.

Banting, Keith and Richard Simeon. *And No One Cheered: Fedealism, Democracy and the Constitution Act*. Toronto: Methuen, 1983.

Barnes, Samuel H. and Max Kaase, et al. *Political Action*. Beverly Hills: Sage Publications, 1979.

Bell, David and Lorne Tepperman. *The Roots of Disunity*. Toronto: McClelland and Stewart, 1979.

Burke, Mike, Harold D. Clarke and Lawrence LeDuc. "Federal and Provincial Political Participation in Canada: Some Methodological and Substantive Considerations" *Canadian Review of Sociology and Anthropology*, 15: 61-75. 1978.

Cairns, Alan C. "Constitution-Making, Government Self-Interest, and the Problem of Legitimacy." In Allan Kornberg and Harold D. Clarke, eds. *Political Support in Canada: The Crisis Years*. Durham, N.C.: Duke University Press, 1983.

Clarke, Harold D., Jane Jenson, Lawrence LeDuc and Jon Pammett. *Absent Mandate: The Politics of Discontent in Canada*. Agincourt, Ont.: Gage Publishing, 1984.

Clarke, Harold D., Allan Kornberg and James Lee. "Ontario Student Party Activists: A Note on Differential Participation in a Voluntary Organization." *Canadian Review of Sociology and Anthropology*, 12:213-20. 1975.

Clarke, Harold D., Allan Kornberg and Marianne C. Stewart. "Parliament and Political Support in Canada." *American Political Science Review* 78, 1984.

Clarke, Harold D., Richard G. Price, Marianne C. Stewart and Robert Krause. "Motivational Patterns and Differential Participation in a Canadian Party: The Ontario Liberals." *American Journal of Political Science*, 22:130-51. 1978.

Converse, Philip E. *The Dynamics of Party Support*. Beverly Hills: Sage Publications, 1976.

Easton, David. *A Systems Analysis of Political Life*. New York: Wiley, 1965.

----------. "A Re-Assessment of the Concept of Political Support." *British Journal of Political Science*. 5: 435-57. 1975.

----------. "Theoretical Approaches to Political Support." *Canadian Journal of Political Science*, 9: 431-48. 1976.

Elkins, David J. and Richard E.B. Simeon. "A Cause in Search of Its Effect, or What Does Political Culture Explain?" *Comparative Politics*, 11: 127-46. 1981.

Fiorina, Morris P. *Retrospective Voting in American National Elections*. New Haven: Yale University Press, 1981.

Gibbins, Roger. *Prairie Politics and Society*. Scarborough, Ont.: Butterworth and Company, 1980.

Gutek, B. "On the Accuracy of Retrospective Attitudinal Data." *Public Opinion Quarterly*, 42: 390-401. 1978.

Inglehart, Ronald. *The Silent Revolution*. Princeton: Princeton University Press, 1977.

----------. "Post-Materialism in an Environment of Insecurity." *American Political Science Review* 75: 880-900, 1981.

Kornberg, Allan, Harold D. Clarke and Lawrence LeDuc. "Some Correlates of Regime Support in Canada." *British Journal of Political Science*, 8: 199-216. 1978.

Kornberg, Allan, Harold D. Clarke and Marianne C. Stewart. "Federalism and Fragmentation: Political Support in Canada." *Journal of Politics*, 41: 889-906. 1979.

----------. "Public Support for Community and Regime in the Regions of Contemporary Canada." *American Review of Canadian Studies*, 10: 75-93. 1980.

Kornberg, Allan, William Mishler and Harold D. Clarke. *Representative Democracy in the Canadian Provinces*. Scarborough, Ont.: Prentice-Hall, 1982.

Kornberg, Allan, Joel Smith and Harold D. Clarke. *Citizen-Politicians Canada*. Scarborough, Ont.: Prentice-Hall, 1979.

Milbrath, Lester and M.L. Goel. *Political Participation*, 2d ed. Chicago: Rand McNally, 1977.

Miller, William L., et al. "Democratic or Violent Protest? Attitudes Towards Direct Action in Scotland and Wales." *Studies in Public Policy* 107. Glasgow: University of Strathclyde Centre for the Study of Public Policy, 1982.

Mishler, William. *Political Participation in Canada*. Toronto: Macmillan of Canada, 1979.

Muller, Edward N. *Aggressive Political Participation*. Princeton: Princeton University Press, 1979.

Muller, Edward N. and Thomas O. Jukam. "On the Meaning of Political Support." *American Political Science Review*, 71: 1561-95. 1977.

Nie, Norman, Sidney Verba and John Petrocik. *The Changing American Voter*. Cambridge, Mass.: Harvard University Press, 1979.

Ornstein, Michael D., H. Michael Stevenson and A. Paul Williams. "Region, Class and Political Culture in Canada." *Canadian Journal of Political Science*, 13: 227-72. 1980.

Pammett, Jon H. "Adolescent Political Activity as a Learning Experience: The Action-Trudeau Campaign of 1968." Jon H. Pammett and Michael S. Whittington, eds. *Foundations of Political Culture: Political Socialization in Canada*. Toronto: Macmillan, 1976.

Pedhazur, Elazar J. *Multiple Regression in Behavioral Research*. New York: Holt, Rinehart and Winston, 1982.

Presthus, Robert. *Elite Accommodation in Canadian Politics*. Toronto: Macmillan, 1973.

Przeworski, Adam and Henry Teune. *The Logic of Comparative Social Inquiry.* New York: John Wiley & Sons, 1970.

Rogowski, Ronald. "Political Support for Regimes: A Theoretical Inventory and Critique." Allan Kornberg and Harold D. Clarke, eds. *Political Support in Canada: The Crisis Years.* Durham, N.C.: Duke University Press, 1983.

Schwartz, Mildred A. *Politics and Territory.* Montreal-Kingston: McGill-Queen's University Press, 1974.

Shingles, Richard D. "Black Consciousness and Political Participation: The Missing Link." *American Political Science Review*, 75: 76-91. 1981.

Simeon, Richard and David J. Elkins. "Regional Political Cultures in Canada." *Canadian Journal of Political Science*, 7: 397-437. 1974.

Sutherland, S.L. *Patterns of Belief and Action.* Toronto: University of Toronto Press, 1981.

Tufte, Edward. *Data Analysis for Politics and Policy.* Englewood Cliffs, N.J.: Prentice-Hall, 1974.

Uhlaner, Carole Jean. "The Consistency of Individual Political Participation Across Governmental Levels in Canada." *American Journal of Political Science*, 26: 298-311. 1982.

Ullman, Stephen H. "Regional Political Cultures in Canada: Part I." *American Review of Canadian Studies*, 7: 1-22. 1977.

----------. "Regional Political Cultures in Canada: Part II." *American Review of Canadian Studies* 8: 70-101, 1978.

Van Loon, Rick. "Political Participation in Canada: The 1965 Election." *Canadian Journal of Political Science*, 3: 376-99. 1970.

Verba, Sidney and Norman H. Nie. *Participation in America.* New York: Harper and Row, 1972.

Verba, Sidney, Norman H. Nie and Jae-on Kim. *Participation and Political Equality.* Cambridge: Cambridge University Press, 1978.

Weir, Blair. "The Distortion of Voter Recall." *American Journal of Political Science*, 19: 53-61. 1975.

Welch, Susan. "Dimensions of Political Participation in a Canadian Sample." *Canadian Journal of Political Science*, 8: 53-59. 1975.

Wilson, John. "The Canadian Political Cultures: Towards a Redefinition of the Nature of the Canadian Political System." *Canadian Journal of Political Science*, 7: 438-83. 1974.

APPENDIX 16.A

MEASUREMENT OF PREDICTOR VARIABLES

Age — This variable is measured as age in years.

Level of Formal Education — A six-category variable is employed: elementary school or less = 1, some secondary school = 2, completed secondary school = 3, post-secondary (technical or junior college) = 4, some college or university = 5, college or university degree (B.A. Level or above) = 6.

Income — Measured as annual family income: under $10,000 per year = 1, $10,000-$19,999 = 2, $20,000-$29,999 = 3, $30,000-$49,999 = 4, $50,000 or more = 5.

Parental Political Involvement — Based on measures of parental political interest and activity: one or both parents interested and active = 2, one or both parents interested or active = 1, neither parent interested or active = 0.

Political Interest — Respondent follows politics "very closely" = 3, "fairly closely" = 2, "not much at all" = 1.

Trust in Political Authorities — A factor score variable based on the following items: (a) "most people in the federal government are dishonest" (agree = -1, disagree = 1, no opinion = 0), (b) "people in the federal government waste a lot of the money we pay in taxes" (agree = -1, disagree = 1, no opinion = 0), (c) "most of the time we can trust people in the federal government to do what is right" (agree = 1, disagree = -1, no opinion = 0), (d) "most of the people running the government in Ottawa are smart people who usually know what they are doing" (agree = 1, disagree = -1, no opinion = 0). The factor analysis of (a)-(d) yielded one factor (eigenvalue = 1.74, percentage of variance explained = 43.4) with the following loadings: (a) = .68, (b) = .60, (c) = .72, (d) = .63.

Perceived Responsiveness of MPs — A factor score variable based on the following items concerning the likely behaviour of MPs: (a) "take into consideration the opinions of people like yourself when making up their mind on an important issue, if they knew your feelings on it," (b) "try hard to do or get something for their riding if people like yourself asked them for it," (c) "try hard to do something about a specific proposal or family problem that a person like yourself approached them with," (d) "make themselves available in their constituency office and in Ottawa to people like yourself." Responses were scored: "very likely" = 1, "somewhat likely" = 0, "not very likely" = -1. The factor analysis of (a)-(d) yielded one factor (eigenvalue = 2.29, percentage of variance explained = 57.4) with the following loadings: (a) = .74, (b) = .79, (c) = .74, (d) = .76.

Federal Government Performance — This is an additive index based on responses concerning judgements re: federal government performance in ten areas of activity, and judgements re: the equity/fairness of federal government performance in eleven areas. Re: the former, items included: (a) providing welfare services, (b) keeping the armed forces strong, (c) providing job opportunities, (d) protecting lives and property, (e) insuring personal liberties and rights, (f) keeping inflation under control, (g) looking after health needs, (h) providing educational opportunities, (i) cleaning up and protecting the environment, (j) supporting culture and the arts. For each of these items respondents were asked if the federal government "should do" the activity, and if so, how well it was performing. Responses were coded: "very well" = 1, "fairly well" or "don't know = 0, "not very well" or "should not do" = -1.

Re: the equity/fairness items, respondents were asked if they agreed or disagreed with the following: (a) "In Canada some people don't pay enough taxes whereas others pay too many" (agree = -1, disagree = 1, no opinion, don't know = 0); (b) "In Canada what people become depends on what they can do, and not on who they are or who they know" (agree = 1, disagree = -1, no opinion, don't know = 0); (c) "In Canada the federal government treats some groups much better than others" (agree = -1, disagree = 1, no opinion, don't know = 0); (d) "Over the years the federal civil service in Ottawa has treated all Canadians equally" (agree = 1, disagree = -1, no opinion, don't know = 0); (e) "Over the years political parties generally have tried to look after the best interests of all Canadians, not just the interests of those who vote for them" (agree = 1, disagree = -1, no opinion, don't know = 0); (f) "In Canada some groups get too much and others get too little" (agree = -1, disagree = 1, no opinion, don't know = 0); (g) "Over the years the federal courts generally have acted speedily and treated people fairly" (agree = 1, disagree = -1, no opinion, don't know = 0); (h) "Parliament in Canada does not represent everyone fairly" (agree = -1, disagree = 1, no opinion, don't know = 0); (i) "In some countries interest groups like business, labour, or farmers' groups may have too much say in politics but this isn't the case in Canada" (agree = 1, disagree = -1, no opinion, don't know = 0); (j) "In some countries there may be one law for the rich and another for the poor, but that's not the way the federal government works in Canada" (agree = 1, disagree = -1, no opinion, don't know = 0); (k) "In Canada many people don't have the opportunity to get the things that make for the good life" (agree = -1, disagree = 1, no opinion, don't know = 0).

To provide equal weighting for the performance and equity/fairness subsets, additive indices based on each of these were standardized and the resulting scores were combined to form an overall index.

Federal Governmental Impact on Personal Well-Being — Judgements of personal well-being were measured using responses to questions regarding material and more general life satisfaction. Responses were scored: "very satisfied" = 2, "fairly satisfied" = 1, "a little dissatisfied" = -1, "very dissatisfied" = -2. These scores were multiplied by those for variables measuring assessments of governmental impact on the two types of satisfaction. The governmental impact variables were scored: "a great deal" = 2, "something" = 1, "not much" or "don't know" = 0. The resulting indices (ranging from 4 to -4) were summed to yield an overall index (range = 8 to -8) of evaluations of governmental impact on personal well-being.

National Regime and Community Support — National regime (the government of Canada) and community (Canada) support measured using thermometer scales. Respondents were asked to think of a thermometer scale ranging from 1 to 100 with 50 designated as the neutral point, and requested to indicate their feelings about several political entities including the government of Canada and Canada. Since feelings about government, in the sense of regime, may be influenced by attitudes toward the "government of the day," we regressed the government of Canada variable on a measure of the strength and direction of party identification and computed residual scores. (Clarke, Kanberg and Stewart, 1984) The regression equation used for this purpose is: Thermometer score = 52.14 + 5.17 party identification, where party identification is a seven-point scale ranging from 3 (very strong Liberal party identifier) to -3 (very strong other party identifier).

Protest Approval and Effectiveness — In both cases two factor-score variables were constructed on the basis of the factor analysis presented in table 16.4A. The first has strong factor-coefficients for the demonstrations and strikes items, while the second has strong factor-score coefficients for the petitions, boycotts, and rallies items.

Protest Approval and Effectiveness Index — Since the equivalent protest approval and effectiveness factor-score variables are highly intercorrelated (.47 and .53 respectively), multicollinearity is a potential problem in the multivariate analyses. To obviate this problem, an overall protest approval/effectiveness index is created by summing the four approval and effectiveness factor scores.

Compliance — Five agree-disagree items are subjected to factor analysis. These are: (a) "people should pay their federal taxes even if they are used to support programmes they don't like," (b) "the laws of Parliament should be obeyed as long as they don't violate people's basic rights," (c) "people should be willing to serve in the armed forces if the government asks them, even if they don't want to," (d) "if a policeman orders you to do something you should do it even if you disagree," (e) "Canadians should be willing to go along with what the federal government decides even if they do not personally support the political party in power." In each case, responses were scored "agree" = 1, "disagree" = -1, "no opinion" = 0. The resulting factor analysis yields two factors as shown in appendix B. The results of this analysis are used to construct two factor-score variables: "federal government compliance" and "armed forces/police" compliance.

Region/Ethnicity — To avoid multicollinearity problems in the multivariate analyses produced by the large concentration of persons of French ethnicity in Québec, dummy region/ethnicity variables are constructed as follows: Atlantic (Newfoundland, Prince Edward Island, Nova Scotia, New Brunswick), Québec-French, Québec-Non-French, Prairies (Manitoba, Saskatchewan, Alberta), and British Columbia. Ontario is treated as the suppressed category.

APPENDIX 16.B
Factor Analysis of Attitudes Toward Political Compliance

	Factor 1	Factor 2
Pay Federal Taxes	.62	.23
Obey Laws of Parliament	.75	-.23
Serve in Armed Forces	.01	.77
Obey Police	.17	.72
Comply with Federal Government's Decisions	.60	.32
Eigenvalue	1.6	1.0
% of variance explained	32.4	20.5

APPENDIX 16.C

Multiple Regression Analyses of Federal Government and Armed Forces/Police Compliance – Significant Predictors Only

	Federal Government Compliance			Armed Forces Police Compliance		
Predicators	b	B	F	b	B	F
Age	.04	.07	8.83[b]	.15	.24	105.31[a]
Education	.04	.06	6.23[c]	+	+	+
Income	+	+	+	.05	.06	5.98[c]
Trust in Political Authorities	.18	.19	55.02[a]	+	+	+
MPs' Responsiveness	+	+	+	.03	.07	8.01[b]
Federal Government Performance	.08	.14	28.30[a]	.05	.09	12.17[a]
Federal Government Impact	+	+	+	.03	.06	7.01[b]
National Regime Support	.00	.08	9.80[b]	+	+	+
National Community Support	.00	.08	10.55[b]	+	+	+
Region/Ethnicity:						
Quebec-French	+	+	+	-.12	-.05	5.13[c]
R =		.35			.33	

a – $p \leq .001$
b – $p \leq .01$
c – $p \leq .05$

\+ – does not enter equation as significant predictor

NOTES ON CONTRIBUTORS

FRANCES ABELE is an Assistant Professor, School of Public Administration and Social Work, Carleton University, Ottawa. Formerly Research Associate of the Arctic Institute of North America and Director of the Native Employment Training Study, she has published a number of articles on northern politics and northern development.

HAROLD D. CLARKE is Professor of Political Science and department head, Virginia Polytechnic Institute and State University. He is co-author of *Political Choice in Canada, Citizen Politicians — Canada, Representative Democracy in the Canadian Provinces*, and *Absent Mandate: The Politics of Discontent in Canada*. His articles have appeared in journals such as the *American Journal of Political Science*, the *American Political Science Review*, the *British Journal of Political Science*, the *Canadian Journal of Political Science*, and the *Journal of Politics*. His current research interests are concerned with the impact of short-term forces on electoral choice in Anglo-American democracies.

BARRY COOPER is Professor of Political Science at the University of Calgary. His publications in political philosophy include *Merleau-Ponty and Marxism*, *Michel Foucault, An Introduction to His Thought*, and *The End of History*. He has published widely on Canadian political thought, is currently completing a biography of Alexander Kennedy Isbister, and is working on a major study of political thought in western Canada.

RONALD S. DICK worked for many years in the educational media. Specializing in international and political affairs, he made some forty documentary films for the National Film Board of Canada, including the series *Commonwealth of Nations* and *Struggle for a Border*. From 1970 to 1977 he was director of research for NFB English productions. Now retired, he devotes his time to research and writing on a variety of topics, including the political and social influence of the media.

LEO DRIEDGER is Professor of Sociology at the University of Manitoba, Winnipeg. He has published several books including *The Canadian Ethnic Mosaic*, as well as contributing many chapters in books, and his articles have appeared in a number of scholarly sociological journals in North America. His major research interests focus on ethnic identity and urban minorities.

MARY EBERTS practices civil litigation with the law firm of Tory, Tory, Deslauriers and Binnington in Toronto. She taught at the Faculty of Law, University of Toronto, from 1974 to 1980 and is the author of numerous publications in the areas of women's rights and civil liberties, including the book *Women and Legal Action* (1984). She has served as a Board of Inquiry under the Ontario and Canadian Human Rights legislation, special counsel to the Canadian Civil Liberties Association, and counsel to the Canadian Advisory Council on the Status of Women in connection with the hearings of the Joint Parliamentary Committee on the Constitution.

THOMAS FLANAGAN is Professor and Head of the Department of Political Science at the University of Calgary. He is the author of *Louis "David" Riel: "Prophet of the New World"* (1979); *An Introduction to Government and Politics*, with Mark O. Dickerson (1982); and *Riel and the Rebellion: 1885 Reconsidered* (1983). With Rainer Knopff, he is currently conducting research on Canadian Human Rights Commissions.

JAMES S. FRIDERES is Professor of Sociology at the University of Calgary. He is co-editor of the journal *Canadian Ethnic Studies* and co-author of a text on *Ethnic Relations in Canada*. His research interests focus on native people in Canada and he is presently completing work on investigative procedures used by the federal Human Rights Commission.

ROGER GIBBINS is Professor of Political Science at the University of Calgary. His publications include *Prairie Politics and Society* (1980); *Out of Irrelevance: A Socio-Political Introduction to Indian Affairs in Canada*, with J. Rick Ponting (1980); *Regionalism: Territorial Politics in Canada and the United States* (1982); and *Conflict and Unity: An Introduction to Canadian Political Life*. His major research activities have focused on regional and aboriginal minorities in Canada.

DALE GIBSON is a Professor of Law at the University of Manitoba. He has written extensively on the subject of human rights, among others, and chaired the Manitoba Human Rights Commission from 1981 to 1984. His chief academic interests are Constitutional Law, Torts, and Canadian Legal History.

RAINER KNOPFF is Associate Professor of Political Science at the University of Calgary. He has published a number of articles on nationalism, public law, human rights and civil liberties, and Canadian political thought. With F.L. Morton, he has recently completed a study entitled "Nation-Building and the Charter" for the Royal Commission on the Economic Union and Development Prospects for Canada and is currently collaborating with Thomas Flanagan on a study of Human Rights Commissions in Canada.

ALLAN KORNBERG is Professor and Chairman of the Department of Political Science at Duke University and editor of the *Journal of Politics*. He is author of *Canadian Legislative Behavior*, co-author of *Influence in Parliament: Canada, Citizen Politicians — Canada*, and *Representative Democracy in the Canadian Provinces*, and editor of *Legislatures in Developmental Perspective* and *Legislatures in Comparative Perspective*. His articles have appeared in journals such as the *American Political Science Review*, the *British Journal of Political Science*, and the *Canadian Journal of Political Science*.

FRANK MacKINNON is Professor Emeritus of Political Science at the University of Calgary. He is the author of numerous articles and five books, including *The Government of Prince Edward Island*, *The Politics of Education*, *Postures and Politics*, and *The Crown in Canada*, and is a past president of the Institute of Public Administration of Canada and of the Atlantic Provinces Economic Council.

F.L. (TED) MORTON is Assistant Professor of Political Science at the University of Calgary. His articles have appeared in *Polity*, the *Canadian Journal of Political Science* and the *Canadian Human Rights Yearbook 1984*, and he edited *Law, Politics, and the Judicial Process in Canada* (1984). He recently co-authored a study on the political impact of the Charter of Rights for the Royal Commission on the economic Union and development Prospects for Canada. His research interests include comparative public law and civil liberties, American government, and modern political thought, and he is currently conducting a qualitative study of judicial implementation of the Canadian Charter of Rights.

NEIL NEVITTE is Associate Professor of Political Science at the University of Calgary. His publications include articles in the *Canadian Journal of Political Science*, the *Canadian Journal of Public Policy* and *Social Compass*, and he has co-edited *The Future of North America: Canada, the United States and Quebec Nationalism* (1979) and *Introductory Readings in Government and Politics* (1984). His research interests include comparative political ideology, electoral behavior and political change.

WILLIAM JOSEPH REEVES is Associate Professor of Sociology at the University of Calgary. He is the author of *Librarians as Professionals*, and his publications have focused on the role of organizations in structuring and defining status groups.

BETH RUSHING is a Ph.D. candidate in the Department of Sociology at Duke University, Durham, North Carolina. Her research interests include work and occupations and theories of power, and her current work focuses on the determinants of midwives' professional power in Canada, the United States and Great Britain.

JOEL SMITH is Professor of Sociology at Duke University. He is co-author of *Citizen Politicians — Canada, Restructuring the Canadian State*, and *Ecology and Demography*, and co-editor of *Legislators in Development*. He has written numerous articles for sociological and political science journals in both Canada and the United States.

MARIANNE C. STEWART is Visiting Lecturer in the Department of Political Science at Virginia Polytechnic Institute and State University. She has contributed to a number of edited books, and her articles have appeared in such journals as the *American Journal of Political Science*, the *American Political Science Review* and the *Journal of Politics*. Her research interests include comparative political participation, political socialization and the methodology of attitudinal survey research.

I NAME INDEX

A.-G. Canada v. Lavell: 40, 45, 50, 61
A.-G. Canada v. Burnshine: 84
A.-G. Nova Scotia v. Bedford Service Commission: 36, 37, 50
A.-G. Quebec v. Blaikie et.al.: 31, 50
Abele, Frances: 25, 243
Abu-Laban, Bahu: 187, 188
Adler, Richard: 177
Adorno: 181
Aharoni, Yair: 121
Aharow: 135
Alexander, David G.: 201
Alliance des Professeurs de Montreal, et.al. v. A.-G. Quebec: 50, 84
Allport, Godron: 116, 117, 162-164
Almond: 295
Arendt, Hannah: 215
Aristotle: 208, 214
Asch: 242
Atcheson, M.E.: 68, 69, 255, 256
Atkinson, Tom: 297
Atwood, Margaret: 212
Audrey: 210
Augustine: 215
Baker v. Carr: 37, 50
Baker, Charles: 254
Baldwin: 182
Banting: 203
Barnes: 275, 279, 290, 296
Bayefsky: 69, 256
Beaudoin, G.A.: 50, 51, 69, 256
Beck, Stanley M.: 85
Bedard: 62, 63, 75, 76
Beetz, Justice: 73, 75, 78
Bell, Daniel: 182, 296
Belobaba: 50
Bennett, Premier: 122
Berger, Justice Thomas: 246, 249-252
Berlin: 115, 118
Bernier, Ivan: 85
Berry: 166, 167
Berton, Pierre: 179, 188, 205
Bey, Salome: 180, 190
Biddiss, Michael: 188
Bisonette, Lise: 221
Blair, Bob: 249
Bliss v. A.-G. Canada: 61, 84
Bliss: 63, 76
Block, W.E.: 105
Bogle, W.E.: 105
Boorstin, Daniel: 176
Borowski v. Minister of Justice for Canada: 69

Borowski, Joseph: 64
Bortnick: 184
Bottomore: 168
Brennan, Justice: 37
Breton: 160
Brown v. Board of Education: 73, 82, 84, 100
Bruce, Mary: 91, 105
Bruner: 115
Burke: 279, 284, 296
Burns, George: 49
Burnshine: 68
Cairns: 205, 209
Calder v. A.-G. British Columbia: 45, 50
Can. Odeon Theatres v. Saskatchewan Human Rights Commission: 43
Canard: 74, 78
Cardinal, Harold: 76, 85, 161, 163
Carpenter, David: 212
Carrothers: 245
Cartwright, Richard: 202
Charlie, Chief Johnny: 247
Cheki: 223
Child: 149
Chris Vogel v. Government of Manitoba: 122
Christian, T.P.: 32, 50
Church: 160
City of Winnipeg v. Barrett: 44, 50
Clarke, Joe: 217
Clarke, Harold: 26, 222, 276-279, 284, 288, 296-297, 303
Clement, Wallace: 182, 185
Clifton: 163
Conklin, W.E.: 32, 50
Connecticut v. Teal: 104
Converse: 259
Conway, J.F.: 205
Cooper, Barry: 23, 217
Cripps, Thomas: 178
Cross: 193
Curr v. The Queen: 58
Dahrendorf: 168
Darwin: 107
Dashefsky: 159
Daudlin, Bob: 87, 91, 195
Davis, William: 217
Dawson, R. MacGregor: 71, 85
Deschenes, Chief Justice: 33, 34
Devereaux: 224
Diamond: 176
Dicey: 73, 74
Dick, Ronald: 21, 22
Dickson, J.: 41
Doeriner: 149
Dosman: 243

Doull, James: 216
Driedger, Leo: 21, 160-164
Drury: 239
Drybones, R.: 50, 61, 68, 73, 74, 76
Dunbar: 217
Dworkin: 108
Dworkin, A.G.: 109
Early, Mary Two-Axe: 77
Easton: 297
Ebert, Mary: 16, 53, 69, 256
Edwards: 149, 223
Eisenhower, President: 82
Elkins: 296
Ellul, Jacques: 205, 217
Federal Republic of German & Rauca: 68
Feenstra: 177
Fiorina: 298
Fischer: 201
Fishman: 187
Flanagan, Thomas: 18, 19, 54, 58, 68, 75, 85, 126-137, 255
Fleming, P.: 190
Francis: 217
Freeman: 107
Friar, Natasha A.: 178
Friar, Ralph E.: 178
Frideres, James S.: 20
Frum, David: 92, 105
Frye, Northrop: 23, 210, 217
Fumoleau, Father Rene: 244
Gardner: 177
Garson, Stuart: 203
General Custer: 249
George, R.: 45, 50
Germscheid, Darlene: 122
Gertner: 50
Gibbins, Roger: 25, 203, 261, 267, 276
Gibson: 16, 19, 35-39, 47, 50, 53, 58, 69, 122, 256
Gilbert & Sullivan: 197
Gilbert: 197
Glazer: 79, 85, 101, 105, 169
Goel: 281, 296
Gold, Marc: 40, 48, 50, 65, 69, 256
Gomez, Henry: 180
Gordon, Milton: 159, 167, 168
Gordon, Rosemary: 178
Government of Canada: 68
Grant, George: 81, 214, 215, 217
Granzberg, Gary: 186, 187, 190
Gray, Herb: 87, 97
Green v. Country School Board: 105
Green, L.C.: 46, 50, 105

Gregg: 217
Grey: 199
Gunderson, Morley: 102, 105
Hagan: 164
Hage: 149
Hall, Justice Emmett: 73, 74
Hamilton, Alexander: 206
Harris, Marvin: 108
Harrison, Marvin: 108
Harrison: 213
Hartz: 81
Hawkins: 148
Head: 189
Hegel: 215, 216
Henry, Jeff: 179, 190
Herberg: 167
Hoffman, Carl: 102, 105
Hofley: 223
Hogg, Peter W.: 35, 40, 50, 71, 85
Horkheimer, 181
Horowitz: 81
Hosek, C.: 48, 50
Hostetler: 168
Hughes: 157
Hunter: 115
Inglehart: 279
Isaac et.al. v. Bedard: 61
Isajiw: 160
Jackson, Jesse: 272
Jackson, John: 168
Jay, John: 206
Joy: 159
Jukam: 297
Juriannsz, Russell: 92, 105
Kaase: 275, 279, 290, 296
Kalbach: 160
Kalin: 166
Kalisch: 175
Kallen, Horace: 148, 158, 167
Kanberg: 303
Kaye: 217
Keeley: 187
Kehoe, John: 186
Kim: 296
King, Martin Luther: 161, 195
Kitchener: 201
Klapper, Joseph: 177, 188
Knopff, Rainer: 17-19, 84, 87, 125, 133-137
Kornberg, Allan: 24, 27, 222, 276, 278, 284, 296, 297
Krause: 296
Kreisel, Henry: 212

La Commission des Droits de la Personne du Quebec: 122
Laporte, Pierre: 193, 201
Laskin, Justice: 58
Latour: 148
Laurier, Sir Wilfred: 78, 82
Lavell: 62, 63, 74-76
Lecker: 213
Leduc: 276, 279, 284, 296, 297
Lee: 296
Levesque, Premier Rene: 78, 80-82, 120, 161
Levine: 162
Lewin, Kurt: 160, 162
Linton: 108
Locke, John: 40, 206
Lynch, Charles: 187
Lysyk, K.: 45, 50
LeDain, Justice: 36
Machiavelli: 206
Mackie: 163, 177
Madison, James: 206
Malcolm X: 161
Mansfield Jr., Harvey: 88, 104, 105
Manuel, George: 76, 85
Manzer, Ronald: 95, 105
Martin: 217
Marx, H.: 50
Marx: 32, 34, 168
Mendel: 107
Mezoff: 163, 164
Michel Wilkinson v. La Ville de Montreal: 122
Milbrath: 281, 296
Mill, John Stuart: 107, 108
Miller, Randall: 178
Mina, E.: 189
Miner: 160
Mishler: 290, 296
Mitchell, W.O.: 217
Montesquieu: 206
Moodie: 217
Morel, A.: 32, 51
Morgentaler: 68
Morrow, Justice: 246
Morton, F.L.: 16, 71
Moynihan: 169
Muller: 284, 297
Munro, John: 84
Muntington: 168
Murdoch v. Murdoch: 62, 69
Murdoch: 63
MacDonald, John A.: 201
MacKay v. The Queen: 68

MacKinnon, Frank: 22
McCormack, Thelma: 222, 224, 226-232, 237-238
McCourt: 212
McDonald: 223
McDougall, Hugh A.: 188
McGee, D'Arcy: 201
McIntyre, Justice: 41
McKay: 50
McKercher, William R.: 80-85
McNaught, Kenneth: 82, 85
McNeil, K.: 45, 47, 50
Nahirny: 187
Nevitte, Neil: 25, 27, 254, 261, 267
Newman: 158, 167
Nie: 281, 296, 297
Nielsen-Ferns: 184
Nisei-Sansei: 184
Niskanen: 119
Offierski v. Peterborough Board of Education: 100
Offierski: 100, 105
Ont. Film & Video Presentation Soc. v. Ont. Bd. of Censors: 33, 51
Operation Dismantle Inc. v. The Queen: 36
Operation Dismantle: 37, 51, 68
Ornstein: 296
Pammett: 296
Park, Robert: 157, 168
Pedhazur: 297
Penton, M. James: 80
Perdue: 213
Perlin: 217
Perrow: 149
Petrocik: 297
Phillips, Rhys D.: 88, 105
Pierson: 201
Piore: 149
Plessy v. Ferguson: 76
Plutarch: 206
Polyviou, P.G.: 40, 51
Porter, John: 158, 175, 182
Posluns, Michael: 76, 85
Prata: 68
Pratt, E.J.: 205
Presthus: 275
Price: 296
Publius Valerius Publicola: 206
Publius: 207-209
Quebec Assoc. of Protestant School Bds., et.al. v. A.-G. Quebec: 33, 44, 51, 84
R. v. Drybones: 40
Rea: 242, 244
Rechnitzer: 224
Reed, John: 102, 105

Rees, Tim: 180, 181
Reeves, William: 20
Reid, Frank: 102, 105
Richmond: 160, 168
Ricou: 213
Rioux: 159, 166
Robertson, Gordon: 79, 92
Robertson, Peter: 89, 105
Roche, George: 92, 106
Rogowski: 297
Roosevelt, President: 49
Rosen: 159
Ross, James: 254
Rousseau, Jean Jacques: 40
Rubel: 168
Rudnyckyj: 171
Rushing, Beth: 24
Ryan Justice: 36
Sager: 201
Sahlins: 241
Sanders, Doulas: 45, 46, 51, 69, 75, 85
Saunders: 223
Sawer, G.: 35, 51
Schmeiser, P.A.: 31, 51
Schorr, Daniel: 188
Schwartz: 296
Scott, Dred: 82
Scott, S.A.: 34, 51
Seabury, Paul: 92
Sheppard, R.: 31, 34, 51
Sheppart, C.-A.: 51
Shils, Edward: 182
Shingles: 296
Simeon: 203, 296
Simmel, George: 168
Simmel: 162
Sklar, Robert: 176, 178
Skulmoski, Sheree: 254
Slattery, B.: 34, 45, 51
Smith, Adam: 208
Smith, Davis: 209
Smith, Joel: 24
Smith: 222, 276, 284, 296
Snowshoe, Charlie: 247-253
Southam: 68
Sowell, Thomas: 92, 95-98, 101-106, 257
Stanley: 158
Stegner, Wallace: 212, 213
Stephens, Donald: 212
Stevenson: 296
Stewart, Marianne: 26, 217, 276, 278, 288, 296, 297, 303
Storing: 217
Strauss, Leo: 217

Strayer, B.C.: 35, 51
Strong, Dennis: 190
Suave, Jeanne: 224
Sullivan: 197
Sutherland: 288, 296
Suzuki, David: 184
Swingewood: 181
Swinton, K.: 35, 51
Symons, T.B.H.: 175
Szasz, Thomas: 107
T'Seleie, Frank: 247, 249, 250-253
Tarnopolsky, Justice Walter: 31, 40, 41, 48-51, 65, 67, 69, 111-114, 125, 138, 148, 256
Taylor: 166, 177
Temple v. Bulmer: 36, 51
The Queen v. Drybones: 84
The Queen: 68
Theresa O'Malley v. Simpson-Sears Ltd.: 104
Thomas, Caroline: 104
Thompson: 254
Tienhaara: 163
Tremblay, Andre: 81, 82
Tribe, L.H.: 35, 51
Troper: 188
Trudeau, Pierre E.: 78, 83, 84, 171, 201
Tutte: 284
Ullman: 296
Ursell, Geoffrey: 203
Vallee, Frank: 158
Valpy: 34
Van Loon: 275, 279, 284, 296
Veenhoven, Willem A.: 106
Verba: 281, 295-297
Vickers, Dr. Jill: 40, 51
Wagley, Charles: 108
Walker, Jack: 119
Walker, M.A.: 105
Wallace, Mike: 176
Ward, Norman: 85
Warkentin: 217
Weir: 297
Welch: 296
White, Lenny Little: 184
Williams: 296
Wilson: 296
Wirth, Louis: 108
Wong, Eugene F.: 178, 179
Woolgar: 148
Young, Donald: 107
Zazlow: 242
Zey-Ferrell: 149
Zimmerman: 147, 148
de Tocqueville, Alexis: 107

II SUBJECT INDEX

Aboriginal Rights: 77
Ad Hoc Committee on Media and Race Relations: 177
Advertising Council: 186
Advisory Committee on Northern Development: 243
Affirmative Action Dir. of the Can. Emp. & Imm. Com. (CEIC): 87
Affirmative Action Policy: 17, 19, 39, 48, 49, 72, 83, 87-104, 125, 132, 137, 152, 257
Alaska Highway: 242
Alaska: 245, 246
Alberta Conservatives: 120
Alberta Indians: 161
Alberta Individual Rights Protection Act: 120
Alberta: 115, 116, 164, 168, 205, 212, 242
Amalgamation: 21, 166, 168-172
American Arctic: 245
American Bill of Rights: 62
American Blacks: 161
American Civil Rights Movement: 25
American Constitution: 158
American Liberalism: 216
American School Boards' Desegregation: 100
American School Desegregation: 79
American South: 101
American Supreme Court: 82, 101
American West: 205
Americans: 263, 266, 267
An Act Respecting the Constitution Act 1982: 34
Anglo: 159
Anglo-Americans: 181
Anglo-Celtic: 157, 166, 170-71
Anglo-Conformity: 157, 166-71
Anglophones: 26, 47, 230, 258, 266-67, 271
Angola: 193
Anti-Chinese Legislation: 80
Anti-Discrimination Legislation: 119
Anti-Discrimination Policy: 107
Anti-Semitism: 111, 185
Asians: 164, 171, 178-79
Asiatic Exclusion: 187
Asiatics: 22, 163, 169
Assemble Nationale de Quebec: 80
Assembly of First Nations: 76
Assimilation: 21, 157-59, 162, 165-72, 245
Atlantic Provinces: 194-200, 286
Atlantic Region: 23, 166
Attorney-General: 137
Ayatollah: 193
Bank Employees Civil Rights Act: 206
Beaufort Sea: 245
Berger Commission: 253
Berger Inquiry into Construction of Mackenzie Valley Pipeline: 239

Berger Inquiry: 25, 239, 246-48, 250-251
Biculturalism Commission: 180
Bilingualism: 180, 209
Bill 101: 82, 166
Bill 62: 80
Bill of Rights 1960: 73, 74
Bill of Rights: 66, 72, 75, 76
Bill of Rights, SS 1(b), S 52: 61
Blacks: 22, 26, 158, 164, 169, 171, 178-81, 257-72
Board of Inquiry: 63
Bona Fide Occupational Qualification: 118
Bona Fide Qualification Principle: 127, 128, 131
British Canadians: 163
British Columbia Human Rights Branch: 137
British Columbia Human Rights Code: 114, 115
British Columbia Human Rights Commission: 137
British Columbia: 113, 166, 212, 258, 286
British Empire: 216
British Maritimers: 163
British North America Act: 111
British North America Act, S. 130: 72
British North America Act, S. 91(24): 72, 74
British North America Act, S. 93(13) 93, 133: 79
British North America Act, S. 93: 72, 77, 78
British North America Act, S. 93, SS 13, S. 93: 77
British: 159
Canadian Association of Statutory Human Rights Agencies: 119
Canadian Bill of Rights: 15, 31, 61, 62, 67
Canadian Bill of Rights, S. 1(b): 40-41, 57-8, 65
Canadian Constitution: 31
Canadian Consultative Council on Multiculturalism: 187
Canadian Courts: 39
Canadian Film Institute: 183
Canadian Human Rights Act: 120, 139
Canadian Human Rights Commission, Complaints & Compliance Br.: 141
Canadian Human Rights Commission: 92, 139, 141, 144, 147-152
Canadian Human Rights Commission, Public Program Branch: 141
Canadian Human Rights Commission, Research and Policy: 141
Canadian Indians: 126, 163, 167
Canadian Parliament: 200
Canadian Radio-Television Telecommunications Commission: 183
Canol Pipeline: 242
Catholics: 72, 78-80, 167, 169
CBC: 182, 185, 190
CEIC: 93-95, 97-99
Charter 1982, Multicultural Clause No. 27: 186
Charter Interpretation: 65
Charter of Rights 1982: 71
Charter of Rights and Freedoms: 21
Charter to the Parliament, SS 32(1): 61
Charter, Litigation: 53
Charter: 14-16, 27, 31, 32, 37, 50, 61, 75, 78, 111-113, 172, 203, 295

Charter, Reasonable Limits Clause, S. 1: 15
Charter, S. 1: 27, 28, 33, 43, 48, 57, 62, 66, 75, 79
Charter, S. 2: 57, 60, 62, 80
Charter, S. 3: 39, 57
Charter, S. 7: 36, 62
Charter, S. 7-15: 60, 80
Charter, S. 14: 39
Charter, S. 15: 16, 34, 40-42, 46, 57-59, 65-68, 71-79, 83-84, 127, 133-136
Charter, S. 16: 43
Charter, S. 16-20: 56
Charter, S. 16-22: 55
Charter, S. 16-23: 43, 62, 72, 83
Charter, S. 20: 39, 43
Charter, S. 21: 43
Charter, S. 22: 43
Charter, S. 23: 33, 39, 44, 45, 81
Charter, S. 24: 38, 39, 44, 60-64
Charter, S. 25: 44, 67, 72, 77
Charter, S. 27: 47, 55, 62, 78
Charter, S. 28: 49, 55, 62
Charter, S. 29: 62, 72, 78
Charter, S. 33: 15, 33, 60, 62, 64, 80, 83
Charter, S. 34: 46
Charter, S. 35: 47, 72, 77
Charter, S. 37: 47
Charter, S. 52: 65
Chile: 193
Chinatowns: 169, 187
Chinese Canadians: 266
Chinese: 22, 164, 181, 187, 258
Chipeweyan Tribes: 242
CHRC, Public Program Branch, Program Analysis & Development: 141
CHRC, Public Program Branch, Information & Production: 141
CHRC, Public Program Branch, Program Delivery: 141
Christian-Non-Christian Groups: 13
Christianity: 241
Civil Rights Act 1964: 105
Civil Rights Movement, United States: 175
Cold War: 242
Collective Rights: 80, 82
Commons Committee on Visible Minorities: 91
Commonwealth Courts: 39
Communist Party: 118, 127
Conciliation: 144
Confederation: 14
Conservatives: 120
Constitution Act 1867, S. 91(24): 45
Constitution Act 1867, S. 93: 31, 56
Constitution Act 1867, S. 133: 31, 43
Constitution Act 1981, S. 25, 35: 74
Constitution Act 1982: 80

Constitution Act 1982, S. 25: 46, 75
Constitution Act 1982, S. 35: 46, 75
Constitution Act 1982, SS 52(1), 52(3): 60
Constitution Act, Part III: 203
Constitution Act, S. 35: 67
Constitution of Canada: 15, 56, 78
Constitutional Act 1982: 203
Constitutional Amendment: 46, 47, 60, 80
Constitutional Conference on Aboriginal Rights 1984: 76
CPR: 24, 205
Criminal Code, S. 250: 64
Cross-Cultural Communications Centre: 183
Crown: 45, 66-68, 246
Cruise Missile: 36
Dene Declaration: 240, 252
Dene Nation: 252, 254
Dene: 25, 239-45, 250-254
Denominational Schools: 56
Department of Indian Affairs and Northern Development: 246
Department of National Health and Welfare: 243
Department of Northern Affairs and National Resources: 243
Diceyean Interpretation: 78, 183
Discrimination: 14-21, 40-46, 59, 77-118, 125-44, 147-51, 157, 163-64, 179-85, 195
Dominion Government: 205, 242
Doukobors: 14, 80, 158, 185
Dutch: 170
Eastern Europeans: 107
Eastern Provinces: 200, 201
English Canadians: 79, 260-267
English Government: 199
Entrenchment: 34, 42-46, 55, 83, 194, 238-40, 252-53
Equal Benefit: 42
Equal Opportunity: 103
Equality of Condition: 40
Equality of Rights: 40
Eskimos: 216
Ethical Humanism: 112
Ethnic Identity: 159, 162, 169
Europeans: 170, 214, 240-42
Executive Order No. 10925: 257
Faction: 208
Fair Practices Act: 115
Federal Court of Appeal: 36, 37
Federal Enforcement: 82
Federal Government: 186
Federalism: 24, 204-206
Feminist Issues: 272
Feminist Movement: 226, 232, 237
First Nations: 77
Fort Good Hope: 247, 249
Fort McPherson: 247

Fourteenth Amendment: 61
Franch Canadians: 169
Franco-Conformity: 166, 171
Francophones: 47, 72, 80, 87, 108, 258-59, 266-67, 271, 278, 294
Frankfurt School: 181
French Canadians: 17, 22, 73, 79, 162-63, 166, 181, 272
French Fact: 78
French Government: 199
French Language Instruction: 39
French Nation: 166
French: 79, 131, 159-61, 171, 203, 215
Front de Liberation du Quebec: 168
Fundamental Freedoms: 84
Fundamental Christians: 78
Gallup Polls: 163
Gang of Eight: 83
General Linear Model: 228
Germans: 158, 160-63, 167, 170
Government Intervention: 26
Governor General in Council: 56, 57
Governor General: 224
Governor, Bank of Canada: 193
Great Britain: 205, 213
Great Depression: 242
Great Slave Lake: 239
Group Rights: 77
Guides to Non-Discriminatory Communication: 179
House Committees: 205
House of Commons: 57
Human Rights Commission, Complaints & Compliance Br.: 20
Human Rights Commission: 18-20, 42, 63, 104, 109, 115, 120, 128
Hutterites: 14, 80, 157-61, 163-64, 168-71, 185
Identity: 183- 210-12
Indian Act: 40, 64, 72, 74-77
Indian Affairs Advisory Committee: 245
Indian Brotherhood: 245, 246, 251-52
Indians: 22, 45, 46, 59, 67, 73, 77, 110, 133-136, 157, 159, 163-64, 169, 172, 178, 181, 196, 239, 242, 246
Individual Rights Protection Act: 120
Individual Rights: 80
Indopakistanis: 171
Institute for Behavioural Research: 297
Inuit: 46, 67, 239, 252
Inuvialuit: 239
Irish Catholics: 169
Irish: 183
Italians: 158, 160, 163-169, 184
Japan: 242
Japanese Canadians: 34, 37, 163, 164, 258, 266
Jehovah's Witnesses: 80, 185
Jews: 78, 112, 157-168, 171

Joint Negotiating Secretariat: 252
Judicial Interpretation: 73
Judicial Policy Making: 78
Judicial Scrutiny: 41
Justice Department: 246
Klondike Gold Rush: 242
Legislative Assembly: 252
Legislature of Quebec: 34, 43
Legislature: 56
Liberals: 120
Linguistic Minorities: 54, 78
Loyalism: 216
Loyalists: 211
Mackenzie Delta: 245
Mackenzie River: 239
Mackenzie Valley Pipeline Inquiry: 251
Mackenzie Valley Pipeline: 25
Mackenzie Valley: 241-246, 251
Majority Faction: 209
Manitoba Act 1870, S. 23: 43
Manitoba Act: 206
Manitoba Government: 137
Manitoba Human Rights Act: 113
Manitoba Human Rights Commission: 115, 120, 128, 135-136
Manitoba School Crisis: 82
Manitoba School Question, Bill 101: 168
Manitoba: 113-116, 212
Maritimes: 120, 200
Mass Society: 181, 187
Media: 22, 176-187, 275, 288, 294
Mennonites: 14, 80, 185
Metis Association: 252, 254
Metis: 22, 46, 67, 178, 211, 239, 252-254
Middle East: 164
Ministry of Communications: 214
Ministry of State for Multiculturalism: 184
Minority Identities: 193
Minority Language Instruction: 39
Missouri Human Rights Commission: 89
Mounties: 244
Multicultural Policy: 182
Multicultural Rights: 47
Multiculturalism: 187
National Election Studies: 297
National Energy Program: 205, 211, 217
National Film Board: 182, 183, 185
National Guard: 82
National Indian Brotherhood: 76
National Policy: 205, 217
National Poll: 163
National Science Foundation: 296

321

National Unity: 183
Native Indians: 171
Natives: 71, 73, 94
Nazis: 169
Neo-Conservatism: 272
New Brunswick Lan. Rights, S. 16.2, 17.2, 18.2, 19.2, 20.2: 43
New Brunswick: 115
New Democratic Party: 120
Newfoundland Human Rights Act: 114
Newfoundland: 116
Non-Diceyean Equality: 74
Non-European: 212
Norman Wells: 242
North America: 215, 257
Northern Ireland: 164
Northwest Territories: 25, 35, 112-116, 239-247, 252-254
Nova Scotia Human Rights Commission: 97
Nova Scotia Supreme Court, Appeal Div.: 37
Nova Scotia: 114, 116, 164
Office of Native Claims: 246, 252
Official Language: 55
One-Party System: 120
Ontario Human Rights Code: 100, 109-115
Ontario Human Rights Commission: 91, 105
Ontario Ministry of Culture and Recreation: 184
Ontario's Divisional Court: 104
Ontario: 112, 113, 166, 211, 212
Parkinson's Law: 199
Parliament Hill: 203
Parliament of Canada: 43, 45, 57, 257
Parliament: 15, 33, 277
Parti Quebecois: 80, 166, 168, 221-224, 236
Peter Principle: 199
Pluralism: 21, 158, 165, 168-172, 182-199
Poles: 161, 164, 187
Politics of Women: 223
Prairies: 166, 212, 287
Prince Edward Island: 115
Proportional Representation: 88
Protestant-Catholic-Jewish-Muslim-Other: 13
Protestantism: 214
Protestants: 72, 78-79, 167
Provincial Authority: 57
Provincial Law: 57
Public Service Commission: 91
Public Service of Canada: 87
Public Service: 96
Puerto Ricans: 169
Puritanism: 214
Quebec - October Crisis: 37
Quebec Association of Protestant School Boards: 81

322

Quebec Government: 137
Quebec Nationalism: 81
Quebec Provincial Rights: 72
Quebec Referendum for Canada: 221
Quebec Referendum: 24, 78
Quebec's Charter of Human Rights and Freedoms: 116
Quebec's Quiet Revolution: 168, 175, 221, 267, 295
Quebec: 18, 27, 34, 56, 79, 80, 111-114, 131, 158-167, 193-196, 209-215, 259, 278
Quebec-French: 287
Quebecois: 71, 77, 161, 169, 226, 260-267, 286-290, 295
Queen's Roman Catholic Subjects: 56
Quotas: 18, 26, 96
Reasonable Limits: 48, 79
Referendum: 222, 235
Religious Minorities: 78
Report of the Royal Commission on Bilingualism & Biculturalism: 182
Republican Party: 82
Roman Catholic Minority of the Queen's Subjects: 57
Rowell-Sirois Report: 204
Royal Canadian Mounted Police: 139
Royal Commission on Bilingualism and Biculturalism: 171
Royal Commission: 81
Royal North-West Mounted Police: 242
Royal Proclamation of Octover 7, 1763: 46, 67
Saskatchewan Bill of Rights: 115
Saskatchewan Commission: 137
Saskatchewan: 24, 112, 205, 212-213, 242
Scandinavians: 170
Scientology: 112
Secretary of State: 187
Segregation: 162
Senate: 205
Separate Schools: 56
Seventh Day Adventists: 112, 126
Shah: 193
Sikhs: 118, 119, 126
Social Credit Party: 120
Southern Europeans: 107
Special Committee on the Mass Media: 176
Special Committee on the Participation of visible Minorities: 177, 257
Special House of Commons Committee on Visible Minorities: 87
Special Senate Committee on the Mass Media: 180
Speech from the Throne in P.E.I. Legislature 1981: 199
St. Lawrence River: 211
Statement on Indian Policy: 245
States' Rights: 82
Status of Women in Canada 1970: 148
Status of Women: 148, 221, 225, 229, 236-237
Supreme Court of United States: 35
Supreme Court: 17, 33, 40-42, 58, 61-64, 73-76, 79, 81, 82, 100, 246
The North: 25, 204, 245, 248, 251

The West: 23-24, 204-216
Toronto Board of Education: 185
Treasury Board of Canada: 87, 94-97
Treaty 8: 242
Treaty Commissioners: 244
Treaty 11: 242
Tribunal: 144
TV Ontario: 185
Two-Party System: 120
U.S. Bill of Rights: 62
U.S. Fugitive Slave Law: 184
Ukrainians: 157-167, 184-185, 227
United Kingdom: 40
United States Congress: 89, 200
United States Constitution: 206
United States Supreme Court 1937: 49
United States Supreme Court: 257
United States, Kerner Commission: 180
United States: 40, 87-91, 98, 107-108, 141, 157, 164, 167-169, 172-180, 210, 213, 226, 245
Upper Canada: 56
Urban Alliance on Race Relations: 180
Valid Federal Objective: 41, 42
Vietnam War: 275
War Measures Act: 37
White Paper: 245
Winnipeg School Division No. 1: 39
Winnipeg: 160-164
Women's Movement: 62
World War I: 169-184
World War II: 34, 37, 163, 164, 169, 222, 242-243, 258
Worldwide Church of God: 112
Yukon Territory: 35, 113-115, 251

Quebec Government: 137
Quebec Nationalism: 81
Quebec Provincial Rights: 72
Quebec Referendum for Canada: 221
Quebec Referendum: 24, 78
Quebec's Charter of Human Rights and Freedoms: 116
Quebec's Quiet Revolution: 168, 175, 221, 267, 295
Quebec: 18, 27, 34, 56, 79, 80, 111-114, 131, 158-167, 193-196, 209-215, 259, 278
Quebec-French: 287
Quebecois: 71, 77, 161, 169, 226, 260-267, 286-290, 295
Queen's Roman Catholic Subjects: 56
Quotas: 18, 26, 96
Reasonable Limits: 48, 79
Referendum: 222, 235
Religious Minorities: 78
Report of the Royal Commission on Bilingualism & Biculturalism: 182
Republican Party: 82
Roman Catholic Minority of the Queen's Subjects: 57
Rowell-Sirois Report: 204
Royal Canadian Mounted Police: 139
Royal Commission on Bilingualism and Biculturalism: 171
Royal Commission: 81
Royal North-West Mounted Police: 242
Royal Proclamation of October 7, 1763: 46, 67
Saskatchewan Bill of Rights: 115
Saskatchewan Commission: 137
Saskatchewan: 24, 112, 205, 212-213, 242
Scandinavians: 170
Scientology: 112
Secretary of State: 187
Segregation: 162
Senate: 205
Separate Schools: 56
Seventh Day Adventists: 112, 126
Shah: 193
Sikhs: 118, 119, 126
Social Credit Party: 120
Southern Europeans: 107
Special Committee on the Mass Media: 176
Special Committee on the Participation of visible Minorities: 177, 257
Special House of Commons Committee on Visible Minorities: 87
Special Senate Committee on the Mass Media: 180
Speech from the Throne in P.E.I. Legislature 1981: 199
St. Lawrence River: 211
Statement on Indian Policy: 245
States' Rights: 82
Status of Women in Canada 1970: 148
Status of Women: 148, 221, 225, 229, 256-257
Supreme Court of United States: 35
Supreme Court: 17, 33, 40-42, 58, 61-64, 73-76, 79, 81, 82, 100, 246
The North: 25, 204, 243, 248, 251

The West: 23-24, 204-216
Toronto Board of Education: 185
Treasury Board of Canada: 87, 94-97
Treaty 8: 242
Treaty Commissioners: 244
Treaty 11: 242
Tribunal: 141
TV Ontario: 185
Two-Party System: 120
U.S. Bill of Rights: 62
U.S. Fugitive Slave Law: 184
Ukrainians: 157-167, 184-185, 227
United Kingdom: 40
United States Congress: 89, 200
United States Constitution: 206
United States Supreme Court 1937: 49
United States Supreme Court: 257
United States, Kerner Commission: 180
United States: 40, 87-91, 98, 107-108, 141, 157, 164, 167-169, 172-180, 210, 213, 226, 245
Upper Canada: 56
Urban Alliance on Race Relations: 180
Valid Federal Objective: 41, 42
Vietnam War: 275
War Measures Act: 37
White Paper: 245
Winnipeg School Division No. 1: 39
Winnipeg: 160-164
Women's Movement: 62
World War I: 169-184
World War II: 34, 37, 163, 164, 169, 222, 242-243, 258
Worldwide Church of God: 112
Yukon Territory: 35, 113-115, 251